THE WESTMINSTER HANDBOOKS
TO CHRISTIAN THEOLOGY

The Westminster Handbook to Reformed Theology

Edited by DONALD K. McKIM

Westminster John Knox Press
LOUISVILLE
LONDON • LEIDEN

Book design by Sharon Adams
Cover design by Cynthia Dunne
Cover art: Monks Copying Manuscripts (Corbis/© Archivo Iconografico)

First edition

Published by Westminster John Knox Press
Louisville, Kentucky

This book is printed on acid-free paper that meets the American National Standards Institute Z39.48 standard. ∞

PRINTED IN THE UNITED STATES OF AMERICA

01 02 03 04 05 06 07 08 09 10 — 10 9 8 7 6 5 4 3 2 1

Cataloging-in-Publication Data for this book is available from the Library of Congress.

ISBN 0-664-22430-X

*Dedicated with gratitude to Alan P. F. Sell,
a Christian who is a wonderful
Reformed theologian and cherished friend*

Contents

Series Introduction

The Westminster Handbooks to Christian Theology series provides a set of resources for the study of historic and contemporary theological movements and Christian theologians. These books are intended to assist scholars and students find concise and accurate treatments of important theological terms. The entries for the handbooks are arranged in alphabetical format to provide easy access to each term. The works are written by scholars with special expertise in these fields.

We hope this series will be of great help as readers explore the riches of Christian theology as it has been expressed in the past and as it will be formulated in the future.

The Publisher

Preface

The Westminster Handbook to Reformed Theology provides easy access to the ways that important theological terms have been understood within the Reformed tradition. Reformed theology is part of the broader stream of Christian theology. Yet Reformed theologians have developed emphases and particular understandings of the ways scripture should be interpreted and theological insights are to be understood. This handbook shows the distinctive accents of Reformed thought while also indicating how the Reformed views fit within the larger framework of Christian theology as a whole.

Reformed theology is the way Reformed persons have articulated their Christian faith. The entries in this volume are drawn from my earlier work, Encyclopedia of the Reformed Faith (Westminster John Knox Press, 1992). In that volume, in addition to the theological pieces, there were entries on persons and events that have held significance for those in the Reformed tradition. The Reformed faith is the living faith of Christian people. Reformed theology is an articulation of that faith using the language and thought forms of Christian theology as a whole. Thus, Reformed theology will always be in dialogue with the larger Christian theological community just as Reformed Christians will always be ecumenically engaged with the fellowship of believers in Jesus Christ throughout the world in the global Christian church.

The following pieces provide a way of understanding Reformed theology based on a study of the "words" of Christian faith. Theological terms are the building blocks and vocabulary by which Christian faith and Christian theology are expressed. The dictionary format of this handbook is meant to enhance understandings of these important terms and to indicate their significance for the Reformed family of Christian believers.

This volume takes its place with other resources for studying Reformed theology. A selection of these works is listed below. The development of Reformed theology as a theological movement is assessed in the present book at the entry on "Theology, Reformed." An invaluable bibliographic guide is found in the Historical Dictionary of Reformed Churches (cited on page 243).

I would like to thank Dr. Richard E. Brown, who, as director of Westminster John Knox Press, was supportive of the idea of extracting the theology articles from my Encyclopedia of the Reformed Faith to form a new volume in The Westminster Handbooks to Christian Theology series. David F. Wright of the Faculty of Divinity of New College, University of Edinburgh was my consulting editor for the Encyclopedia of the Reformed Faith, and so a number of the articles here have been helped by his work. My colleagues on the staff of Westminster John Knox Press have done their usual superb work in bringing this book into print.

My love goes out, as always, to my family, LindaJo, Stephen, and Karl, who bring joys and meaning to life shared together.

This volume is dedicated to Alan P. F. Sell. Alan has served the church and Christian scholarship as a splendid Reformed theologian. He has also been a very dear friend. I am grateful for his care and support throughout the years.

My hope is that this new offering will be an important resource for students, pastors, and scholars of Reformed theology and the Reformed faith.

Donald K. McKim
Germantown, Tennessee
Lent, 2001

Contributors

Mark Achtemeier
Assistant Professor of Systematic
    Theology
University of Dubuque Theological
    Seminary
Dubuque, Iowa

Brian G. Armstrong
Formerly Professor of History
Georgia State University
Atlanta, Georgia

William V. Arnold
Associate Pastor
Bryn Mawr Presbyterian Church
Bryn Mawr, Pennsylvania

J. Wayne Baker
Professor of History Emeritus
University of Akron
Akron, Ohio

Robert Benedetto
Associate Librarian and Associate
    Professor of Bibliography
Union Theological Seminary &
    Presbyterian School of Christian
    Education
Richmond, Virginia

Hendrikus Berkhof[†]
Formerly Professor of Theology Emeritus
University of Leiden
Leiden, Netherlands

Donald G. Bloesch
Professor of Theology Emeritus
University of Dubuque Theological
    Seminary
Dubuque, Iowa

Fred O. Bonkovsky
Vienna, Austria

R. Douglas Brackenridge
Professor Emeritus, Department
    of Religion
Trinity University
San Antonio, Texas

Geoffrey W. Bromiley
Professor of Church History Emeritus
Fuller Theological Seminary
Pasadena, California

Robert McAfee Brown
Professor of Theology and Ethics
    Emeritus
Pacific School of Religion
Berkeley, California

Donald J. Bruggink
James A. H. Cornell Professor of
    Historical Theology Emeritus
Western Theological Seminary
Holland, Michigan

John E. Burkhart
Professor of Systematic Theology
    Emeritus
McCormick Theological Seminary
Chicago, Illinois

Eberhard Busch
Professor of Reformed Theology
University of Göttingen
Göttingen, Germany

David G. Buttrick
Drucilla Moore Buffington Professor
    of Homiletics and Liturgics
    Emeritus
Vanderbilt Divinity School
Nashville, Tennessee

Carnegie Samuel Calian
President and Professor of Theology
Pittsburgh Theological Seminary
Pittsburgh, Pennsylvania

Cynthia M. Campbell
President and Cyrus McCormick
    Professor of Church and Ministry
McCormick Theological Seminary
Chicago, Illinois

Anna Case-Winters
Associate Professor of Theology
McCormick Theological Seminary
Chicago, Illinois

Arthur C. Cochrane
Professor of Theology Emeritus
University of Dubuque Theological
    Seminary
Dubuque, Iowa

Harvie M. Conn[†]
Formerly Professor of Missions
    Emeritus
Westminster Theological Seminary
Philadelphia, Pennsylvania

Jane E. A. Dawson
John Laing Lecturer in the History
    and Theology of the Reformation
University of Edinburgh
Edinburgh, Scotland

John W. de Gruchy
Robert Selby Taylor Professor
    of Christian Studies
University of Cape Town
Cape Town, South Africa

James A. De Jong
President and Professor of Historical
    Theology
Calvin Theological Seminary
Grand Rapids, Michigan

Dawn DeVries
John Newton Thomas Professor of
    Systematic Theology and Director
    of Graduate Studies
Union Theological Seminary and
    Presbyterian School of Christian
    Education
Richmond, Virginia

Edward A. Dowey Jr.
Archibald Alexander Professor
    of the History of Christian
    Doctrine Emeritus
Princeton Theological Seminary
Princeton, New Jersey

Richard H. Drummond
Professor of the History of Religion
    Emeritus
University of Dubuque Theological
    Seminary
Dubuque, Iowa

Carlos M. N. Eire
Professor of History
Yale University
New Haven, Connecticut

Gabriel Fackre
Abbot Professor of Christian Theology
    Emeritus
Andover Newton Theological School
Newton Centre, Massachusetts

Benjamin Wirt Farley
Eunice Witherspoon Bell Younts
    and Willie Camp Younts Professor
    of Bible, Religion, and Philosophy
    Emeritus
Erskine College
Due West, South Carolina

Nathan P. Feldmeth
Associate Dean for Extension and Assistant Professor of Church History
Fuller Theological Seminary
Pasadena, California

Janet F. Fishburn
Professor Emerita, The Theological School
Drew University
Madison, New Jersey

David Foxgrover
Pastor, Congregational Church
Batavia, Illinois

John M. Frame
Professor of Systematic Theology
Reformed Theological Seminary
Orlando, Florida

Paul R. Fries
Professor of Foundational and Constructive Theology
New Brunswick Theological Seminary
New Brunswick, New Jersey

Mary McClintock Fulkerson
Associate Professor of Theology
Duke University Divinity School
Durham, North Carolina

Richard B. Gaffin Jr.
Professor of Biblical and Systematic Theology
Westminster Theological Seminary
Philadelphia, Pennsylvania

Richard C. Gamble
Professor of Systematic Theology
Reformed Theological Seminary
Orlando, Florida

Timothy George
Dean and Professor of Divinity
Samford University Divinity School
Birmingham, Alabama

John H. Gerstner[†]
Formerly Professor of Church History Emeritus
Pittsburgh Theological Seminary
Pittsburgh, Pennsylvania

Catherine Gunsalus González
Professor of Church History
Columbia Theological Seminary
Decatur, Georgia

W. Fred Graham
Professor of Religious Studies Emeritus
Michigan State University
East Lansing, Michigan

Thomas M. Gregory[†]
Formerly Professor of Religion and Philosophy Emeritus
Westminster College
New Wilmington, Pennsylvania

Donald D. Grohman
Professor of Religion and Philosophy
Knoxville College
Knoxville, Tennessee

Shirley C. Guthrie Jr.
Professor of Systematic Theology Emeritus
Columbia Theological Seminary
Decatur, Georgia

Douglas John Hall
Professor of Christian Theology Emeritus
McGill University
Montreal, Quebec, Canada

Charles E. Hambrick-Stowe
Minister of Worship and Stewardship, Church of the Apostles (United Church of Christ), and Adjunct Professor of Church History, Lancaster Theological Seminary
Lancaster, Pennsylvania

Trevor A. Hart
Professor of Divinity and Dean of the Faculty of Divinity
St. Mary's College
University of St. Andrews
St. Andrews, Scotland

W. Ian A. Hazlett
Senior Lecturer in Ecclesiastical History
University of Glasgow
Glasgow, Scotland

Alasdair I. C. Heron
Professor of Theology
University of Erlangen
Erlangen, Germany

I. John Hesselink
Albertus C. Van Raalte Professor
  of Systematic Theology Emeritus
Western Theological Seminary
Holland, Michigan

J. David Hoeveler Jr.
Professor of History
University of Wisconsin
Milwaukee, Wisconsin

Philip C. Holtrop
Professor of Religion Emeritus
Calvin College
Grand Rapids, Michigan

Philip E. Hughes[†]
Formerly Professor, Westminster
  Theological Seminary
Philadelphia, Pennsylvania

Merwyn S. Johnson
Professor of Historical and Systematic
  Theology
Erskine Theological Seminary
Due West, South Carolina

Christopher B. Kaiser
Professor of Historical and Systematic
  Theology
Western Theological Seminary
Holland, Michigan

Douglas F. Kelly
J. Richard Jordan Professor of System-
  atic Theology
Reformed Theological Seminary
Charlotte, North Carolina

William J. Klempa
Formerly Principal, Presbyterian
  College
Montreal, Quebec, Canada

John H. Leith
Professor of Theology Emeritus
Union Theological Seminary
Richmond, Virginia

Robert Letham
Pastor, Emmanuel Orthodox
  Presbyterian Church, Wilmington,
  Delaware
Adjunct Professor of Systematic
  Theology, Westminster Theological
  Seminary
Philadelphia, Pennsylvania

Alan E. Lewis[†]
Formerly Professor of Constructive
  Theology
Austin Presbyterian Theological
  Seminary
Austin, Texas

Robert D. Linder
Professor of History
Kansas State University
Manhattan, Kansas

David Little
T. J. Dermot Dunphy Professor of
  the Practice in Religion, Ethnicity,
  and International Conflict
Harvard Divinity School
Cambridge, Massachusetts

Bradley J. Longfield
Dean and Professor of Church History
University of Dubuque Theological
  Seminary
Dubuque, Iowa

C. T. McIntire
Professor of the History of Religions
University of Toronto
Toronto, Ontario, Canada

Elsie Anne McKee
Archibald Alexander Professor of
  Reformation Studies and the
  History of Worship
Princeton Theological Seminary
Princeton, New Jersey

Donald K. McKim
Academic and Reference Editor
Westminster John Knox Press
Germantown, Tennessee

LindaJo H. McKim
Pastor, Cordova Presbyterian Church
Cordova, Tennessee

Joseph C. McLelland
Professor Emeritus
McGill University and the Presbyterian
    College
Montreal, Quebec, Canada

Bruce M. Metzger
George L. Collord Professor of New
    Testament Language and Literature
    Emeritus
Princeton Theological Seminary
Princeton, New Jersey

Daniel L. Migliore
Charles Hodge Professor of Systematic
    Theology
Princeton Theological Seminary
Princeton, New Jersey

Glenn T. Miller
Waldo Professor of Ecclesiastical History
Bangor Theological Seminary
Bangor, Maine

John M. Mulder
President and Professor of Historical
    Theology
Louisville Theological Seminary
Louisville, Kentucky

Richard A. Muller
P. J. Zondervan Professor of Historical
    Theology
Calvin Theological Seminary
Grand Rapids, Michigan

Roger Nicole
Professor of Systematic Theology
Reformed Theological Seminary
Orlando, Florida

Rick Nutt
Associate Professor of Religion
Muskingum College
New Concord, Ohio

Hughes Oliphant Old
Center of Theological Inquiry and
    Adjunct Professor
Princeton Theological Seminary
Princeton, New Jersey

Richard R. Osmer
Thomas W. Synnott Professor of
    Christian Education and Director of
    the School of Christian Education
Princeton Theological Seminary
Princeton, New Jersey

M. Eugene Osterhaven
Albertus C. Van Raalte Professor of
    Systematic Theology Emeritus
Western Theological Seminary
Holland, Michigan

Douglas F. Ottati
M. E. Pemberton Professor of Theology
Union Theological Seminary and
    Presbyterian School of Christian
    Education
Richmond, Virginia

James I. Packer
Board of Governors Professor of Theology
Regent College
Vancouver, British Columbia, Canada

Robert J. Palma
Professor of Religion Emeritus
Hope College
Holland, Michigan

Thomas D. Parker
Professor of Theology Emeritus
McCormick Theological Seminary
Chicago, Illinois

Charles Partee
P. C. Rossin Professor of Church History
Pittsburgh Theological Seminary
Pittsburgh, Pennsylvania

Barbara A. Pursey
Formerly Adjunct Assistant Professor
University of Dubuque Theological
    Seminary
Dubuque, Iowa

Andrew Purves
Associate Professor of Pastoral
    Theology
Pittsburgh Theological Seminary
Pittsburgh, Pennsylvania

W. Stanford Reid[†]
Formerly Professor of History Emeritus
University of Guelph
Guelph, Ontario, Canada

Jack B. Rogers
Vice-President for Southern California
    and Professor of Theology Emeritus
San Francisco Theological Seminary
Pasadena, California

H. Martin Rumscheidt
Professor of Theology
Atlantic School of Theology
Halifax, Nova Scotia, Canada

Letty M. Russell
Professor of Theology
Yale University Divinity School
New Haven, Connecticut

Jean-Loup Seban
La Chapelle Royale
Belgium

Alan P. F. Sell
Professor of Christian Doctrine and
    Philosophy of Religion
United Theological College
Aberystwyth, Wales

M. Richard Shaull[†]
Formerly Professor of Ecumenics
Princeton Theological Seminary
Princeton, New Jersey

Donald W. Shriver Jr.
President Emeritus
Union Theological Seminary
New York, New York

Donald Sinnema
Professor of Theology
Trinity Christian College
Palos Heights, Illinois

Wayne R. Spear
Dean of the Faculty and Professor of
    Systematic Theology and Homiletics
Reformed Presbyterian Theological
    Seminary
Wilkinsburg, Pennsylvania

Gordon J. Spykman[†]
Fomerly Professor of Theology
    Calvin College
Grand Rapids, Michigan

John W. Stewart
Ralph B. and Helen S. Ashenfelter
    Associate Professor of Ministry
    and Evangelism
Princeton Theological Seminary
Princeton, New Jersey

Jack L. Stotts
President and Professor of Christian
    Ethics Emeritus
Austin Presbyterian Theological
    Seminary
Austin, Texas

George W. Stroup
J. B. Green Professor of Theology
Columbia Theological Seminary
Decatur, Georgia

Charles M. Swezey
Anne Scales Rogers Professor of
    Christian Ethics
Union Theological Seminary and
    Presbyterian School of Christian
    Education
Richmond, Virginia

Eugene TeSelle
Professor of Church History and
    Theology Emeritus
Vanderbilt Divinity School
Nashville, Tennessee

Peter Toon
President, The Prayer Book Society of
    the USA
Carrollton, Texas

John C. Vander Stelt
Professor of Theology and Philosophy
    Emeritus
Dordt College
Sioux Center, Iowa

Ronald J. VanderMolen
Professor of History
California State University Stanislaus
Turlock, California

Kenneth L. Vaux
Professor of Theological Ethics and
    Co-Director of the Center for Ethics
    and Values
Garrett-Evangelical Theological
    Seminary
Evanston, Illinois

Lukas Vischer
Formerly Office protestant pour
    l'oecuménisme en Suisse
Evangelische Arbeitsstelle Oekumene
    Schweiz
Bern, Switzerland

Derk Visser
Professor of History Emeritus
Ursinus College
Collegeville, Pennsylvania

Arvin Vos
Professor of Philosophy
Western Kentucky University
Bowling Green, Kentucky

John R. Walchenbach
Pastor
First Presbyterian Church
Fort Walton, Florida

Dewey D. Wallace Jr.
Professor of Religion
George Washington University
Washington, D.C.

Louis B. Weeks
Professor of Historical Theology and
    President in the Walter W. Moore
    Foundation Presidential Chairs
Union Theological Seminary and
    Presbyterian School of Christian
    Education
Richmond, Virginia

Charles C. West
Stephen Colwell Professor of Christian
    Ethics Emeritus
Princeton Theological Seminary
Princeton, New Jersey

James A. Whyte
Emeritus Professor of Christian Ethics
    and Practical Theology
St. Mary's College
University of St. Andrews
St. Andrews, Scotland

Preston N. Williams
Professor of Theology and
    Contemporary Change
Harvard Divinity School
Cambridge, Massachusetts

E. David Willis
Charles Hodge Professor of Systematic
    Theology Emeritus
Princeton Theological Seminary
Princeton, New Jersey

Marianne L. Wolfe
Formerly Stated Clerk, Pittsburgh
    Presbytery
Presbyterian Church (U.S.A.)
Pittsburgh, Pennsylvania

David F. Wright
Professor of Patristic and Reformed
    Christianity
New College
University of Edinburgh
Edinburgh, Scotland

---

†Deceased

Abbreviations

AIB   Jack B. Rogers and Donald K. McKim, *The Authority and Interpretation of the Bible* (San Francisco: Harper & Row, 1979)

AP   *American Presbyterians*

ARG   *Archiv für Reformationsgeschichte*

ARH   *Archive for Reformation History*

BC   *Book of Confessions* [Presbyterian Church (U.S.A.)]

BCP   *Book of Common Prayer*

CD   Karl Barth, *Church Dogmatics* (Edinburgh: T. & T. Clark, 1936–69)

CF   Friedrich Schleiermacher, *The Christian Faith* (1821–22; 2nd ed. 1830–31; ET 1928)

CFI   Hendrikus Berkhof, *Christian Faith: An Introduction to the Study of the Faith*, rev. ed. (Grand Rapids: Wm. B. Eerdmans Publishing Co., 1986)

CH   *Church History*

CO   *Ioannis Calvini Opera qui supersunt omnia*, ed. W. Baum, E. Cunitz, and E. Reuss, 58 vols. (Brunswick and Berlin: Schwetschke, 1865–1900)

CR   *Corpus Reformatorum* (Berlin and Leipzig, 1834–)

Creeds   *The Creeds of Christendom*, ed. Philip Schaff, 3 vols. (1877)

CTJ   *Calvin Theological Journal*

DD   Alan P. F. Sell, *Defending and Declaring the Faith: Some Scottish Examples, 1860–1920* (Colorado Springs, Colo.: Helmers Howard Publishers, 1987)

DNB   *Dictionary of National Biography,* and supplements (London, 1885–)

EPM   Patrick Collinson, *The Elizabethan Puritan Movement* (1967; repr. New York: Routledge, Chapman & Hall, 1982)

ET   English translation

FD   Otto Weber, *The Foundations of Dogmatics*, 2 vols. (ET Grand Rapids: Wm. B. Eerdmans Publishing Co., 1982–83)

Gr.   Greek

HC   Heidelberg Catechism

HCC   Philip Schaff, *History of the Christian Church*, 12 vols. (1883–93)

Inst.   John Calvin, *Institutes of the Christian Religion*

JPH   *Journal of Presbyterian History*

LCC   Library of Christian Classics, 26 vols.

NIV   New International Version

NSH   *The New Schaff-Herzog Encyclopedia of Religious Knowledge*, 13 vols. (New York, 1908–12; repr. Grand Rapids: Baker Book House, 1949–50); supplement, *Twentieth Century Encyclopedia of Religious Knowledge*, 2 vols. (1955)

NT	New Testament	*SJT*	*Scottish Journal of Theology*
OT	Old Testament	TEV	Today's English Version
PCUS	Presbyterian Church in the United States	*TRE*	*Theologische Realenzyklopdie,* ed. G. Krause and G. Müller (Berlin, 1977–)
PCUSA	Presbyterian Church in the United States of America	*TZ*	*Theologische Zeitschrift*
PC(USA)	Presbyterian Church (U.S.A.)	UPCNA	United Presbyterian Church of North America
RCA	Reformed Church in America	UPCUSA	United Presbyterian Church in the U.S.A.
RD	Heinrich Heppe, *Reformed Dogmatics,* ed. Ernst Bizer (ET 1950; repr. Grand Rapids: Baker Book House, 1978)	WARC	World Alliance of Reformed Churches
		WCC	World Council of Churches
		WCF	Westminster Confession of Faith
RGG	*Die Religion in Geschichte und Gegenwart,* 2nd ed., 5 vols. (1927–31); 3rd ed., 6 vols. (1957–65)	WLC	Westminster Larger Catechism
		WSC	Westminster Shorter Catechism
RSV	Revised Standard Version	*WTJ*	*Westminster Theological Journal*
SCJ	*Sixteenth Century Journal*		

Words set in bold and italics are also listed as a separate entry.

Accommodation Latin rhetoricians and jurists used "accommodation" (Lat. *accommodatio*) for the process of adapting, fitting, and adjusting language to the needs and capacities of their hearers. This meant accounting for an audience's situation, character, intelligence, and emotional state.

Rhetorically trained early church theologians such as Origen, Chrysostom, and *Augustine* used the concept when dealing with difficulties in the Bible. Calvin, a classicist, expanded this and used accommodation to explain every relationship between *God* and *humanity.* Given the great gulf between God and humankind, by virtue of God's transcendence and human finiteness, God's holiness and human sinfulness, for God to communicate with humanity and God's *revelation* to occur, God must condescend to communicate in ways humans can understand, according to the limits of human capacities. This method of revelation of God's speaking and acting in human forms is God's accommodation.

Calvin saw accommodation as grounded in scriptural portrayals of God as Father, teacher, and physician. Three specific scriptural uses of accommodation are the *law* (*Inst.* 2.11.13), the Lord's Prayer (*Inst.* 3.20.34), and the *sacraments* (*Inst.* 4.1.1). Through these, the divine message of *salvation* is conveyed, just as, more generally, in the language of *scripture* itself. God "lisps" in speaking of who God is to "accommodate the knowledge of [God] to our slight capacity" (*Inst.* 1.13.1). Using parental imagery, Calvin quoted Augustine: "We can safely follow Scripture, which proceeds at the pace of a mother stooping to her child, so to speak, so as not to leave us behind in our weakness" (*Inst.* 3.21.4). Calvin used accommodation to deal with God's nature (*Inst.* 1.13.1), *creation* (*Inst.* 1.14.3) and function of angels (*Inst.* 1.14.11), fate (*Inst.* 1.16.9), and God's ways with humans (*Inst.* 1.17.12–13). The supreme instance of accommodation, however, is Jesus Christ. In Christ, God has fully entered into the human by becoming a person.

Calvin commented: "In Christ God so to speak makes himself little (*quodammodo parvum facit*), in order to lower himself to our capacity" (*ut se ad captum nostrum submittat*; Commentary on 1 Peter 1:20). For Calvin, human limitations were not barriers to hearing and understanding God's revelation and message of salvation, since God used humans to express the written *Word of God* in scripture.

F. L. Battles, "God Was Accommodating Himself to Human Capacity," *Interpretation* 31, no. 1 (January 1977): 19–38; Rogers and McKim, *AIB.*

DONALD K. MCKIM

Adoption The theologoumenon of adoption (or filiation) is that biblical understanding of the ultimate divine purpose in redemption which sees human persons as drawn into a peculiar relationship with *God* as Father, through a relationship with God as Son and as *Holy Spirit.* As such, it is a soteriological motif inseparable from the doctrines of the *incarnation* and the *Trinity.*

Biblical. Properly speaking, the language of adoption (Gr. *huiothesia*) is found only in the Pauline corpus (esp. Rom. 8; Gal. 4), though the idea of Christians as "sons" of *Abba* (God the Father) lies at the heart of Jesus' own message and *ministry.* The precedent for Paul's language can be discovered in the Jewish belief that Israel, through its *election* and rescue from Egypt by Yahweh, progressed from a status of slavery to one of "sonship" (a transition paralleled in the Christian's *experience* of redemption from sin). But it is equally clear that, for Paul, the "adoption" proper to Christian experience is rooted ontologically in the decision of God to send God's own Son into the world as a human being and is no mere metaphor. It is through union with *Christ* and living "in him" that Christian existence consists in adoption, since it is precisely being given to share in the hitherto unique filial relation of love with the Father in the Spirit.

Patristic. Among the early Christian

theologians, several took this central biblical theme and developed it theologically, being careful to distinguish the "adopted" sonship of Christians from the "natural" Sonship of him who is "consubstantial" with the Father, yet seeing the two as inseparably linked. It is within this context, as the christological thinking of the *church* developed, that the term "deification" (Gr. *theopoiēsis*) was introduced as a radical statement of the ultimate meaning of adoption, or filiation, clarifying the implication that human beings are given to share or participate in the very inner life of the *Trinity* as "sons" (children) of the Father. It was precisely to safeguard this soteriological insight that the early theologians insisted that if Christ is thus to save us, he must be fully God as well as fully human.

Reformed. Reformed **theology** has often presented the God-human relationship in primarily judicial rather than filial categories, perhaps because it has traditionally focused rather more on that which human persons have been saved "from" by God than that which they have been saved "for." Yet, from John Calvin onward, there has always been a recognition of the importance of the theme of adoption and of the ultimately prospective purpose of God in Christ in "bringing many sons to glory." Even the **Westminster Confession,** the overall framework of which is unmistakably judicial, contains a separate chapter on adoption. What has sometimes been lacking, however, is clear recognition that the Trinitarian and filial understanding of God must, if it is taken seriously, provide the proper context for understanding the judicial side of God's activity rather than vice versa.

TREVOR A. HART

Analogy Designation for a type of predication between univocal ("having the same meaning") and equivocal ("having different meanings") predication. A term is analogous when it names a quality that is partly the same and partly different in two or more subjects. Its theological significance is to explain how language that is derived from creatures can be applied to *God.*

In John Calvin, as in the church fathers, there is no systematic treatment of analogy as a type of predication. Yet it is implied in Calvin's *doctrine* of the **knowledge of God** (*Inst.* 1.5–6). God's essence is incomprehensible, but there are innumerable evidences of God in *creation.* So God is known from similarities in creatures which are dissimilar to God. After the fall, no true knowledge of God is possible from nature but only through *revelation.*

In later Reformed theologians such as A. Quenstedt, one discerns the influence of Thomas Cajetan, a commentator on Aquinas. Essence, substance, spirit, and the like are terms predicated of both God and creatures by an analogy of intrinsic attribution. In other words, "essence" belongs to both God and creature but in different ways and because the creature has its essence from God.

In the twentieth century, Karl Barth asserted that the only means for understanding God is by the analogy of faith (*analogia fidei*), not by any human, philosophical category (*analogia entis*). A word applied to a creature and then to God has similarity in its meaning, partial correspondence and agreement, only because it has been chosen by God.

Barth, *CD* II/1; B. Mondin, *The Principle of Analogy in Protestant and Catholic Theology* (1963).

ARVIN VOS

Apologetics Christianity has always had its cultural despisers. In every age Christian apologists have attempted to rebut objections or restate and refine Christian belief to make clearer its claims of *knowledge of God.* Apologetics seeks to benefit the criticized and the critic by preserving the integrity of *God,* who has been revealed in human thought forms as Supreme Truth.

Before and after the Reformation, apologetics often built a defense of Christianity on the same *philosophy* used by the unbeliever. When philosophy was willing to be a servant to *faith,* the result was frequently a clearer reformulation of the faith, as seen in *Augustine* and Thomas Aquinas. The Reformation, however, brought a crisis in apologetics as well as in theology. The prevailing method of defending the faith, *scholasticism,* became an uncomfortable option for the Reformers. They perceived that it had been diverted from its proper objective of safeguarding the truth of God to the purpose of bolstering an organization that made itself the judge of truth. They recognized that philosophy was no longer willing to be a "handmaiden" to theology and could not be used to defend Christianity without excessive qualification of the faith.

Reformed thought thus introduced a paradigmatic change in apologetics. Shifting from a philosophy that stressed the priority of metaphysics and being, it embraced an outlook that put epistemology and truth first in preserving the *authority* of God in God's objective self-revelation. John Calvin was a conscious exponent of this new approach with his stress on knowledge (*Inst.* 1). He observed that a knowledge of ourselves is mutually connected with the knowledge of God because self-knowledge arouses us to seek God. The epistemological connection is firmly seen when Calvin points out that the clarity and the truthfulness of self-knowledge, which stimulates us to seek God, are dependent upon knowing God's majesty and our own sinful pride and recognizing that God is the sole standard by which we know ourselves. Further indication of this paradigm shift is in Calvin's distinction of a twofold knowledge of God, which became the definitive ordering principle of the structure of his *Institutes.*

At the heart of the Reformed apologetic stressing the reception of truth from God was a new conception of the place of the Bible. *Scripture* was projected to purvey a comprehensive view of the world and life in it given by God, powerful enough to accommodate scientific and cultural change without being negatively shaped by it. Because of *sin,* scripture was necessary, and because it was from God it was authoritative and sufficient as a source of faith and life. Proclamation and exposition of the *Word of God* became the apologetic, because there could be no knowledge of God that is not basically conceptual.

The Bible was viewed as "properly basic," as self-authenticating. The task of *reason* was not to validate such acclaim but to provide insight for biblical interpretation or application. Self-authentication meant that the Bible contains truths that are patent and can persuade to belief without supplementary aid. Thus, the aim of apologetics was to set forth in a winsome fashion the promises of God and God's redemptive action in Christ. God had accommodated his truth to human capacity in order to meet human need. Scripture gives rise to distinctive beliefs that satisfy human hopes and fears. The judgments of scripture are believed, not because philosophy or a church council validates them, nor simply because they are helpful, but because they are accepted as truths from God. Assenting to them as true is the mediate cause of their power to arouse and satisfy religious need, and the *Holy Spirit* is the immediate cause of the believing.

Though centered in promulgating the biblical message, this apologetic may employ external reasons, or evidences, to achieve its purpose. Arguments that the Bible was an ancient book wonderfully preserved and coherent, and that nature, human culture, and *science* display amazing complexities inconceivable without divine wisdom as their source, may bring assurances. But they are not the essence of the matter; knowledge of God is the crucial issue.

Under the pressure of Deism and rationalism in the seventeenth and eighteenth centuries, many Reformed apologists exploited external evidence or reverted to the use of postulates common to Deism and rationalism in attempting to defend Christianity. For a consistent Reformed apologetics, however, these indices cannot be the ground for accepting the claims of the Bible as true, since the defensibility of these supporting reasons would reappear in one's conception of God and would not be serving God, or God's Word, as the Supreme Truth.

Reformed apologetics may also use reasons integral to humanity's internal consciousness to enhance faith. Here assumptions about human nature that are found in scripture are drawn upon. Calvin speaks of an understanding of the divine majesty implanted in all persons, and Augustine holds that there are innate principles that even the skeptic cannot deny. But while this internal illumination may be very helpful in providing fortification for the faithful in the face of atheism, it is not the ground for the individual's believing the truth of God's Word. The apologetic witness does not arise out of, or appeal for ultimate *justification* to, internal phenomena. It is dependent upon the appeal of truth itself as from God and vouchsafed by the Holy Spirit.

External and internal evidence for believing the Christian message in the scriptures can and should be provided as circumstances require, but the lack of them does not invalidate the testimony of God revealed in the Bible. Hebrews 4:12 shows the apologetic thrust of God's Word: "For the Word of God is living and active. Sharper than any double-edged sword, it penetrates even to dividing soul and spirit . . . ; it judges the thoughts and attitudes of the heart" (NIV). Reformed apologists need only to realize that their method is not irrational and is honoring to the God whose being is truth.

G. Clark, *Three Types of Religious Philosophy* (1989); T. Halyburton, *An Essay Concerning the Nature of Faith* (1798); P. Helm, *Varieties of Belief* (1973); J. Owen, *The Reason of Faith* (1677); A. Plantinga, "Advice to Christian Philosophers," in *Faith and Philosophy*, ed. A. Plantinga (1964).

THOMAS M. GREGORY

Arminianism   Emerging from the influence of the Dutch theologian Jacobus Arminius (1560–1609), Arminianism proposed a substantial revision of the Reformed doctrines of *predestination* and *grace*. The five Remonstrant Articles (1610) developed Arminius's ideas, only to meet emphatic repudiation at the *Synod of Dort* (1618–19).

Reacting against the lack of Christocentricity in the *supralapsarianism* of his erstwhile teacher Theodore Beza, Arminius argued that *election* was subsequent to grace. *God* determines to save all whom God foresees will repent and trust Christ. Election is thus conditional on God's *foreknowledge* of a person's response. Moreover, the fallen will remains free. Humans can believe or resist grace. Thus, saving grace is sufficient but not irresistible. Humans cooperate. The possibility of a true believer falling from grace totally or finally Arminius left open.

The Remonstrant Articles affirmed these claims: Election is seen as conditional on God's foreknowledge, Christ died for all but only believers are saved, grace is necessary to *salvation* but is resistible, and further investigation is needed into whether all the regenerate will persevere.

The Synod of Dort condemned the articles, removing and exiling the Remonstrant ministers. It appeared to the contra-Remonstrants that Arminianism threatened to destroy the doctrine of *assurance* by questioning perseverance, that it introduced a semi-Pelagian doctrine of grace and a conditional gospel that would undermine the *atonement* and *justification*.

The atonement demonstrates a substantive difference between Arminianism and orthodoxy. While some form of penal substitution was at least implicit in the limited atonement taught by the Synod of Dort, Arminianism held that Christ suffered for all but did not actually pay the penalty for their sins, since all are not saved. Rather, Christ's death permits the Father to forgive all who repent and believe. Hugo Grotius, a Dutch jurist, soon developed the governmental theory of the atonement, teaching that the cross was necessary as a wise means of upholding God's moral administration of the universe and was not required by virtue of anything inherent in God's nature.

Despite suppression, Arminianism eventually spread widely throughout the world, pervading many fundamentalist circles in North America. Methodism has been a particular base since the impetus provided by John Wesley. While holding to total depravity, Wesley taught the universality of Christ's work, the sufficiency of grace, and the ability of *humanity* to cooperate in appropriating it, expressly accepting the possibility of falling from grace.

The Arminian challenge posed questions for the Reformed church. Further debate on the nature of predestination and God's grace followed the controversy. Moïse Amyraut (1596–1664) and the French Reformed theological school at Saumur developed a modified predestinarianism that met with much resistance. Arminius's reconstruction of election with Christ as foundation resulted in particular problems. Hitherto, election and *Christology* had frequently been integrated in *Reformed theology.* Now there was a reluctance to integrate them. Arminius had stolen the idea. Reformed predestinarianism was to move in a more speculative direction.

J. Arminius, *Works,* 3 vols. (1825); C. Bangs, *Arminius* (rev. ed. 1985); A. W. Harrison, *Arminianism* (1937); R. Muller, *God, Creation, and Providence in the Thought of Jacob Arminius: Sources and Directions of Scholastic Protestantism in the Era of Early Orthodoxy* (1991).

ROBERT LETHAM

Ascension The entry into *heaven* of the Lord Jesus Christ in his *resurrection* body in order to sit at the right hand of *God* the Father as the Mediator who is to us king, priest, and prophet. There are three views of when this ascension occurred.

1. On Easter morning. The resurrection was the first part of the one act of God exalting Jesus to heaven from the grave. Thus, Jesus ascended when he was resurrected. In this view, all the resurrection appearances are of Jesus from heaven, and the last (Acts 1:11) is a dramatic symbolic presentation of what has happened to Jesus already.

2. On Easter evening. This view is based on John 20:17 and Luke 24:50ff. Jesus rose from the dead on Easter morning, and after appearing to his disciples he ascended from Bethany in the evening. Later resurrection appearances are from heaven, and the last (Acts 1) is symbolic (as in view 1).

3. On the fortieth day after his resurrection, the day the *church* has celebrated as Ascension Day. This, the traditional view, does not indicate where Jesus was when he was not with his disciples. It takes the appearance and departure recorded in Acts 1 as the actual account of the ascension of Jesus into heaven (symbolized by the Shekinah cloud of glory) as witnessed by the disciples and angels.

There is, of course, a major element of mystery in this event, for we are dealing with what is unique and supernatural. Most modern Reformed theologians favor the first view in one or another form, expounding it in relation to the resurrection and heavenly session of our Lord.

J. G. Davies, *He Ascended into Heaven* (1958); D. Farrow, *Ascension and Ecclesia: On the Significance of the Doctrine of the Ascension for Ecclesiology and Christian Cosmology* (1999); P. Toon, *The Ascension of Our Lord* (1984).

PETER TOON

Assurance of Salvation One of the great benefits of the Reformation was the recovery of the doctrine of the Christian believer's assurance of eternal security in Christ.

The developed Roman Catholic system opposed this *doctrine.* (1) It taught that the blood of Jesus availed only for the purging of sins committed before *baptism*; hence the need for the performance of penitential deeds and, after this life, purgatorial fire to deal with postbaptismal sin. (2) It distinguished between venial and mortal sins, according to which the committing of mortal *sin* resulted in the loss of the *grace* of *salvation*. (3) It conceived of justifying grace as infused grace rather than as the grace of Christ's righteousness imputed to the believer, so a person was regarded as either totally holy or, through the forfeiting of infused grace, totally unholy before *God*. (4) It held that a person's *justification* depended not only on the work of Christ but also on one's own good works performed before and after justification as meritoriously contributing to and also increasing one's justification (semi-Pelagianism).

From this teaching no one could be sure that the grace possessed today might not be lost tomorrow or that one would not die in a graceless state of mortal sin. Because of the finite fallibility and fallenness of the human creature, for salvation to depend in part on the merit of one's own good works and not wholly on the merit of Christ's work of redemption left everything in uncertainty. In the sixteenth century the Roman Catholic Council of Trent asserted the uncertainty of salvation inherent in its teaching, declaring that "each person, when he regards himself and his own indisposition, may entertain fear and apprehension concerning his own grace, inasmuch as no one can know with a certainty of faith, which cannot be subject to mistake, that he has obtained the grace of God" (Sess. 6, canon 2), and also anathematizing any person who taught that the sinner is justified by faith alone, apart from the cooperating merit of good works (Sess. 6, canon 9).

The Reformers contended *scripture* teaches that the blood of Jesus Christ cleanses from all sin, not just from sin committed before baptism (1 John 1:7); that the believer's security is based solely on the atoning work of Christ, which, since it is the work of God on our behalf, cannot fail or come to nothing (2 Cor. 5:17–21; Phil. 1:6); that Christ himself promised that no one could pluck those who are his out of his hand (John 10:28); and that the biblical doctrine of the *election* of the redeemed in Christ also ensured the final *perseverance* and glorification of those who are called and justified by God (Rom. 8:29–30). In short, the redemption of sinners is, from beginning to end, the work of God by virtue of the saving grace that freely flows to the believer from the cross of Jesus (*sola gratia*). This is the sole and solid ground for the Christian assurance of the believer's security in Christ for all eternity.

J. Beeke, *Assurance of Faith: Calvin, English Puritanism, and the Dutch Second Reformation* (1991); R. Zachman, *The Assurance of Faith: Conscience in the Theology of Martin Luther and John Calvin* (1993).

PHILIP E. HUGHES

Atonement   As the work of reconciliation wrought by *God* in Christ, atonement has been central in the Reformed tradition. Interpretations of this saving deed have ranged from an encompassing at-one-ment of God and the world accomplished by a manifold *ministry* of Christ (the threefold office) to a delimited focus on a penal substitution carried out on Calvary to render the sinner acceptable to God. Whether broad or narrow in scope, the Reformed understanding of the atonement has always stressed the "cruciality of the cross" (P. T. Forsyth).

The term "atonement" is English in origin, appearing in Elizabethan literature as the bringing of concord between persons or groups. In the Geneva Bible (1560) the word is used interchangeably with "reconciliation" in association with the root *kpr* (Lev. 23:28; Num. 15:28), though the latter is more often translated in its cultic context as "expiation." In both the Genevan and the King James (1611) versions its single NT appearance is in

Rom. 5:10–11 (*katallassō; katallagē*), where "atonement" and "reconciliation" are used synonymously. In theological discourse its equivalents in both non-English and English traditions are "the work of Christ," "the office of Mediator," "the work of reconciliation (redemption, *salvation*)," and "objective soteriology."

Over the centuries, Reformed commentary on the doctrine of atonement was marked by accents on the radical character of sin as judged by the holiness of God; divine sovereignty as source of the work executed; OT prefiguration of the ways of reconciliation; ethical implications of atonement; and interconnections of Christ's life and teachings, suffering and death, *resurrection* and *ascension.*

The Anselmic portrayal of Christ's redeeming work as satisfaction of God's offended honor was recast by the Reformers in forensic terms. Christ stood in our place to receive punishment meted out on *sin* by a just judge. John Calvin notably describes Christ's vicarious work blending priestly imagery (Heb. 9:14, 25–26) with law court metaphors (Gal. 3:13):

> Because a deserved curse obstructs the entrance, and God in his character of judge is hostile to us, expiation must necessarily intervene, that as a priest employed to appease the wrath of God, he may reinstate us in his favor. Wherefore, in order that Christ might fulfill this office, it behooves Him to appear with a sacrifice. . . . God could not be propitiated without the expiation of sin. . . . By the sacrifice of his death He wiped away our guilt and made satisfaction for our sin. (*Inst.* 2.15.6)

Sacrifice and penal substitution become refrains in Reformed *confessions* and *catechisms.*

> The Lord Jesus, by his perfect obedience and sacrifice of himself, which he through the eternal Spirit once offered up unto God, hath fully satisfied the justice of his Father; and purchased not only reconciliation, but an everlasting inheritance in the kingdom of heaven, for all those whom the Father hath given unto him. (WCF, 8.5)

Q. 37. What do you understand by the word "suffered"?

A. That throughout his life on earth, but especially at the end of it, he bore in body and soul the wrath of God against the sin of the whole human race, so that by his suffering, as the only expiatory sacrifice, he might redeem our body and soul from everlasting damnation, and might obtain for us God's grace, righteousness, and eternal life. (HC)

Calvin, and the confessional tradition after him, followed the trajectory of sacrifice into the lower regions, interpreting the descent into *hell* of the Apostles' Creed as Christ's experience of the torments that befit human sin.

The "finished work" of passion, death, and descent is succeeded in Reformed teaching by a "continuing work" of the resurrected and ascended Lord whose intercession before the Father secures for the elect the benefits of oblation. In *Reformed theology,* substitution is active as well as passive, the fulfillment of the law's requirements as well as acceptance of the penalty for its violations. Hence, Christ "removed the enmity between God and us . . . through the whole course of his obedience" (*Inst.* 2.16.5). The merit of Christ transferred to the elect therefore is twofold: a righteousness of life exhibited in perfect holiness through his "active obedience" and a righteousness in *death* in which Christ suffers the consequences of our sin through his "passive obedience."

The extended range of Christ's mediatorial work to "the whole course of his obedience" is also expressed through Calvin's imaginative development of the *munus triplex*: "Therefore that faith might find a solid ground of salvation, and so rest in him, we must set out this principle, that the office which he received from the Father consists of three parts" (*Inst.* 2.15.1). Christ, the Anointed

One, fulfills the promise of reconciliation embodied in the OT types of prophet, priest, and king, each called by unction into their respective offices. Thus, the prophetic teacher and herald and the royal ascended Lord join the priestly Savior of Calvary in a total saving deed. Following Calvin, atonement has been conceived in these encompassing terms in Reformed confessions and catechisms (WCF, 8.1; HC, qq. 31–32; WSC, qq. 23–26) and by its theologians from the post-Reformation scholastics to Karl Barth.

While Zwingli cannot rank with Calvin in either influence or profundity, he sought to give systematic expression to the work of Christ. In doing so, he voiced an aspect of the *doctrine* of atonement often neglected in traditional formulations but taken up in the nineteenth century by the *Mercersburg Theology* (John Williamson Nevin and Philip Schaff) and also in more recent Reformed thought. Zwingli wrote:

> Wishing at length, then, to help this desperate case of ours, our Creator sent one to satisfy His justice by offering Himself for us—not an angel, nor a man, but His own Son, and clothed in flesh in order that neither His majesty might deter us from intercourse with Him, nor His lowliness deprive us of hope. For being God and the Son of God, He that was sent as deputy and mediator gives support to hope. For what cannot He do or have who is God? (*Commentary on True and False Religion,* 6)

Here the incarnational presupposition of the atonement—the affirmation that "God was *in* Christ, reconciling the world" (2 Cor. 5:19)—is forcefully stated, calling into question popular portrayals of a retributive deity punishing a loving Jesus.

Subsequent Reformed theology continued the Reformers' themes, drawing out implications and making applications according to contemporary issues. The accent on the divine sovereignty soon came to prominence in *Socinian* and *Arminian* controversies. It took form as the assertion of a *pactum salutis* between the Father and the Son in which by inscrutable decree the Second Person is sent to execute in the human nature of Christ a "limited atonement" for the elect, with the others, the reprobate, passed over. This position is sometimes described by use of the acronym TULIP: *Total depravity,* Unconditional *election,* Limited atonement, *Irresistible grace,* and *Perseverance of the saints*—five points made at the *Synod of Dort* (1618–19) against the Remonstrants who defended human choice against Calvinist interpretations of divine sovereignty. More recently, the double decree and vicarious sacrifice have been restated by Barth as the election and rejection of Jesus Christ, with all of *humanity, de jure,* a participant in the "humiliation of the Son of God" and the "exaltation of the Son of Man."

Early Reformed thought gave considerable attention to the equivalency of punishment for fallen humanity's offense against the *law* of God, executed on the cross. This "penal substitutionary theory" came to the fore in the debate with exemplarist and Abelardian notions that ignored both the gravity of sin and the rigor of God. Included in the attack on the latter were "four point Calvinists" and others who held that the redemption won was sufficient for all but applied only to some.

The Reformed inheritance includes an activist emphasis on the *response* to the mandates of the divine majesty rather than its initiatives, turning away from the objectivity of both election and penal substitution and toward an obediential subjectivity. It found expression, variously, in the seventeenth-century "governmental theory" of Hugo Grotius (influential also in the *New England Theology*) that views Jesus' sacrifice as upholding the sanctity of the law by exhibiting the consequences of its breach by a sinful humanity rather than execution of an equivalent punishment; the "moral influence theory" (expressed in nineteenth-century theology in the early Bushnell), in which the life and the death of Christ are viewed as an exemplification of the divine love, the incentive required to change us rather than a suffering undergone to alter God's relationship to a sinful world.

Reformed accents on either the indicatives or the imperatives of divine sovereignty have been regularly assailed by critics for, on the one hand, the "horrible decree" of double **predestination** in which speculation on the majesty of God overwhelms the biblical witness to the love of God, or for, on the other hand, a preoccupation with the call to obedience that obscures both the impossibilities of human sin and the possibilities of divine **grace.** Challenges to the Reformed tradition continue, as in a "hermeneutics of suspicion" which charges that the historic emphasis on atonement for individual sin by a personal savior overlooks the struggle against oppression and the work of Jesus the liberator or asserts that the centrality of the cross entails the picture of a wrathful Father punishing an innocent Son and must be rejected as "child abuse theology."

Under the banner of *semper reformanda,* Reformed response has acknowledged reductionist tendencies in its tradition, both speculative excesses and subjectivistic lapses. In an attempt to be faithful to both its "world-formative" (N. Wolterstorff) character and sobriety about sin, and striving to learn from the suspicionist critique, it holds the full work of redemption to include the rule of Christ over, and our call to resist, oppressive political, economic, and social powers and principalities (see contemporary statements and confessions of Reformed churches in Vischer, ed., *Reformed Witness Today,* and statements of the WARC). And it seeks to recover its own classical teaching about the unity of person and work, asserting that God does not inflict suffering on another but receives into the divine heart the painful consequences of human sin.

Calvin's threefold office returns time and again to provide a vehicle for integrating the various accents of the Reformed tradition and for developing a more ecumenical framework for understanding the atonement. In this inclusive rendering, Christ the prophet engages ignorance and error by the disclosure and embodiment of truth, Christ the priest meets sin and guilt by vicarious sacrifice, and Christ the king conquers suffering and death by his liberating power. The partnership of roles invites the correction of reductionist tendencies: The exacting punishments of the penal theory are reconceived in terms of a *holy* love; the naïvetés of exemplarism are challenged by the *tough* love of accountability to the divine holiness; the militant metaphors of ransom, victory, and liberation learn from the *tender* love of Galilean *agapē* and from the realism of Calvary's sacrifice about the sin that persists in the champions of justice as well as its foes. Inclusivity also joins **incarnation** and atonement and affirms the Trinitarian life together, precluding the temptation to distribute what is done between a punitive deity and a perfect human sacrifice or between a wrathful Father and a loving Son.

While Reformed theology has given attention to the narrative sequence of the offices—a prophetic ministry in Jesus' life, teachings, and healings; a priestly ministry in passion and death; and a royal ministry in resurrection and ascension—it has also stressed their coinherence: the priestly and royal character of Christ's prophetic work in its vulnerable and victorious love; a prophetic and royal priesthood—the king who reigns and the Word that is proclaimed from the cross; and the royal rule of a suffering servant. The theme of mutuality persists in the concurrence of the offices in the continuing work of Christ as it applies the benefits of this finished work: the prophetic proclamation of the Word to us, the priestly intercession for us, and the royal rule over us.

R. S. Franks declared that Calvin's articulation of the threefold office is one of the lasting contributions of the Reformation. Its continuing significance is demonstrated by such twentieth-century expositions as Barth's magisterial restatement and application of prophetic, priestly, and royal roles to the ministry of the laity in both Protestant and Roman Catholic theology. So might a doctrine of atonement, Catholic and Reformed, contribute to the reconciliation about which it speaks and for which it hopes.

Barth, *CD* IV/1–3; P. T. Forsyth, *The Work of Christ* (1910); R. S. Franks, *The Work of Christ* (1918; repr. 1962); Heppe, *RD*; H. D. McDonald, *The Atonement of the Death of Christ* (1985); A. E. McGrath, *Iustitia Dei: A History of the Christian Doctrine of Justification*, vol. 2 (1986); R. S. Paul, *The Atonement and the Sacraments* (1960); L. Vischer, ed., *Reformed Witness Today* (1982); J. S. Whale, *Victor and Victim* (1960).

GABRIEL FACKRE

Augustine and Augustinianism

Augustine (354–430), a major influence on Catholic and Protestant theology and *doctrine*, was born and educated in North Africa. After teaching in Rome and Milan, where he was converted to Catholic Christianity (386) through the influence of Ambrose, he returned to Africa, where he became a presbyter and then bishop in Hippo. The *Confessions* interpret his life up to his *conversion* and *baptism* and the death of his mother, Monica. His sermons (about 750 survive) and his controversial, expository, and theological writings (chief among which are *The Trinity* and *The City of God*) were widely used during the Middle Ages.

As Adolf von Harnack suggested, there are three "circles of thought" in Augustine's theology, successively elaborated: (1) a Neoplatonist quest for direct contemplation of *God,* which enabled Christians to affirm both human *reason* and the spiritual aspirations of non-Christians; (2) a Catholic insistence on *revelation,* the *authority* of the *church,* and indispensability of the *sacraments,* reflected in the controversy against the Donatists' claims of personal holiness; and (3) a Pauline emphasis on the

bondage of the will, the need for *grace,* and the role of *predestination* in *salvation,* all elaborated against the Pelagians' defense of *freedom* and merit. In the practical realm, we should not overlook Augustine's influence in extending the monastic life to the clergy, who lived "the common life" under a rule. *The City of God* offered a Christian perspective not only on human *history* but on political life; it was variously interpreted through the centuries to support clericalism, "political realism," or a quest for secular *justice.*

Augustine's writings, edited by Johannes Amerbach and Erasmus and printed in Basel, became a major influence after 1500. Luther, Zwingli, and Calvin all ascribed their "conversions" to their reading of Augustine. But tensions among the different emphases in Augustine's thought also emerged. The humanism of the "Northern Renaissance" looked to Augustine's interest in rational and religious quests, sometimes in isolation from Christian or churchly concerns; Roman Catholicism to his affirmation of authority, the church, and the sacraments; and Protestantism to the more individualistic themes of predestination and grace. None followed Augustine uncritically. Calvin, who made much use of Augustine's writings in thinking about predestination, grace, the unity of OT and NT, the church, and the sacraments, judged him to be in error about purgatory and celibacy and took more radical positions on predestination, *original sin,* and *justification;* Calvin also disliked Augustine's use of allegory and numerology in exegesis, preferring Chrysostom's more literal method of interpretation.

The "Scripture principle" limited Protestant loyalty to Augustine. Post-Tridentine Catholicism nourished a more vigorous development of Augustinian anthropology, which also became the focus of major doctrinal debates within the Catholic Church. One concerned nature and grace. Against those who tended to superimpose grace upon nature, the Augustinians stressed their interpenetration, affirming both a human "desire for God" and the freedom or "gratuity" of God's invitation. Another concerned *free will* and grace. Against the Thomists, who asserted that grace moves the will "physically"—that is, without its own action—the Jesuits, following Augustine, saw it acting "morally," through suggestion, inclination, and consent. A third debate concerned predestination. While assuming that predestination is based in God's will rather than human merit, Luis de Molina argued that God takes into account what human beings "would do" if offered grace, and Francisco Suárez suggested that God gives grace in a way "congruous" to their inclinations—both on the basis of passages in Augustine. The refined concepts that were introduced during these debates influenced Protestant as well as Catholic theology after 1600.

Jansenism, a more extreme form of Augustinianism in seventeenth-century France, was similar to *Calvinism* in its insistence on the unconditional necessity of predestining grace; it is often blamed for a grim and pessimistic strand in French Catholicism. The more authentic Augustinian tradition is the other one, which developed in Catholic and then Protestant theology, anticipating many themes in the theology of Moïse Amyraut and Jonathan Edwards, liberalism, and twentieth-century Catholicism.

M. Bendischioli, "L'agostinismo dei riformatori protestanti," *Revue desétudes augustiniennes* 1 (1955): 203–24; C. Boyer, "Jean Calvin et Saint Augustin," *Augustinian Studies* 3 (1972): 15–34; P. Brown, *Augustine of Hippo* (1967); J. Cadier, "Calvin et Saint Augustin," in *Augustinus Magister. Actes du Congrès international augustinien* (1954–55), 2:1033–56; J. Fitzer, "The Augustinian Roots of Calvin's Eucharistic Thought," *Augustinian Studies* 7 (1976): 69–98; A. Fitzgerald, ed., *Augustine through the Ages* (1999); A. von Harnack, *History of Dogma*, vol. 5 (1891); H. de Lubac, *Augustinianism and Modern Theology* (1969); and *The Mystery of the Supernatural* (1967); O. J.-B. du Roy, "Augustine, St.," *New Catholic Encyclopedia* (1967), 1:1041–58; R. P. Russell, "Augustinianism," *New Catholic Encyclopedia*, 1:1063–71; L. Smits, *Saint Augustin dans l'oeuvre de Jean Calvin*, vol. 1: *Etude de critique littéraire*, vol. 2: *Tables des références augustiniennes* (1957–58); E. TeSelle, *Augustine the Theologian* (1970); B. B. Warfield, *Calvin and Augustine* (1956); and *Studies in Tertullian and Augustine* (1930); F. Wendel, *Calvin* (1965).

EUGENE TESELLE

Authority In Reformed thought, Christian belief is not based on a rational *philosophy* devised by the human mind but on divine *revelation*, which is the scriptures of the OT and the NT. The biblical writers were divinely inspired when they wrote their history, songs and psalms, and theological expositions. Consequently, their writings are the recorded *Word of God*. The message of the Bible is that *God* is the sovereign creator, judge, and redeemer of the world and its inhabitants.

While the Bible is quite explicit in stating that it is the Word of God, no one comes to a recognition of this unless enlightened by the *Holy Spirit*, who opens one's eyes to the Bible's character. In Reformed thought, no one is able to understand the meaning and teaching of the scriptures unless and until the Holy Spirit enlightens one's mind. When this happens, the reader of the scriptures recognizes their authority and also comes to an understanding of how their teachings should be applied to one's view of the world and life in it.

From this belief in scripture's inspiration and the enlightenment by the Holy Spirit has developed the Reformed tradition, based largely on the work of ancient church leaders such as *Augustine*, medieval thinkers such as Bernard of Clairvaux, but especially the early modern theologian John Calvin, who set forth the doctrinal position of what became known as the Reformed churches. However, over the years there have been modifications in some areas of Calvin's doctrines. Consequently, while there have been variations in Reformed points of view, the requirement is always to go back to the scriptures as a check on the "Reformed" doctrines.

This raises the question of the nature and place of human *reason.* Some even in the Reformed tradition have tended to refuse to give any credence to the use of reason, but generally most have held that God by *grace* has given humans the power to use their reason in a limited sense but not to be able to give an ultimate explanation of reality apart from the teachings of the Bible. Thus, in the fields of *science, economics,* and so forth, one does have a certain freedom to use reason, but without the guidance of the scriptures, one is doomed to misuse or misapply much of its rationally gained knowledge. Reason enlightened by the Holy Spirit, however, has a true understanding, although always limited because no human has reached perfection in this life.

D. G. Bloesch, *A Theology of Word and Spirit* (1992); P. T. Forsyth, *The Principle of Authority,* 2nd ed. (1952); Rogers and McKim, *AIB.*

W. STANFORD REID

Baptism Reformed churches have understood baptism as a covenant sign, whereby the washing of water in the name of the Father, and of the Son, and of the *Holy Spirit* seals to those who receive it the promises of the gospel (cf. HC, qq. 65–74; Second Helvetic Confession, ch. 20; WSC, qq. 92, 94).

Baptism in scripture. Since *Reformed theology* affirms that the *worship* of the *church* must be according to *scripture,* the manner in which certain scripture passages regarding baptism have been understood is the key to its teachings on the subject. At the beginning of all four Gospels we read of the baptism of Jesus, who, bearing the name Joshua, was baptized in the Jordan, leading the new covenant people of God into the promised kingdom. This baptism as John the Baptist preached it was a baptism of *repentance,* a washing away of *sin,* leaving it behind, and an entering into the new life of the *kingdom of God.* At his baptism, Jesus received the Holy Spirit, for only by the power of the Spirit can one live the Christian life. Christ's baptism, as the Reformers understood it, is the pattern of Christian baptism. Huldrych Zwingli made this point early in the Reformation, and though it was a radical departure from scholastic theology, which understood John's baptism as being quite different from the apostles' baptism, Zwingli's approach was followed by Reformed theology rather generally. Martin Bucer made the point that baptism stands at the beginning of the Christian life, just as it stands at the beginning of the Gospel, a prophetic sign of what that life will be, namely, a turning away from the ways of this world and an entering into the life of the Spirit, a sign and seal of our *conversion.* One often asks where John the Baptist got this rite and why he used it in his ministry. Most recent scholarship has tended to dismiss the idea that it was borrowed from the Hellenistic mystery religions and favors the idea that John saw his rite in terms of Jewish proselyte baptism. This would explain why John's baptism was such a scandal to the Jews; it implied that even Jews needed to be converted to enter the messianic kingdom.

Before his *ascension,* Jesus gave his disciples the commission to open up his kingdom to all the peoples of the earth by baptizing them in the name of the Father, and of the Son, and of the Holy Spirit, teaching them to observe all things he had commanded, and with this commission he gave the covenant promise that in their doing this he would be with them (Matt. 28:18–20). They were to baptize in the name of the Father, that all peoples might be received into the household of faith; in the name of the Son, that they be joined to Christ in his *death* and *resurrec-*

tion; and finally in the name of the Holy Spirit, that they receive the gift of the Holy Spirit.

In the book of Acts, the apostles do just this. Peter preached the gospel to all nations, offering them baptism with the assurance that the promises of the new covenant were not only for the children of Israel but for the Gentiles and their children as well (Acts 2:38–39; cf. Calvin's commentary here). Throughout Acts, it is carefully noted that Gentiles were baptized and therefore made part of the covenant community: a group of Samaritans (Acts 8:4–11); an Ethiopian (8:26–40); a Roman centurion and his household (ch. 10); Lydia, a Greek businesswoman (16:14–15); and the Philippian jailer and his household (16:29–34). In Luke's various accounts, the sign was given rather quickly. One does not hear of long preparations or of waiting until conversion has become profound. Baptism marks a beginning. Often Paul found it necessary to point out to his Gentile converts that Christian baptism was not to be confused with the initiation rites of different Hellenistic mystery religions. In Rom. 6:1–14, he makes it clear that the rite of Baptism does not confer *salvation* simply by the performing of a ceremony in such a way that one's moral behavior is irrelevant to one's salvation. Baptism joins us to Christ in his death and his resurrection, not by means of a dramatic reenactment of his burial and resurrection, but by *faith* in Christ expressed in the living of the Christian life. The apostles obviously understood baptism as a covenant sign, and because baptism is a covenant sign, it commits us to the Christian life. The ceremonial view of salvation fostered by the mystery religions is likewise attacked in 1 Cor. 10:1–13, where Paul is clear that even those who had been baptized in the sea and in the cloud during the exodus were not automatically saved.

At the core of the NT understanding of baptism are the OT types of the sacrament. The Reformers sensed that the early church thought of the *sacraments* in terms of OT imagery (Bullinger, *Decades,* 5:6–8; Calvin, *Inst.* 4.14.20–26; 4.15.9). Paul presents crossing through the Red Sea as a type of baptism (1 Cor. 10:1–2). Baptism sets us on the pilgrimage that leaves behind the land of sin and heads out toward the land of promise. In 1 Peter 3:20–21, the flood is presented as a type of baptism. This type emphasizes God's sovereign demand for *justice* and righteousness among all the peoples of the earth as well as God's gracious gift of a new beginning. Reformed theology from the very beginning has found circumcision to be a particularly important type of baptism (HC, q. 74). Circumcision is, like many of the liturgical usages of the OT, a shadow of things to come (Col. 2:17). In Rom. 4:11, Paul speaks of the relation of circumcision to faith. This passage has encouraged Reformed theologians to understand the sacraments generally as covenantal signs. In Rev. 1:5–6, the various rites involving washing with water and sprinkling of blood, particularly in the *ordination* of the Levitical priesthood, are seen as types of baptism that set Christians apart to the service of *God* under the new *covenant.*

Rite of Baptism. In Reformed worship, the rite of Baptism is understood to have four parts.

The washing of water with the Word (Eph. 5:26). This is the core of the rite. The Reformers, as the medieval schoolmen and the church fathers before them, gave great importance to following the institution of Jesus, baptizing in the name of the Father, and of the Son, and of the Holy Spirit (Matt. 28:19). These words of institution are read in the course of the rite to make clear that the church is acting at the bidding of Christ. The washing may be administered by immersion, pouring, or sprinkling, but it is understood primarily as a sign of washing and only secondarily as a sign of birth (Titus 3:5), illumination (Heb. 6:4), or burial (Rom. 6:4). A fundamental concern of Reformed churches has been that the sign of washing not be confused or obscured by additional symbolic acts such as exorcism, anointing with oil, renunciation of Satan, or the consecration of the font. With this giving of the sign, the sacrament is complete. But it entails the remaining three parts of the rite.

Prayers. First there are prayers of confession and repentance in which we cry out to God for our salvation. The prayers of confession found in the regular worship service begin the rite of Baptism, and indeed such prayers of lamentation whenever we pray them throughout the whole of our earthly life are part of the baptismal dimension of the Christian life. Then there is the baptismal invocation at the time of the administration of the sacrament in which we ask that the outward sign be fulfilled by the inward work of the Holy Spirit. Finally, the rite is concluded by the giving of a benediction to the newly baptized.

Teaching what Christ commanded. This is understood both in terms of formal catechetical instruction and in terms of lifelong study and discipleship. In the Netherlands, there is a tradition of catechetical **preaching** on Sunday evenings for the whole congregation.

Vows of faith. These are formally made before the church and maintained by a constant Christian witness. The Apostles' Creed traditionally expresses these vows, though a simple statement such as "Jesus Christ is my Lord and Savior" is sufficient. The Reformed understanding of baptism sees the sacrament as a sign at the beginning of the Christian life that unfolds throughout the whole of life.

Baptismal controversies. Through the centuries, certain problems have arisen in regard to the theology and administration of baptism to which Reformed churches have given fairly consistent answers.

Baptismal regeneration. The NT assumes that one must be baptized to be counted a Christian (Acts 2:41), yet the story of the thief on the cross would indicate that the necessity of baptism is not so absolute as to imply that God cannot save anyone without it. We are saved by grace through faith (Eph. 2:8), not by going through some religious ceremony (1 Cor. 10:1–13; 1 Peter 3:21). If Reformed theology does not teach baptismal regeneration, neither does it teach decisional regeneration (John 1:13; Rom. 9:16). Salvation is God's work of grace abundantly poured out upon us through the Holy Spirit working faith in our hearts and uniting us to Christ in his death and resurrection.

Infant baptism. Beginning with Zwingli, Reformed theologians have found good reason for believing that infants were baptized in the NT church. If it is true that this is not specifically stated, it is also true that the NT does not record the baptism of anyone raised in the church. The question of how the second generation became Christian is not addressed. Throughout scripture, covenant signs were given to children with their parents. Circumcision, which the NT clearly regards as a type of baptism, was normally administered to infants. In Jewish proselyte baptism, the infants of converts were baptized because it was a well-established principle that children belong with their parents to the covenant community (cf. 1 Cor. 7:14). Jesus healed children as well as adults and at least once on the basis of the faith of a parent (John 4:50). The New England Puritans were even willing to admit the children of the larger Christian community to the sacrament, though this so-called **Half-Way Covenant** was a problem for later generations. Following the Cane Ridge revival, the question was raised again and vigorously debated by Alexander Campbell and Nathan Rice. Horace Bushnell made a significant defense of infant baptism in *Christian Nurture* (1847). During the Nazi ascendancy, Karl Barth recommended that with the weakening of the state-supported Protestant churches of Europe, infant baptism be discontinued, though he never denied its validity. While at first his suggestion was followed in certain circles, his position elicited significant rebuttals by Oscar Cullmann and Joachim Jeremias, with the result that both European and American Reformed churches have continued infant baptism, finding it a significant witness to the sovereignty of grace.

Minister of baptism. Essential to the nature of the baptismal sign is that one is baptized by another; one does not baptize oneself. Far more than a symbolic profession of faith whereby the believer indicates his or her decision for Christ, baptism is, above all, a sign and seal of Christ's washing us from our sin and is therefore given us by a minister of the gospel acting in the name and under the *authority* of Christ (Matt. 28:18–19; Acts 2:38; 10:48). For this reason, "emergency baptisms" by persons other than ministers are not recognized by Reformed churches. Likewise, since it is what Christ does that is crucial, baptism is not invalidated through the unworthiness of the minister.

Mode of baptism. Whether baptism should be administered by immersion or sprinkling has aggravated American Protestantism unduly. If it is true that in classical Greek the word for baptism means to submerge, it is also true that in the popular Greek of NT times, the same word was used to refer to a number of different Jewish rites of purification involving washing (cf. the Gk. text of Mark 7:3–4; Luke 11:38; Heb. 6:2). Whatever mode of baptism is used, the sign of washing should be clear.

Rebaptism. In the ancient church, persons who committed grave sins after baptism or who under pressure of persecution had apostasized often asked to be rebaptized and received back into the fellowship of the church. While the church gradually developed disciplines of penance and readmission to regular Communion, it decided against rebaptism. Likewise, Reformed churches have taught that baptism is to be administered but once. Because Reformed churches have an abiding faith in God's faithfulness to the promises made in the sacrament itself, they regard rebaptism as constituting a sacrilege, implying that God had been unfaithful. The covenantal promises of God are not compromised by

our confusion about the true nature of the sacrament, the immaturity of our faith, or our unfaithfulness to God. In the same way, baptism is not invalidated by liturgical faux pas. Reformed churches have usually been rather generous in recognizing baptisms administered by other Christian churches.

Water and Spirit. Baptism with water is an outward sign of an inward reality, namely, the baptism of the Holy Spirit. To imagine that some Christians have received only water baptism, while more advanced Christians have been baptized by the Holy Spirit is quite alien to the NT. Ephesians 4:5 teaches that there is but one baptism, and Reformed theologians therefore have always guarded against dividing water and Spirit. Water signifies the giving of the Spirit, just as much as it does the washing away of sin (Ezek. 36:25–27). To add to the sign of washing some sort of anointing or to regard *confirmation* as a sacrament for the conferring of the Holy Spirit is to rob the original baptismal sign of half its meaning.

Barth, *CD* IV/4; G. W. Bromiley, *Children of Promise* (1979); O. Cullmann, *Baptism in the New Testament* (ET 1950); E. B. Holifield, *The Covenant Sealed* (1974); J. Jeremias, *Infant Baptism in the First Four Centuries* (1960); G. W. H. Lampe, *Seal of the Spirit* (1967); H. O. Old, *The Shaping of the Reformed Baptismal Rite* (1991); R. Schnackenburg, *Baptism in the Thought of St. Paul* (1964); U. Zwingli, *Refutation of the Tricks of the Catabaptists*, ed. E. Peters (1972).

HUGHES OLIPHANT OLD

Barmen, Theological Declaration of Representatives of Lutheran, Reformed, and United churches constituted the first Confessional Synod of the German Evangelical Church in Wuppertal-Barmen (May 29–31, 1934). The Roman Catholic Church and the so-called Free Churches (Baptist and Methodist churches) did not participate because they were not members of the Evangelical Church in Germany.

The Barmen Declaration was unanimously adopted to withstand the errors of "German Christians" and attempts of the Reich church government "to establish the unity of the German Evangelical Church by means of false doctrine, by the use of force, and insincere practices." It became the theological basis of the true evangelical *church*, commonly called the Confessing Church. It was the point of departure for subsequent *synods* held in Dahlem (1934), Augsburg (1935), and Bad-Oeynhausen (1936). It was binding upon the Church's Council of Brethren and administration in the conduct of the struggle against the Reich church bishop and church committees appointed by the government. It was adopted by the Second Free Reformed Synod, in Siegen (March 26–28, 1935), and is numbered among the historic *confessions* of the Reformed Church in Germany. Most constitutions of the Lutheran and United Churches in Germany have incorporated Barmen with varying degrees of authority. The United Presbyterian Church in the U.S.A. included the Barmen Declaration in its *Book of Confessions* (1967).

The "Faith Movement of the 'German Christians'" wanted to unite the twenty-nine regional churches into a state church after the pattern of the Church of England, with a bishop at its head. Claiming to stand on "Positive Christianity," the German Christians castigated godless Marxism, the Catholic Center Party, a mission to the Jews, intermarriage between Jews and Germans, pacifism, internationalism, and Free Masonry. All was based on the belief that "race, nationality and the nation [are] orders of life granted and entrusted to us by God." The German Christian Movement represented a syncretism of Christianity and the ideology of national socialism or Hitlerism.

The Nazi state was well aware the Confessing Church was opposed to its totalitarian claims and neopaganism. The Confessing Church was an illegal, minority church inasmuch as the German Christians had won an overwhelming victory—with the aid of the Nazi propaganda machine—in the church elections (July 26, 1933). L. Müller had been elected Reich bishop at a National Synod of the German Evangelical Church that met in Wittenberg.

The Synod of Barmen did not call its six articles a confession of *faith* but a theological explanation of the present situation in the church. It explicitly stated, "It was not our intention to found a new church or to form a union." On the contrary, "precisely because we want to be and to remain faithful to our various confessions, we may not keep silent."

On the other hand, Barmen did say, "We are bound together by the confession of the one Lord of the one, holy, catholic and apostolic church" and "we confess the following truths." Thus, Barmen confessed with its intention of declaring the right understanding of the Reformation confessions in a concrete situation. It confronted a decision concerning the ground, nature, and task of the church and of the state.

As Hans Asmussen said in his address on the Barmen Declaration: "We are raising a protest against the same phenomenon that has been slowly preparing the way for the devastation of the Church for more than two hundred years. For it is only a relative difference whether—beside Holy *Scripture* in the *church*—historical events or reason, culture, aesthetic feelings, progress, or other powers and figures are said to be binding claims upon the Church" (Cochrane, 255).

R. Ahlers, *The Barmen Theological Declaration of 1934* (1986); A. C. Cochrane, *The Church's Confession under Hitler* (1962); Eberhard Jüngel, *Christ, Justice, and Peace: Toward a Theology of the State* (1992).

ARTHUR C. COCHRANE

Basel Confession   Also called the First Confession of Basel (1534) to distinguish it from the Second Confession of Basel (1536; or *First Helvetic Confession*). Both documents belong to early Reformed history influenced by the theology of

Zwingli rather than that of Calvin, a second-generation reformer.

The Basel Confession was drafted by John Oecolampadius, principal Basel reformer, and was finalized by his successor, Oswald Myconius. It has twelve articles: (1) *God*, (2) the fall, (3) divine *providence*, (4) the natures and person of Jesus Christ, (5) *church* and *sacraments*, (6) the Lord's Supper, (7) *church discipline*, (8) civil authority, (9) *faith* and works, (10) *judgment*, (11) of things forbidden and permitted, and (12) against the errors of Anabaptists.

A. C. Cochrane, ed., *Reformed Confessions of the 16th Century* (1966); Schaff, *Creeds* 1:385–88; J. Rohls, *Reformed Confessions* (1998).

CHARLES PARTEE

Belgic Confession The oldest creed of the Reformed Church of the Netherlands and its daughter churches, the confession (1561) was written by French-speaking Guido de Brès (d. 1567) from what is now Belgium. It was to show Spanish authorities that Reformed people were not rebels but law-abiding Christians. The confession sets itself against both Roman Catholic and Anabaptist doctrinal errors. It exemplifies Reformed confessional writing after the earlier creed of the Reformed Church of France.

The Belgic Confession was translated into Dutch (1562) and adopted by synods of Antwerp (1566), Wesel (1568), and *Dort* (1619). It was translated into English by John W. Livingston of the Reformed Church in America (1768).

The topical order is traditional: *God* and how God is known (arts. 1–11); *creation* and *providence* (arts. 12–13); fall and *election* (arts. 14–16); *salvation* in Christ (arts. 17–21); *justification* and *sanctification* (arts. 22–26); the *church* (arts. 27–29); church order (arts. 30–32); *sacraments* (arts. 33–35); church and state (art. 36); and last things (art. 37). Distinctive Reformed emphases are: *scripture* as normative; the sovereignty of God and God's *grace*; *sin*; salvation in Christ alone, including sanctification and good works; the *law* of God as a help in Christian living; Calvin's view of the sacraments; and the state as instrument of God and vehicle of God's grace.

A. C. Cochrane, ed., *Reformed Confessions of the 16th Century* (1966); P. J. Los, *Tekst en Toelichting van de Geloofsbelijdenis der Nederlandsche Hervormde Kerk* (1929); M. E. Osterhaven, *Our Confession of Faith* (1964); J. Rohls, *Reformed Confessions* (1998).

M. EUGENE OSTERHAVEN

Brief Statement of Faith "A Brief Statement of Faith: Presbyterian Church (U.S.A.)" is the eleventh and most recent (1991) confession in the *Book of Confessions* of that denomination. It developed from the reunion of the PCUS and the UPCUSA (1983). The Articles of Agreement stipulated that former confessional standards of the denomination should be combined and augmented by a fresh statement of the new church's convictions.

The Brief Statement stands firmly within the Reformed heritage. One of the tradition's characteristics is its commitment to the importance of confessing its *faith* anew upon occasions of significant moments. The reunion of churches was a gift of *God* testifying to the partial recovery of the oneness of the *church* for which Christ prayed. When Reformed churches unite or reunite they seek a common voice to confess their common faith. The drive rises from the Reformed claim that the church is under obligation to state its faith in contemporary terms as well as hold firmly to the historic affirmation of the ecumenical *creeds*. But it also derives from the present need to assure the uniting churches that their coming together has a theological integrity at its core. Union between churches cannot be reduced in meaning to a merger based solely on the values of efficiency and cost effectiveness. A "new" church in the Reformed tradition articulates its foundational beliefs as and when it adopts a new statement of faith.

The Brief Statement is Reformed in confessing the one faith of the one church. Thus, the Trinitarian character of faith is affirmed explicitly: "We trust in the one triune God." The *Trinity* also provides the structure of the Statement with the apostolic benediction ordering its flow. The Statement follows the *Confession of 1967* and the *Barmen* Declaration in beginning with the Second Person of the Trinity and subsequently taking up the First Person and Third Person before concluding with the traditional formula of the Gloria Patri.

A Reformed confession addresses the contemporary situation. The Brief Statement does so in its contemporary idiom. Gender-inclusive language about humans is incorporated. Gender-inclusive language about God is addressed. The introduction of male and female images of God enriches the confessional heritage. A line that affirms that women and men are called to all the ministries of the church locates the *ordination* of women in the confessional standards of the church for the first time.

The Brief Statement's contemporaneity is noted in its urgent recognition of the possibility of humans' inflicting, through nuclear holocaust or ecological assault, death to life as we know it on this planet. The positive inference from one of its lines, "We threaten death to the planet entrusted to our care," is a transformed understanding of what is required for *stewardship* of the planet.

The Brief Statement was written in a form to make sections readily usable in *worship*. Its evocative, seminarrative style makes it a useful educational tool, inviting discussion and development of more complete meanings. Only as the Brief Statement lives its way into the church's life through these and other methods will it play an identity-forming and identity-reforming role in the church and thus be truly a Reformed creed.

Austin Presbyterian Theological Seminary, *Insights: A Journal of the Faculty of Austin Seminary* (Fall 1990); W. C. Placher and D. Willis-Watkins, *Belonging to God: A Commentary on A Brief Statement of Faith* (1992); J. L. Stotts and J. D. Douglass, eds., *To Confess the Faith Today* (1990).

JACK L. STOTTS

Calling   *see* **Vocation**

Calvinism   While Calvinism bears the name of John Calvin as the system of theology he set forth during the Reformation, he was by no means the inventor of it, for its roots go back to the Bible and to the interpretations of such early church theologians as Chrysostom and *Augustine* and to medieval thinkers such as Bernard of Clairvaux. This is clear in Calvin's theological works and commentaries. Yet Calvin added much to the earlier *tradition* by his studies and Christian thought. So Calvinism is a summing up of the earlier tradition by an able and committed theologian of the sixteenth century.

To understand Calvin's part in this development, it is necessary to know something of his background. He came from a Roman Catholic family and planned to become a lawyer. To this end he studied first at the University of Paris, then at Orléans and Bourges. During this latter period he was influenced by the Reformation movement. The result was his setting forth Protestant views. Trained in the current methods of humanism in reading ancient authors, he applied the same methods to his reading of OT and NT scriptures, seeking a literal interpretation of the biblical text.

The Bible. To Calvin, *scripture* was the **Word of God.** Therefore, it was to be taken literally in its presentation of God's rule over history. Calvin was not, however, a literalist in his understanding of what today would be called natural science, as for instance in his view of the biblical account of *creation.* He viewed the Genesis statements as setting forth creation, but in a way that even the "rude and ignorant" could understand. At the same time, he stressed that *God* was the creator of everything, though God has not revealed the methods by which creation occurred. Thus, to Calvin, the Bible as the Word of God is the final *authority* for the Christian's view of the world and life in it.

How does one come to recognize the Bible as the Word of God and understand it? Calvin's answer was by the work of the *Holy Spirit,* the Third Person of the *Trinity,* who opens humanity's eyes so that many are able to recognize the Bible as divinely inspired. Further, one understands the message of the scriptures by the enlightening action of the Spirit, who enables God's people not only to understand but also to apply what the scriptures teach. This meant to Calvin that the Bible must be interpreted historically and literally, with no place for the common practice of medieval exegesis in allegorizing biblical passages.

The Bible's prime characteristic is as the self-revelation of God. God has been revealed in creation, nature, and history as God has providentially watched over and directed the physical and human aspects of creation. But because of human sinfulness, this is not enough. Humans need direct and specific *revelation* to enable them to know and understand their relationship to God. To this end, God has given specific and direct revelation in the Bible so that *humanity* has in scripture an inspired record of God's dealings with creation.

To Calvin, the Bible, however, was not just a record of history and how God had dealt with creation in the past. It is a revelation of God today, as it tells much concerning God's plans and purposes throughout history. It also provides humankind with a knowledge of God's redeeming work in Christ that took place two millennia ago as well as God's providential and redeeming work today. Therefore, the Bible's message is not only to be read as history but to be applied faithfully to one's life now. At the same time, Calvin stressed the mystery of God's own being and purpose, constantly quoting Deut. 29:29 that one

might not reduce biblical teaching to some form of a purely human, rational system, for God can be known only as God is revealed to human creatures.

God. The God of whom Calvin wrote and spoke is the God of the Bible. God is the only God, but at the same time God is the God who is a trinity of persons: Father, Son, and Holy Spirit, who are the same in substance and equal in power and glory. Here Calvin followed biblical teaching as formulated and expressed in the early church *confessions.* But this *doctrine* was absolutely basic to his whole system of thought, and as a result he was sometimes more consistent in his theological exposition than others who, while professing a Trinitarian theology, were subordinationist in their application of the doctrine.

Equally important in Calvin's thought was the belief that God is sovereign. God is eternal, without beginning or end; God is also infinite, an attribute on which Calvin laid great stress. This in turn means that God is self-sufficient and does not depend upon either physical forces or human cooperation to accomplish the divine purposes. God works all things after the counsel of God's own will. This brought Calvin into conflict with some other Protestant leaders and has been one of the main points of disagreement between Calvinists and other Christians since the Reformation. Because God is sovereign, God is the source of all in the universe.

On this basis, Calvin saw God as the creator and sustainer of all things. Throughout his writings, and especially in his Genesis commentary, Calvin was very insistent that nothing has come into existence by chance or accident but only in the plan and purpose of God. Further, he rejected any Deistic view that God created all and then left creation to run by itself. Rather, he is equally insistent that God is the sustainer of everything, so all physical laws are expressions of God's constant care and the result of God's sovereignty. This applies not only to the physical universe. God also rules over humanity, guiding and directing history in God's foreordained fashion. In this, Calvin laid the foundation for a Christian interpretation of *science* and history.

Humanity. Calvin saw humans as the peak of creation, since they are made in God's own image, an honor conferred on no other creature. To Calvin, the image of God in humanity was not physical but spiritual, intellectual, and volitional. Moreover, God made humans capable of free choice and decision, while placing them in the position of ruling over creation as God's deputies. The deputy status comes through a *covenant* relationship in which humans are commissioned to rule over the creation while also required to serve God wholly in the world. Humans receive God's blessing as long as they obey God's commands.

Desiring to be independent of God, however, humans went their own ways and broke God's command. To the question, How could they do this if God is sovereign? Calvin admitted this was a mystery. But he insisted that human responsibility and God's sovereignty are always mysterious in their relationship. Yet both are set forth in scripture. When humans broke their covenant relationship with God, they came under divine condemnation and rejection. The result is that they are now at enmity with God, going their own ways and doing as they please, for Adam's rebellion has become characteristic of the whole human race. Humans themselves are unwilling to repent and return to their covenant relationship with God.

Though Satan through the serpent (Gen. 3) led humans astray, God's purpose for humanity still remains. God, by God's *grace,* has from all eternity chosen a great multitude of the human race to be brought back into relationship with God. Yet *atonement* had to be made for humanity's rebellion, and it was for this purpose that the Son, the Second Person of the Trinity, came into the world to bear its sins. Whether Calvin would have accepted the later doctrine of "limited atonement" may be questioned, as he

seems to have believed that Christ's atonement was sufficient for all but efficient only for the elect. He did stress, however, that individuals came to accept Christ's atonement in faith only as the result of the effectual *calling* of the Holy Spirit. They were then regenerated and placed their faith in Christ, to whom they gave their obedience as Lord and King. Thus, *salvation* was entirely by the grace of God. Without divine grace, *hell* is the only human destiny.

In stressing that the sinner was justified by faith alone, Calvin agreed fully with Luther and other reformers. He held firmly that it was only as one placed one's faith in Christ, trusting in Christ as the one who paid the penalty for sin and whose righteousness was imputed to the believer, that the individual would find *forgiveness* and acceptance by God. Throughout Calvin's writings, one finds constant rejection of the Roman Catholic doctrine of merits through good works. In this, Calvin was very explicit.

Calvin did not, however, believe that the Christian was without moral standards and not required to perform good works. Rather, the Christian is to manifest the grace of God in all of life. As one entered into a covenant relationship with God, one was to exhibit this in all aspects of human activity. This meant not only witnessing faithfully to God's grace but manifesting the Christian faith and life in all actions and seeking to persuade others to do the same. If this were done, society as a whole would be influenced to seek to do God's will and this would have an influence on the form of government, laws, economy, and every other element of daily life.

While the individual would seek to bring about such a revolution in human society, the body that was especially appointed to this office was the *church.* Composed of all who profess faith in Christ as Lord and Savior, along with their children, who were to be received into the visible church by the sign of *baptism,* the church, governed by elected *elders,* was to proclaim the gospel to all people across the world. By this means, it fulfills Christ's commission to the apostles before his *ascension*. On this, Calvin was very insistent and did much to forward missionary work in his own day. In this way, he presented a very practical agenda for Christians to follow in this life.

Calvin's influence has continued long after his death, as many accepted his teachings as being truly biblical. He gained a large following in many countries in Europe, and from there his teachings spread to America, Africa, and Asia. His theology influenced not only individuals but whole societies as well, and it continues to do so. Notable individuals in many fields of human endeavor—government, science, education, and the arts—testify to the influence of Calvin's thought, and through their efforts Calvinism has had a significant impact on world history.

A. Duke, G. Lewis and A. Pettegree, eds., *Calvinism in Europe 1540–1610: A Collection of Documents* (1992); A. Kuyper, *Calvinism* (repr. 1931); J. T. McNeill, *The History and Character of Calvinism* (1954); A. Pettegree, A. Duke, and G. Lewis, eds., *Calvinism in Europe 1540–1620* (1994); M. Prestwich, ed., *International Calvinism, 1541–1715* (1985).
W. STANFORD REID

Calvinism in America   Originating in sixteenth-century German- and French-speaking Switzerland, *Calvinism* gradually spread to other areas of both eastern and western Europe where strongholds developed in the Netherlands and the British Isles. The Puritans in Holland and England, and the Scotch-Irish, were especially successful in transplanting Calvinism to America. The Puritan and Scotch-Irish forms of Calvinism were organized into Congregational, Presbyterian, and Baptist churches. The Dutch Reformed, German Reformed, and other immigrant groups also established American churches during the eighteenth century.

Calvinism is both a cultural system and a theology. As a theology, American Calvinism owes much to its European heritage. This heritage is rooted in the Augustinian tradition and in the Reformation-era biblical and theological works of John Calvin, especially his *Institutes of the Christian Religion* (1559). The Reformation-era movement was also shaped by the work of others, including Theodore Beza of Geneva, Huldrych Zwingli and Heinrich Bullinger of Zurich, John Oecolampadius of Basel, and John Knox of Scotland. The theology of these reformers was further developed and summarized in important *confessions* and *catechisms*, particularly the *Scots Confession* (1560), the *HC* (1563), the *Second Helvetic Confession* (1566), and the *WCF* (1647).

During the post-Reformation period, a number of continental European and English theologians also produced important summaries of Calvinistic thought that reflect changing cultural, social, political, and scientific views. These presentations of Calvinism include works by the Puritan theologians William Perkins, William Ames, and John Owen; by the great Swiss scholastic Francis Turretin (1679–85); by Dutch Reformed thinkers Abraham Kuyper and Herman Bavinck; and by Swiss theologians Karl Barth (1932–67) and Emil Brunner (1946–60). Recently, Jürgen Moltmann, Helmut Gollwitzer, T. F. Torrance, and other Reformed thinkers have opened new perspectives. While many of the central concepts of Calvinism, such as the power and activity of *God* as creator and sustainer of the world, as redeemer, and as Lord of *history,* can be found in the works of Calvin, many post-Calvinian ideas and diverse cultural expressions have also shaped the Reformed tradition.

As a cultural system, American Calvinism emphasizes learning and stresses the importance of higher education. Approximately seventy-five American colleges were founded by Presbyterian, Congregational, and German and Dutch Reformed churches prior to the Civil War. A disproportionately high number of college and university faculty, trustees, and presidents have also been affiliated with the Reformed tradition. Reformed churches also emphasize the centrality of the OT and the NT as the *authority* for Christian living. The biblical witness is viewed as the basis for cultural transformation sought through social, political, and evangelical means. The Calvinistic worldview was certainly a primary influence in the life of John Witherspoon and other patriots who participated in the American Revolution and influenced the development of democratic institutions, for example.

Traditionally, Calvinism has also stressed simplicity and hard work. While there has been much debate on the relationship between Calvinism, capitalism, and the Protestant work ethic, many scholars now see the contributing aspects of *Reformed theology* as one important factor among several that led to the development of capitalism. In its various organizational forms, Calvinism relies on a shared leadership of ministers and laity working together in partnership. Often theologically factious and divisive, the Presbyterian and Reformed denominations are also characterized by their emphasis on corporateness and catholicity. This emphasis fostered cooperative educational and mission programs, a commitment to church union, especially among Reformed churches, and development of important ecumenical organizations.

During colonial times, Calvinistic ideas flowered in the works of Puritans who settled New England and became Congregationalists. The classic exposition of early American Puritanism is found in the lectures of Samuel Willard (1640–1707) on the Westminster *Shorter Catechism*. Published posthumously (1726) as *A Compleat Body of Divinity*, the lectures fill over one thousand double-columned pages. This great summa of *New England Theology* centers around the *covenant* idea (God's chosen people), which permeated all aspects of early New England life, including *church*, society, *politics*, and the Puritan view of history.

The most important historical work written from a New England Calvinist perspective is certainly Cotton Mather's *Magnalia Christi Americana* (1702). By recording the "wondrous works" of God in the churches of New England, Mather glorified the past and tried to halt the decline of his own day. While flawed in its presentation of history, the *Magnalia* contains aspects of Puritan thought and passages of literary excellence that make it a great work. Other important works were written by Jonathan Edwards, a seminal theologian and philosopher, including *Religious Affections* (1746), *Freedom of the Will* (1754), and *Original Sin* (1758). In these and other writings, Edwards displays philosophical and ethical insight equaled by few, if any, American theologians.

The decline of New England Puritanism was hastened by the growth of Baptist, Quaker, and other churches alongside and within the "holy commonwealth." It soon became apparent that the religious uniformity sought by the founders was not possible. At the same time, many second- and third-generation Puritans refused church membership. This erosion from within led to adoption of the *Half-Way Covenant*. Religious pluralism, the Half-Way Covenant, the revivalism of the Great Awakening, and other troubles led to a fragmentation of the theological and social aims of the commonwealth. As a result, the "New Divinity" theologians who followed Edwards found themselves in a more theologically diverse landscape. This landscape included traditional Scotch-Irish Calvinism, which rejected revivalism and pressed for a return to a pre-Awakening theology; the *New Haven Theology* of N. W. Taylor, which made some concessions to revivalism but maintained Calvinistic orthodoxy; and the liberal Calvinism of William Ellery Channing (1780–1842) and others who rejected Trinitarianism, *original sin,* and the *atonement,* and identified with the Unitarian movement.

Amidst this growing diversity, Horace Bushnell emerged as a mediating figure. He tried to find a middle way between

Old Calvinism and Unitarianism and between *science* and revivalism. In *God in Christ* (1849) and other works, Bushnell concentrated on the nature of language, which he viewed as poetry and symbol rather than science. He favored the romanticism of Friedrich Schleiermacher and was extremely critical of the theological rationalism and disciplinary system of his New England forebears. In *Christian Nurture* (1847) he presented a case for the gradual, catechetical process through which *faith* is nurtured and argued against individualism, revivalism, and the need for a *conversion* experience. He also broke with more orthodox views in *The Vicarious Sacrifice* (1866) by arguing that Christ's atonement was an example of God's love rather than a reconciling act.

Bushnell, like other Presbyterian and Reformed theologians during the nineteenth century, wrestled with advances in many fields of knowledge. Scientific discoveries, including evidence of human evolution and the antiquity of the earth and solar system, were startling. New disciplines such as Freudian psychology, and new methods of biblical study using textual, literary, and historical methods, presented many challenges. Also, the growing interaction of Christianity with other world religions posed new questions. The industrial revolution, urbanization, development of communist ideology, and the issue of slavery also presented additional questions for theology.

Many in the Reformed community viewed these discoveries and developments with great alarm, seeing them as challenges to both traditional Calvinism and Christianity itself. In response, many embraced the conservative *Princeton Theology,* which defended the views of the Old Calvinism.

The Princeton Theology held sway at Princeton Theological Seminary from its founding in 1812 through the fundamentalist/modernist controversy of the 1920s. It was probably the most dominant form of American Calvinism during this period. Archibald Alexander, Charles Hodge, and B. B. Warfield were its prin-

cipal proponents, though Archibald Alexander Hodge and J. Gresham Machen popularized many of its doctrines. Through Charles Hodge's detailed *Systematic Theology* (3 vols.; 1872–73) and Warfield's numerous articles, especially "Inspiration" (1881), the Princeton Theology became known for its high view of biblical authority and inspiration and defense of Old School Calvinism. While many considered the Princeton Theology to be "pure Calvinism," in reality its theological method was influenced by the work of Turretin, by Scottish *common sense philosophy,* and by many of the challenges cited above.

The Princeton theologians also held a static view of orthodoxy that failed to recognize the importance of historical development. In spite of its shortcomings, the Princeton Theology was *the* theology of many Presbyterian and Reformed churches during the nineteenth and early part of the twentieth century.

The South was influenced by the Princeton Theology and by Turretin, whose theological textbook, *Institutio theologiae elencticae,* was used by Presbyterian seminaries in Virginia and South Carolina. Old School views were also transmitted by the two dominant theologians of the nineteenth-century South, James Henley Thornwell and Robert Lewis Dabney. Dabney's *Systematic and Polemic Theology* (1871) and Thornwell's *Collected Writings* (4 vols.; 1871–73) were of primary importance in shaping southern Calvinism through the 1930s. In his understanding of Old School Calvinism, however, Thornwell differed from the Princeton theologians in ecclesiology and *doctrine* of "the spirituality of the church." The latter doctrine holds that the church is a purely spiritual entity and should not involve itself in social or political issues. While this doctrine proved to be very influential in theological circles, in practice many southern Presbyterians took conservative positions on the controversial issues of the day, including slavery, women's suffrage, temperance, and Sabbath observance.

In the German Reformed tradition, American scholars such as John Williamson Nevin and Philip Schaff broke new ground by developing the *Mercersburg Theology*. In two major works, *The Anxious Bench* (1843) and *The Mystical Presence* (1846), Nevin criticized revivalism, stressed the corporateness of Christian belief, and pointed to the centrality of the *sacraments*. In these and other works, the Mercersburg Theology was presented as an alternative to, and critique of, both revivalism and the Princeton Theology, which were viewed as extremes. As a theological system, the Mercersburg Theology was also important because of its attempt to reconcile German idealism with the American Reformed tradition.

More progressive in their theology were "evangelical liberals" such as William Adams Brown and the *Social Gospelers*. Brown held decidedly Christocentric views. In his textbook *Christian Theology in Outline* (1906), Brown recognized the centrality of Christ and the value of the Reformed tradition but also discarded old worldviews and "scholastic phraseology" in his attempt to present a modern Calvinism in dialogue with modern science and *philosophy*. Brown wanted to be both Christian and modern. Social Gospelers, led by Walter Rauschenbusch (1861–1918), and Congregational ministers Washington Gladden (1836–1918) and Josiah Strong (1847–1916), pressed for a number of social reforms, including labor and economic reform, in a movement that lasted from the 1890s to the 1920s. This movement was allied with the theological liberalism of William N. Clarke (1840–1912) and others who stressed education, morality, and social change.

The Niebuhr brothers, Reinhold and H. Richard, were important figures in the American neo-orthodox movement of the 1930s and 1940s. In *Moral Man and Immoral Society* (1932), Reinhold Niebuhr criticized both liberal theology and the Social Gospel for their overly optimistic view of *humanity* and failure to take *sin* seriously. In *The Nature and Destiny of Man* (2 vols.; 1941–43), he developed a theology of sin and *grace* in which the struggle for social reform is paramount. H. Richard wrote a number of important works. *The Kingdom of God in America* (1937) traced the kingdom theme in American life, and *Christ and Culture* (1951), a classic work of Christian ethics, argued for the transformation of culture.

S. E. Ahlstrom, ed., *Theology in America* (1967); G. G. Atkins and F. L. Fagley, *History of American Congregationalism* (1942); J. D. Bratt, *Dutch Calvinism in Modern America* (1984); F. J. Hood, *Reformed America: The Middle and Southern States, 1783–1837* (1980); B. Kuklick, *Churchmen and Philosophers from Jonathan Edwards to John Dewey* (1985); J. H. Leith, *An Introduction to the Reformed Tradition* (rev. ed. 1981); L. A. Loetscher, *The Broadening Church* (1954); J. T. McNeill, *The History and Character of Calvinism* (1954); A. C. Piepkorn, *Profiles in Belief*, vol. 2, pt. 3, "Reformed and Presbyterian Churches" (1978); J. Smylie, *A Brief History of the Presbyterians* (1996); E. T. Thompson, *Presbyterians in the South*, 3 vols. (1963–73); R. E. Thompson, *A History of the Presbyterian Churches in the United States* (1895); L. J. Trinterud, *The Forming of an American Tradition* (1949); D. F. Wells, ed., *Reformed Theology in America* (1985).

ROBERT BENEDETTO

Cambridge Platform/Synod

Cambridge Platform/Synod New England Puritans in the mid-seventeenth century, though generally holding to Reformed doctrine, were not unanimous in their views on church government. In the Massachusetts Bay Colony, many Congregationalist ministers and laity strongly desired to distinguish their concept of the autonomous local *church* from the *polity* of Presbyterianism, Separatism, and Brownism. The outbreak of the English Civil War and the significant influence of a Presbyterian faction in the English Parliament led some Congregationalists to call for a "Presbyterian" church order (1645). Fearing a loss of distinctiveness, the General Court of Massachusetts Bay

Colony called a *synod* composed of *elders* (ministers) and messengers (laity). They came from twenty-nine different churches to Cambridge, Massachusetts, and became the Cambridge Synod (1646).

The Synod's Congregationalist church government statement became known as the Cambridge Platform. This highly influential document made it clear that councils and synods have a valuable advisory role but no legal authority in local church government. On the other hand, the Platform affirmed a state-church union where civil authorities could and should discipline *heresy* for the sake of unity.

The elders and messengers carefully defined and delineated basic concepts such as "the catholic church," "the visible church," and the nature of the church covenant. They set guidelines for election of church officers, *ordination* of ruling elders and pastors, and the admission, discipline, and excommunication of church members. In other doctrinal matters, the Synod adopted the *WCF* as its standard.

H. S. Smith et al., *American Christianity: An Historical Interpretation with Representative Documents* (1960), 1:128–40; W. Walker, *Creeds and Platforms of Congregationalism* (1893; repr. 1960).

NATHAN P. FELDMETH

Canon of Scripture

With reference to the Bible, "canon" means the list or collection of books that were received as divinely inspired and therefore serve as the rule or standard for belief and practice. Though recognition of the canon of the OT and the NT was of momentous consequences, history is silent on exactly how, when, and by whom such recognition was brought about. Nevertheless, it is generally agreed that the process involved the following stages of development.

Canon of the OT. Authoritative legal and prophetic literature grew up by degrees and was carefully preserved. Eventually the books of the Hebrew Bible came to be regarded as twenty-four in number, arranged in three divisions. The first, and primary, division is the *Torah* (Law), comprising the five "books of Moses." The second division is the *Nebiim* (Prophets), further subdivided into Former Prophets (Joshua, Judges, Samuel, and Kings) and Latter Prophets (Isaiah, Jeremiah, Ezekiel, and the Book of the Twelve). The third division is the *Kethubim* (Writings) and comprises Psalms, Proverbs, Job, Song of Solomon, Ruth, Lamentations, Ecclesiastes, Esther, Daniel, Ezra-Nehemiah (reckoned as one book), and Chronicles. These twenty-four books are identical with the thirty-nine of the Protestant OT; the difference in reckoning arises from counting the twelve ("minor") prophets separately and dividing Samuel, Kings, Chronicles, and Ezra-Nehemiah into two each.

The Septuagint, the Greek translation of the Hebrew Scriptures made in the centuries just preceding the Christian era, includes several additional books and parts of books not present in the Hebrew Bible. These are Tobit, Judith, Wisdom of Solomon, Ecclesiasticus (the book of Jeshua ben Sira), Baruch (including as ch. 6 the Letter of Jeremiah), 1 and 2 Maccabees, as well as six additions to Esther, and three additions to Daniel (Susanna; Prayer of Azariah and the Song of the Three Young Men; and Bel and the Dragon). These several texts were widely used in the early *church* and eventually were translated into Latin, becoming part of the OT as received by the Roman Catholic Church. In Protestant Bibles these books, along with 1 and 2 Esdras and the Prayer of Manasseh, were gathered together and placed between the OT and the NT in a section entitled Apocrypha (see WCF, 1.3).

Reasons that led the Reformers to adopt the Hebrew canon of the scriptures rather than the expanded canon of books in the Greek Septuagint and the Latin Vulgate included the following considerations: (1) Neither Jesus nor any of the writers of the NT make any direct quotation from any of these books. (2) Some of the Apocrypha contain texts that support purgatory (2 Macc. 12:43–45) and the efficacy of almsgiving in covering one's sins (Tobit 4:7–11; 12:8–9; 14:10–11; Sir. 3:30; 35:2).

Canon of the NT. The apostolic church received from the Jews a written rule of faith, the Jewish Scriptures. Besides these writings, the oldest Christian communities accepted another authority, the words of Jesus as these were handed down, first by oral *tradition* and later in written Gospel. There also circulated copies of apostolic letters giving explanations of the significance of the person and work of Jesus Christ for the lives of believers. At first a local church would have copies of only a few apostolic letters and perhaps one or two Gospels. In the collections that were gradually formed, a place was found for two other kinds of books—the Acts of the Apostles and the Apocalypse of John (or Revelation). Thus, side by side with the old Jewish canon, and without in any way displacing it, there sprang up a new Christian canon.

The church had the task not only of collecting but also of sifting and rejecting—for many other gospels, acts, letters, and apocalypses circulated in the second, third, and succeeding centuries. Finally, after many years, during which books of local and temporary *authority* came and went, the limits of the NT canon were set forth for the first time by Bishop Athanasius of Alexandria (A.D. 367). But not all in the church were ready to follow him, and in the following centuries there were minor fluctuations in the canon, such as temporary acceptance by the Armenian church of Paul's Third Letter to the Corinthians and inclusion of the spurious Letter to the Laodiceans in the eighteen German Bibles printed prior to Martin Luther's translation.

The criterion of canonicity of books of the NT appears to have been apostolic authorship or near-apostolic status, antiquity, orthodoxy, and usage throughout the churches. According to non-Reformed churches, the canon is an authoritative collection of books, whereas for Reformed churches it is a collection of authoritative books; the books had their authority before they were collected. In the most basic sense, neither individuals nor councils created the canon; instead, they came to perceive and acknowledge the self-authenticating quality of these writings, which imposed themselves as canonical upon the church. This conviction of divine authority "is from the inward work of the Holy Spirit, bearing witness by and with the Word in our hearts" (WCF, 1.5).

R. Beckwith, *The Old Testament Canon of the New Testament Church* (1985); F. F. Bruce, *The Canon of Scripture* (1988); L. M. McDonald, *The Formation of the Christian Biblical Canon* (1995); B. M. Metzger, *The Canon of the New Testament* (1987).

BRUCE M. METZGER

Catechism

A form of instruction in the basics of the Christian faith, usually by question and answer, greatly used in Reformed and other churches. The word derives from the Greek word *katēchein,* "to instruct" (1 Cor. 14:19). In the early *church,* a well-developed catechumenate prepared candidates for *baptism* (described in Hippolytus's *Apostolic Tradition* [c. 215] and reflected in a series of catechetical homilies by Cyril of Jerusalem, John Chrysostom, and others). The later prevalence of infant baptism called for catechesis after baptism, and in the medieval era a wide variety of aids, normally focusing on the Ten Commandments, the Lord's Prayer, and the Apostles' Creed, were used.

Martin Luther's Small Catechism (1529) fixed the name of a new genre of Christian literature. It was part of his response to the ignorance exposed during church visitations in Saxony (G. Strauss, *Luther's House of Learning* [1978]). It set a pattern that became classical, built around the traditional elements of the Decalogue, the Creed, the Lord's Prayer, and the *sacraments* (with confession separating Baptism and the *Lord's Supper*), with appendixes on household religion and daily Christian living. It was intended for children. Luther also stressed the importance of verbatim repetition and memorization in instructing the young. From the Small Catechism, those who were adequately taught should move to his Large Catechism, which was not in question-and-answer form.

During the Reformation numerous catechisms were compiled, not only by leading reformers (e.g., John Oecolampadius and Heinrich Bullinger) but also by pastors whose works were never published. These catechisms served not only as general purpose tools of Christian teaching but also specifically as preparation for *confirmation,* which under the lead of Martin Bucer took on a new lease of life as the occasion when children gave an account of their *faith* (*Inst.* 4.19.4, 13). Inevitably, the catechisms of the Reformation and the post-Reformation reflected the distinctive emphases of contemporary controversies and so fulfilled a confessional function also. This is true even of the brief catechism of Thomas Cranmer that was included in the *BCP* (1549). It requires recitation of the Creed, the Decalogue, and the Lord's Prayer. Only the section on the sacraments, added in 1604, used short questions and answers. It was drawn largely from one of the much-used catechisms of Alexander Nowell (d. 1602), dean of St. Paul's Cathedral, London.

Within the Reformed tradition, deserving special mention are Calvin's *Geneva Catechism* for the Genevan church and the *Heidelberg Catechism.* Calvin's illustrates the artificiality of the question-and-answer form; too many questions are "leading," and some become statements that the child endorses with "Correct"! The Heidelberg Catechism still enjoys wide admiration for its warm *piety* and doctrinal clarity.

No Reformed catechism has been more influential than the *Shorter Catechism* of the Westminster Assembly (1648). Largely the work, it seems, of the

English Puritan Anthony Tuckney, it comprises 107 questions and answers that present a structured account of Christian belief (not based on the Creed) from *God* and *creation* to the final *resurrection* before dealing with the Decalogue, the sacraments, and the Lord's Prayer. Its distinctive emphases (e.g., the decrees of God and the Sabbath commandment) and weaknesses (e.g., on the church) are not hard to find, but its noble start ("Q. 1. What is the chief end of man? A. Man's chief end is to glorify God, and to enjoy him forever") and general dignity and economy merited the treasured place it held for centuries in church and school in Presbyterian Scotland and elsewhere.

Alongside the catechism went the practice of catechizing—the inculcation of Christian knowledge by interrogation and testing, often in families on a Sunday afternoon in response to the morning sermon. Though in recent years various attempts have been made to revive both catechisms and catechizing (e.g., the Church of England's Revised Catechism [1962]), they have rarely enjoyed much success. Yet in the "post-Christian" West, even if learning by memorization and repetition is not in vogue, appropriate catechetical instruction is urgently needed.

K. Barth, *The Faith of the Church: A Commentary on the Apostles' Creed according to Calvin's Catechism* (1958); K. Barth, *The Heidelberg Catechism for Today* (1964); I. J. Hesselink, *Calvin's First Catechism: A Commentary* (1997); T. F. Torrance, ed. and trans. *The School of Faith* (1959); and Presbyterian Church (U.S.A.), *Book of Catechisms: Reference Edition* (2001).

DAVID F. WRIGHT

Christian Education The institutional patterns and processes by which the *church* educates its members. It includes (1) handing on the Christian faith to adult converts and children of believers to support their ongoing growth in the Christian life; and (2) relating the Christian faith to the general education of the church's members. These internal and external dimensions have been important parts of the Reformed tradition.

Christian education prior to the Reformation. The first use of "Christian education" (Gr. *en Christō paideia*) is in Clement of Rome (c. A.D. 96). In Paul's writings, however, Christian parents are told to bring their children up "in the discipline and instruction of the Lord" (Eph. 6:4). As the church spread around the Mediterranean and adapted to new cultures, it sought continuity with the original teachings of Jesus and instructed children and adults in the Christian way of life.

While much Christian education took place through *preaching* and, indirectly, through participation in the *liturgy,* the early central focus was the catechumenate for adult converts. Lasting several years, the catechumenate involved a well-structured period of formation and instruction. Entry into the church meant a radical break with the ways of the surrounding pagan culture and an internalization of the attitudes, behaviors, and beliefs of the community of *faith.*

Since pagan culture was held suspect during this period, it is ironic that the church did not form its own schools. Children and youth of believing families simply attended already established schools, based on the traditions of classical humanism, to receive a general education. The only explicitly Christian "schools" to emerge were communities gathered around leading theologians to study Christian *doctrine.* These were not sponsored by the church but did contribute significantly to the emergence of theology as a "sacred science" comparable to the reflection of the pagan philosophers.

With the Roman Empire's collapse and the subsequent decline of the schools it had supported, the church had to assume functions previously carried out by other agencies. The rise of the monastic schools was a particularly important trend. To study and pray *scripture,* children and unlearned novices had to be taught to read. Similarly, bishops were forced to provide candidates for the priesthood with an elementary as well as a *theological education.* By the sixth century, the church's involvement in general education spread beyond the bishop to the rural parishes, where priests were ordered by the Second Council of Vaison to educate "worthy successors to themselves."

Christian education during the Middle Ages built on this foundation. Most formal education was for persons who were involved in an ecclesiastical function, and it occurred in monastery or cathedral schools. These schools were also important centers for theological study and writing. The prevalence of infant *baptism* and the gradual separation of initiation and catechesis led to the demise of the catechumenate, leaving ordinary Christians with limited involvement in formal Christian instruction.

During the late Middle Ages, *scholasticism* dominated Christian education, emphasizing logic (dialectic) in a manner mirroring the prevalent style of theological disputation. The Renaissance challenged this style of education, restoring the ideals of classical humanism. John Calvin, Johannes Sturm, and other Reformed educators were deeply influenced by this movement, incorporating into their educational reforms its emphasis on rhetoric, use of classical models for grammar and composition, and acceptance of historical and philological modes of investigation.

Christian education in the Reformed tradition. The Reformation was a watershed in the history of Christian education. Reformation churches took renewed interest in the education of their own members and the general populace. Calvin believed that if the Reformation was to succeed, it must find ways to support the emergence of an educated laity and a learned clergy. All persons must have direct access to the Bible and receive a basic foundation in Christian doctrine if they were to order their lives according to the purposes of God. Moreover, the general populace must be educated in the virtues of citizenship and instructed in how to find and hold their place in the social order. Accordingly, Calvin greatly emphasized both the internal and external dimensions of Christian education.

Following the lead of Martin Luther, Calvin attempted to renew the catechumenate of the early church, focusing now on the task of teaching children the basic doctrines of the Christian faith. The family and the church were to cooperate in forming Christian *piety* and understanding early in life. Calvin also encouraged ministers to teach the laity through sermons, reviving the practice of didactic preaching associated with catechesis in the early church. To carry out these tasks, ministers were to receive the best general and theological education. In part, Calvin's desire for a learned clergy lay behind his strenuous efforts to establish a first-rate system of education in Geneva, culminating in the Geneva Academy.

Yet his motivation went beyond this. Equally important was his belief that literacy was necessary for a healthy laity and citizenry. From the start, Calvin attempted to establish a system of education open to all, rich and poor. Here, instruction in the faith and general education were to commingle, for education in citizenship and occupation were inseparable from a theological understanding of Christian *vocation.* Church and magistrate were to cooperate.

Calvin's comprehensive interest in education permanently affected the Reformed tradition. Virtually everywhere it appeared, the Reformed tradition spawned vital educational institutions. John Knox, who studied at the Geneva Academy, gave careful attention to education in his Book of Discipline for the Scottish Reformed church. As in Geneva, church and state were to cooperate to provide universal education and institutions of higher education for the gifted. General education and education in the faith were to cooperate in such institutions. Likewise the church's internal education of its own members followed Calvin's lead, placing great emphasis

on catechetical instruction and didactic preaching.

The close relationship between the Reformed tradition and Christian education is also found in Holland, England, and France. In Holland, Abraham Kuyper's theology of "sphere sovereignty" undergirded a revitalization of education both inside and outside the church.

In America, the Puritans continued this legacy. Ministers frequently functioned as the first teachers in a town. By the 1650s, the villages of Massachusetts were required to provide a school for the education of the community's children. Similarly, in the middle and southern colonies, Presbyterian ministers of Scottish descent were responsible for much of the formal education. Many of the first colleges in America were established to provide a learned clergy, and eventually there were colleges to train people for teaching and other professions. Reformed churches produced a variety of educational resources, including *catechisms* for children and primers that included moral and religious material.

The disestablishment of religion, however, created a new situation to which Reformed churches had to adapt. They could no longer expect the state to cooperate with the church, at least in a manner favoring a specific denomination. Three different approaches to Christian education emerged in the Reformed churches in response to this situation, each legitimately drawing on Calvin's legacy.

First, some churches, such as the Christian Reformed Church in North America, have opted for parochial schools. In the mid-1800s, this approach was feasible for many in the Presbyterian Church and was sharply debated in the *General Assemblies.* Between 1846 and 1870, Presbyterians founded 264 parochial schools.

A second response has been to accept the separation of Christian education and general education and confine the church's educational efforts strictly to its own members, leaving their general education to the public schools. The cooptation of the Sunday school movement by the major denominations (late 1900s) has been a key part of this strategy. Many in the Reformed tradition have argued theologically for the universal education that the common school represents, recalling the examples of Calvin and Knox.

The third response is a mixture of the first two. In general, the separation of Christian education and general education is accepted as a necessary evil, but recognition of the difficulties involved in really separating moral and religious dimensions from public education is acknowledged. The need to teach civic virtue, for example, is seen as necessitating a religious or quasi-religious foundation. Many half measures have been tried: grounding civic duty in a "generalized" religious stance and teaching religion off school grounds or after school.

All three approaches to Christian education have been important in Reformed churches in the United States and continue to represent viable options. In an increasingly pluralistic society where Christians confront a number of conflicting beliefs and values, the need to continue the Reformed tradition's strong emphasis on Christian Education is perhaps more important than ever.

Eby, *Early Protestant Educators* (1931); H. I. Marrou, *A History of Education in Antiquity* (1956); R. R. Osmer, *A Teachable Spirit: Recovering the Teaching Office in the Church* (1990); L. J. Sherrill, *Presbyterian Parochial Schools 1846–1860* (1932); J. Westerhoff and O. C. Edwards, eds., *A Faithful Church: Issues in the History of Catechesis* (1981).
                                    RICHARD R. OSMER

Christology As the study of who Jesus of Nazareth is in relation to *God* and *humanity,* Christology is pursued not in isolation from what Jesus achieved for humanity (the work of Christ) but in close association with it. There is a unity of the person and work of Christ, for Christ came to humanity in and through his saving work. Thus, Calvin united the person and work by presenting Christ in the threefold office of prophet, priest, and king. For conceptual purposes it is, however, convenient to look at the person and work separately. The following examines the person of Christ.

Patristic creeds. The most important doctrinal statement concerning the identity and nature of Jesus produced by the early *church* is the Chalcedonian Definition (A.D. 451). This christological formula was taken up by sixteenth-century Reformed theologians as a faithful reflection and statement of that to which *scripture* pointed concerning the person of Christ. The Definition first emphasizes the unity of the person of Christ by use of "one and the same" and "the same": He is "one and the same Son, the same perfect in Godhead, the same perfect in manhood, truly God and truly man, the same consisting of a rational soul and body."

Second, and of more significance, the duality of the two natures, human and divine, is underlined. "One and the same Christ, Son, Lord, Only-begotten, made known in two natures without confusion, without change, without division, without separation; the difference of the natures having been in no wise taken away by reason of the union but rather the properties of each being preserved, and both concurring into one *prosōpa* and one *hypostasis*—not parted or divided into two *prosōpa* but one and the same Son and Only-begotten, the divine Logos, the Lord Jesus Christ."

The four "withouts" serve as "No Road" notices for false paths in patristic theology (e.g., Nestorius [without division; without separation]; Arius [without change]; and Eutyches [without confusion]). Nestorianism was seen as commending a double personality in Christ as if there were two persons, not one, living inside his skin. Arianism was seen as teaching that the Logos was passible and mutable because it attributed all that was said of Jesus (e.g., his growth, temptations, and suffering) to the Logos, not the human nature. Finally, Eutyches was interpreted as teaching "two natures before the union, one nature afterward," thereby indicating that the humanity of the incarnate Logos was hardly real.

The Council of Chalcedon claimed that the incarnate Lord must be described as one person (Gr. *hypostasis* or *prosōpa)* in two natures *(physis)*. Thus, it was necessary to give an account of the way in which the Logos/Son could be described as the ultimate subject of two disparate natures. Thus, the *doctrine* of *enhypostasia* (often unhappily referred to as "the doctrine of impersonal humanity") was developed in order to show that the *hypostasis* of the Logos (who is Creator) sufficed as the *hypostasis* of the humanity (the created) because the latter, never having existed on its own, had no independent *hypostasis* of its own. This means that the divinity of Christ is not really the divine nature (common to all three Persons of the **Trinity***)* but the Person of the Logos/Son, the deity under the personal determination of the Logos. Thus, it was not the divine nature that became flesh but the Logos of the Second Person of the Trinity who became flesh.

Further, in terms of the assumed human nature of the Logos, the third Council of Constantinople (681) taught (against the Monothelites) that it retains, in its unimpaired integrity, a separate will and intelligence, and thus in the one Person of the Logos there are two wills, divine and human (dyothelitism), with the latter being subject to the former.

Reformed confessions. During the Protestant Reformation, the Reformed churches took up the christological teaching of the Nicene Creed, the Chalcedonian Definition, the Quicunque Vult, together with the doctrines of *enhypostasia* and dyothelitism, and applied it to their contemporary situations to present sound doctrine and set aside error and **heresy**. Further, they added to their use of patristic statements of dogma many scripture citations to make clear they accepted the patristic dogma because it

was scriptural. For example, the **Belgic Confession** (1561) said the Son is one of the three Persons of the eternal Godhead (art. 8), eternally begotten of the Father (art. 9), and thus neither made nor created (thus anti-Arian in emphasis). Further, Christ's *incarnation* is said to be a real and true assuming of a full human nature, body and soul, with all its infirmities, **sin** excepted (art. 18). Thus, the error of the Anabaptists who teach that Christ did not really take flesh from Mary must be rejected. If this is antidocetic in emphasis, then the next article is antimonophysite, for it clearly teaches the unity and distinction of the two natures in the one Christ in Chalcedonian style. The reality of the (now immortalized) human nature after the **resurrection** is affirmed and the section ends with this declaration: "We confess that he is *very God* and *very man*: very God by his power to conquer death and very man that he might die for us according to the infirmity of his flesh."

The **Second Helvetic Confession** (1566) deals with Christology (ch. 11) by affirming the Christology of the first four ecumenical councils, in particular the Chalcedonian teaching. It rejects the impious doctrine of both the ancient Arius and the modern Servetus that Jesus was not coequal and consubstantial in his divine nature with the Father. Further, it insists against all ancient and modern forms of docetism that Jesus had "a soul with its reason and flesh with its senses" and suffered real pain. This human nature, while immortalized and spiritualized through resurrection and **ascension,** is not localized in **heaven** and is not (as some Lutherans taught in connection with the real presence of Christ in the sacrament) present in this world.

The disagreement with the Lutherans about the **ubiquity** of the human nature of the exalted Lord Jesus is also expressed in the **Heidelberg Catechism** (1563). Here it is taught that "Christ is true man and true God. As a man he is no longer on earth, but in his divinity, majesty, grace, and Spirit, he is never absent from us"

(HC, 47). This is possible because "divinity is incomprehensible and everywhere present" and thus "beyond the bounds of the humanity which it has assumed" (HC, 48). In other words, while the glorified human nature of Christ is localized in heaven, his infinite and eternal divine nature cannot be localized even though it is always perfectly united with his localized human nature.

This doctrine was taught by Calvin himself. While Luther particularly insisted on the unity of the person, Calvin emphasized the integrity of the two natures, fearing it was possible to destroy both natures by insisting too much on the unity of the person. Thus, Calvin opposed the Lutheran exposition of the *communicatio idiomatum* ("communication of properties") and taught that the human nature was not capable of being divinized and given the property of omnipresence. Calvin revived a form of teaching from patristic sources that, when the Logos became incarnate as Jesus, he did not relinquish the divine attribute of omnipresence but continued to fill the whole cosmos and thus to be outside as well as inside the human nature he had assumed (the *extra calvinisticum*).

Yet it was from Lutheran sources that Reformed theologians borrowed the important concept of the two states of Christ, though they interpreted it differently. One problem with using the categories of the Chalcedonian Definition was that they are static and seem far removed from the dynamic Jesus who is encountered through the Gospels and the epistles. However, the adoption of the concept of the threefold office of prophet, priest, and king, along with that of the two states, helped give a more rounded character to Reformed Christology. On the basis of Phil. 2:5–11, Jesus as the incarnate Word (not the human nature alone but the Logos become flesh) has been presented as first in a state of humiliation (suffering, death, burial, and descent into Hades) and then in a state of exaltation (resurrection, ascension, session, and parousia). This approach provided an answer to the question, Who is the subject about whom the statements of the Chalcedonian Definition are made?

It has been noted that while classic Christology relies heavily on abstract nouns, the NT (as well as the Apostles' Creed) makes use primarily of verbs in presenting the person of Jesus. The doctrine of the two states also focuses attention on the verbal dimension—he suffered, he arose, and so forth. But Phil. 2:7, "he emptied himself," has been much discussed over the centuries, and from it what are known as kenotic theories of the incarnation have been propounded, especially by Lutherans and only rarely by Calvinists. Is the subject of the self-emptying either the preexistent Logos (as in some nineteenth-century formulations) or the Logos incarnate (Lutheran dogmaticians of the seventeenth century)? The former was a bold attempt to seek to do justice to the figure of Jesus in the Gospels, who had obvious limitations in terms of his knowledge, and it may be judged to have failed because of its reducing and limiting of the Godhead in the divine nature of Jesus.

From above and from below. In modern times, there has been a determined attempt by some theologians to do justice to the true manhood of Jesus and thereby to construct a Christology from below, that is, from the account of Jesus and his ministry in the Gospels (as viewed through modern biblical criticism). In this approach, Jesus is really and truly a man (human) without reserve or ambiguity. The human experiences recorded in the texts and those that are not recorded but that all accept as belonging to humankind must be taken into account. So although Jesus, because of the quality of his life and deeds, is presented as God's Man and also God's Son, nothing must detract from the fact that he was first and foremost a man. Thus, the patristic transition from God's Son to God the Son is seen as a false step. In this approach, the divine disclosure took place through a man who was utterly open and transparent throughout his whole being to the living God. That man who thus lived for God is therefore God for us. His union with God is a matter of relation, function, and activity, and a matter of degree not of kind. As the contemporary biblical scholar John Knox put it: "We can have the humanity without the pre-existence and we can have the pre-existence without the humanity. There is absolutely no way of having both" (*The Humanity and Divinity of Christ* [1967], 106).

Classic Christology begins from the side of God—from above. Within **Reformed theology,** the best modern presentation is undoubtedly that of Karl Barth, whose great commitment to the Bible as the witness to God's *revelation* ensures a more biblical presentation than the classical statements of the fifth and sixth centuries (see *CD* I/1; I/2; IV/1; IV/2). Barth employed the ontological framework of the classic statements but was always careful to ensure that Christology is much more than the manipulation of logical categories. The various stages in his argument are carefully checked by reference to the person and work of Christ as a whole and from the reality of Jesus Christ as fact and event. Barth's contemporary, Emil Brunner, believed that Barth had not clarified adequately or successfully the difference between person (*hypostasis*) and personality (as used in modern psychology). Brunner addressed this in *The Mediator* (1927; ET 1934, 345ff.) and argued for the inclusion of personality within nature (*physis*) and not connected with person (*hypostasis*).

Obviously, to the believer who searches for truth, this whole subject has the aspects of both mystery and paradox. One is led to exclaim with Thomas, "My Lord and my God!" (John 20:28).

D. M. Baillie, *God Was in Christ* (1948); G. C. Berkouwer, The Person of Christ *(1954);* D. G. Bloesch, Jesus Christ *(1997);* A. C. Cochrane, ed., Reformed Confessions of the 16th Century *(1966);* Heppe, RD; J. Rohls, Reformed Confessions *(1999);* H. Schwarz, Christology *(1998);* D. F. Wells, The Person of Christ *(1984).*

PETER TOON

Church   The following four quotations suggest some landmarks in addressing a Reformed understanding of the church. The church as a theological community is the subject of the first two. The church as a dynamic community/institution is indicated by the third. And the contemporary context as important for a Reformed understanding of the church is suggested by the last.

Q. 54. What do you believe concerning "the Holy Catholic Church"?

A. I believe that, from the beginning to the end of the world, and from among the whole human race, the Son of God, by his Spirit and his Word, gathers, protects, and preserves for himself, in the unity of the true faith, a congregation chosen for eternal life. Moreover, I believe that I am and forever will remain a living member of it. (HC, in *BC* 4.054)

To be reconciled to God is to be sent into the world as his reconciling community. This community, the church universal, is entrusted with God's message of reconciliation and shares his labor of healing the enmities which separate men from God and from each other. Christ has called the church to this mission and given it the gift of the Holy Spirit. The church maintains continuity with the apostles and with Israel by faithful obedience to his call. (Confession of 1967, in *BC* 9.31)

Ecclesia reformata semper reformanda. "The church reformed and always being reformed."

Clearly, the meaning of one's life for most Americans is to become one's own person, almost to give birth to oneself. (Bellah, 82)

The church as a theological community. A Reformed understanding of the church begins not with the church but with God's gracious call to be the church and, as the people of **God,** to be engaged in God's mission in the world. This polarity of being the church and being in mission has been nuanced differently in different historical periods. The missional element rises to more prominence, for example, in the nineteenth and twentieth centuries, as suggested by the quotation above from the *Confession of 1967* (C-67). The *Heidelberg Catechism,* on the other hand, suggests the church as a people called into a community where there is mutual nourishment and consolation. Both statements reflect not only enduring facets of the *doctrine* of the church but different social and cultural environments. Heidelberg arises from a religious culture where the issue was joined between and among religious communities. C-67 reflects a church in a society where religion, including the Christian faith, has become an option, not an assumption.

The central point of agreement between Heidelberg and C-67 is a theological point, not perhaps unique to the Reformed heritage but nevertheless central to it: The church must be understood theologically in the context of the doctrine of *election.* The core identity of the church is its confession that it is a people chosen through Jesus Christ and by the work of the *Holy Spirit.* It cannot, therefore, be self-defining. Its identity is given by the being and activity of God. The church is a theocentric community.

The church visible and invisible. "We must leave to God alone the knowledge of his church, whose foundation is his secret election," wrote Calvin (*Inst.* 4.1.2). Calvin, the engendering agent of the Reformed heritage, grounds the church in God's action but provides for a distinction between the invisible and the visible church. The former is the true and full church. But it is known only to God. Hence, one must be cautious in making judgments about others and humble about one's own condition. The invisible church is the whole number whom God has chosen, living and dead, the *communion of saints,* perhaps even those who appear to our eyes as reprobate, and excluding some who appear to be genuinely righteous and godly. But to say the church is invisible is to rest its identity solely in God.

The visibility of the church is, however, equally as important as the church invisible. Indeed, to separate the two

would be as great an error as to identify them as one. For the visible church, with all its deficiencies and *sins,* is grounded upon God's gracious provision for our lives, individually and corporately. It is the visible church that Calvin strikingly calls "our mother." "For there is no other way to enter into life unless this mother conceive us in her womb, give us birth, nourish us at her breast, and lastly, unless she keep us under her care and guidance until, putting off mortal flesh, we become like the angels [Matt. 22:30]. Our weakness does not allow us to be dismissed from her school until we have been pupils all our lives" (*Inst.* 4.1.4).

The visible church is absolutely essential. It is not an option. It is God's provision for our fallen world, God's *accommodation* to our fallen state. God's election creates a people who live in this world, not in some other. This is the good news associated with the church as we know it. It is not only a house of hypocrites. It is a community/institution that God provides as an agency for God's saving, justifying, and sustaining activity. It is, to use Karl Barth's striking phrase, "the earthy-historical form of existence of Jesus Christ Himself" (*CD* IV/1, 661). It is, to use the biblical metaphor, the body of Christ. Clearly, the dangers in such a proposal are immense—pride, self-congratulation, and *idolatry.* But since Jesus Christ is the center of the church, the head of the body, the visible church is defined by one who emptied himself, taking the form of a servant (Phil. 2:7). The true church is instrumental to God's mission of serving.

In the Reformed heritage, the church is both visible and invisible, sometimes more and sometimes less visible! Yet its authenticity rests not upon itself but upon its center—Jesus Christ, who calls this people into being and gives them life through the power of the Holy Spirit. Through the Spirit, the people know their election in Jesus Christ and render their thankful praise and service. Such knowledge is cause for rejoicing but not boasting. It is grounds for serving, not being served.

The one church. Theologically, the church in the Reformed tradition claims that its commitment is to the ecumenical church. What it holds in common with other traditions is more important than what separates it. A Reformed understanding of the church includes, therefore, the four classical, theological characteristics associated with the ecumenical church. The church that is Reformed is one, holy, catholic, and apostolic.

To say the church is one is to assert that all churches find their unity not in their common practices but in their common source—Jesus Christ. The oneness of practices and understanding is not unimportant. Far from it. But these matters are subordinate to the fact that in Christ all are one. To be "in" Christ is to be a member of the church. Such deficiencies of unity and scandals of separation as there are in the visible church are negative reminders of the oneness given in Christ. Oneness is an eschatological dimension of the church, avidly to be sought now and to be received in the future.

Similarly, the church's holiness is not its perfection or purity. Holiness is the holiness of Jesus Christ, who bestows upon the church the righteousness it cannot attain for itself. Therefore, to be holy is to depend on Christ, who "is daily at work in smoothing out wrinkles and cleansing spots. . . . The church is holy, then, in the sense that it is daily advancing and is not yet perfect" (*Inst.* 4.1.17). The Holy Spirit leads the church into righteousness. But this leading of the church into righteousness is not only the *sanctification* of the believers. It is the believers' engagement, individually, corporately, and with others in reaching out to and transforming the "unholy," in seeking to build community among all, the so-called sheep and goats, and in doing *justice* in the world. It is the engagement through Christ and in Christ with the struggles for a world where the hungry are to be fed, the homeless to be sheltered, and the lost to be found. It is, as C-67 puts it, allowing the life, death, *resurrection,* and promised coming of Jesus

Christ to "set the pattern for the church's mission" (*BC* 9.32).

The church is catholic. This affirmation locates the church simultaneously in relationship to Jesus Christ and to Jesus Christ's being confessed. Ignatius of Antioch wrote, "Wherever Jesus Christ is, there is the catholic church" (*Smyrneans* 8.2). So understood, catholicity or universality is, like holiness and oneness, grounded in the universal Lordship of Jesus Christ. The given universality in Jesus Christ leads the church to be inclusive in its life and leaves no realm of life exempt from the Lordship of Christ. The church as catholic understands Christ's Lordship as embracing all geographic arenas and all spheres of life within geographic units. Jürgen Moltmann writes: "The goal of the church's mission remains universal. In the new people of God the divisions that destroy mankind will be deprived of their force here and now. The barriers which people set up against each other . . . will be broken down through mission and fellowship" (Moltmann, 351).

The church is apostolic. By *apostolic* is meant both the legitimate source of the church's message and its mission. By *source* is meant the apostolic witness to Jesus Christ as received in the scriptures. These testimonies are the touchstone for current apostolic faithfulness. Where the church does find its legitimacy is in its consistency with the message of those who saw the Lord "face to face." The church is apostolic as it is instructed and disciplined by the apostles and as it carries into the whole inhabited earth the good news that all, including the church, need to hear. It is apostolic as it fulfills its purpose, put simply by H. Richard Niebuhr, as the increase of the love of God and the neighbor among humans (Niebuhr, 31).

In the Reformed tradition, thinking about the nature of the church holds firmly to these marks of self-understanding: one, holy, catholic, and apostolic. The church that is centered in Jesus Christ is instructed and commissioned by the apostolic witness; it proclaims by word and deed the universal rule of God in Jesus Christ; it trusts in God's Spirit to lead it into and to contribute to the holiness God intends for all the world; and it clings to the unity it has in Christ and that it seeks institutionally. For Reformed Christians, the church is, therefore, inevitably ecumenical, engaged with the world, and informed and held under scrutiny by the words and deeds of the earliest witnesses.

The church as a dynamic community/ institution. Inasmuch as the church is a human instrument, indeed, an "earthen vessel," there is need to attend to such matters as *ministry, sacraments,* and church order. These are by no means issues of indifference to the Reformed way of thinking. They are, in some cases, distinctives. They are means of *grace* God provides and uses to provide for the church and the world. They are necessary furnishings for the visible church.

Calvin wrote: "From this the face of the church comes forth and becomes visible to our eyes. Whenever we see the Word of God purely preached and heard, and the sacraments administered according to Christ's institution, there, it is not to be doubted, a church of God exists" (*Inst.* 4.1.9). Such a statement does not resolve all *confessions* or disagreements. Persistent questions remain. The Reformed acceptance of two sacraments—*Baptism* and the *Lord's Supper*—sets it apart from the Roman Catholic Church. Disagreement about the meaning of these two sacraments divided and still divides today Reformed Protestants from Lutheran and Anabaptist Protestants. But these visible marks of the true church are central to the Reformed understanding of the church. Note that the "preaching" mark of the church includes both *proclaiming* and *hearing*. This interactive setting emphasizes the responsibility of the whole people of God to discern the Word that God speaks by the power of the Spirit. Word, Spirit, and people are inextricably tied together. All

in the church are active participants in discernment.

The Reformed tradition today embraces a high view of the church as a people whom God calls. It endorses the perspective that two marks of the church are as stated above. But there is as well a third mark associated with this tradition—discipline.

The *Scots Confession,* following a description of the first two marks of the church as true *preaching* and the right administration of the sacraments, affirms another mark: "lastly, ecclesiastical discipline uprightly ministered, as God's Word prescribes, whereby vice is repressed and virtue nourished" (*BC* 3.18). *Church discipline* is instrumental to faithful discipleship.

Since it is a Reformed insistence that the church is to be ordered by the Word and Spirit, the issue of how that ordering is to be done is not a trivial matter. While there is no one *polity* or system of discipline mandated for every Reformed community, there are shared points of agreement among them.

One agreement is the importance of the *elder* as an agent of the church's disciplines. This lay officer shares with the minister of Word and Sacrament in the positive task of providing for the spiritual well-being of the church. Further, there is agreement that discipline is the constructive task of providing for the structures, processes, and programs that build up the church and enable it to carry forward its mission. Such discipline is exercised through a series of ascending governing bodies, in which clergy and laity share responsibility in a representative system.

Some features of discipline, of course, must be determined in the light of changing conditions. The flexibility of church discipline illustrates the motto that is identified widely with a Reformed understanding of the church: *Ecclesia reformata semper reformanda* ("The church reformed and always being reformed").

Within this Reformed understanding of the church there is the affirmation of the church as a dynamic community, dependent upon a living Lord as it seeks to be in mission in a changing world. One should note that the subject of the reform of the church is not the church. The church is the object of reform—it is "always being reformed." The agent of legitimate reform is the Holy Spirit. It is the dynamic element of the Spirit's work that emboldens the church to be open to and to seek new forms of discipline, including new **confessions of faith.** Calvin wrote: "Our constant endeavor, day and night, is not just to transmit the tradition faithfully, but also to put it in the form we think will prove best" (*Defense against Pighius*). So Reformed churches understand themselves as part of an open tradition. In such a tradition, one understands, for example, confessions of faith as necessary disciplines for the church's life and mission. But one also knows that such confessional standards and other forms of discipline arise under specific conditions and address needs of a particular time and place. Subordinate to **scripture,** such disciplines order and inform the life and convictions of the church.

The church in the Reformed tradition understands itself in a dynamic tension with the culture and the state. As the Lord of the church is the Lord of the world, so the church is called to discern and respond to God's creating, redeeming, and ordering work in the world. The church seeks the public good. With reference to **civil government,** for example, there is a high view of the calling of the state. It is to provide for justice, order, **freedom,** and **peace,** to enact and enforce policies that liberate those who are oppressed or victimized. But the church has the positive task of addressing the state and society as to what the church believes makes for peace, justice, freedom, and order.

In the Reformed tradition, the church is the communion of saints. It is the communion of Christians of all times and all places. But this phrase is something more. It points to the church as a community marked by mutual care and bearing of burdens. It is the community where sins are forgiven, encouragement is shared, and faith is deepened and corrected. It is the people who know and live as members one of another because they are members of Christ's body. It is the community of the elect who exercise toward each other and toward all neighbors the love and justice of Jesus Christ. It is the community of the Holy Spirit.

The challenge of individualism. Perhaps one of the greatest challenges to the corporate view of the church in the United States, and possibly in the world, is indicated by the concluding quotation at the beginning of this entry. "To become one's own person" and "to give birth to oneself" reflect a view of the self and community where the community drops away or recedes so far into the background that only the separate and self-reliant individual comes into focus. This self is the individual who has no necessary relationships of mutuality, whose individual accomplishments overshadow the sense of gifts received, where one "makes it" alone or not at all, where consuming goods takes precedence over public responsibility, where the church as our mother is replaced by self-birthing.

To this radical individualism as a cultural value the Reformed understanding of the church addresses a good word. It is the word that true life is life in community. It is the good word that life in community rests firmly on a foundation that endures, the gracious calling into the community of all of God's creation, through Jesus Christ and by the power of the Holy Spirit. That is a hard word to hear for the radical individualist in and outside the church. But beyond that, it is a graceful Word, full of truth. For the nature of the church is finally not a doctrine but a life lived in, from, and by the **Word of God.** It is the life of a people who are in relationship with each other because they share a relationship with Jesus Christ that defines who they are—children of God and sisters and brothers in Christ.

Robert R. Bellah et al., *Habits of the Heart* (1985); G. C. Berkouwer, *The Church* (1976); E. Clowney, *The Church* (1995); T. George,

ed., *John Calvin and the Church* (1990);
H. Küng, *The Church* (1967); J. T. McNeill,
The History and Character of Calvinism (1954);
J. Moltmann, *The Church in the Power of the
Spirit* (1977); H. R. Niebuhr et al., *The Purpose
of the Church and Its Ministry* (1956); R. S.
Paul, *The Church in Search of Its Self* (1972);
L. Vischer, ed., *Reformed Witness Today* (1982).

JACK L. STOTTS

Common Sense Philosophy   Also
called common sense realism, it was an
intellectual product of the Scottish
Enlightenment associated with Thomas
Reid and Dugald Stewart and also with
George Campbell and James Beattie. It
had major influence in the United States,
both in the academic culture of the late
eighteenth and nineteenth centuries and
in several theological traditions.

Reid published *An Inquiry into the
Human Mind on the Principles of Common
Sense* (1764) and expanded its ideas into
later volumes. Influenced by Francis
Bacon and John Locke, Reid wished to
combat the influence of David Hume and
the dangerously speculative philosophical tendencies he believed Hume had
influenced. Reid's epistemology was
grounded in the conviction that perception is always of existing objects, that
knowledge is not restricted to perceptions in the mind alone. More important
for its religious use, Reid's *philosophy*
adhered to a rigorous dualism of material and spiritual being.

Common sense philosophy emerged
in the American colonies when John
Witherspoon, a product of the evangelical movement in Scotland, became president of Princeton College (College of
New Jersey) in 1768. Witherspoon discovered the ideas of George Berkeley in
fashion at the college and worked to dis-
credit them through a philosophy of realism. He laid the foundations for a long
tradition of academic philosophy in the
United States; by the early nineteenth
century, works in the common sense
genre were in wide use in American colleges. Stewart's *Elements of the Philosophy*

of the Human Mind (3 vols.; 1792–1827)
was a popular text.

Within the Reformed tradition, common sense philosophy was particularly
important at Princeton Seminary
(founded 1812), the major citadel of
"orthodox" Presbyterianism in the United
States. The Scottish influence was evident
in Charles Hodge, Samuel Miller, and
Archibald Alexander. The *Princeton Theology* opposed metaphysical influences
associated with certain varieties of German philosophy and American transcen-
dentalism and sought to temper the
excesses of revivalism by establishing
faith on a strong intellectual base. Building on the empirical data of consciousness,
and deriving moral and spiritual laws
from this source, the inductive method of
the Scots, in the tradition of Bacon, helped
accommodate Reformed thinking to a
new spirit of *science* and a new challenge
from scientific methodology.

Common sense philosophy was
remarkably adaptable. It fortified conservative theology, as at Princeton, but was
widely implemented in more liberal
movements. It influenced the *New Haven
Theology* of N. W. Taylor and the Unitarianism of William Ellery Channing.
Channing was introduced to Scottish philosophy at Harvard and used Reid's
dualism to defend a rational belief in the
supernatural against rival philosophies
of materialism. Common sense philosophy was a kind of Protestant *scholasticism* that gave something of a common
base to Reformed and non-Reformed religious intellectual traditions.

T. D. Bozeman, *Protestants in an Age of Sci-
ence: The Baconian Ideal and Antebellum
American Religious Thought* (1977); D.
Meyer, *The Instructed Conscience* (1973);
Rogers and McKim, *AIB*; D. Sloan, *The Scot-
tish Enlightenment and the American College
Ideal* (1971).

J. DAVID HOEVELER JR.

Common Sense Realism   *see* Com-
mon Sense Philosophy

Communion of Saints

The Apostles' Creed's *sanctorum communio* can have seven grammatical translations. Three major theological interpretations have emerged. The sacramental, prominent in the Middle Ages, linked the believer to *salvation* through "participation in holy things"—the *sacraments.* Second, the phrase can mean the *church* here and now, the "union of saints" in fellowship and mutual love. A further Reformed emphasis, however, is the whole company of God's people—past, present, and future. This is a comprehensive picture of "church," grounded in God's *election* (*Inst.* 4.1.3).

DONALD K. MCKIM

Confession of 1967

Part of the *Book of Confessions* in the *Constitution* of the PC (USA), representing the first major revision of formally approved *doctrine* in American Presbyterianism. The Confession of 1967 (C-67) is founded on the biblical doctrine of reconciliation (2 Cor. 5:18ff.), a fundamental motif comparable to, and almost identical with, the doctrine of *justification* at the time of the Reformation. Classical Trinitarian and christological doctrines are "recognized and reaffirmed" but not restated—as they appear in other parts of the *BC* as described in the Preface of C-67.

Part I, "God's Work of Reconciliation," begins with the *ministry* as well as the death and *resurrection* of Jesus Christ and affirms the universality of Christ as savior and judge. This point of departure leads to a doctrine of universal *sin,* from which Christ is the sole redeemer, and thence to *creation* as a work of the same universal and sovereign love of *God* known in Christ. Next, "The Communion of the Holy Spirit" describes the "new life" of the Christian, which results when Christ's cross becomes "personal crisis and present hope." It is always a life in community (the *church*), still in conflict with sin, but finding its direction and pattern in the life of Jesus, and trusting that "God's purpose rather than man's schemes will finally prevail." Also under the teaching on the Spirit is a section on the Bible, which is "received and obeyed" as the Spirit's "authoritative witness" to "the one sufficient revelation of God" in "Jesus Christ, the Word of God incarnate." This founding of *authority* in the Word revealed in Christ, rather than on the inspiration of a sacred text, was an intentional development beyond the *WCF* (1647). C-67 then presents the NT as the confessional access to the OT and requires "literary and historical understanding" of the "views of life, history, and the cosmos," found in various documents that make up *scripture.* The persistence of the Word through "diverse cultural situations" gives confidence that God "will continue to speak through the Scriptures in a changing world and in every form of human culture."

Part II, "The Ministry of Reconciliation," deals first with the "direction" of the church's mission and the "forms and order" that take shape from the message preached and the "pattern" of the life, death, resurrection, and promised coming of Jesus Christ, carried forward in different times and places. C-67 is compressed, but it is quite elaborate about characteristics and norms of the church as an institution.

"Revelation and Religion" deals with the mission encounter with *world religions,* confessing that the gospel judges also the "Christian religion" but is to be carried to the whole human race. The mission of "Reconciliation in Society" offers four paradigms that have to do with racial injustice, *war,* poverty, and sexual anarchy, in which the church "seeks to discern the will of God and learn how to obey." Here church responsibility toward social evil in addition to that of private Christians represents a development beyond other documents in the *BC.* This section, together with that of scripture, was the focus of thorough study and considerable controversy in the adoption process. "The Equipment of the Church" for its mission is presented under the topics "Preaching and Teaching,"

"Praise and Prayer," "Baptism," and the "Lord's Supper."

Part III, "The Fulfillment of Reconciliation," is a brief *eschatology* of the kingdom, which images Christian *hope* as "the triumph of God over all that resists his will and disrupts his creation." The concluding words are the ascription of praise from Eph. 3:20.

E. A. Dowey, Jr., *A Commentary on the Confession of 1967 and an Introduction to "The Book of Confessions"* (1968); and "Reconciliation and Liberation—The Confession of 1967," *JPH* 61, no. 1 (1983); J. B. Rogers, *Presbyterian Creeds* (1985).

EDWARD A. DOWEY JR.

Confessions of Faith   see Creeds and Confessions

Confirmation/Admission to the Lord's Supper   John Calvin regarded confirmation as one of the five "bastard Sacraments" of the Roman Church. It has no institution in the *Word of God*, and it is "a noted insult to baptism." Martin Luther also regarded confirmation as "a human invention" and considered it "preposterous to think confirmation could add something to baptism that baptism lacked." Calvin, nevertheless, believed it was an ancient custom that those baptized as infants should, in adolescence, be examined in the *catechism* and blessed. "This laying on of hands, which is done simply by way of benediction, I commend, and would like to see restored to its pure use in the present day" (see *Inst.* 4.19.4–13). He was decisively rejecting any view that the laying on of hands had a sacramental quality or conferred a special *grace.*

In the Western church, confirmation, as distinct from *Baptism,* arose when one of the ceremonies by which Baptism had been elaborated came to be reserved to the bishop and administered at a later date. Since anointing or the laying on of hands (and there is always dubiety as to what the "matter" of confirmation is) was intended to symbolize and underline the work of the *Holy Spirit* in Baptism, its separation from Baptism could not detract from the fullness of that rite, and there have been few, until recent times, who would have argued that it did.

Once the rite of confirmation had been separated from Baptism, the problem was to find a meaning for it. The medieval view that confirmation confers an increase of grace can be traced back to the fifth century and was given definition by Thomas Aquinas in the context of his view of *sacraments* as conferring special graces for the different stages and states of life.

This was rejected by all the Reformers, but the proposal of Erasmus, Bucer, and Calvin to link the service in some way with catechizing and profession of *faith* came to be accepted. In the Church of Scotland, young people were catechized by the kirk session and admitted to Communion, and this was seen as a disciplinary rather than a ritual matter. In the Church of England, confirmation was reserved for the bishop and the medieval view prevailed until, beginning in the late nineteenth century, a radically new view was propounded that separated the gift of the Holy Spirit from Baptism and attached it solely to confirmation: "In baptism, he is the agent, in confirmation the gift." This view, associated with the names of F. W. Puller, A. J. Mason, L. S. Thornton, and Gregory Dix, has had support among Anglo-Catholics but not in official statements. The view was ably countered by G. W. H. Lampe (*Seal of the Spirit* [1951]).

In other Reformed churches, notably the Church of Scotland, admission to the Lord's Table began to take place at public *worship,* and in the orders of service that were provided, the word "confirmation" began to be used. The most widely influential of these was in the *Book of Common Order* (1940). The Scoto-Catholics who produced that book were vague enough about the meaning of "confirmation" but tended toward the medieval view rather than the view of Mason and Dix—as did the Church of Scotland's Panel on Doctrine in a 1967 report. The result is a vague idea of confirmation as conferring something by the hands of the minister. Such a mechanical, clerically operated view of grace is strangely out of place in a Reformed church. The recovery of a Reformed understanding of God's prevenient grace might yield a more robust theology of Baptism and remove the need for a medieval theology of confirmation.

The place of confirmation has become even more problematic with the increasing tendency of Reformed churches to welcome children to the Lord's Table at an age much younger than admission (or confirmation) has traditionally been granted.

J. D. C. Fisher, *Confirmation Then and Now* (1978); R. R. Osmer, *Confirmation: Presbyterian Practices in Ecumenical Perspective* (1996).

JAMES A. WHYTE

Conscience   Paul's allusions to conscience (Rom. 2:15; 1 Cor. 4:4) assured this topic a place in *Reformed theology,* where the condemning conscience ("the worm of conscience") has been more prominent than the guiding conscience.

John Calvin defined conscience as a "sense of the divine judgment" and a "medium between God and man" that "does not allow a person to suppress what he knows" (*Inst.* 3.19.15). However, the Reformers also stressed that "peace of conscience," or "good conscience," is possible through—but only through—faith in God's free redemption in Christ.

Romans 2:15 and 1 Cor. 4:4 display a tension always present in Reformed treatments. "Written on their hearts" (Rom. 2:15) could mean that conscience is a faculty of the soul that pronounces God's verdict on the morality of an act or decision. But when Paul says (1 Cor. 4:4) he is not acquitted even though his conscience is clear, he suggests that conscience is relative to God's *judgment.* For Calvin, conscience mediates and can even anticipate God's judgment but cannot be separated from God's judgment.

After Calvin, conscience continued to be important in Reformed thought, especially in William Ames's "cases of conscience" and with others who dealt with "assurance of salvation" as well as with conscience providing guidance in making moral decisions. The emphasis on the practical syllogism and conscience as an act of practical reason are reminiscent of medieval discussions. Some might argue that these theologians returned to conscience as linked to the will or *reason* rather than seeing it as a description of the whole person before *God*. However, the works of Francis Turretin show that this latter idea was still present among Reformed thinkers.

Later Reformed theologians, such as Friedrich Schleiermacher, continued to treat the concept. For Schleiermacher, conscience "expresses the fact that all . . . activity arising from our God-consciousness . . . confront[s] us as moral demands" (*CF*). Conscience is important because it is directly related to the central concept of the feeling of dependence.

Among twentieth-century Reformed theologians, conscience has not been a significant topic. This is clearly due to Freud's criticisms. For him, the guilty conscience was the result of parental and societal injunctions and the price paid for civilization. However, Reinhold Niebuhr defined conscience as the "sense of being . . . judged" by God, and he frequently criticized the "easy conscience" of contemporary persons.

Paul Lehmann attempted to reclaim conscience as an important ethical concept by redefining conscience in dependence on Reformation insights, while taking account of the criticisms presented by modern psychology. For him, conscience "forges the link between what God is doing in the world and man's free obedience to that activity" (*Ethics in a Christian Context,* 350).

Studies of the sociological and psychological stages of moral development by psychologists critical of Freud may foster a renewed interest in conscience among Reformed theologians.

W. Ames, *De conscientia* (1622; 1630; ET *Conscience with the Power and Cases Thereof* [1639]); K. E. Kirk, *Conscience and Its Problems* (repr. 1999); P. L. Lehmann, *Ethics in a Christian Context* (1963); Reinhold Niebuhr, *The Nature and Destiny of Man*, 2 vols. (1941–43); R. Zachman, *The Assurance of Faith: Conscience in the Theology of Martin Luther and John Calvin* (1993).

DAVID FOXGROVER

Consensus of Geneva   John Calvin composed this treatise to defend his *predestination* teachings, and it was subscribed to by the Genevan pastors (1552). The work responded to antipredestinarian critiques by Roman Catholic Albertus Pighius (1542) and the temporary Protestant, onetime colleague of Calvin who became his fierce enemy, Jerome Bolsec, as well as by one George of Sicily. Pighius and George advocated a semi-Pelagian view of the *freedom* of the human will, and Bolsec held that Calvin's view of divine sovereignty and human inability made *God* the author of *sin* and encouraged immorality.

Reminiscent of Romans 9—11, Calvin replied that there is no moral standard of *judgment* outside and above the character and will of God by which humans can negatively assess God's choices. God's sovereign *election* of sinners is the most solid foundation for believers' assurance, and through divine "passing by" the lost is in accord with God's righteousness, which requires God to punish sin, not obligating God to save anyone.

Though Calvin hoped for support from pastors and civil authorities of other Swiss cities, the strident and sometimes bitter polemical tone of the Consensus prevented its acceptance beyond Geneva. Other Protestants, such as Heinrich Bullinger and Philip Melanchthon,

desired a more moderate and irenic predestination statement.

CO 8:249–366; H. A. Niemeyer, *Collectio Confessionum* (1840), 218–310; J. K. S. Reid, ed., *Concerning the Eternal Predestination of God* (1961); Schaff, *Creeds*, vol. 1.

DOUGLAS F. KELLY

Consensus Tigurinus   ("Agreement of Zurich") A statement of *faith* composed principally by John Calvin and Heinrich Bullinger to provide concord on eucharistic theology and practice between the French-speaking and German-speaking Swiss Reformed churches. The need arose from intense disputes over the *Eucharist* between Zwinglians and Lutherans. In international *politics*, the militant Roman Catholic maneuvers against the Reformers demanded a united Swiss Protestant response. Calvin and William Farel traveled to Zurich (May 1549) to sign the accord with Bullinger and other city ministers. The document reflected several years of extensive negotiations between Calvin and Bullinger.

The Consensus (1551) had twenty-six articles. It was eventually adopted by the other Swiss Reformed churches, providing an important step toward the *Second Helvetic Confession* (1566). It states that Christ truly "exhibits" himself to believers in the *Lord's Supper*, which is a mark or badge of the Christian life. However, apart from faith, the *sacraments* are nothing but "empty masks." Sacramental efficacy is thus related to the *doctrine* of *predestination*: "God does not exert his power indiscriminately in all who receive the sacraments, but only in the elect." A materialist view of the Eucharist is rejected by emphasizing spiritual communion with Christ and the lifting of the believer's heart to *heaven* (*sursum corda*) by the power of the *Holy Spirit*.

The Consensus brought Swiss Reformed churches closer, but it occasioned still another eucharistic controversy as Calvin was forced to defend it against renewed assaults from the Lutherans. The meaning of the Consensus has been debated by subsequent Reformed theologians such as Charles Hodge and John Williamson Nevin.

U. Gäbler, "Das Zustandekommen des Consensus Tigurinus im Jahre 1549," *Theologische Literaturzeitung* 104, no. 5 (1979): 321–32; T. George, "John Calvin and the Agreement of Zurich," in *John Calvin and the Church*, ed. T. George (1990); P. Rorem, *Calvin and Bullinger on the Lord's Supper* (1989); O. Strasser, "Der Consensus Tigurinus," *Zwingliana* 9, no. 1 (1949): 1–16.

TIMOTHY GEORGE

Conversion   The experience of God's *forgiveness* and love and the reorientation of an individual's life away from *sin* to *grace* and *faith.* Though the Hebrew and Greek biblical texts rarely use the word for "conversion," the Bible is filled with references embodying the root meaning—to turn or to turn around. All understandings of conversion involve three dimensions: the act of *repentance,* the experience of grace, and a new life of discipleship.

The history of *Reformed theology* has been marked by sharp and bitter debates about the nature of conversion. While John Calvin conceded that *knowledge of God* and knowledge of self were so intertwined that they could not be separated, scholastic *Calvinism* increasingly insisted on a more rigid view of God's sovereignty and humanity's inability to do anything to achieve *salvation.* This debate over human will and *free will* lay at the heart of the *Arminian* controversy and continued to shape Reformed attitudes toward evangelicalism and revivalism in the eighteenth, nineteenth, and twentieth centuries.

The conversion debate decisively molded New England Puritanism and its *doctrine* of the *church.* At first, membership was restricted only to persons who could recount conversion experiences; later, the *Half-Way Covenant* was introduced to extend baptism to children of unregenerate parents. Central was the dispute over whether the church should include only persons who have been converted or whether its fellowship should extend to persons who have not yet had a definable and describable grace experience.

At the heart of the broad movement of Protestant evangelicalism, conversion was understood as a particular event in one's life. Though many, such as Charles G. Finney and Alexander Campbell, rebelled against scholastic Calvinism's determinism and *predestination* emphasis, others, such as Horace Bushnell, questioned the legitimacy of defining grace in terms of solitary events. He insisted that children should grow up never knowing themselves to be anything other than Christians.

Whether it is predestined by *God* or is an act of individual submission, whether it is one event or a series of experiences over a lifetime, whether it should be the primary requirement for church membership instead of a confession of faith, conversion remains a mystery of God's grace. In John 3, Jesus does admonish Nicodemus to be "born anew" or "born again." But when Nicodemus asks how this is possible, Jesus replies, "The wind blows where it chooses, and you hear the sound of it, but you do not know where it comes from or where it goes. So it is with everyone who is born of the Spirit" (John 3:8).

Conversion becomes the sign of a turning away from sin and doubt to a new life of joy and faith through the work of the *Holy Spirit.* The Reformed tradition also stresses that this inner *regeneration* is accompanied by a life of discipleship and service. The link between conversion and witness is one of the distinctive marks of Reformed *piety.*

W. E. Conn, ed., *Conversion: Perspectives on Personal and Social Transformation* (1978); B. R. Gaventa, *From Darkness to Light: Aspects of Conversion in the New Testament* (1986); W. James, *The Varieties of Religious Experience* (1902); A. D. Nock, *Conversion* (1933).

JOHN M. MULDER

Cosmology   The study of the arrangement and dynamics of the sun, the moon, planets, comets, and stars. At the time of the Reformation, European schools had been teaching Aristotle's cosmology for three centuries. The earth was at rest, the cosmos was finite, and speculation about what lay beyond its outermost sphere was problematic.

John Calvin wondered why the earth should be attracted to a bare point at the center of the cosmos and remain perfectly motionless in the midst of the huge revolving spheres around it. These must be signs of the particular *providence of God,* he argued. Though he left nothing in writing about the heliocentric theory of Copernicus (1543), Calvin ridiculed the very suggestion that the earth might be moving as a subversive ploy of skeptics like Sebastian Castellio to cast doubt on the truth of biblical *faith.*

Copernicus restructured Western cosmology by setting the earth in motion, placing the sun at the center, and greatly increasing the distance to the stars, now "fixed" at the circumference of the cosmos. The English Protestant Thomas Digges (1576) first suggested that an infinite expanse of stars was suited to the infinite power and majesty of their creator. Calvin's commitment to Aristotelian cosmology was easily forgotten!

The dynamics of the moving planets were worked out by Isaac Newton (1687). Though mathematical and predictable, they still required *God* for their origin and maintenance. Within a century, however, God was no longer needed for either reason. The French agnostic, Pierre Simon Laplace, was largely responsible for convincing the scientific world that a completely mechanical cosmology was feasible.

In the early eighteenth century, Reformed theologians such as Isaac Watts and Jonathan Edwards had already accepted the Epicurean notion that the formation of all aspects of the world—inanimate ones, at least—was explicable in purely mechanical terms. A Scottish astronomer, James Ferguson, even anticipated Laplace's theory that the formation of the solar system could be explained by the clustering of atoms in accordance with Newton's law of gravitation. Such was the skill of the Creator in giving motions and powers to the atoms in the beginning!

Though belief in *creation* was not ruled out, particular providence had disappeared from scientific cosmology by the end of the eighteenth century. Thomas Chalmers, leader of the Free Church of Scotland, was one who questioned the completeness of Laplace's account of things and because of this favored catastrophist understandings of natural history. Singularities and instabilities regained prominence in twentieth-century cosmology, but the debacle of nineteenth-century catastrophism has made most Reformed theologians shy away from the issue.

C. B. Kaiser, "Calvin's Understanding of Aristotelian Natural Philosophy," in *Calviniana,* ed. R. V. Schnucker (1988), 77–92.

CHRISTOPHER B. KAISER

Covenant   In *Reformed theology,* "covenant" usually refers to God's gracious promise to Abraham and his spiritual descendants that *God* will be a God and father to them and that they, enabled by God's *grace,* will live before God in *faith* and loving obedience. It has a richer theological meaning and more frequent usage in the Reformed tradition than in any other.

Though both the expression and that which it denotes lie at the heart of both Testaments, there was no development of the *doctrine* until the sixteenth century, and that development was confined to Reformed theology. Zwingli and Bullinger were the first to emphasize scriptural teachings on the covenant, reacting to Anabaptism in and around Zurich. Thereafter, Reformed theologians, including Calvin, made increasingly frequent mention of God's covenant with *humanity.*

In the seventeenth century, a "covenant theology" was developed that received heavy emphasis and sometimes played a dominant role in the system of doctrine expounded. Thus, Johannes Cocceius wrote *Doctrine of the Covenant and Testament of God* (1648), Hermann Witsius entitled his three volumes on God's relationship to the human race *The Oeconomy of the Covenants* (1685), and the Westminster Standards gave the theology of the covenant prominence in 1646–48 (WCF, chs. 7, 29, 30, 32.3; WLC, qq. 20; 30–36; 57; 79; 80; 97; 162; 165–66; 174; 176; WSC, qq. 12; 16; 20; 92; 94). Inasmuch as Puritanism embraced this covenant, or federal, theology, it was woven into the fabric of New England's early church life and played an important role in Presbyterian and Dutch Reformed churches.

Though the etymology is unclear, "covenant" probably comes from the Assyro-Babylonian and Hebrew word meaning "to bind" or "to fetter"; hence, the two covenant parties are bound together by oath. Originally the word was applied to two contracting human partners. When "covenant" came to be used in a religious meaning among the Hebrews, the meaning shifted to a divine bestowal of grace by which God took chosen people into fellowship, telling them that God would be their God and they should live as God's people. In some Reformed theology, the covenant was seen as a relationship that God bestowed on humankind as a reflection of a covenantal relationship thought to subsist among the three Persons of the *Trinity.*

As this emphasis on God's interaction with humanity in *history* developed in Reformed circles, attention was shifted away from the theology of the divine decree and *predestination,* which was prominent from the time of Calvin's controversy with Jerome Bolsec to the *Synod of Dort* in the next century. A connecting link between the divine decree and God's covenant with humanity was the covenant of redemption, which many Reformed theologians defined as the eternal pact between the Father and the Son whereby the Father commissioned the Son to be the Savior and gave him a people. The Son agreed to fulfill all righteousness and give his life for the *salvation* of humankind. Thus, before the foundation of the world a covenantal relationship existed in the Godhead as the archetype of that which was to appear later in history. Scriptural support stemmed from John 3:16; 5:20, 22, 36; 10:17–18; 17:2, 4, 6, 9, 24; Ps. 2:7–8; Heb. 1:8–13.

Covenant of works. In elaborating the theology of the covenants, some Reformed theologians taught a covenant of works as God's first covenant in history. This consisted of the promise of eternal life and confirmation in righteousness for Adam if he would be obedient throughout a probationary period and death if he were disobedient. As the father of all humankind, Adam was a public person and not acting only for himself. His fall, therefore, affected all who were to come after him, so we are all conceived and born in sin. The problem in the covenant of works is the promise to life, an idea not found in *scripture,* though Rom. 10:5 and Gal. 3:12 have been cited as support. Moreover, some feel the covenant of works to be a legitimate inference from that which has been revealed.

Covenant of grace. This covenant, beginning with the call of Abraham (Gen. 12–13; 15; 17:1–7), lies at the heart of scripture. Frequently mentioned in the Psalms (Pss. 89; 105) and the prophets (Jer. 31:31–34), it was given a new form and richer meaning by Jesus Christ (Matt. 26:28; Mark 14:24; Luke 22:20; 1 Cor. 11:25). Appearing often in the epistles (2 Cor. 3:6; Heb. 8—10; 12:24; 13:20), the teaching of the covenant that God established with the people of God and sealed with the blood of Jesus Christ is a major

NT theme, just as its fundamental idea was at the center of Israel's religious life. It runs throughout the two Testaments as a golden chain holding them together, with Jesus Christ the connecting link. Thus, Paul saw both OT Israel and believers in his day as bound together in Christ. That was God's intention with the call of Abraham; the covenant made with him was eventually to include Gentile nations. In Abraham all families of the earth would be blessed. This promise Paul recalled in Gal. 3:7–9, 14, 27–29.

The continuity of the two covenants, Old and New, is portrayed by Paul through the figure of an olive tree. Some natural (Jewish) branches were broken off; Gentile branches were grafted in. The tree itself, spanning both dispensations, is the continuing community of those who know and serve God (Rom. 11:17–24). Jesus' parable of the wicked husbandmen (Matt. 21:33–46) teaches the same truth, climaxing with Jesus' words to Jewish leaders: "The kingdom of God will be taken away from you and given to a nation producing the fruits of it" (v. 43). That nation, or people (alternative translation), can be none other than the Christian *church*, which is now God's covenant community. The new covenant, that is, the new form of the old covenant with Abraham, has been established with it.

In Jer. 31:31–34, God promises a new covenant with God's ancient people. In Hebrews 8, that passage is quoted to teach that the covenant promised to Israel has been given to the church. The author clearly understood the Christian church to be the covenant people of God. Jesus had instituted the *Lord's Supper* before his crucifixion by saying, "This is my blood of the new covenant which is shed for many for the remission of sins" (Matt. 26:28). Thus, the author wrote that "for this cause he is the mediator of a new covenant" (Heb. 9:15; cf. 7:22). So Paul reminded the Corinthians that Christ had made them "ministers of a new covenant" (2 Cor. 3:6). New Testament writers were aware that the new form of the old covenant had been promised to

Israel and claimed that this promise had been fulfilled in the church.

This is the uniform NT teaching. Since Christ has come and established the new form of the covenant, distinctions formerly prevailing in Israel are no longer binding. The old dietary laws became obsolete (Acts 10:28, 34–35). One is not a Jew who is one outwardly; the real Jew is the person whose heart is right with God (Rom. 2:28–29). The "dividing wall of hostility" that once separated Jews and Gentiles is said to have been removed. Gentiles are no longer "alienated from the commonwealth of Israel, and strangers to the covenants of promise, . . . no longer strangers and sojourners, but . . . fellow citizens with the saints and members of the household of God, built upon the foundation of the apostles and prophets, Christ Jesus himself being the cornerstone, in whom the whole structure is joined together and grows into a holy temple in the Lord" (Eph. 2:11–21). The temple is the church, which traces its descent from Abraham, the father of all the faithful. Believers in the Lord Jesus Christ are the Israel of this age.

Sinaitic covenant. Within Israel's history before the coming of Christ, God implemented and strengthened the earlier covenant. At Sinai (Ex. 19–24) the covenant assumed a national form with many commandments and prohibitions and with special stress on the *law* of God. This was not to lessen the gracious character of the earlier covenant (Gal. 3:17–18) but to train Israel until God would appear in its midst. The Davidic covenant (2 Sam. 7; 1 Chron. 17; Ps. 80) also is no break in the Abrahamic covenant but a high moment in the latter's realization, to come to fruition in David's greater son, the Lord Jesus.

Mediator of the new covenant. When Christ fulfilled the OT promises by his perfectly obedient life, sacrificial *death*, and *resurrection*, he became the mediator of the new covenant, that is, the new and better form of the covenant of grace. Jesus is mediator by virtue of his saving work (Heb. 8:6; 9:15; 12:24) and not only because he is the arbitrator between God and humankind. Because in Jesus salvation is sure, Jesus is called the "surety" or "guarantee" of a better covenant than that which came from Moses (Heb. 7:22). There is a direct relationship between Hebrews 7 and 8 and the institution of the Lord's Supper (Matt. 26:28; Luke 22:20) and the sealing of the Sinaitic form of the covenant (Ex. 24). Moses sacrificed an animal and sprinkled its blood on the altar and the people. Christ must have had that in mind when he said his blood was poured out for his people for the *forgiveness* of their sins.

This teaching of the unity of the covenant of grace is fundamental to the Reformed understanding of the church. The Christian church is the new covenant form of the people of God, the Israel of this age. It lives as the body of Christ, in communion with its head. It is as much a holy people, separated unto God, as was Israel of old. It is *in* the world but not *of* it. Its present existence is a pilgrimage, its destination eternal life with God.

Practical application. The application of the doctrine of the covenant for life is that Christians, who are members of Christ (1 Cor. 12:12–27; John 15:1–8; Eph. 4:4–16), are not their own but belong to Christ (1 Cor. 6:19–20). They live in union with Christ and glorify him through the power of his Spirit (Rom. 6; Matt. 5—7; Col. 3:1–17; Rom. 8). The fruit of the Spirit is evident in their lives (Gal. 5:22–25), and they are lights to shine in a dark world so others may see their good works and glorify God (Matt. 5:14–16). In the Reformed tradition, this practical aspect of living for the Lord is known as "calling" or "vocation," an idea inherited from Luther and developed in *Calvinism.* As children of the covenant and members of Christ, Christians are to dedicate their lives to Christ as "a chosen race, a royal priesthood, a holy nation, God's own people" (1 Peter 2:9–10).

L. Berkhof, *Reformed Dogmatics* (1941); E. M. Emerson, "Calvin and Covenant Theology," *CH* 25 (1956): 136–44; Heppe, *RD*; E. Kutsch, *Neues Testament—Neuer Bund?* (1978); C. S. McCoy, "Johannes Cocceius: Federal Theologian," *SJT* 16 (1963): 352–70; M. E. Osterhaven, "Calvin on the Covenant," in *Readings in Calvin's Theology,* ed. D. K. McKim (1984); J. Rohls, *Reformed Confessions* (1999); G. Schrenk, *Gottesreich und Bund im älteren Protestantismus* (1923; repr. 1967); H. H. Wolf, *Die Einheit des Bundes* (1958).

M. EUGENE OSTERHAVEN

Covenant Theology   *see* Federal Theology

Creation   Understandings of creation within the Reformed tradition include classical emphases found in other Christian traditions, revisions due to modern developments also affecting other traditions, plus its own characteristics. Emphases shared with other traditions include belief in creation as a free act of **God** performed through the eternal Word, creation of the world along with time out of nothing, a very good creation, and God's continuing sustenance and governance of the created order. Through these emphases is the pervasive belief that the creation is neither absolute nor divine but is forever contingent upon the eternal and self-existent creator.

Along with other Christian traditions, the Reformed understanding of creation has been altered by consequential modern developments, including the rise of historical-critical biblical studies, the Copernican revolution, Darwin's evolutionary theories, Einstein's theories of relativity, the emergence of process thought, and, more recently, the big bang cosmogony. These fostered a diminution of Christian cosmogonic and cosmological commentary, the differentiation of divinely revealed truth and obsolete worldviews through which it was conveyed, plus a movement away from literalistic interpretation of biblical accounts of creation to more textually informed interpretations.

The confessional sources of the Reformed **doctrine** of creation include

Calvin's *Geneva Catechism* (1541), the *Scots Confession* (1560), the *Belgic Confession* (1561), the *Heidelberg Catechism* (1563), the *Westminster Confession of Faith* (1647), and, more recently, the *Confession of 1967*. Major theological contributions to the Reformed understanding include those of John Calvin, Jonathan Edwards, Herman Bavinck, Karl Barth, Emil Brunner, and T. F. Torrance. While these *confessions* and theologians certainly do not constitute a uniform Reformed witness, there are prevailing Reformed perspectives on creation.

Beginning with Calvin and the HC and culminating in Barth, God the Creator is believed to be our Father because of Christ the Son who is also the Creator. Closely allied with this is the belief in creation found in Calvin and the WCF as the work of the triune God. Another persistent emphasis is on the close connection between creation and *providence*, made so clear in the HC and in the *Second Helvetic Confession*, where a chapter on providence precedes one on creation. The Reformed emphasis on God's ongoing involvement in creation is a kind of *creatio continua* held alongside a *creatio ex nihilo*. Allied with this emphasis is the epistemological role given to the created order in general *revelation*. Here we have Calvin's glorious or beautiful theater that as a mirror reflects God's power, wisdom, and goodness. But human wickedness, consequent ignorance, and error suppressed God's truth and negated this revelation. The Reformed view is also very theocentric in that creation's ultimate purpose is the glorification of God through humankind serving God, to which end other creatures were made for the sake of humankind. This emphasis, plus a belief in an active Creator who continues to be faithfully involved with the creation, has fostered sustained inquiry into its workings.

Barth, *CD* III/1–4; Berkhof, *CFI*; L. Gilkey, *Maker of Heaven and Earth* (1959); P. K. Jewett, *God, Creation, and Revelation* (1991); J. Orr, *The Christian View of God and the World* (repr. 1989); T. F. Torrance, *The Ground and Grammar of Theology* (1980).

ROBERT J. PALMA

Creeds and Confessions

The people of *God* have always paused at critical historical moments to summarize and declare who they are and what they most deeply believe. These high moments are remembered and passed on to succeeding generations to preserve the identity and vitality of the community.

Precursors of Creeds in Scripture

Old Testament. Deuteronomy 6:4–9 records one such moment. God had rescued the *covenant* people from slavery. They had disobeyed and wandered forty years in the wilderness. Now they were finally about to enter the Promised Land. The *law* had been given on Sinai. The issue was how to keep the law and prosper as a nation in the new land. All that they had experienced and been taught was summed up in one stirring sentence: "Israel, remember this! The LORD—and the LORD alone—is our God" (TEV). Then came the exhortation to put that declaration into practice: "Love the LORD your God with all your heart, with all your soul, and with all your strength." That was followed by the necessary injunction to teach this to their children by building it into the fabric of their daily lives.

The ritual offering of the firstfruit of the harvest was a time for remembering God's greatness and goodness. The story of God's deliverance was recited at the time of presenting an offering to the priest. Deuteronomy 26:5–9 records an early faith affirmation in narrative form beginning with the words "My ancestor was a wandering Aramean."

New Testament. Those close to Jesus, at certain crisis moments, came to stark clarity in response to his questions. Jesus asked Peter, "Who do you say I am?" Peter replied, "You are the Messiah, the Son of the living God" (Matt. 16:15–16). After Lazarus's death, Martha ran to meet Jesus, sorrowing that he had not been present to prevent the tragedy. Jesus declared to Martha, "I am the resurrection and the life," and then asked her, "Do you believe this?" Martha confessed, "Yes, Lord! . . . I do believe that you are the Messiah, the Son of God, who was to come into the world" (John 11:25–27).

In 1 Corinthians and Romans, Paul makes brief summary statements of the significance of Christ's life, death, and *resurrection* for our sake (1 Cor. 15:3–4; Rom. 1:3–4). He urges the verbal confession of these succinct statements of essential Christian truth (Rom. 10:9; 1 Cor. 12:3). Philippians 2:11 retains what is possibly the oldest crystallized confession of the early Christian community in the phrase "Jesus Christ is Lord."

No formal creeds, confessions, or *catechisms* are found in *scripture*. Present, however, is a common body of belief, accepted by all, as the faith affirmation of the Christian community (Kelly, 23–24). This pattern of commonly accepted affirmation set the stage for the development of formalized and repeated creeds in the first centuries of the church's life. A creed, confession, catechism, statement, or declaration is, therefore, a formal statement of a group's set of beliefs (Plantinga, 5).

Ancient Creeds of the Early Church

The early church built on the biblical examples of terse affirmations of *faith* and developed "creeds." The Latin word *credo* means "I believe" and points to the personal character of the earliest creeds.

Individual confession at baptism. When early converts asked how they could become part of the Christian community, the answer was: By being baptized. This *baptism* took place according to Christ's command: "in the name of the Father, the Son, and the Holy Spirit" (Matt. 28:19). Candidates for baptism became catechumens, learners, instructed in the meaning of this belief in one God in three persons. After a training period, the initiates recited a creed summarizing the truth they were going to profess.

Reciting a creed in this context was equivalent to taking a sacred oath, the original meaning of the word "sacrament." Another common name for the

creed was "symbol." It was a sign pointing Christians back to their baptism and their solemn oath of trust in the triune God.

By the second half of the second century, Christians generally knew a summary of Christian *doctrine* called "the rule of faith." Because of fear of persecution, this was not written down. It was, however, memorized and recited, often in connection with the *sacraments* of baptism and the *Lord's Supper.*

First to take definitive form in a local area was the Old Roman Symbol. Toward the end of the second century, this expansion on the Trinitarian baptismal formula became known and used. The Apostles' Creed is a descendant of this Roman creed. The present form of the Apostles' Creed is an expanded version that developed in the south of France between the fifth and the eighth century. By the ninth century, the Creed in its present form was sanctioned for use in Christian instruction by the Holy Roman Emperor, Charlemagne, and incorporated into the Roman liturgy by the papacy.

Community identity through church councils. The Nicene Creed, from the fourth century A.D., has a different beginning and serves some additional functions. It begins, "We believe . . . " and primarily proposes to solidify the identity of the Christian community. When differing interpretations of scripture threatened the unity of the *church,* it became necessary to identify orthodoxy (correct opinion) and differentiate it from *heresy* (choosing another way). After two church councils convened by emperors (Nicaea, A.D. 325; Constantinople, A.D. 381), the Nicene Creed developed to affirm the full deity and humanity of Jesus Christ and the reality of the *Holy Spirit.*

Creeds are a way of passing on the Christian tradition. There is risk involved. The Latin word *tradere* can mean "to hand on" and also "to betray." The responsibility to pass on the truth of the Christian *tradition* necessitates objectifying the *experience* of a people so that subsequent generations can analyze and, it is hoped, appropriate it as their own (Routley, 1, 4). Creeds intend to describe the faith of the whole, undivided Christian church. They are symbols of unity and givers of identity. They become vehicles of praise to God; are used in the *worship* of God, especially in connection with the sacraments; and serve as standards for *preaching* and instruction. Creeds are also guides in the interpretation of scripture, indicating how the church has read its Holy Books in the past. They clarify the identity of the community by demarcating orthodoxy and rejecting heresy. They become a testimony, a witness, sometimes even a battle cry, as the church encounters the world (Leith, "History," 35–39).

Reformation Confessions

The intent to be catholic. Confessions presuppose creeds. Often they explicitly affirm their adherence to the ancient creeds. Whereas creeds are brief summary statements of the belief of the whole church, confessions are more elaborated statements intended as the application of Christian faith to one group or region. During the Protestant Reformation of the sixteenth century, the renewal of the church took shape along national lines. Nations often used confessional documents to clarify their Christian and national identity.

National confessional distinctives. These confessions not only affirmed generic, catholic Christianity but also objectified the differences between a particular national church and others. All Protestants distinguished themselves from the Roman Catholics. *Justification* by *grace* through faith became a Protestant distinctive, a virtual thirteenth article of the creed (Routley, 11). Internal Protestant differences quickly arose. German Lutherans made clear their distinctions from the Swiss Reformed. The Swiss Reformed distanced themselves from both the German Lutherans and the Anabaptists in their midst. The Anglicans declared what they perceived to be a more excellent middle way between Protestantism and Catholicism.

Most of the Reformers did not intend or desire to be sectarian in any way. They wished only to articulate the undivided catholic faith in their confessions. They hoped all Christians would come to agree with the rightness of their formulations. But because these confessions were developed in differing historical and theological contexts, they inevitably took on distinctive colorations, tones and textures. There came to be theological traditions within Protestantism—for example, Lutheran, Anglican, Anabaptist, and Reformed. Within each tradition, national and regional groups produced their own distinctive confessional statements.

The sixteenth century also saw the production of catechisms. These were teaching tools, often in question-and-answer form, intended to guide preaching and instruct the young. Luther's Small Catechism was widely used. Calvin's *Geneva Catechism* (1541) provided the basis for a dialogue on Christian faith between a minister and a child. The *Heidelberg Catechism* (1563) became the chief theological standard for the Reformed communities in Germany, Hungary, Belgium, and the Netherlands. In 1609, Dutch explorers brought it as the first Reformed statement of faith in the New World. It was approved for use in Presbyterian congregations in the United States in 1870. The Westminster Larger Catechism (for preachers) and the Westminster Shorter Catechism (for children) proved influential in the Anglo-Saxon world from the seventeenth to the mid-twentieth century.

Reformed confessions. Of all the Protestant theological traditions, the Reformed has been the most prolific in producing confessional documents. Anglicans find their theology primarily in the liturgy. The Lutherans will interpret the Augsburg Confession (1530) but refuse to change or supplement it. The Anabaptists have statements such as the Schleitheim Confession (1527) and the Dordrecht Confession (1632). But they find their distinctiveness more in their way of life than in their confessional documents.

Sixteenth-century Reformed groups and their descendants have taken seriously their motto *Ecclesia reformata semper reformanda*. They have attempted both to be Reformed, rooted in a tradition, and always open to being further reformed according to the **Word of God** and the call of the Spirit. Reformed communities produced at least fifty confessional documents of some substance in their first fifty years of existence. Harmonies of Reformed confessions have sometimes been produced to show general doctrinal agreement among them. The *Second Helvetic Confession* was used as an outline for the Harmony of Reformed Confessions (1581; ET 1842; see Leith, *Creeds*, 128–29; see Dowey, 243ff., for a harmony of the *BC*). The WARC issued a collection of thirty-three Reformed statements of faith produced in many countries in the twentieth century (see Vischer).

Contemporary Reformed Confessions

New forms to meet new needs. In the twentieth century, another theological genre came into use. The *Theological Declaration of Barmen* (1934) was an "explanation," or "clarification," of the meaning of previous creeds and confessions. It applied Reformed principles to the menacing intrusion of German national socialism into the churches' life. Using only biblical and theological language, it made clear that the affirmation "Jesus Christ is Lord" meant that Adolf Hitler is not Lord.

The *Confession of 1967* in the United States followed the style and substance of the Barmen Declaration. Though much longer, it was structured around one doctrine, reconciliation. It was not to be a summary statement of Christian doctrine but applied the doctrine of reconciliation to the pressing social problems of the time, including *racism, war,* poverty, and anarchy in sexual relations.

A Brief Statement of Faith. In the late twentieth century, the Presbyterian Church (U.S.A.) developed "A Brief Statement of Faith." A Special Committee was called into being by the reunion of northern and southern branches of American Presbyterianism (1983). After a year of wrestling with its task, the committee concurred that a primary need was for a renewed sense of identity in the reunited church. The form chosen was a brief, liturgically usable document. The models were not Barmen or the Confession of 1967 but the Apostles' Creed and the Nicene Creed. The Statement was simply to summarize the Christian faith in its Protestant and Reformed expression in contemporary terms.

Although there was no intention of breaking new ground, the writers were compelled to extend the Reformed tradition into new areas. They introduced into Reformed confessional literature a narrative of Jesus' life and *ministry*; a clear assertion of the equality of women and men in the image of God and their fitness to be called to all the ministries of the church; a warning of the sins that threaten death to the planet entrusted to human care; and a modeling of both masculine and feminine imagery in speaking about God.

How We Confess the Faith Today

Contemporary Reformed Christians take their confessional documents very seriously but not with slavish literalism. Office-bearers are asked to "receive" and "adopt," to be "instructed" and "led." In most Reformed churches they are not required to subscribe to every word of every confession. Rather, they are asked whether they stand "in this succession, recognizing the road marked out by these confessions as that of a church obedient to its calling" (Smart, 6). Charles Hodge declared that subscription to the Westminster Standards asked one to affirm that she or he was Christian, Protestant, and Reformed (quoted in Leith, "History," 44). Contemporary creedal affirmation is a way of saying there is latitude within limits. Confessions are subordinate standards to the *revelation* of God in Jesus Christ recorded in scripture. But they are standards. They represent the careful reading of scripture by our parents in the faith. They cannot be treated casually. Governing bodies have the right to use them as a measure of whether or not someone is willing to function with integrity as a member of the community. Yet there must be responsible latitude for creative expression of theological thought alongside the essential affirmations. It is not every historically conditioned detail or the nuance of a word prescribed by a particular theological school that is definitive in the confessions. Rather, it is the common themes, the continuing principles, the central affirmations of the Reformed confessions that form the essential tenets or set the parameters that point us to the center of the Reformed tradition we share (Rogers, 24–26).

E. A. Dowey, Jr., *A Commentary on the Confession of 1967 and an Introduction to "The Book of Confessions"* (1968); J. N. D. Kelly, *Early Christian Creeds*, 3rd ed. (1981); J. H. Leith, "A Brief History of the Creedal Task: The Role of Creeds in Reformed Churches," in *To Confess the Faith Today*, ed. J. L. Stotts and J. D. Douglass (1990); J. H. Leitl, ed., *Creeds of the Churches*, 3rd ed. (1982); R. Muller, "Reformed Confessions and Catechisms," in *The Dictionary of Historical Theology*, ed. T. A. Hart (2000); W. Niesel, *Reformed Symbolics* (1962); C. Plantinga, *A Place to Stand* (1979); J. B. Rogers, *Presbyterian Creeds: A Guide to The Book of Confessions* (1985); J. Rohls, *Reformed Confessions* (1999); E. Routley, *Creeds and Confessions* (1962); Schaff, *Creeds*; J. D. Smart, "The Confession of 1967: Implications for the Church's Mission," *Monday Morning* 33 (6 May 1968): 15–30; T. F. Torrance, *The School of Faith* (1959); L. Vischer, ed., *Reformed Witness Today* (1982).

JACK B. ROGERS

Crypto-Calvinism A sixteenth-century term using "crypto" (Gr. *kryptos*, hidden, secret, concealed) as a prefix to describe Lutherans in Germany and Scandinavia who privately held or sympathized with Calvinist tenets and, less commonly, in France to those professing Roman Catholics accused of secretly being Calvinists. In Germany particularly, charges of crypto-Calvinism had

serious repercussions for the future of Lutherans and Calvinists. After Luther's death (1546), as Lutheranism struggled to define itself, Lutheran rigorists (Gnesio-Lutherans) often accused Philipp Melanchthon and his followers (Philippists or Melanchthonians) of covertly holding Calvinist views or tolerating those who did.

The controversy that erupted divided Lutheranism theologically and politically. Theologically, it centered on the *Lord's Supper* concerning which Melanchthon and many Lutherans held views similar to those of Calvin. Thus, Melanchthon changed his Augsburg Confession to omit from its article on the Supper the phrase "truly present" and its condemnation of differing views (1542). Hard-line Lutheran theologians suspected that Melanchthon had decided to embrace Calvin's rejection of the *doctrine* of *ubiquity* (omnipresence) in which the resurrected Christ was believed to be corporeally present in the eucharistic elements, and instead accepted a real spiritual presence made possible through the intermediary of the *Holy Spirit.*

In political terms, the controversy made cooperation among various Lutheran German states more difficult in the last half of the sixteenth century. This was especially true when Electoral Saxony was governed successively by two Philippist Lutherans (Augustus, 1553–86; Christian I, 1586–91) who knowingly harbored Calvinist sympathizers before strict Lutheran orthodoxy was reestablished by succeeding rulers. This, in turn, made it harder for German Protestants to maintain a common front against Rome and its allies. However, the theological consensus achieved by the Formula of Concord (1577) enabled a reunion of the various Lutheran factions, and after 1600, crypto-Calvinism was no longer a vital theological concern of Lutheranism.

T. Klein, *Der Kampf um die zweite Reformation in Kursachsen, 1586–1591* (1962); R. D. Linder, "The French Calvinist Response to the Formula of Concord," *Journal of Ecu-*

menical Studies 19 (Winter 1982): 18–37; J. Moltmann, Christoph Pezel (1539–1604) und der Calvinismus in Bremen (1958); R. D. Preus, The Theology of Post-Reformation Lutheranism, vol. 1 (1970); D. Visser, ed., Controversy and Conciliation: The Reformation and the Palatinate, 1559–1583 (1986).

ROBERT D. LINDER

Deacons   The diaconate in the Calvinist *tradition* is one of four church offices (pastor, teacher, elder, and deacon). Its responsibility is institutional leadership in caring for the poor and those who physically suffer. Calvin identified two diaconal functions: administration of benevolence and personal care for the needy, tasks he believed were scripturally assigned to men and women (Acts 6:1–6; 1 Tim. 3:8–13; 5:9–10; Rom. 12:8; 16:1–2). Following sixteenth-century cultural biases, women were subordinated to men. Deacons, who should be ordained by the laying on of hands, are ministers of the *church*, not deputies of the pastor. Deacons do not preach or administer the **sacraments** independently but may appropriately collect the offering (alms) and offer the cup in the **Lord's Supper,** as expressions of the spiritual character of their charitable *ministry.* Calvin insisted that the office of deacons is permanently necessary for right church order.

The distinctiveness of the Calvinist diaconate is seen by comparison and contrast with: (1) the *vocation* of all Christians and (2) other diaconates.

1. Calvinists, like other Christians, teach that every believer is called to *diakonia,* love of neighbors. The diaconate is the institutional expression of *diakonia,* leading and giving structure but not replacing individual service to neighbors. (2) In medieval Catholicism, the diaconate was a sacramental ministry; money matters were considered inappropriate for a church ministry. Protestants insisted that charity is a religious ministry but disagreed about who is responsible for it. This is particularly evident in the differences between the two branches of the Reformed tradition itself. For Zwinglians, church order was based on the OT as well as the NT. As in Israel, church and state were not clearly distinguished, so Christian rulers were responsible for all practical ministries, including poor relief. In many Zwinglian churches, organized *diakonia* eventually lost its ecclesiastical roots and became simply a part of secular government. For Calvinists, church order was based on the NT, where ecclesiastical offices are distinguished from civil ones; thus the diaconate should be distinct in theory, though not necessarily in practice, from state welfare. Deacons are essentially ministers of the church. In a Christian state, civil welfare and ecclesiastical diaconate may coincide or cooperate, but the Calvinist diaconate is not dependent upon the state for its existence.

Calvinist practice and theory of the diaconate varied in different places and times. Often the responsibilities of *elders* and deacons were not clearly distinguished. A few churches experimented with women deacons, but most diaconates were exclusively male (as was Geneva's, to Calvin's regret). Formal diaconates continued in many places, but sometimes later churches were established without diaconates, though *diakonia* might be done by voluntary associations loosely related to churches. Today's most significant factors are the concern for *justice* as well as charity, **ordination** of women as full deacons, and participation in the ecumenical renewal of the diaconate.

R. M. Kingdon, "Social Welfare in Calvin's Geneva," ARH 62 (1971): 50–69; E. A. McKee, John Calvin on the Diaconate and Liturgical Almsgiving (1984); and Diakonia in the Classical Reformed Tradition and Today (1989); J. E. Olson, Calvin and Social Welfare (1989).

ELSIE ANNE MCKEE

Death   *Scripture* reveals the *"living God"* who creates life and then re-creates it in Jesus Christ. Death appears in Genesis 3 as an unnatural interloper. Death is both universal and final. It comes to humans and beasts, rich and poor, wise and foolish (Ps. 49; Eccl. 3:19–20). In the OT, believers sought *God* for prolongation of life, for Sheol separated them from God's presence (Ps. 6:5). The NT teaches continuation of life beyond the grave and *resurrection* of the body. Paul says death is the "wages" of *sin* (Rom. 6:23), experienced in solidarity with Adam (Rom. 5:12–21). But in Christ we are resurrected to eternal life (1 Cor. 15). Death is the last enemy to be destroyed (1 Cor. 15:26). Then all *creation* will share our perfection (Rom. 8:18–19).

Augustine's *doctrine* of *original sin* tightly knitted sin and death. The Vulgate text of Rom. 5:12 says, "In Adam all sinned." First Corinthians 15:22 says, "In Adam all die." Thus death, the punishment for Adam's sin, is inherited by all of Adam's children. This view persisted through the medieval period, the Reformation, and to our own times.

The classic Reformed doctrine, taught by John Calvin, the *WCF,* Charles Hodge, and A. A. Hodge, is that death came into the world through human sin: the spiritual death of sin led to physical death. In death, mortal body and immortal soul are severed. In the general resurrection, body and soul will unite again—unto eternal life or eternal death.

Karl Barth, Emil Brunner, G. C. Berkouwer, Hendrikus Berkhof, and others have revised classic ideas of the relation of sin to death. New translations of Rom. 5:12 removed the genetic inevitability; death extends to all because all have sinned (RSV). From a modern scientific perspective, suffering, Death, and struggle were in the world long before *humanity* appeared. All creatures are finite; death is biologically *natural* and necessary. It seems that God's good creation is provisional—perfection lies ahead, not in the past. Unlike the beasts, we know we will die—and death always seems *unnatural.* We live and die before God. Jesus in his death and resurrection delivers us out

of the nexus of sin, guilt, and death. For Christians, death remains a sign of *judgment,* but it has lost its sting. Through *faith* in Christ, death becomes a "gracious ending," free of sin's curse.

Death also refers to the process of *sanctification* in both the NT (Rom. 6—8) and the Reformed tradition. For Calvin, death teaches Christians not to cling to this life but to live in communion with Christ. Through Christ's death we enjoy both liberation from the power of death and mortification of our old nature through self-denial (*Inst.* 2.16.7). Through faith the horror of death is overcome and we may face with courage the afflictions that are the harbingers of death.

Barth, *CD* III/2, sec. 47.5; Berkhof, *CFI*; R. S. Wallace, *Calvin's Doctrine of the Christian Life* (1959); Weber, *FD.*

BARBARA A. PURSEY

Decree(s) of God

Decree(s) of God   Reformed scholastic *doctrine* rooting in God's sovereignty (power) is the theological starting point. The focus is on God's determining in God's eternal decree (plan) whatever occurs in *heaven* and earth. In the background is Aristotle's fourfold causality: the decree as efficient cause; Christ as material; *faith* (Spirit) as instrumental; and the glory of *God* as final cause (*Inst.* 3.14.17, 21; *Commentary* on Eph. 1:4; continued in Theodore Beza and the Canons of *Dort*).

Nature of the decree. The decree is finally one, and equated with God's "purpose" in the destinies of people. Some are chosen "before the foundation of the world . . . for the praise of his glory" (Eph. 1:4, 11–12), while others are condemned. Moreover, by God's "most wise and holy counsel," God did "freely and unchangeably ordain whatsoever comes to pass" (WCF, 3.1). The Reformed scholastics focused on God in God's self and not in covenantal relations. God foresees all things *because* God decrees them eternally. Against semi-Pelagians and Arminians, the decretal theologians taught that God's predeterminations do not *depend* on God's *foreknowledge* of free agents. These thinkers also distinguished God's immanent works (*opera ad intra*) from God's extrinsic (*ad extra*) and limited the decree to the latter—including all reactions of free creatures. God effects some of these directly but renders others certain by God's "permissive decree." The blame for *sin* rests on "secondary causes" or "instruments" (again, à la Aristotle).

The scholastics said this decree roots in God's essential attributes—including a balance of love/hate or mercy/justice. They inadequately appreciated that these qualities imply a relation to creatures in *history.* They distinguished sharply God's decree to act (eternal "cause") and humanity's activity ("secondary cause") and thus the decree itself and its execution. Beza particularly made this distinction, though it is already present in medieval nominalism.

Characteristics of the decree. This decree is founded in God's wisdom ("counsel") and presumes a consultation in the *Trinity,* a rational actualization in history, and immutability throughout the ages. Its "parts" are related logically but not chronologically. Nevertheless, the proponents have frequently used chronological language. The decisive action occurs in a "prior" eternity, and history "effects" what God has (already) "caused." Faith is the product of the decree—and Christ is the "executor" or ground for assurance of *salvation* (the "mirror of election"). Christ is in the decree, instead of the decree in him (as "author"). Finally, the decree is the starting point for all theological reflection. The idea of *reprobation* "naturally follows from the logic of the situation," since "the decree of election inevitably implies the decree of reprobation" (L. Berkhof, 116). The fall (*lapsus*) is therefore necessary for God to realize both mercy and justice in history.

Neo-Reformed scholars, such as Karl Barth, Emil Brunner, Gerrit Berkouwer, Otto Weber, Hendrikus Berkhof, James Daane, Neal Punt, and Harry Boer, have rejected this view of reprobation. They contend—in line with Jerome Bolsec (early 1550s)—that the Bible does not teach eternal reprobation and subjection of Christ to the decree. But traditional *Reformed theology* has gone in two directions here. *Supralapsarianism* began with Beza and included Franciscus Gomarus, Peter Martyr Vermigli, Girolamo Zanchi, William Perkins, and recently Herman Hoeksema. *Infralapsarianism* arose as a reaction, though still presuming the necessity of the *lapsus.* It included Pierre Viret, Petrus van Mastricht, Francis Turretin, and more recently Herman Bavinck and Louis Berkhof. The Reformed creeds are infralapsarian. The difference between these two views relates to this question: Did God regard the objects of *election* and reprobation as not-yet-created or as already-created-and-fallen? Supralapsarians say the former and put the *lapsus* "before" *creation* in God's mind, while infralapsarians say the latter and set the fall logically "after" creation. But both have stressed the sequence from eternity to time and contended that God's decisive action occurred in the former (thus a certain metaphysics is implied).

Objections to decretal theology. 1. Is decretalism consistent with human moral *freedom*? Reformed thought has distinguished between necessity and compulsion: Free agents act necessarily, according to their disposition and God's decree, without being externally coerced. Freedom is incompatible with compulsion but entails the necessity to act in terms of who we are (Jonathan Edwards). The question is finally this: Is a previous certainty consistent with free agency? Reformed decretalism has underscored the distinction between determination and determinism.

2. Does decretalism eliminate incentives for human effort? If all things are necessary, does human responsibility make sense? Reformed theologians have said God's initiative requires human response and the "final cause" is only attained through the "means" of obedience and disobedience. It is also an

empirical fact that Reformed *piety* has usually been dynamic. The glory of God is the highest motivation.

3. But is God the "author of sin"? Decretalism has maintained that God creates free agents, who are themselves culpable. Again, it has used the distinction of "efficient" and "permissive." The neo-Reformed have argued that mechanical "causality" is inappropriate to the personal relations of God and human beings, and sin is a "riddle" that cannot be rationalized (Barth, Berkouwer). Some scholastics have responded that God has "deemed it wise, for the purpose of His self-revelation, to permit moral evil, however abhorrent it may be to His nature" (L. Berkhof, 108). Others have said that sin is necessary for God to realize God's glory by revealing both mercy and wrath (Beza).

The neo-Reformed have rejoined that we cannot speak of God's decree apart from God's *revelation* in the historical Christ. There is no *decretum absolutum.* Faith enables us to see that God has eternally willed to give people the dignity of being God's "covenant partners." There is no eternal decree of reprobation (for Barth, this implies an incipient *universalism*). Election in Christ "before the foundation of the world" suggests that nothing in this world can shake the salvation we have in him (Rom. 8:18ff.; esp. vv. 38–39; again this presumes a different metaphysics of "causality" and the relation of eternity and history). With Calvin in the *Institutes,* the neo-Reformed have refused to focus on God in God's self and have limited their discussions to God in creation, redemption, and history. Instead of a triumph of power, they want a "triumph of grace" (Berkouwer's description of Barth).

In past years, some theologians have interpreted Calvin (too much) in a quasi-Barthian way (Berkouwer, Weber, Daane). But others have argued (too much) that the early Reformed were not guilty of abstract decretalism (Muller). One thing is clear: One's view of the decree lies at the heart of what it means to be Reformed.

Calvin, *Inst.* 1.17.3, 13–14; 2.12.1; 2.17.1; 3.21–23. For Reformed scholasticism: T. Beza, *The Sum of All Christianity* (1555); J. Wolleb and F. Turretin selections, in *Reformed Dogmatics,* ed. and trans. J. W. Beardslee III (1965); C. Hodge, *Systematic Theology,* vol. 1 (1871); L. Berkhof, *Systematic Theology,* 4th rev, and enl. ed. (1949); H. Hoeksema, *Reformed Dogmatics* (1966).

For older Reformed theologians: Heppe, *RD.* For a more covenantal approach: J. Edwards, *Freedom of the Will* (1754). For the neo-Reformed: Barth, *CD* II/2; E. Brunner, *The Christian Doctrine of God* (1946; ET 1950); G. C. Berkouwer, *Divine Election* (1960); and *Sin* (1971); Berkhof, *CFI*; Weber, *FD*; J. Daane, *The Freedom of God* (1973); N. Punt, *Unconditional Good News* (1980); H. R. Boer, *The Doctrine of Reprobation in the Christian Reformed Church* (1983). Also, R. A. Muller, *Christ and the Decree* (1986); P. C. Holtrop, *The Bolsec Controversy* (1991).

PHILIP C. HOLTROP

Descent into Hell   Christ's descent into *hell* after his crucifixion (Matt. 12:40; Eph. 4:9; 1 Peter 3:19) appeared in the Creed by the fourth century. Understood as the release of the OT faithful, it became a graphic element in medieval belief. The Protestant Reformers generally rejected this "limbo of the fathers," believing that pre-Christian saints went immediately to God's presence, but otherwise disagreed on the meaning of the descent. Lutheran theology (though not Luther) affirmed a descent to triumph over the power of hell. *Reformed theology* offered several alternatives to a spatial descent. Huldrych Zwingli and Heinrich Bullinger thought Christ's descent meant that his saving work extended spiritually to the pre-Christian righteous. The modern theologian Emil Brunner found *hope* for those who never heard of Christ in this interpretation. Martin Bucer and Theodore Beza, echoed by Charles Hodge in the nineteenth century, considered the descent synonymous with Christ's death and burial. John Calvin, however, interpreted it psychologically: Christ, on the cross, suffered in soul the wrath of God, or "hell." Many Puritans accepted this view; Karl Barth developed a modern form of it. Seventeenth-century philological scholarship concluded that the Hades/Sheol of the descent was the state and power of *death*, under which Christ's human soul remained until his *resurrection*. Reformed *scholasticism* distinguished a strict meaning (the grave and persisting under the power of death) from a metaphorical one (suffering God's wrath) and held, against Lutheran orthodoxy, that the descent belonged to Christ's humiliation rather than to his exaltation.

D. D. Wallace, Jr., "Puritan and Anglican: The Interpretation of Christ's Descent into Hell," *ARG* 69 (1978): 248–87.

DEWEY D. WALLACE JR.

Dialectical Theology Theological perspectives developed about 1920 in German-speaking territories under the leadership of Karl Barth, Emil Brunner, Rudolf Bultmann, Friedrich Gogarten, Eduard Thurneysen, and to a lesser extent Paul Tillich. Those outside the movement called it "dialectical theology," a term that only partially characterized its concerns. The leaders, however, understood their concern as a "theology of the Word of God," since Barth and Thurneysen saw the impulse for it not in a problem of thought but in the problem of *preaching*. Because of the movement's relation to the crisis mentality existing in the spiritual and cultural milieu after the end of World War I, it was also called "theology of crisis" (Tillich). It communicated through the periodical *Zwischen den Zeiten* (1922–33), and its chief document was Barth's *Der Römerbrief* (2nd ed., 1922). Rather than a unified school of thought with its own program, from the beginning it existed only as a loose working fellowship.

This fellowship was initially united by its fundamental critique of the previous era of theology and *church*, summarily named "neo-Protestantism." The critique applied both to the "positive," that is, the more conservative or orthodox form of neo-Protestantism as well as to its liberal form, out of whose school the leaders of the new movement had come. Its protest was directed point-blank "against the forfeiture of theology at the hands of the theologians" (Moltmann, *Anfänge*, 1:ix). Bultmann formulated it in a way that also faithfully represents the conviction of Barth and Gogarten: "The object of theology is God, and the charge against liberal theology is this: that it did not deal with God, but rather with humans" (*GV*, 2). The goal of the critique was not that there be more speaking about *God* but that speaking about God had to mean something different from "talking about humanity in a somewhat elevated tone" (Barth, *WG*, 164). According to the critique, neo-Protestant theology's shortcoming was that in its speaking about God it was actually only speaking about "something" in *humanity* and its world and therefore not speaking of God. So a "No" was said to a dissolving of God into human religion, morals, and culture. This threatened dissolution was understood as an unavoidable consequence of the titanic attempt of humanity to take God into its possession and disposition.

What united the circle of dialectical theology on the constructive side was its determination to break away from neo-Protestantism in order to forge a new basis for evangelical theology. However, this circle believed it first had to accomplish some essential preparatory tasks. They saw themselves in a time "between the times" (Gogarten; see Moltmann, *Anfänge*, 2:95). As the theme of theology, discourse of humanity about itself did not qualify, nor did discourse about God as a factor in human life. It had to be strictly the *Word of God* directed to humanity, identical with the "Word in the words" of the Bible (Barth, *Römerbrief*, xiii). It is therefore really impossible for us to speak of God. For us remains only the recognition that God is the "wholly other," that "God is God" (Barth, *Wort*, 85; *Römerbrief*, 326). God is not a God of mere otherworldliness, for the otherworldly is a part of the given reality of the world as its converse. Also, God is not God simply by virtue of being different from humans, who could then be simply left to their own devices. God is neither this-worldly nor otherworldly; God is "the one who, doing without all the qualities of an object, is the source of the *krisis* of all objectivity," of all actualities, of all holding tight to what exists as though one could possess it (Barth, *Römerbrief*, 57). As the wholly other, God is not distant from humanity but rather "reveals" God's own self in humanity. God does this, not in order thereby to inaugurate a new kind of "possessing," but rather in this way to carry out toward humanity the *krisis* of all "possessing"! Therefore, God reveals God's self "as the unknown God" (Barth, *Römerbrief*, 88), as the crucified, as the judge, in "radical denial and dissolution of humanity" (Bultmann, 2). Yet in this way God actually does make God's self known. The crucified is also the risen one. *Judgment* is also *grace*. The "No" is also the "Yes" for humanity and the *krisis* is also the "source" of the unity of God and humanity. To be sure, this "Yes" is only given in the "event" of the Word of God, which cannot be viewed, cannot be deduced, and in this sense comes "vertically from above." This "Yes" is given to humans strictly in *faith* and hope, only in "the justification of the sinner," never as a kind of visible possession. On the side of what can be viewed, no reality can be ascertained, but rather there is only "vacant space" (Barth, *Römoerbrief*, 17), only allusion and parable. In these principles, dialectical theology believed it was renewing *Reformed theology*. The expression "dialectical theology" is appropriate insofar as here the structure of the relation of God to the reality of humanity is thought of dialectically. That is, it is thought of as a paradoxical conjuncture of transcendence and immanence, of *revelation* and veiling, of judgment and grace, of the invisible "Yes" and the visible "No." The dialectic is not to be understood as though what is posited and what is negated could be gathered together intellectually in a higher unity (Hegel). It is understood, rather, that the conjuncture of both, existing only through God in the event of a word, always remains a paradox for our thinking (Kierkegaard). Because of this, dialectical theology holds that theological thinking itself has to be dialectical and constantly has to "correlate every position and negation one against the other, to clarify `Yes' by `No' and `No' by `Yes,' without persisting longer than a moment in a rigid `Yes' *or* `No'" (Barth, *Wort*, 172).

The breakup of the circle of dialectical theology (1933) over opposing stances to the new political conditions in Germany clarified long-standing differences among its leaders, or even a "productive misunderstanding" (Barth, in *Zwischen*, 1933, 54) existing from the beginning over what they wanted to do. Though they were united against neo-Protestantism, there was a deep difference: either to maintain methodologically over against the subjectivism of neo-Protestantism the *category* of "Word," or "Reality" (Gogarten), or "Event" (Bultmann), or "I-Thou relationship" (Brunner), or—in concern about the threat from this direction of a new anthropological fettering of theology—to base everything referring to the "Word," "Reality," "Event," and "I-Thou relationship" on the revelation of God (Barth, Thurneysen). While united against neo-Protestantism in recognizing that God is not at our disposal, there were also deep differences: either to postulate from this recognition a secular world as a law unto itself (Gogarten); or, in conjunction with renunciation of direct speech about God, to talk of human existence that is capable of receiving this speech (Bultmann); or to understand the reality of God as a critical counterreality to the present worldly reality, with divine reality acting in contradiction to the present reality to bring it into correspondence with itself (Barth). In Barth's unique conception, it is apparent that influences of Calvin's theocentric thought were at work as well as the *eschatology* of Johann Christoph Blumhardt and Christoph Blumhardt. However this may be, dialectical theology showed itself to be a theology "between the times," whose unforgettable impetus for taking seriously the Godness of God had to lead, and did lead, beyond the immediate impetus to further clarification and development.

G. Merz, ed., *Zwischen den Zeiten* (periodical; Munich, 1923–1933); K. Barth, *Der Römerbrief* (1919; 1922²; 1923³; ET 1932); and *Das Wort Gottes und die Theologie* (1924; ET 1928); R. Bultmann, *Glauben und Verstehen*, vol. 1 (1933; ET 1969); J. Moltmann, ed., *Anfänge der dialektischen Theologie*, vols. 1–2 (1962–63; ET, see *The Beginnings of Dialectic Theology*, vol. 1, ed. J. M. Robinson, 1968); T. Siegfried, *Das Wort und die Existenz: Auseinandersetzung mit der dialektischen Theologie*, 3 vols. (1930–33); C. Van Til, *The New Modernism* (1946); H. Urs von Balthasar, *Karl Barth* (1951; repr. 1961); C. Gestrich, *Neuzeitliches Denken und die Spaltung der dialektischen Theologie* (1977); W. H. Ruschke, *Entstehung und Ausführung der diastasen Theologie in Barths zweiten "Römerbrief"* (1987); M. Beintker, *Die Dialektik in der "Dialektischen Theologie" Karl Barths: Studien zur Entwicklung der Bartschen Theologie und zur Vorgeschichte der "Kirchlichen Dogmatik"* (1987); W. Pannenberg, "Dial. Theol.," *RGG*³ 2:168–74. Cf. W. Haerle, "Dial. Theol.," in *TRE* 9:683–96.

EBERHARD BUSCH

Discipline, Church Church discipline has always been a major concern within the new Reformed churches. Three basic issues were involved. First, would the new Reformed churches discipline their members with excommunication as in the past? Second, would discipline fall under the jurisdiction of the civil magistrate or an ecclesiastical court? Third, how would the *church* relate to the civil com-

munity? The proposed solutions to the problem resulted in three basic types of church discipline and *polity* within the Reformed tradition.

Reformed Protestantism began in Zurich (1520s) under the leadership of Huldrych Zwingli. Zwingli and Heinrich Bullinger, his successor, developed a theory of discipline that was the basis for the system in Zurich. They saw Zurich as a single, unified Christian community, where the civil magistrate held supremacy over all external matters. Clergy had no coercive power. There was no separate church discipline, not even excommunication. The church and the Christian were equivalent to the civil community and the citizen. Civil magistrates thus ruled over both the church and the civil community.

John Oecolampadius offered the Basel magistrates a second solution (1530). He unsuccessfully proposed, first, that excommunication was an absolute necessity for a fully Reformed church; and, second, that excommunication and other forms of church discipline must be imposed by an ecclesiastical court of *elders* or presbyters, chosen from the clergy and the laity.

Martin Bucer, who originally agreed with Zwingli on discipline, came to Oecolampadius's viewpoint (early 1530s). Partially because of Bucer, and perhaps because of Oecolampadius's writings, John Calvin came to advocate the newer ideas on church discipline.

Calvin attempted to implement his more developed Oecolampadian version of discipline in the Ecclesiastical Ordinances (1541). The Geneva Consistory was composed of all pastors and twelve lay elders. It was to be in charge of church discipline, which consisted of admonishing offenders and, if necessary, excommunicating them. For Calvin, the goals of church discipline were those of protecting the purity of the church, shielding the good Christian from the influence of the wicked, and the *repentance* of sinners.

While Calvin tried to impose this discipline on Geneva, all Protestant cities in

Switzerland, and many South German cities, had a system similar to Zurich's, with the *civil government* in control of Christian discipline, supreme in its control over the entire community. But Calvin's concept distinguished between civil and ecclesiastical jurisdictions. Though not denying the proper *authority* of the magistrate, he proposed a separate church discipline under Consistory control. It took Calvin nearly fifteen years to establish the independence of the Consistory in Geneva and make the system work.

In the second half of the sixteenth century, the Calvinist and Zwinglian approaches came into conflict in the Swiss cities, Germany, England, and the United Provinces. One key battle was at Heidelberg, where Thomas Erastus, a disciple of Zwingli and Bullinger, defended Heidelberg's current Zurich style against Calvinists who wanted to establish a Genevan system. The Calvinists won. The Zwinglian approach to the Christian community and discipline was thereafter often called Erastianism.

In French and Scottish Reformed churches, the Calvinist discipline system developed into Presbyterianism. In France, a Presbyterianism loosely modeled on the Genevan system emerged under the guidance of Theodore Beza. Andrew Melville was responsible for the fully developed Presbyterian church discipline and government in Scotland.

In 1562, Jean Morély suggested a third approach to discipline for the French Reformed church, Congregationalism, where discipline would be imposed by the local congregation. Beza's party defeated the proposal.

In England, under Elizabeth I, the established Erastian system met opposition from "Congregationalists" such as Robert Browne and "Presbyterian" advocates such as Thomas Cartwright and Walter Travers. At the Westminster Assembly (1640s), the Presbyterians appeared to be triumphant, but the Congregationalists won in the end. The religious settlement under Oliver Cromwell

(1652) established Congregationalism in England. These events also had an impact on the American colonies, especially those in New England, where Congregationalism prevailed.

During the seventeenth and eighteenth centuries, the three Reformed approaches to discipline continued to compete for acceptance. However, the Zwinglian approach, Erastianism, was doomed to failure because it could function only in a unified Christian community. It could not adjust to a modern pluralistic community, where the civil government did not impose religious uniformity. Presbyterianism, though it was similarly wedded to the idea of a Christian commonwealth, could operate independently of government. There had been an implicit separation between the ecclesiastical jurisdiction and the civil jurisdiction since Calvin's time. Therefore, when forced, Presbyterian discipline could exist and even flourish in a pluralistic society. Congregationalism was less wedded to the concept of a unified Christian society. By definition, each congregation was self-governing and self-disciplining. It was therefore easily adaptable to a pluralistic milieu.

J. W. Baker, "Calvin's Discipline and the Early Reformed Tradition," in *Calviniana: Ideas and Influence of Jean Calvin* (1988), 107–19; R. M. Kingdon, *Geneva and the Consolidation of the French Protestant Movement* (1967); J. T. McNeill, *The History and Character of Calvinism* (1954); A. Simpson, *Puritanism in Old and New England* (1955).
                                J. WAYNE BAKER

Dispensationalism

Also called dispensational premillennialism, it is a scheme of *history* based on a complex literal interpretation of the prophetic books of the Bible. Developed primarily by the Englishman and Plymouth Brethren John Nelson Darby (1800–1882) in the mid-nineteenth century, dispensationalism was popularized in the United States by annual Bible and prophetic conferences initiated in 1875, publication of *The Scofield Reference Bible* (1909), and at schools such as the Moody Bible Institute.

Though there are various dispensational schemes, most divide world history into seven eras or dispensations, including the historical "parenthesis" of the current church age. In this plan, the present age will steadily deteriorate until the secret rapture of the *church,* the return of Christ, and the establishment of God's kingdom. Included too is a strict division between Israel and the church.

Early dispensationalist leaders were largely drawn from Presbyterian and Baptist communions, and most of the early dispensationalists were broadly Reformed. However, the *General Assembly* of the PCUS (1944) condemned dispensationalism as "out of accord" with the church's confession.

Dispensationalism continued to attract interest and adherents in the late twentieth century, especially in fundamentalist circles, as evidenced by the immense popularity of Hal Lindsey and C. C. Carlson's dispensationalist book, *The Late Great Planet Earth* (1970), which has sold millions of copies.

J. H. Gerstner, *Wrongly Dividing the Word of Truth: A Critique of Dispensationalism* (1991); E. R. Sandeen, *The Roots of Fundamentalism* (1970); H. H. Rowdon, "Dispensationalism," in *The Dictionary of Historical Theology,* ed. T. A. Hart (2000); C. C. Ryrie, *Dispensationalism Today* (1965); T. P. Weber, *Living in the Shadow of the Second Coming* (1983).
BRADLEY J. LONGFIELD

Doctrine   The term derives from the Latin word *docere* ("to teach"). In contemporary usage it may mean the general teaching of the *church* (e.g., Christian doctrine), teachings of a church or *tradition* (e.g., Presbyterian; Reformed doctrine), or a specific tenet of *faith* (e.g., the doctrine of *predestination*). Doctrine may be seen as constitutive, authoritative, normative, and/or descriptive. A given doctrine or doctrinal system may be judged true or false, sufficient or deficient, essential or nonessential.

The Reformed tradition from its beginning acknowledged that the formulation of doctrine is an appropriate and necessary task of the church. In accord with the *sola scriptura* of the Reformation, the Reformers taught that doctrine must derive from and communicate the truth of the Bible. Thus, the formulation of doctrine is not an endeavor that builds on a prior interpretation of *scripture* but is offered as the initial interpretation itself. It is a primary rather than a secondary hermeneutical endeavor. Calvin's *Institutes of the Christian Religion,* for example, was written as a summary of the Christian religion for use by theological students in their biblical studies. Thus, there is no prior norm for doctrine imposed on scripture; the *Word of God* provides both the content and the norm for the teachings formulated from it.

Doctrine is thus viewed by the Reformed reformers as an organized statement of the teaching of scripture for the use of the church. Every aspect of the church's life must be grounded in the Word of God: Doctrine is the link between the Bible and the *preaching,* teaching, *worship,* order, and service of the Christian community. Formation of doctrine is not an end in itself but is undertaken for the sake of the church and the believer. When it is understood in this way, defining the duties of the *deacon,* for example, is as much a doctrinal matter as a confessional statement concerning election.

In the sixteenth and seventeenth centuries, doctrine in the Reformed tradition was articulated through *confessions.* Since then, with a few exceptions (such as the United Church of Christ in the United States), Reformed churches have continued to be confessional churches, with a flowering of new confessions in the twentieth century. Confessions are not intended to be innovations but faithful expositions of biblical and apostolic faith. Consequently, most Reformed churches are also creedal, subscribing to the Apostles' Creed and the Nicene Creed and, less commonly, the Athanasian Creed. Apostoli-city in the Reformed tradition is not invested in the office of bishop but in the confessions of the church. Twentieth-century confessions seek to formulate biblical teachings in terms relevant to the issues of our time and also to present a range of ethical concerns confessionally.

Reformed theology and *polity* have placed responsibility for sound doctrine in certain offices of the church: doctor, minister of the Word, and governing *elder.* Most Reformed bodies no longer recognize a distinct teaching office, subsuming the responsibilities of the doctor under the minister of the Word. The minister of the Word has been specifically charged to preach and teach the doctrines of the Bible, in some cases through the requirement that theological points of a confessional statement be systematically presented. A responsibility of those ordained to the office of governing elder is to ensure the faithful performance of this task.

Since the Reformation, doctrine has been understood in a variety of ways. Already in the sixteenth century, Reformed *scholasticism* began to distill sharply defined doctrinal propositions from scripture and organize them in logical systems that today seem often to distort rather than faithfully represent biblical teaching. The development of biblical scholarship as a discipline placed responsibility for determining the teaching of scripture in the hands of those pursuing scientific knowledge. Early in the nineteenth century, the understanding of doctrine was recast by Friedrich Schleiermacher, who taught that the doctrines of the Christian faith are descriptive rather than constitutive. Karl Barth, in opposition, held that the community of faith is created only by the Word given testimony in scripture, and apart from the teachings of the Bible, neither faith nor church can exist. Jürgen Moltmann's emphasis on the doctrine of *hope* has resulted in a focus on sound practice (*orthopraxis*) alongside sound teaching (*orthodoxy*). Liberation, feminist, and minjung theologies claim that doctrine

may be articulated only by persons who experience a certain kind of oppression.

Barth, *CD* I, II; H. Berkhof, *Introduction to the Study of Dogmatics* (1985); Heppe, *RD*; Weber, *FD*; G. Lindbeck, *The Nature of Doctrine* (1984).

PAUL R. FRIES

Dort, Synod of   This assembly, the most significant national *synod* of the Reformed Church of the Netherlands, settled the *predestination* controversy between Arminians and Calvinists by condemning *Arminianism.*

After Jacob Arminius's death, the Arminians (or Remonstrants) drew up a Remonstrance (1610) that presented their views in five articles. These became the basis of the increasingly bitter controversy that climaxed at the Synod of Dort. Convened at Dordrecht by the States General of the Netherlands, the synod lasted 180 sessions (November 13, 1618, to May 29, 1619). Its Dutch delegates included fifty-eight ministers and *elders* sent by provincial synods and five theologians (including Arminius's adversary Franciscus Gomarus) from different Dutch academies. The States General sent eighteen civil delegates to protect government interests. Also represented were twenty-six Reformed theologians from eight foreign lands (Great Britain, the Palatinate, Hesse, Switzerland, Nassau-Wetteravia, Geneva, Bremen, and Emden), giving the synod an international character. Leeuwarden pastor Johannes Bogerman was chosen president.

The synod summoned thirteen Remonstrant leaders, not to be delegates but so that the synod could examine and pass judgment on their views. Prior to their arrival, the synod dealt with issues of Bible translation, catechism *preaching,* catechetical instruction, *baptism* of slaves, the status of theology students, and censorship.

The arrival of the Remonstrants on December 6, headed by Leiden theologian Simon Episcopius, initiated five weeks of procedural wrangling. The Remonstrants protested the synod's *authority* to act as judge and called for a conference between equals. Though both sides made procedural concessions, Remonstrant failure to cooperate fully led ultimately to their expulsion from the synod. After a government decision that the Remonstrants be judged from their writings, Bogerman expelled them with an angry speech (January 14).

For the next three months, the synod studied the issues before making its judgment. The debate was sometimes heated, especially between the *supralapsarian* Gomarus and the English and Bremen delegates. On the basis of reports from all nineteen delegations, a committee of nine drafted the Canons of Dort, which condemned Remonstrant views and affirmed: *God* elects and reprobates, not on the basis of foreseen belief and unbelief but by his sovereign will, though the reprobate perish by their own fault; Christ's *death* was sufficient for all but effective only for the elect; by the fall, *humanity* was totally corrupted, though it remained human; God's *grace* works effectively to convert the unbeliever, though not by coercion; and God preserves believers so they cannot totally fall from grace. These have been popularly described by the acronym TULIP: *Total depravity,* Unconditional *election,* Limited *atonement,* Irresistible grace, and *Perseverance of the saints.* The Canons, signed by all delegates, accommodated significant theological diversity among them and represented the triumph of a moderate *Calvinism.*

Then, after approval of the *Belgic Confession* and the *HC,* the foreign delegations returned home. The remaining sessions, beginning on May 13, dealt with such church matters as revision of the church order, liturgical forms, and Sunday observance.

The Synod of Dort's decisions on doctrine and church order defined the Dutch Reformed church for two centuries and continue to shape Reformed churches of Dutch heritage.

Acta Synodi . . . Dordrechti (1620); G. Brandt, *History of the Reformation . . . in . . . the Low*

Countries (1733; repr. 1979, 4 vols. in 2), vol. 3; Schaff, *Creeds,* vols. 1 and 3.

DONALD SINNEMA

Economics The study of patterns of production, exchange, and consumption of "goods" to fulfill human needs and desires. In European civilization, no religious people paid more systematic attention to economics than the Calvinists.

Unlike their medieval predecessors, Calvinists neither downgraded nor episodically concerned themselves with poverty, wealth, and questions of economic *justice.* Instead, they sought to bring the economic realm—like every other human realm—into conformity with the realm of God.

Indeed, says R. H. Tawney, *Calvinism* "is perhaps the first systematic body of religious teaching which can be said to recognize and applaud the economic virtues. Its enemy is not the accumulation of riches but their misuse for purposes of self-indulgence or ostentation. Its ideal is a society which seeks wealth with the sober gravity of men who are conscious at once of disciplining their own characters by patient labor, and of devoting themselves to a service acceptable to God" (Tawney, 105).

Calvin's Geneva was the laboratory of this development. Its church and government leaders devised and enforced an economic discipline that touched all facets of that city's material life. Laws requiring church attendance and the education of children combined with laws for public sanitation, family health practice, and the founding of new industry. Under Calvin and the Councils, Genevans acquired latrines and balcony railing in their houses, better home-heating systems, licensed dentists, new hospitals, and their first textile factory (McNeill). Most of all, they acquired theology, law, and active church-state controls of the ancient human vice of greed as practical in the new commercial culture of capitalism. "The hungry are defrauded of their rights," said Calvin, "if their hunger is not relieved." Therefore, charging the poor high prices for bread when bread is scarce may be market ethics, but not Christian ethics.

Calvinism's influence in shaping capitalism has elicited much scholarly debate. Like the parallel dispute regarding its contribution to the emergence of democracy, its contribution to capitalistic theory and practice over the centuries is undoubtedly partial and complex, a mixture of affinity and antagonism. Calvinists have to begin their thinking about economic life with a certain cluster of unambiguous general principles. For example, there can be no "autonomous sphere" of economics in a world governed wholly by a sovereign God; rules of justice and fairness apply to market exchanges just as much as to any other human relationships; God loves poor people as much as rich people but requires of the rich particular concern for the needs of the poor; greed remains a besetting human *sin*, and the rich are especially vulnerable to it. These principles root in a biblical tradition more ancient than Calvinism—the Bible, where Calvinists mean to start their cultivation of an economic ethic.

Max Weber believed that the only powerful surviving modern fruit of this rootage is the "Protestant ethic" and its associated personal character—the frugal, hardworking, wealth accumulator who became Karl Marx's stereotype of the capitalist. Tawney, in accusing Weber of oversimplifying this history, underscored the truth in it when he observed that Calvinists, from the Puritans to modern Presbyterian businesspersons, have progressively suffered from the atrophy of one-half of their ethical roots: They acquired freedom of economic striving and lost collective discipline of that striving. Calvinism's "theory had been discipline; its practical result was liberty," in both Puritan England and Protestant America.

The ironic result of this four-century erosion of the sense of social justice, social control, and social responsibility of all economic enterprise has been the clamor, in America of the 1990s, for a new "business ethic." Modern adherents of the Reformed tradition have much thinking to do if they are to combine the old, basic Calvinist principles with the new world of global economics and multinational corporations. They will probably have to begin their recovery of *tradition* and their new thinking about it in the company of fellow church members rather than exclusively in the company of associates in business. In the former company, they are more likely to become sensitive to the basic ethical-theological wisdom of Tawney, a practicing economic historian and practicing Christian, when he wrote:

> If . . . economic ambitions are good servants, they are bad masters. Harnessed to a social purpose, they will turn the mill and grind the corn. But the question, to what end the wheels revolve, still remains; and on that question the naive and uncritical worship of economic power . . . throws no light. . . . For the condition of effective action in a complex civilization is cooperation. And the condition of cooperation is agreement, both as to the ends to which effort should be applied, and the criteria by which success is to be judged. (Tawney, 282)

W. J. Bouwsma, *John Calvin: A Sixteenth-Century Portrait* (1988); J. T. McNeill, *The History and Character of Calvinism* (1954); *Presbyterian Social Witness Policy Compilation* (Advisory Committee on Social Witness Policy—PC[USA], 2000), ch. 7; R. L. Stivers, ed., *Reformed Faith and Economics* (1989); R. H. Tawney, *Religion and the Rise of Capitalism* (1926; repr. 1962); M. Weber, *The Protestant Ethic and the Spirit of Capitalism* (1904–5; ET 1930; repr. 1958).

DONALD W. SHRIVER JR.

Ecumenism   The movement through which divided churches seek to manifest afresh the unity given and willed by Jesus Christ. The term "ecumenism" is from the Greek word *oikoumene*, meaning the "inhabited earth." The noun "ecumenism" is a construct of relatively recent date, coming into general use through the Second Vatican Council.

Reformed churches are divided in their attitude toward the ecumenical movement. While the majority participate with great openness and can be considered to be a driving ecumenical force, others are skeptical or even hostile toward it. Basic for the Reformed understanding of ecumenism is that the Reformers did not intend to found a new *church* but sought reform of the whole church. Reformed churches open to the ecumenical movement see it as an opportunity to resume the dialogue with other churches that was prematurely disrupted in the sixteenth century. In a certain sense, the ecumenical movement is the fulfillment of the deepest intentions of the Reformation.

John Calvin considered unity to be part of the nature of the church. His fourth book of the *Institutes* is a vivid expression of this conviction: "On the True Church with whom We are to Cultivate Unity because She is the Mother of all faithful" (*Inst.* 4.1). He made repeated efforts to avoid the final rupture with the Church of Rome. In particular, he worked indefatigably for the unity of the various Reformation churches. In this respect, his assumption was that as long as agreement on the essentials of *faith* was assured, diversity among the local churches was admissible. The *Consensus Tigurinus* (1549) made it possible to maintain fellowship with the Reformation of Zurich, but for centuries it created an obstacle to the rapprochement with the Lutheran tradition.

When separate Reformed churches had been established, the question of the status of other churches arose. In what did the Reformed church claim to be or to represent the church of Jesus Christ? French theologians (primarily) developed the concept of the church of Jesus Christ being alive in all churches, in some purer and in others in less pure form. "Identifying a particular church with the *una sancta* is as inappropriate as calling the sea of Bretagne the whole ocean" (Philippe Duplessis-Mornay [1549–1623]). The one church consists of several Christian communions that are one in the essentials of the faith and recognize one another on this basis (Pierre Jurieu [1637–1713]). Reformed theologians persisted in hoping that one day the divided churches would gather in a universal council and confess together the fundamental truths of the gospel.

In the course of the centuries, Reformed churches were at the origin of many initiatives toward unity—both internal and intraconfessional. The hardening of the Reformed tradition into *Reformed orthodoxy* in the seventeenth and eighteenth centuries and resulting splits provoked countermovements. Both in Pietism and the revival movement, the quest for unity was alive. At the beginning of the nineteenth century, the Disciples of Christ movement split from the Presbyterian Church because it wanted to provide a platform for intraconfessional unity. Reformed Christians actively participated in the foundation of the Evangelical Alliance (1846).

Reformed theologians played an outstanding role in the beginnings and shaping of the modern ecumenical movement (e.g., F. F. Ellinwood, William Paton, Wilfred Monod, Adolf Keller). The first two general secretaries of the WCC were from Reformed churches (W. A. Visserát Hooft, Eugene Carson Blake). The thought of some Reformed theologians had a decisive influence on the nascent ecumenical movement (e.g., Karl Barth, Josef Hromádka, John Mackay, Lesslie Newbigin, Hendrikus Berkhof).

An important step was taken after World War II with the decision of the WARC to consider itself an instrument in the service of the ecumenical movement. The General Council at Princeton (1954) developed the idea that "Jesus Christ himself breaks down all barriers of separation and, in obedience to him, the various forms of faith and life become means of serving the unity of the Spirit in the bond of peace." The Council declared that the Reformed churches recognized the *ministry,* the *sacraments,* and members of all churches that, according to the Bible, confess Jesus Christ as Lord and Savior and that they were prepared to invite all members of such churches to participate in the celebration of the *Lord's Supper.* Not all Reformed churches shared this emphasis on openness. In 1946, the Reformed Ecumenical Synod (since 1988 the Reformed Ecumenical Council) was founded, an association of Churches with a clear allegiance to the classic Reformed *confessions.* A militant opponent of the ecumenical movement has been the Presbyterian pastor Carl McIntire, founder of the International Council of Christian Churches.

Reformed commitment to the ecumenical movement also found expression in bilateral dialogues. On the basis of extended theological conversations, European Reformed churches declared "church fellowship" with the Lutheran churches (Leuenberg Agreement, 1973). At the international level, dialogues were conducted with the Disciples of Christ (concluded 1988), the Anglican Communion (1984), Baptist World Alliance (1982), Lutheran World Federation (1989), World Methodist Council (1988), and Mennonite World Conference (1984). While these conversations aimed at full communion, dialogues with the Roman Catholic Church (1990) and the Orthodox Church (started in 1988) served the purpose of better mutual understanding. Analogous conversations took place with all partners at the national level. In the course of the twentieth century, several Reformed churches decided to enter into united churches in countries such as Canada, India, and Australia.

Internal division, however, remains a characteristic of the Reformed family. While in some countries reunion of divided Reformed churches was successfully achieved (United States, Holland), the movement of dividing continues in other countries (e.g., Korea). The WARC has in recent years recognized the problem, which was one of the major themes

at the 22nd General Council in Seoul, Korea (1989). At the same time, the Alliance emphatically confirmed its commitment to the ecumenical movement.

H. E. Fey, ed., *The Ecumenical Advance: A History of the Ecumenical Movement 1948–68,* 2nd ed. (1986); J. L. Mangina, "Ecumenical Theology," in *The Dictionary of Historical Theology,* ed. T. A. Hart (2000); H. Meyer and Lukas Vischer, eds., *Growth in Agreement: Reports and Agreed Statements of Ecumenical Conversations on a World Level* (1984); R. Rouse and S. C. Neil, eds., *A History of the Ecumenical Movement 1517–1948,* vol. 1, 3rd ed. (1986); L. Vischer, *The Reformed Family Worldwide* (1999); G. Wainwright, ed., *Dictionary of the Ecumenical Movement* (2000).

LUKAS VISCHER

Effectual Calling   *see* **Predestination**

Elders   The Calvinist office of elders is one of four church ministries. With pastors and teachers, elders are presbyters; the fourth office is the diaconate. Presbyterial functions include *preaching,* teaching, administering the *sacraments,* and governing. Pastors, who have all functions, share government with the lay elders, and together pastors and elders form a governing council called the consistory (session). Church government is usually identified with "discipline" but this concept must be rightly understood. *Discipline* is not primarily punishment but guidance, counseling, rebuke, reconciliation, and only finally excommunication if other measures have not brought *repentance* and renewal. Traditionally, discipline has been based on Matt. 18:15–18, and usually the "church" (v. 17), which disciplines the unrepentant sinner, has been understood as a body representing, acting for, the whole. John Calvin believed that in Matthew, Jesus was speaking of a Christian version of the Sanhedrin; he considered Rom. 12:8, 1 Cor. 12:28, and 1 Tim. 5:17 to be Pauline references to lay Christians elected to share church government with pastors. Modern study of Calvin's Geneva Consistory reveals that its work went far beyond "discipline" as rebuke, to include religious education, corporate counseling, and efforts to build and rebuild Christian community.

The office of elder was the most controversial of Calvin's four; its distinctive Calvinist Reformed character is best seen by comparison with other Christian agencies of discipline. Until the Protestant Reformation, Matt. 18:17 was normally read as assigning discipline to the clergy, but control of excommunication became a source of contention in Christendom, as princes vied with bishops for the power to exclude citizen-Christians from common life. Protestants expanded the interpretation of Matt. 18:17 to include laity, but after some hesitation most groups concluded that discipline should be handled for the community by senior members (men). Differences arose primarily over which laity should represent the *church*. Zwinglian Reformed (like Lutherans) assigned discipline to Christian rulers. Zwinglians based church order on the OT as well as on the NT; 2 Chronicles 19 was a favorite text supporting magisterial control of ecclesiastical discipline. Calvinist Reformed insisted on the NT model for right church order, distinguished church and state, and advocated and struggled for autonomy in ecclesiastical government. The same person might be Christian magistrate and elder, but the offices are different and distinct.

The elders' office has a varied history, partly because of its nontraditional character as a "lay ecclesiastical" office. In some places, the responsibilities of elders and *deacons* were not clearly distinguished. Where congregationalist *polity* developed, elders were discontinued. Today, in many churches, women as well as men serve as elders. However, though communal oversight of personal life has come to seem an invasion of privacy, and practice of discipline has changed, the Reformed office of elders continues to represent the importance of corporate responsibility for the quality of Christian life.

P. De Klerk, ed., *Renaissance, Reformation, Resurgence* (1976), 63–84 (F. W. Monter), 95–106 (R. M. Kingdon); R. M. Kingdon, "Calvin and the Establishment of Consistory Discipline in Geneva," *Nederlandsch Archief voor Kerkgeschiedenis* (1990); E. A. McKee, *Elders and the Plural Ministry* (1988); L. Vischer, ed., *The Ministry of the Elders in the Reformed Church* (1992).

ELSIE ANNE MCKEE

Election *see* **Predestination**

Eschatology The *doctrine* of "the last things" (called "eschatology" only since the nineteenth century), often appearing last in expositions of Reformed faith. It has traditionally dealt with the end of the world: the return of Christ—before, after, or without a millennium, the last *judgment,* and the end of a person's life: *death* and the hereafter, *heaven* and *hell.* In contrast to these terminal and individual emphases, one finds, partly in Calvin and most fully in contemporary **Reformed** *theology,* the recovery of a more dynamic and cosmic eschatology.

Pre-Reformation. Original anticipations of the ascended Christ's immediate return soon yielded to the task of being his *church* in the interim before history's certain but possibly distant culmination. Some retained apocalyptic visions, often based on the "thousand years" of Revelation 20, of an earthly triumph for God's saints over the pagan powers. Others denounced this *millennialism* (or chiliasm) as too literal, materialist, and chronological, and a more figurative, spiritual, dehistoricized eschatology dominated the Middle Ages. For *Augustine,* the millennium represented the whole Christian era, whose eventual ending, with the judgment of Antichrist, would halt *history* rather than renew it, as time gave way to eternity. Meanwhile, the City of **God** could be distinguished from the city of the devil not by visible, worldly marks but by spiritual and inward ones: love of God, not of self.

Reformation. Events around them convinced the Reformers that God was actively redeeming history. Luther expected Christ's cataclysmic return, to resolve the conflict between God and the devil. Yet his "two kingdoms" preserves the unhistorical inwardness of Augustine's "two cities." To live by *faith* in the kingdom of Christ means inner warfare between gospel and *law. Hope* provides more consolation until the world is overcome than anticipation that the world shall itself be sanctified.

Calvin envisaged more clearly creation's restoration. *Predestination* does not rob history of meaning in subjection to God's eternal will but promises that history has a destiny and goal. Dismissing a millennium as too brief an earthly rule, Calvin still affirmed that Christ would come again, and the renovation of the world had "in a manner" already begun, in Christ's glorified *humanity.* As Christ Ascended awaits his final reign, the church, in union with him, waits too. That means humiliation for now, but we treat our sufferings with contempt and meditate on the future life, when we shall share Christ's glory (*Inst.* 3.9, 25). Meanwhile, the church advances and actively engages with the world, promoting a godly commonwealth as visible firstfruits of Christ's dominion.

Yet Calvin's eschatology (and that of the Reformed *confessions*) is often individualistic, propounding the biblically questionable view that at death the immortal soul is separated from the body. Still, this immortality is not a Platonic divine essence but God's gift to humanity, grounded in *creation* and redemption. In his early *Psychopannychia* (1534), Calvin affirms that the departed soul is not asleep but awake to enjoy God's presence and anticipate everlasting joy (or, in the case of the impious, fearfully to await damnation). Like the later confessions, he teaches that the souls of the elect will be reunited at the end with their now transfigured bodies.

Post-Reformation. As Calvinists struggled against oppression, futuristic hopes sometimes arose. Jonathan Edwards foresaw a millennium beginning in New England, while some seventeenth-century English Puritans grounded their revolutionary *politics* in the impending reign of Christ and defeat of the papal Antichrist. The contemporaneous Westminster Assembly, though, was more Augustinian than millenarian (cf. WLC, q. 191).

The WCC, embodying a *covenant* framework shaped by Johannes Cocceius, exemplifies Reformed orthodoxy's efforts to develop Calvin's historical instincts. Yet covenant theology often lapsed into *dispensationalism* (which periodized history and found eschatological significance only in the final epoch) or else reduced the interval from *resurrection* to last judgment to a static, necessary outworking of Christ's completed work. This left *Calvinism* ill-placed to resist the post-Enlightenment reduction of eschatology to secular progress or to liberalism's moralized, this-worldly *kingdom of God.*

Contemporary. Reformed theologians led twentieth-century interpretation in quite new directions, embracing eschatology as the key to biblical reality. Karl Barth's *Commentary on Romans* (1919; 1922^2; 1923^3; ET 1932) emphasized the alienness of the kingdom. Eschatology articulates God's eternal Otherness, which intersects time and subverts human hopes. Later, in his *Church Dogmatics,* Barth set the judgment of last things firmly within the graciousness of Christ, the Last One; yet he never conceded that the future could add anything new, beyond fuller disclosure of the *revelation* already completed. Jürgen Moltmann has since given priority to hope and promise over fulfillment; conceived of the future, in its tension with the present, as a "new paradigm of transcendence"; and, with others, has extended

Barth's rethought doctrine of God not as static "being" but as a process of "becoming" through the still unfinished "history" of the *Trinity.*

Like Barth, Moltmann draws radical political conclusions from eschatology. Because the ultimate future rests with God, not with human planning or ideals, we are freed and summoned to struggle for penultimate, human *justice* corresponding to the coming triumph of God's righteousness. Contemporary eschatology relativizes individual concerns and questions of chronology. Yet inheritors of Reformed millenarianism still predict imminent Armageddon, interpreting the nuclear threat, for example, as fulfilling biblical prophecies. Between such literalism and the disavowal of a realistic second coming altogether, Reformed eschatology still struggles to take history and the future seriously yet to affirm not their annihilation but their consummation.

Barth, *CD* III/2, 437–511, IV/3, 274–367; and *The Christian Life* (1981); H. Bavinck, *The Last Things* (ET 1996); G. C. Berkouwer, *The Return of Christ* (1972); A. Hoekema, *The Bible and the Future* (1979); D. E. Holwerda, "Eschatology and History," in *Readings in Calvin's Theology,* ed. D. K. McKim (repr. 1998); J. Martin, *The Last Judgment in Protestant Theology* (1963); J. Moltmann, *Theology of Hope* (1967); H. Quistorp, *Calvin's Doctrine of the Last Things* (1955); H. Schwarz, *Eschatology* (2000); P. Toon, ed., *Puritans, the Millennium, and the Future of Israel* (1970); T. F. Torrance, *Kingdom and Church* (1956).

ALAN E. LEWIS

Eternal Punishment   *see* Hell

Ethics, Social   To speak of social ethics in general and in the Reformed tradition in particular involves making arbitrary distinctions. In a basic sense, all ethics is social because it involves the interaction of human beings, even when it concerns their motivations and charac-

ter. All social ethics is personal, for the same reason.

The Reformed tradition cannot be exclusively defined. Reformed theologians have always made ecumenical claims for their insights and developed their ethics in interaction with the perspectives and *experience* of other branches of the Christian *church.* At best, one can speak of a Reformed emphasis within the common enterprise of Christian ethics based in *scripture* and informed by the whole *tradition* of the church catholic and ecumenical.

Nevertheless, social ethics is understood as dealing with the corporate or collective life of society in areas such as the church and in structures of government and economic life. The Reformed tradition is that movement of theology and church life which, with roots in scripture and the church catholic during the first fifteen centuries, sought and still seeks the reformation of that church from the sixteenth century to the present. Its formative theologians were John Hus, Martin Luther, and John Calvin, with their sixteenth-century colleagues and the church *confessions.* It is a living tradition, constantly criticized and reformed to the present.

Christian life in the church. All ethics in the Reformation tradition is rooted in the message of the apostle Paul, reasserted by Luther, that the Christian lives by free and grateful response to God's *grace* in Jesus Christ, which justifies and transforms a sinful world. This is a radical protest against all forms of human self-justification and *sanctification,* even those that bear the name "Christian." Humans are not saved by works—of personal virtue, social justice, or sacramental order—important as these are as faithful, fallible witnesses to God. Calvin applied this insight directly to the church. *Ecclesia semper reformanda*—the church always being reformed by the living *Word of God*—meant first that no human *authority* or structure is finally authoritative. The church is one, catholic and universal, the given reality of the body of Christ being built up in love. But it has no head except Christ. Its forms must continually be sought by faithful, fallible human work.

This principle caused much tension and struggle. Yearning for a final human authority to define the Word of God and the order of the church has not ceased. A "verbally inspired" Bible, a particular confession, a new episcopal order, and the people in their various self-expressions have been suggested. Reformed and Lutheran churches have divided over these issues. An open, free, and reformable ecclesiology, however, reaffirmed in the twentieth century by such theologians as Karl Barth, Reinhold Niebuhr, Dietrich Bonhoeffer, and Jürgen Moltmann and by modern church confessions, continues as the Reformation tradition's basic witness.

Second, the triune *God* alone is the source of truth and Lord of the *conscience*. The *doctrine* of the church is confessional, the living response to the Word of God revealed in scripture that a historical time and place requires. There is authoritative doctrine that includes authoritative ethics, but it must continually be expressed anew as redeemed but sinful human beings, inspired by the *Holy Spirit*, discern in each time and place the Word of God that judges and saves the world.

Third, the task of ordering the church is political and constitutional. Power and authority must be so balanced as to allow the Word of God to prevail over human emotions and interests. Calvin, adapting NT prototypes, developed the structure of ministers, *elders*, and *deacons* still used today. Teachers and current church leaders in *presbytery* were given a special role in the selection of new officers but always in the presence, and with the confirmation, of the people. Authority lies not with the ministers, the elders, or even the people, but with the process, informed by the Holy Spirit, whereby the church seeks guidance in the selection of its leaders, in the form of its confession,

and in its witness to the world on public policy.

Christian responsibility in politics. The sixteenth-century Reformers were not democrats, nor were individual rights a center of their concern. For both Luther and Calvin, the *freedom* of a Christian is given by grace through *faith* in the community of believers. It is not therefore a freedom to pursue self-interest, or even to assert just claims, by political action. Governments are ordained by God to establish just order and restrain the anarchic drives of human sin. Still, no general *right of resistance* to unjust and tyrannous authority is permitted. God will judge and destroy tyrants in God's way. Christians must speak prophetic words to governors about the governors' misuse of authority, but Christians must crown their witness by suffering under, rather than seeking to overthrow, those governors.

Nevertheless, political ethics in the Reformed tradition has developed in ways undergirding modern democracy and superseding the teachings of the Reformers. The reason lay most deeply in the life of the church itself and the model it offered for a changing world. The model was neither democratic nor hierarchical but constitutional. In analogy to the *covenant* of God with the company of believers, the Puritans in seventeenth-century Massachusetts attempted to establish constitutional structures for government. Suspicious of all unchecked human authority and power, they sought to balance that power by denying the clergy political office and providing for popular participation in the choice of political leaders and legislation. Aware that structures of government, like those of the church, must always be reformed, they provided processes for amendment and change. By analogy with the calling of the Christian to be a servant of others in love, they based participation in the political process on a calling to responsible citizenship. Similar developments took place in Scotland, England, and Holland. Furthermore, this calling led, beginning in a limited way with Calvin and

Knox, not to the right but to the duty of active citizens to resist unjust tyrannous authority for the sake of the God-ordained function of government itself.

This theology made its contribution both to revolution and to democratic political constitutions in Europe, America, and Africa from the sixteenth century to the twentieth. In modern times, however, it has undergone a decisive transformation. Though government continues to be described by some as deduced from (and limited by) the sovereignty of God (Abraham Kuyper) or an order of *creation* (Emil Brunner), the trend has been to understand it in the context of the Lordship of the risen Christ in human affairs and the promise of his coming again. For Bonhoeffer, government is a mandate, an area of human life to be organized responsibly, in penultimate witness to the reality of Christ taking form in the world. For Barth, political relations should be secular parables of the *kingdom of God* in the world in the way they organize *justice* and preserve freedom in the civil community. Reinhold Niebuhr understood government's task to be the coercion of competing vitalities and powers in society into a relative justice, subject to the continual *judgment* and inspiration of the higher mutualities of love revealed in Jesus Christ. *Politics* in these and other modern expressions of the Reformed tradition is a relative, sinful yet promising area for the achievement of those forms of provisional, reformable justice that bear external witness to the realization of human community and love in Jesus Christ.

Economics and the gospel. In *The Protestant Ethic and the Spirit of Capitalism* (ET 1930), Max Weber argued that Calvinist-Puritan theology created the ethos of inner-worldly asceticism in which modern capitalism developed. *Calvinism,* he claimed, stressed the importance of successful work, organizing this world to the glory of God, as evidence of saving grace at work among God's chosen people. The energy and the discipline this released has propelled the commercial and industrial development of the modern world and was an implicit sanctification of the capitalist system. R. H. Tawney, in *Religion and the Rise of Capitalism* (1926), presented a more subtle version of the thesis. He showed that Calvin and later Calvinists, though positive toward the developing economy of their time, attempted to exercise moral and ecclesiastical control over it. Laws governing rates of interest and conditions of loans, just wages and prices, the conditions of labor and limitation of profits, were all part of the Puritan ethic, and the *sin* of avarice was under constant surveillance.

Only when the church lost its disciplinary power to enforce an economic ethic, when social control gave way to individual admonition, did the Protestant work ethic turn into the sanctification of economic success. Individualism and private spirituality took over in the sphere of *economics* from the Reformed ethic.

The twentieth century witnessed a recovery from this failure, in the form of an ecumenical economic ethic to which the Reformed tradition has made a substantive contribution. Swiss reformers Hermann Kutter and Leonhard Ragaz joined with Americans Washington Gladden and Walter Rauschenbusch, the German Christoph Blumhardt, and British Anglicans Charles Gore and William Temple among others to define the *Social Gospel.* Reinhold Niebuhr and John Bennett in the United States gave the movement greater realism and depth, analyzing economic power as a social expression of human sin and proposing strategies of prophetic witness and action to confront this power with the command and promise of God. American church studies and denominational statements on social questions continue to follow their guidance. Reformed economic ethics today must, on the one hand, avoid idealism that judges all existing economies against an absolute standard of loving and sinless human community, and, on the other hand, blessing successful economic power however unjust and inhuman its consequences for the disadvantaged of the world. Its principles here also are: no unquestioned human authority, whether revolutionary or conservative, but the church's continual participation in the search for more just and responsible ways of producing and distributing the goods and services of an economy, with special concern for the poor, while cultivating our common environment in the power and promise of God "in the economy of the fullness of times to gather up all things in Christ" (Eph. 1:10).

G. L. Hunt, ed., *Calvinism and the Political Order* (1965); P. Lehmann, *The Transfiguration of Politics* (1975); A. Miller, ed., *A Christian Declaration on Human Rights* (1977); H. Richard Niebuhr, *Christ and Culture* (1951); Reinhold Niebuhr, *An Interpretation of Christian Ethics* (1935); M. Stackhouse, *Christian Social Ethics in a Global Era* (1995); Ronald H. Stone, ed., *Reformed Faith and Politics* (1983); WARC, *Theological Basis of Human Rights* (1976); N. Wolterstorff, *Until Justice and Peace Embrace* (1983).

CHARLES C. WEST

Ethics, Theological   Theological ethics in the Reformed tradition has stressed the active power and presence of *God* and the need for conscious response in *piety* to God's rule. As a result, this tradition has emphasized the need to comprehend and order all life in faithfulness to the One made known in Jesus Christ and in ancient Israel. These themes are not exclusive to the Reformed tradition; they are grounded in *scripture* and expressed in the wider Christian community. Still, they came to forceful expression in the movement that emerged from Geneva and were further developed in Puritanism.

Calvin emphasized the radical priority of God's power and presence to human response. God is the creator from whom comes every good gift, the governor who rules the whole of nature and history, and the redeemer whose present purposes shall finally be vindicated. Piety is the conscious human response to God's power and presence, an attitude of heart and mind that inclines the believer to faithfulness and the subordination of self-concern in the service of God's reign. The Christian life is envisioned as a "sentry post" at which the Lord has posted us, which we must hold until God recalls us (*Inst.* 3.10.6). In the language of the sociologist Max Weber, Calvin's thought supports an attitude of "inner-worldly asceticism"; called to God's service in this world, Christians are under divine orders to use the goods of the world to God's glory.

The priority of God and the need for piety also are reflected in Calvin's distinctive understanding of the law. For Calvin, the divine *law* disclosed in scripture includes the moral precepts of natural law and equity, which are universally distributed. Found in the Decalogue, these are intensified and extended in Jesus Christ. God's law shows sinners how short they fall of God's purposes, and it restrains *sin* and evil. Its principal use, however, is to provide guidance for renewed hearts and minds who seek to follow God's will. In this sense, the law limits and directs faithful living in political and economic institutions as well as in family and *church.*

The movement that emerged with Calvin soon faced significantly changed social conditions. In the midst of bitter religious conflicts, different national governments supported different branches of Christianity. Calvinist churches sought recognition and toleration in hostile lands. The result was a modification of theocratic impulses and development of the church as a voluntary community, often in tension with its dominant society.

Covenant theology flourished under these conditions, especially among Puritans in England and America who endorsed the theology of the Calvinist Reformation—the priesthood of all believers, *justification* by *faith,* the *sanctification* of believers, and the *authority* of scripture—while emphasizing the sovereignty of God who calls humans to service in the world. The Puritan movement was fueled by piety, an affective orientation of the heart that led to introspection and the need for a narratable *conversion* experience as well as to practice. Indeed, if it is defined as those influenced by the theology, piety, and traditions that emerged from Geneva, Puritanism encompasses a broad range of figures and communities, from the Presbyterians and Thomas Cartwright to Roger Williams and the Rhode Island experiment.

As apparent from the writings of William Perkins, William Ames, William Preston, Richard Baxter, and others, Puritans used the language of the *covenant* to refer to the proper ordering of the entire nexus of human relations under God. Covenants bound parties together by mutual agreements made with respect to the natural order and special circumstances. *Marriage* and friendship, as well as business and political relations, were defined and understood as partnerships with reciprocal interactions, responsibilities, and obligations. For example, covenant theology emphasized mutual companionship as the chief end of marriage. Eventually, it also led to a nonhierarchical view of church *polity*, separate and distinct from *civil government* and the economic sphere. Nevertheless, Puritan ecclesiastical life came to be imbued with democratic tendencies that had broad political and economic consequences. Indeed, following the Puritan revolution, covenant thinking led toward republican government, as Puritans and their sometimes secular descendants argued first for toleration and then, in America, for a separation of church and state, which culminated in the notion of a limited state and separation of government powers. In the economic sphere, the covenant theology that linked the call of the sovereign God to service in the world became associated with a market free of excessive control by family or by state. Throughout the Puritan movement, covenantal thinking was accompanied by a casuistry that talked of particular vocations and cases of *conscience* with critical scrutiny, exemplified in Perkins's *Whole*

Treatise of Cases of Conscience (1606) and Baxter's *Christian Directory* (1673).

During the Great Awakening in America, Jonathan Edwards developed an understanding of the moral life based in true charity or love of God as a new affective principle and sense of the divine excellence that results from regenerating *grace* and reorients the person. Transformed by grace, the moral agent is inclined toward virtuous participation in the universal system of being under God rather than toward some limited participation in a restricted or limited circle, for example, one's family or nation. The sinfully contracted moral sensibilities, judgments, and discernments of the person are thereby enlarged and corrected so that life may be ordered in a fashion that is more truly responsive to God's sovereign reign.

Many of the intellectual challenges facing *Reformed theology* and ethics at the beginning of the nineteenth century were set by the impact of modern *science* and a growing confidence in the powers of human reason. In opposition to what they regarded as the credulity of traditional religion, proponents of the Enlightenment and their heirs claimed that human reason, by itself, could furnish a universal ethic, unencumbered by superstition. Friedrich Schleiermacher responded by claiming that human affections are central for ethics, and Christian ethics is based, not in universal reason, but in the historically particular qualifications of human inclination wrought by the specific form of piety expressed in the Christian community and its tradition. Thus, for Schleiermacher, Christian ethics is grounded in the Christ-shaped or Christ-determined feeling of absolute dependence on God. This becomes the foundation for a particular way of life, and Christian ethics is the reflective work of describing what a person whose emotions are formed in this way will be inclined to do.

From about the mid-nineteenth century through the early twentieth century, challenges provoked by the growing differentiation of Western societies and the growth of industrialization came to the fore. In the United States, proponents of the *Social Gospel* movement included representatives of many Protestant churches who focused attention on faithful service in the midst of interdependent social relations. For example, Richard T. Ely, an economist with theological concerns who was raised a Presbyterian and later became an Episcopalian, developed an idea of "social solidarity," or the notion that we are not isolated individuals but participants in a vast matrix of interests, possibilities, and responsibilities. This idea, he said, was beginning to be glimpsed by social *philosophy* and the sciences, though its longer heritage includes biblical understandings of human community before God and the organic unity of the church. Combining social solidarity with a prescription to love God and neighbor, Ely promoted a social ethic concerned with works of *justice* and reform in law and government, business and labor, education, and housing. These and similar concerns found institutional embodiments in both denominational and ecumenical bureaucracies that continue to be important today.

The twentieth century witnessed not only the ongoing impact of urbanization and industrialization but also the advent of totalitarianism, severe world economic crises, and two world wars. In response to these and other challenges, Karl Barth sought to protect the sovereignty of God by founding Christian ethics on the *Word* and command *of God* alone. In the *Theological Declaration of Barmen* (1934), he contrasted idolatrous reliance on cultural norms with genuine Christian faithfulness. The Declaration, adopted by the Confessing Church in Germany, acknowledged the "divine appointment" of the state to work "for justice and peace," yet insisted the state should not "become the single and totalitarian order of human life, thus fulfilling the Church's vocation as well" (BC 8.22, 23).

Against the separation of law and gospel espoused by some European the-ologians, Barth insisted that "law is a form of the Gospel." He also stressed the particularity of the divine command. "Nothing either outward or inward," including principles or rules, can anticipate the command and so reduce God's sovereign *freedom* to command. Nevertheless, Barth maintained these commands are given within certain "spheres" of human interaction and that genuine faithfulness is more likely to receive these commands if it attends to "prominent lines" or directions in scripture. In sum, Barth insisted on God's sovereignty over all of life, or over the multiple spheres of human conduct in which the command is given, and the urgency of genuine faithfulness.

In America, H. Richard Niebuhr argued that Christian ethics is based in faith as trust in and loyalty to the universal God who creates, governs, and redeems all things. Like Edwards, he argued that such a faith renders one responsive to the entire community of being. It is radically monotheistic in that it expands the community of moral responsibility beyond all partial contexts and so both affirms and relativizes our allegiances to lesser objects and communities. Informed by radical faith, cultural pursuits in religion, *politics*, and science are practiced with a kind of universal intent that opposes the constricted and hegemonic tendencies that arise when they are practiced in the service of idolatrous devotions to less than radical objects, for example, church, nation, or race. The moral life becomes the effort of persons and communities to order their lives appropriately in response to God in the midst of mundane relations and interdependencies.

Important challenges continue to face the Reformed community at the close of the twentieth century. In South Africa, where Calvinist *doctrine* has often been used in the service of racial oppression, a number of Reformed ministers and theologians currently are engaged in the work of reclaiming a tradition of conscience, justice, and compassion. In

Northern Ireland, an unrelenting spiral of violent conflict has occurred among Roman Catholic, Reformed, and other Protestant factions. The churches of central Europe, recently released from decades of official suppression, must once again ponder their appropriate roles in public life. The Reformed communities in the United States, along with other progressive churches and synagogues, need to devise distinctive and engaging interpretations of their increasingly secular and pluralistic society within a matrix of global interdependence. In these and many other contexts, Reformed churches and their theologians will remain true to a rich and distinctive heritage to the extent that they are able to connect a vigorous piety with the vision of a sovereign God who calls persons to faithful service in every area of life.

J. Edwards, *Ethical Writings,* ed. P. Ramsey, *The Works of Jonathan Edwards,* vol. 8 (1989); J. Gustafson, *Theology and Christian Ethics* (1974); D. Little, *Religion, Order, and Law: A Study in Pre-Revolutionary England* (1969); R. W. Lovin, *Christian Faith and Public Choices: The Social Ethics of Barth, Brunner, and Bonhoeffer* (1984); P. Miller, *The New England Mind: The Seventeenth Century,* 2 vols. (1939; repr. 1961); D. F. Ottati, *Meaning and Method in H. Richard Niebuhr's Theology* (1982); F. Schleiermacher, *An Introduction to Christian Ethics,* trans. J. C. Shelley (1989); E. Troeltsch, *The Social Teaching of the Christian Churches* (1912; ET 1931).

CHARLES M. SWEZEY

Eucharist *see* **Lord's Supper**

Evangelism Evangelism as a message is the authoritative summons of *God* to *repentance* and *faith* in the crucified and risen Christ, the inaugurator and consummator of the eschatological *kingdom of God.* Evangelism as a method is so to present Christ that, by the power of the *Holy Spirit,* people may come to God through him, grow in Christ, and serve him as Lord in the fellowship of his *church* and in the extension of his reign in the world. Various components of these definitions are stressed in the Reformed community; others are held in common with other theological traditions.

The God-centered message. Calvin with Luther rediscovered the message of evangelism—*grace* alone, faith alone, Christ alone. Not our work, but God's electing love redeems: "Salvation is of the Lord." Calvin also emphasized our obligation to demonstrate the Lordship of Christ in all life—society, *politics,* family, and church. The Puritans underlined this in their vision for the "wilderness" of America where the garden of God would be planted.

An invitation to a new birth. In the face of spiritual decline in the colonies, the Great Awakening (which peaked in the 1740s) called for the revival of holiness and a new birth, for a living, personal faith in Christ. Jonathan Edwards married the Puritan message on God's eschatological consummation to evangelism as a method, an invitation to accept Christ and become part of his new earthly community. The mission was to call people to fulfill God's predestined design—*a creation* fully subject to its creator's eternal purposes.

Foreign missions and new struggles. Following European Pietism and British Calvinists like William Carey, the nineteenth century brought a new emphasis on the kingdom of God's global extension. Puritanism's "grand scheme" was to be exported to the ends of the earth. This emphasis brought two movements that began to erode Calvinism's earlier emphases. Charles G. Finney's revivalism, shaped by Arminian theology, began to overpower Puritanism's holistic *ministry* and reduce evangelism to special meetings and new techniques. Calvin's emphasis on *conversion* as a "continuous process" of the whole person was reduced to a simple, one-step decision, which the "old side" Calvinist viewed with growing skepticism.

Theological liberalism also began to question earlier commitments of the lostness of *humanity* and the uniqueness of

Christ. In the United States, it overwhelmed Calvinism's interest in society and became identified with the *Social Gospel* movement. Evangelism was transformed into an emphasis on social reform and change.

Contemporary emphases and reinforcements. At least four themes have become focuses of the message and methodology of Reformed evangelism in the twentieth century: (1) renewed interest in the kingdom of God as the comprehensive evangelistic message of Jesus; (2) renewed connection between evangelism and incorporation into the life of the institutional church, an emphasis of the Church Growth school; (3) growing recognition by a now-global church of evangelism's ethnocultural dimensions and a new sensitivity to the cultural lines along which the Holy Spirit works in evangelism; and (4) expanding concern for relating evangelism to *justice* and the special needs of the poor and oppressed.

Agenda issues for the future. Theological pluralism and the global shape of the Reformed community raise these issues:

1. Who are the objects of evangelism? The traditional category of the lost, the poor and oppressed, or both?
2. What is the connection between verbal proclamation and social responsibility? Word or deed, orthopraxy or orthodoxy, or both?
3. Where is the boundary between the church and the world? Which is the main arena of God's activity? What is the role of the church in the world?
4. How do we see the place of Jesus in terms of other religions? Historic *Reformed theology* has stressed his uniqueness. Modern trends press for a universal extension of God's *salvation* that incorporates, not excludes, the world's faiths.

W. J. Abraham, *The Logic of Evangelism* (1989); D. Bosch, "Evangelism," *Mission Focus* 9, no. 4 (1981): 65–74; C. L. Chaney, *The Birth of Missions in America* (1976);

M. Green, *Evangelism in the Early Church* (1970); D. L. Guder, *Be My Witnesses* (1985); and *The Continuing Conversion of the Church* (2000); A. B. Lovell, ed., *Evangelism in the Reformed Tradition* (1990).

HARVIE M. CONN

Ex opere operato   The phrase meaning "from the work worked" is from the Council of Trent (1545–63; decree on *sacraments,* seventh session), where if any say that "grace is not conferred by the performance of the rite itself," they should be anathema. This seeks to affirm that the objective efficacy of the Christian sacraments is not dependent on the subjective worthiness of the recipient. In a way, this extends Augustine's argument (against the Donatists) that the unworthiness of the minister does not affect sacramental validity. It contrasts to those who affirm that the efficacy of the sacraments derives "from the work of the worker" (*ex opere operantis*). By implication, the notion of *ex opere operato* is sometimes understood to suggest that the power and the efficacy of the sacraments are intrinsic, that the sacraments "contain" *grace* and work almost automatically (or "magically"), apart from God's Spirit or human *faith.*

For John Calvin, as for *Augustine, God* is the true minister of the sacraments, and Calvin (critiquing Trent) questions the *ex opere operato.* While the sacraments are among the "means" by which God promises to give grace, God is not "tied" to the sacraments. While through God's gracious *ministry* the sacraments give what they signify, they do not (in and of themselves) have any power. Not magical, the sacraments work, as instruments of God's grace, only where they are received in faith.

G. C. Berkouwer, *The Sacraments* (1969); J. Calvin, *Tracts and Treatises Relating to the Reformation,* trans. H. Beveridge, vol. 3 (repr. 1959); J. Martos, *Doors to the Sacred* (1982); R. P. McBrien, ed., *Encyclopedia of Catholicism* (1995); K. Rahner, *The Church and the Sacraments* (1963); Schaff, *Creeds,* 2:118–22; 3:285–89.

JOHN E. BURKHART

Experience Etymological roots of "experience" suggest testing or experimenting to ascertain the truth. Current English usage defines experience as the state of being consciously affected by something or the conscious content of the life of an individual, group, or community. Theologically, the term is used in all three senses.

The Reformed tradition has expressed ambivalence about the role of experience in theology—an ambivalence traceable to John Calvin. He speaks of experience as common human experience and specifically Christian experience. Either may be probative. The ambivalence arises in trying to discern whether in a specific context Calvin values experience as such and finds it trustworthy or whether he sees it vitiated by *sin* and needing *judgment* and *grace.*

In the *Institutes,* Calvin speaks positively about common human, and specifically Christian, experience. Common human experience can tell us that the seed of religion has been planted in every human being (1.4.1), that *God* is Father (1.5.3), that the world is governed by *providence* (1.16.3), and that our will is not completely free (2.2.3). Christian experience convinces us of the authenticity of *scripture* (1.7.5), the need for the Sabbath (2.8.32), that though *faith* is always mixed with unbelief it cannot be conquered by it (3.2.4, 37), and that God is faithful even in the midst of adversity (3.8.3). However, Calvin also speaks negatively of both kinds of experience. Common human experience tells us that our understanding always reaches for the truth but, left to its own devices, cannot attain it (2.2.12). The daily experiences of Christians do not always assure them of their *election*; rather, Christians must turn from themselves to the *Word of God,* specifically to Christ (3.24.4, 5).

Friedrich Schleiermacher was interested in common human religious experience but saw the thematization of Christian experience as the actual task of dogmatics (*CF,* sec. 15). Scripture records the original, and therefore normative, expression of encounter with Christ. In this sense, it is the first in a series of presentations of Christian experience but retains its uniqueness because all subsequent presentations can only be developments of the apostolic *preaching* (*CF,* sec. 129). Scripture and experience, therefore, are not antithetical as independent sources of the *knowledge of God.*

Karl Barth picks up more of Calvin's negative statements about experience. Theology does not reflect on the experience of believing Christians but on the Word of God (*CD* I/1, 198–227). While people may have an experience of God's Word (i.e., for their existence to be determined by it), it is impossible for that experience to come from themselves. Nothing in human beings as such connects with the Word of God. God's image in *humanity* has been annihilated and must be created anew by God in Christ (*CD* I/1, 238–40). Therefore, to speak about human experience in dogmatics is to miss the real object of theology: God's self-revelation in Jesus Christ.

Neither Schleiermacher nor Barth precisely reproduced Calvin's own ambivalence about experience. Schleiermacher perhaps did not fear the self-deception that, because of sin, is still a part even of Christian experience. Barth, though, did not do justice to Calvin's recognition that there is a knowledge of God in common human experience: "Scripture, gathering up the otherwise confused knowledge of God in our minds, having dispersed our dullness, clearly shows us the true God" (*Inst.* 1.6.1).

J. E. Smith, *The Analogy of Experience* (1973).

DAWN DEVRIES

Extra Calvinisticum The so-called *extra calvinisticum* is the *doctrine* that after the *incarnation,* the Eternal Word by whom all things were made continues to be present and active also beyond the flesh (*etiam extra carnem*) united to himself. This teaching was widely held in the Catholic tradition, but in debates among Lutherans it came to be referred to as that "Calvinistic extra" (*extra calvinisticum*). The term appears to have been used first in controversies in the 1620s between the rival Lutheran schools at Tübingen and Giessen. Both sides agreed that in the incarnation the divine nature's power to be everywhere was communicated to the human nature. The Tübingen school maintained that during the period of his earthly ministry Christ simply hid his power of bodily **ubiquity**. The Giessen school maintained that during that period Christ actually emptied himself of that power. To teach the latter position, objected T. Thumm of Tübingen (1623), would be to reintroduce *illud extra calvinisticum*. Two years earlier, Balthasar Mentzer had employed the synonymous *extra calvinianum*. The term, in whatever form, reflects the assumption among many Lutherans and, by the 1620s, Lutheran and Reformed representatives. By 1564, in polemical debate, "Calvinist" had become the equivalent of "Zwinglian" to refer to opponents classified as the "sacramentarians," namely, those who taught that Christ was only "sacramentally," not really, present in the **Eucharist**. This classification was inaccurate, since Calvin himself objected to the sacramentarian position thus understood. He taught (*CO* 9, cols. 194–95, 507) that the whole Christ, but not everything that is Christ's (*Christus totus sed non totum*), is really (*realiter*) present in the **Lord's Supper** by the power of the **Holy Spirit**.

These eucharistic debates undoubtedly saw overzealous denials, almost Eutychian in tendency, of the teaching that even after the incarnation the Eternal Word was present and active also beyond the flesh. The debates, however, undoubtedly also saw the use, almost Nestorian in tendency, of exaggerated arguments that too often emphasized the "beyond the flesh" at the expense of the confession of the unity of the Person who, after all, the doctrine was meant to serve. Nonetheless, the occasional abuse of this doctrine does not alter the fact that the so-called *extra calvinisticum* was taught in some form by almost all the most prominent theologians of the Catholic tradition. Even a partial list includes Athanasius (*On the Incarnation* 17), **Augustine** (*Letters* 137.2, *To Volusian*), Cyril of Alexandria (*Ep.* 17), Peter Lombard (*Sentences* III, d. 22, 3), and Thomas Aquinas (*Summa Theologica* 3.10.1, ad 2). In fact, so widespread is the doctrine that it could just as well be called the *etiam extra catholicum*.

The term's origin, accuracy, and prominence in the **tradition** is how this commonly held doctrine can function differently in diverse historical settings. At least in Calvin's theology (e.g., *Inst.* 2.13.4; 4.17.30) and in the **HC** (q. 48), the doctrine does not function to encourage speculation about some other Word than the one united to the flesh to constitute the one Person. In Calvin's thought, it functions to support a fully Trinitarian doctrine of the **knowledge of God** and of self. It strengthens the confession of the identity of the redeeming Word and the Word by whom and with whose Spirit all things are created. Werner Krusche rightly argues that Calvin's doctrine of the Holy Spirit reinforces these Trinitarian functions of the *extra calvinisticum*. This is the same function the doctrine also appears to serve in most of the theologians of **Reformed orthodoxy**.

Barth, *CD* I/2, 159–71; IV/1, 180–81; A. Heron, "Extra Calvinisticum," *Evangelisches Kirchenlexikon: Internationale Theologische Enzyklopädie* 1 (1986): 1247–48; W. Kreck, "Extra Calvinisticum," *Evangelisches Kirchenlexikon: Kirchlich-theologisches Handwörterbuch* 1 (1956): 1245–46; W. Krusche, *Das Wirken des heiligen Geistes nach Calvin* (1957); W. Niesel, *The Theology of Calvin* (1956); F. Wendel, *Calvin* (1950); E. D. Willis, *Calvin's Catholic Christology: The Function of the So-called Extra Calvinisticum in Calvin's Theology* (1966).

E. DAVID WILLIS

Faith Christian faith is trust in *God,* whose steadfast love and free *grace* are decisively revealed in Jesus Christ. Because faith is a personal response of confidence in and fidelity to the living, gracious God, it is altogether different from blind submission to church teachings or mechanical adherence to a set of religious beliefs and practices. While some sort of faith—in oneself, family or friends, some ideal or cause, or simply in the worthwhileness of life—is often claimed as a necessary element in all human *experience* and development, faith in the NT sense refers more specifically to a free and wholehearted trust in God, whose goodness, mercy, and faithfulness are disclosed in Christ.

Emphases of a Reformed understanding of faith. **Reformed theology** is not primarily concerned to secure its distinctiveness among the various Christian traditions of faith. Its aim is ecumenical as well as evangelical, that is, to recover the truth of the gospel message as attested in *scripture* for the continual reform and renewal of the *church* catholic. With this proviso, several prominent emphases of the understanding of faith in Reformed theology may be identified.

1. The object of faith is *God alone,* whose grace is known to us supremely in Jesus Christ through the witness of scripture illuminated by the **Holy Spirit.** According to Calvin's celebrated definition, faith is "a firm and certain knowledge of God's benevolence toward us, founded upon the truth of the freely given promise in Christ, both revealed to our minds and sealed upon our hearts through the Holy Spirit" (*Inst.* 3.2.7). Only the living and sovereignly gracious God is to be the object of our faith. To elevate anything else to this position— whether nation, culture, reason, religious experience, church doctrines, or the text of scripture itself—is *idolatry.*

2. The subject of faith is the *whole* person—mind, affections, and will—in response to God's goodness, faithfulness, and *forgiveness* of sins in Christ. Faith is a response of the "heart" and not the mind alone (cf. Calvin's emblem of the Christian life as a flaming heart offered to God). To be sure, there is a cognitive dimension of faith; it is "knowledge" of the truth and not a blind leap in the dark or mindless assent to whatever the church teaches (in this sense the notion of "implicit faith" was rejected by the Reformers). That faith seeks understanding and is no enemy of *reason* is a familiar motif of Reformed theology. Yet this emphasis goes hand in hand with the insistence that true *knowledge of God* is inseparable from the spirit of *piety,* that is, a reverence for and love of God, a readiness to be taught and guided by God's Word and Spirit, a valuing of *prayer* as "the chief exercise of faith" (*Inst.* 3.20), and a humble recognition that "we are not our own; we are God's" (*Inst.* 3.7.1).

3. Faith is both a *gift of God* and a *free human response.* For Reformed theology, faith is a gift of God (Eph. 2:8–9) rather than a human achievement. We receive the grace of God with empty hands and have no grounds for boasting. Yet as the gift of the Holy Spirit who works liberatively rather than coercively, faith is also an act of human *freedom.* Genuine human freedom and humility before God stand in direct rather than inverse proportion. We are never more truly free than when we live by the grace of God alone. As a gift of God, faith brings liberation from all idols of self and world, empowering us for new life and service.

4. Faith comes from *hearing the gospel* of Christ (Rom. 10:17). While faith may arise in unpredictable ways and widely diverse circumstances, it is ordinarily fostered and strengthened in the life of Christian community where the **Word of God** is rightly preached and heard, the **sacraments** properly administered, and Christian discipleship responsibly cultivated. Reformed theology sees the awakening and nourishing of faith as a profoundly communal rather than individualistic process. This is summed up by Calvin's description of the church as the "mother" of our faith (*Inst.* 4.1.1).

Faith in God is intertwined with life in community and fidelity in personal relationships.

5. We are saved by grace through faith alone, but such faith is always coupled with *works of love* and service to the glory of God. While the Reformers objected to the view that faith is mere assent to the church's teachings and must therefore be perfected by our acts of love, they nevertheless insisted that true faith expresses itself naturally and unpretentiously in love and service of God and the neighbor, just as a healthy tree bears good fruit. Motivated by thankfulness (cf. HC, pt. III), authentic faith does not fail to produce works of love (Gal. 5:6). Hence, for Reformed theology there is no contradiction between the Pauline *doctrine* of *justification* by faith (Rom. 3:27) and James's warning that faith without works is dead (James 2:26). Justification is the basis of *sanctification,* and sanctification the goal of justification (hence the characteristically Reformed "third use of the law").

6. Faith and *hope* are inseparable. While God has acted decisively for the world in Christ, the work of redemption is not yet complete. At present, believers see in a mirror dimly (1 Cor. 13:12) and do not yet experience the promised triumph of God's grace throughout the whole *creation* (Rom. 8). *Sin* and suffering are still evident in the world and in the lives of believers. Thus, together with the groaning creation, believers pray for God's kingdom, struggle against injustice, and work for the transformation of all things. Faith and hope are mutually supportive, for faith without hope becomes arrogant and triumphalistic, and hope without faith falls victim to religious escapism or secular utopianism.

7. Within the Reformed tradition, faith in God's grace is not only personally renewing but *world transforming.* While faith is no mere projection of the ideas, wishes, and interests of believers, it nevertheless seeks transformation of all things to the glory of God and thus acts as a *catalyst of human creativity, imagination, and permanent reformation* in all spheres of culture. The steadfast and holy love of God manifest in Christ continually illumines, judges, revolutionizes, and transforms our understandings of God, the world, and ourselves. This world-transforming view of faith informs the characteristic participation of Reformed Christians in many social, political, and cultural reform movements.

8. Recognition that our Christian faith, love, and hope are also *always in need of reform* is a hallmark of Reformed theology. As evident in the *BC,* Reformed churches have produced many *confessions of faith* in different times and places. They have underscored the freedom and responsibility of a believing community to bear witness to its faith in timely words and pertinent deeds to meet the challenges and needs of new situations. Faith is no mere inner disposition that remains indifferent to the crises and possibilities of the public domain. By courageous witness and concrete forms of costly discipleship, faith seeks to shape life and culture in the direction of the coming reign of God.

History of Reformed theologies of faith. The history of Reformed theological reflection on faith shows continuity and diversity. For the sake of simplicity, five major periods can be distinguished:

1. The period of the sixteenth-century Reformation when in the wake of Luther's reform movement Calvin, Bullinger, Beza, Zwingli, Knox, and others recovered the biblical understanding of faith as reliance on the gracious promise of God contained in the biblical witness and centered in the reconciling work of Christ.

2. The period of seventeenth-century *Reformed orthodoxy,* represented in Europe by Francis Turretin, Amandus Polanus, and Johannes Cocceius and defended in nineteenth-century North America by the old Princeton school of Charles Hodge and B. B. Warfield, which tended to stress the cognitive side of faith and the propositional nature of *revelation.*

3. The period of eighteenth-century Reformed evangelicalism and nineteenth-

century Reformed liberalism, which attempted in very different ways to recover the affective and ethical components of faith (cf. Jonathan Edwards's sensitivity to the importance of the affections in the life of faith and Friedrich Schleiermacher's association of faith with the "feeling of absolute dependence").

4. The period of neo-Reformed theology (*neo-orthodoxy*), led by Barth and Brunner, which in opposition to all historicist, psychological, and cultural domestications of faith, reasserted the freedom of God's grace and the orientation of faith on the revelation in Christ.

5. The contemporary period of Reformed theology, whose emphases include H. Richard Niebuhr's radically theocentric description of faith; Jürgen Moltmann's recovery of the critical and transformative significance of hope in God's promise for every aspect of Christian faith and discipleship; and the interpretation of Reformed faith as liberative, contextual, and oriented to "political" praxis (cf. Paul L. Lehmann, A. A. Boesak, Letty Russell).

Barth, *CD* IV/1, 608–42, 740–49; G. C. Berkouwer, *Faith and Justification* (1954); A. A. Boesak, *Black and Reformed* (1984); S. Guthrie, *Always Being Reformed: Faith for a Fragmented World* (1996); Heppe, *RD*; J. Moltmann, *Theology of Hope* (1967); H. R. Niebuhr, *Faith on Earth* (1989); B. Pitkin, *What Pure Eyes Could See: Calvin's Doctrine of Faith in Its Exegetical Context* (1999); N. Wolterstorff, *Until Justice and Peace Embrace* (1983).

DANIEL L. MIGLIORE

Federal Theology   Federal or covenant theology (Lat. *foedus*, "covenant"), is a theological approach depicting the divine-human relationship as covenantal. It became an important school of *Reformed theology* in the seventeenth century and influenced Reformed thought and practice in many areas.

God's *covenant* with Israel is a central theme of the Bible, and occasionally it appeared as a theme in patristic exegesis. Some late-medieval theologians, especially Nominalists, thought in covenantal terms, arguing that God's absolute power was constrained by God's ordaining to act in certain stipulated ways with respect to *creation*. In the early Reformation, Martin Luther and Huldrych Zwingli, claiming to return to a more biblical outlook, gave renewed importance to the covenant.

Heinrich Bullinger, the leading theologian of Zurich after Zwingli's death, devoted a whole treatise to the subject, making it central in his thought. Bullinger followed Zwingli in seeing in the Bible and the church's history one long story of God's covenant relationship with humankind: *God* promised *grace* to Adam and the patriarchs, revealed "types" of it in the *law* of Moses, and fully manifested it in Christ. The histories of Israel and the *church* belonged to this covenant scheme and consisted of periods of decline and revival as God's people were more or less obedient to the divine will. The Reformation, like the time of King Josiah in ancient Israel, was seen as a period of the overthrow of *idolatry*. To Bullinger, God had made but one covenant with humankind, that of grace, known by anticipation before Christ and remembrance thereafter. Each period had its own *sacraments*, circumcision being a sacrament of anticipation that had been replaced by *Baptism*. The covenant was mutual and conditional: God willed to redeem those who fulfilled its terms of *faith* and *repentance*, though Bullinger also thought God's grace made such fulfillment possible. His theology was thus built upon the history of *salvation*, and the covenant was the chief principle for interpreting the Bible and understanding God's rule in history. The covenant also had social implications for Bullinger: In a truly Christian society, covenant obligations of *justice* and pure *worship* would be met.

Calvin gave the covenant less attention than did Bullinger and emphasized its testamentary quality as God's promise of grace more than its conditionality. For Calvin too there was but one covenant—grace—administered differently in OT and NT times. For Calvin, as well as for Zwingli, Bullinger, and later Reformed theologians, the covenant was entirely compatible with *predestination* (many of the strictest double predestinarians were also federal theologians). Though federal theology spoke of God's will as conditional, the covenant was always regarded as the means, in historical time and through human volition and secondary causality, by which God effected his unconditional will. But it did supplement the predestinarianism of Reformed theology with a biblical language stressing *history* and human responsibility.

A new idea entered covenant thinking at the end of the sixteenth century with the appearance of a covenant of works separate from and antecedent to the covenant of grace. This view first appeared with the Heidelberg theologians Zacharius Ursinus, Caspar Olevianus, and Franciscus Junius, then with those who came under their influence, including the English Puritans Thomas Cartwright and Dudley Fenner. Later Reformed scholastic theologians further developed it. According to this view, God made a covenant of works with Adam, the "federal head" of all *humanity,* enjoining obedience to a perpetually binding moral law identified variously with the Ten Commandments (known to Adam before being given to Moses) and the law of nature. After Adam and his posterity with him fell, salvation was no longer available through the first covenant, so God established the covenant of grace, in which Christ fulfills the law and atones for its breach, becoming the "federal head" of believers. This covenant of grace was given as promise in the OT and fulfillment in the NT. Both covenants are "one-sided" insofar as God ordained them but "two-sided" insofar as by them humankind became God's covenant partner. All are under the covenant of works as obligation, but elect believers are also under the covenant of grace and thereby confront obligations of the covenant of

works not only as condemnation but also as a pattern for a devout life possible for them through sanctifying grace. Thus, the covenant of works became a means for regarding certain moral obligations as universally binding. Since these obligations included those of the Decalogue, Reformed Sabbatarianism, especially evident among the Puritans, can be seen as related to federal theology.

By the mid-seventeenth century, the double covenant was a commonplace of Reformed theology. It appeared in the *WCF* (1646) and became the central organizing principle in the writings of Hermann Witsius and Johannes Cocceius in the Netherlands. Cocceius developed yet a third covenant, that of redemption, whereby Christ made a pact with the Father to atone for the sins of the elect. This pushed the covenant pattern back into the inner life of the *Trinity.*

The Puritans, who produced numerous sermons and treatises on the covenant, removed it from abstract theology and related it to personal *piety.* It enabled them to stress the obligations of *conversion* and holiness as well as the assurance found in consideration that God dealt predictably with humankind. Federal theology had significant social ramifications: The disciplined society that Reformed thinkers envisaged was rooted not only in the moral demands made upon believers but also in universal moral obligations of humankind. Moreover, covenanting was applicable to congregational and political life, as evidenced in English Congregationalist *polity* and Scottish Presbyterian political protest. The contractual model it entailed influenced political philosophy, as in John Locke, and led to notions of responsible, democratic government.

J. W. Baker, *Heinrich Bullinger and the Covenant* (1980); M. McGiffert, "Grace and Works: The Rise and Division of Covenant Divinity in Elizabethan Puritanism," *Harvard Theological Review* 75, no. 4 (1982): 463–502; and "From Moses to Adam: The Making of the Covenant of Works," *SCJ* 19, no. 2 (1988): 131–55; J. Von Rohr, *The Covenant of Grace in Puritan Thought* (1986); D. A. Weir, *The Origins of the Federal Theology in Sixteenth-Century Reformation Thought* (1990).

DEWEY D. WALLACE JR.

Feminist Theologies

Feminist theologies reflect on *God* as God is known in and through the *experience* of those who advocate the full *humanity* of women together with men. Fully consistent with the Reformed tradition of searching out reconciliation in the midst of "a ferment" of the world, feminist theologians are exposing the cause of painful divisions and calling for *repentance* and new life in the *church* (*BC* 9.54).

There is no one description of feminist or one type of feminist theology. But there is a consensus that feminist theologies seek to act and reflect upon the search for liberation from all forms of dehumanization, joining God in advocating full human dignity for each and every person. Such advocacy includes all women and men, not just white educated inhabitants of North Atlantic nations. Although I write theology as a white, middle-class woman from the northeastern part of the United States, raised in the Reformed tradition, as a feminist I am committed to working for the equality of all women and men of every race, class, and nationality.

Many feminist theologies use a style similar to other *liberation theologies* such as Latin American, black, and Asian liberation theologies. The reflection begins with the *commitment* to act on behalf of the oppressed in the light of God's liberating action in the exodus and the *resurrection*. It is based in a concrete situation or *context*, asking about the problems, questions, and insights that arise in that context. Because of their incarnational nature, these theologies are rooted in a variety of contexts and traditions on all continents, and therefore there is no *one* feminist theology but rather a host of feminist theologies.

The style is often *communal* as well. Everyone involved in a particular community of *faith* and struggle is invited to take part in the action and reflection. Pastors, lay people, activists, teachers, and students are asked to reflect together on the work of the church in the world. Groups of women often gather in Bible studies and develop their own theological perspectives using this communal process.

The process is also *critical*, since it seeks to test the *authority* and the *tradition* of the church and reinterpret biblical tradition in the light of the experience of women and all people struggling to be free. Here an aspect of Reformed tradition appears in the stress on an educated congregation where all are able to read the Bible and to guard the Word through a process of active discernment. This style of committed, contextual, communal, and critical theological reflection is very much suited to a continuation of the Reformation in our own time.

Unlike the Reformed tradition that begins with God's *revelation,* the method of feminist theologians is to begin with the experience of those struggling against oppression and ask how God is involved in that struggle. After analyzing this experience to understand the social, economic, historical, and ecclesial causes of the oppression, they begin to look at the biblical and church traditions from this perspective of marginal and voiceless persons in society. In the light of this, they ask in what ways the tradition needs reinterpretation and reshaping and what God is calling us to do in response to this understanding of faith. The understanding here is not that God is slighted in the name of women's experience but that God is often known among those "of low estate" and that the gospel message is often discerned through a theological process of action and reflection.

Like Reformed theologies, feminist theologies take seriously the present reality of *sin* and need for a strong *eschatology* that affirms the reality of God's love, which is stronger than sin, *death,* and domination. Women can appeal to the authority of their experience, but this experience is primarily of the old creation and the structures of patriarchy in church and society. They do not yet know what real live children of God will look like (Rom. 8:19).

Nevertheless, many feminist theologies struggle to express a vision of God's intention for a mended *creation*, and this *hope* helps women "keep on keeping on." In an important sense, Christian feminists only have this future, for the patriarchal structures that have shaped *scripture*, tradition, church, and theology are such that the process of reconstruction of women's place in man's world requires a utopian faith that understands God's future as an impulse for change in the present.

C. P. Christ and J. Plaskow, eds., *Womanspirit Rising* (1979); S. McFague, *Models of God* (1987); R. R. Ruether, *Sexism and God-Talk* (1983); L. M. Russell, *Household of Freedom: Authority in Feminist Theology* (1987); L. M. Russell and J. S. Clarkson, *Dictionary of Feminist Theologies* (1996); L. M. Russell, et. al., eds., *Inheriting Our Mothers' Gardens* (1988); E. Schüssler Fiorenza, *Bread Not Stone* (1984); P. Trible, *God and the Rhetoric of Sexuality* (1978); J. W. H. Van Wijk-Bos, *Reformed and Feminist* (1991); J. L. Weidman, ed., *Christian Feminism* (1984).

LETTY M. RUSSELL

Finitum non capax infiniti   Some (H. Baucke, W. Elert, F. Loofs) have argued that the differences between Lutheran and Reformed *Christologies* reflect a more fundamental philosophical difference over whether the finite is capable of receiving the infinite. The Reformed, they say, reject the *doctrine* of Christ's bodily *ubiquity* because they apply to the *incarnation* the philosophical principle that the finite is incapable of receiving the infinite (*finitum non capax infiniti*). This principle supposedly influences the whole of *Reformed theology* for which, finally, there remains an unbridgeable distance between *God* and *creation*.

There is, understandably, a paucity of documentation in Reformed materials to confirm the presence of this philosophical principle. Maintaining that the distinction (not the distance) between God and the creature is common to all Christian theology and Reformed theology is not an exception (cf. the section on the attributes of God in Heppe, *RD,* 57–104). Central to Reformed theology is the conviction that the triune God is known (*Inst.* 1.5.9; 3.1.1) precisely because God does not stay to God's self but *accommodates* God's self to create and redeem. God does more than draw near the creature. In the incarnation, God is united to the flesh; by the bond of the *Holy Spirit,* believers are united to Christ (*Inst.* 3.11.10). This presence of God is the infinite creating in the finite conditions for reception and transformation. In terms of the philosophical formula, this means that by *grace* the finite, is indeed made capable of the infinite, but, more pointedly, it means that out of God's covenanting fidelity, the finite is taken up and transformed in God's freedom to be human—*Deus capax humanitatis.*

Barth, *CD* I/2, 484–91; H. Bauke, "Christologie II: Dogmengeschichte," *RGG²,* vol. 1, col. 1628; G. C. Berkouwer, *The Person of Christ* (1954); W. Elert, "Über die Herkunft des Satzes 'Finitum infiniti non capax,'" *Zeitschrift für systematische Theologie* 16 (1939): 500–504; F. Loofs, "Christologie," *Realenzyklopädie für protestantische Theologie und Kirche,* 3rd ed. (1896–1913), 4:54; A. Schweizer, *Die Glaubenslehre der evangelischreformirten Kirche,* vol. 2 (1847), 296, 303; E. D. Willis, *Calvin's Catholic Christology: The Function of the So-called Extra Calvinisticum in Calvin's Theology* (1966).

E. DAVID WILLIS

Foreknowledge   God's knowledge of all future possibilities, contingencies, and actualities. John Calvin defined it from God's point of view (similar to Duns Scotus): "All things always were, and perpetually remain, under his eyes, so that to his knowledge there is nothing future or past, but all things are present" (*Inst.* 3.21.5).

In classical Reformed thought (*scholasticism*), this is the logical correlate of omniscience and a conclusion from biblical texts stressing the "perfection" of God's knowledge (concerning the outcome of human actions, the world, etc.). God's "almightiness" is emphasized against immanentistic or pantheistic thought.

Some important distinctions are the following:

1. Reformed scholasticism has said that while God's "necessary" foreknowledge (by virtue of being God) logically precedes God's decree, God's "free" foreknowledge (of things happening) logically follows. This implies a sharp distinction of eternity and history, decree and execution, where the former terms precede logically (if not chronologically) the latter. It presumes a "sequential" metaphysics of eternity and time.

2. Foreknowledge means more than intellectual precognition (prescience) and implies God's will concerning the destinies of people (*predestination*). That raises the question of *freedom*. Reformed thought responds that the human will is not indeterminate (to be turned in any direction) but roots in human nature—being connected with humanity's deepest instincts and personality ("heart").

3. Freedom is reasonable self-determination, not indifferent choice (arbitrariness). A free person is reliable—acting necessarily in accord with who one is but not by external compulsion. Thus, traditional Reformed thought has tried to combine foreknowledge with a viable concept of freedom.

L. Berkhof, *Systematic Theology*, 4th rev. and enl. ed. (1949); C. Hodge, *Systematic Theology*, vol. 1 (1871).

PHILIP C. HOLTROP

Foreordination   Part of the cluster of doctrines to explain and defend the absolute sovereignty of *God* in *creation* and *providence, grace* and redemption, and *faith* and *election*. As such, it must be

correlated with divine *foreknowledge* and human *free will,* cause and effect, necessity and permission, and so forth.

"Foreordination" is used in Rom. 8:29–30, 1 Cor. 2:7, Eph. 1:5, 11, and Acts 4:28. The Greek root word *horizō* means to determine, to ordain, or to appoint. With the prefix and when applied to divine determination, *proorizō* is translated "to predestine" or "to foreordain."

The *doctrine* of foreordination is understood as a theologically legitimate extension of belief in "God Almighty" by whose will all things are not only created but governed.

In *scripture,* foreordination and foreknowledge (e.g., Rom. 8:29) emphasize the marvelous grace of the loving God toward the faithful rather than God's determining power over the world. Sometimes God's foreknowledge has been asserted without foreordination. That is, God's omniscience is taken to include everything that happens, but events that occur within God's *omnipotence* are not considered directly determined by God's will.

While Calvin affirmed human free will, *sin,* and evil, his chief insistence was on God's continual governance of all things. God's providence is "the determinative principle of all things in such a way that sometimes it works through an intermediary, sometimes without an intermediary, sometimes contrary to every intermediary" (*Inst.* 1.17.1). This view is not an abstract speculation but a doxological confession.

In recent times, human *freedom,* choice, and responsibility have been affirmed in such ways that God's foreordination, and doctrines closely associated with it, while seldom directly denied, are rather deemphasized in *Reformed theology.*

CHARLES PARTEE

Forgiveness   The *doctrine* of forgiveness (or *justification*) affirms that in Christ sinful people are accounted righteous before *God*, spared divine condemnation, and made fellow heirs with Christ of eternal life in his heavenly kingdom.

Reformed theology presupposes the ubiquity of *sin* in human life, good works included, making need for divine forgiveness universal. It shares the general Protestant affirmation that such forgiveness is wholly the gift of divine *grace*, given apart from any consideration of merit or worthiness in the recipient. God effects this forgiveness by crediting sinners with the righteousness of Christ as a gift. This "alien" or "imputed" righteousness therefore lacks any foundation in the sinner's good works, being entirely the product of Christ's obedience. Believers appropriate forgiveness by *faith* alone, apart from any necessity of ceremonial or priestly absolution.

While God's gift of forgiveness is not based in works, Reformed theology characteristically insists that it is not separable from works either. Forgiveness is one aspect of the total work of divine grace in the sinner's life. Other manifestations include faith, *repentance*, holiness of life, and obedience to God's commands.

G. C. Berkouwer, *Faith and Justification* (1954); H. Bushnell, *Forgiveness and Law* (1840); P. L. Lehmann, *Forgiveness* (1940); H. R. Mackintosh, *The Christian Experience of Forgiveness* (1927); W. Niesel, *The Theology of Calvin* (1956).

P. MARK ACHTEMEIER

Free Will Historical discussion has made "free will" a systematically ambiguous phrase. It is used to mean:

1. Free agency, that is, ability to make and execute one's own decisions, thus incurring accountability for what one does. All Western philosophies and theologies assert free will in this sense, except behaviorism, which sees mental and volitional acts as by-products of physical processes. The assertion means we are not robots, nor are we programmed by some other mind, as computers or persons under hypnotism are, nor are our actions mere conditioned reflexes like those of Pavlov's dogs. But we are moral agents expressing our authentic selves in our conduct. The will is here conceived psychologically and dispositionally as the directedness of human nature whereby preferences, resolutions, and impulses come to be acted out. Free agency is entailed by the scriptural insistence that humans are answerable to *God*, the judge of all.

2. Ability to trust, obey, and *worship* God, that is, power to respond to God heartily and happily in service that shows a loving desire for God's company and a purpose of exalting and honoring God. *Reformed theology*, following *Augustine*, Luther, Calvin, and Edwards, unanimously denies the existence of free will in this sense in any except the regenerate, in whom this capacity is partly restored now and will be perfected and confirmed in *heaven*. Augustine first schemed out the fourfold state of humans as *freedom* in Eden to *sin* (Lat. *posse peccare*), no freedom in our fallenness not to sin (*non posse non peccare*), partial freedom in the present life of *grace* not to sin (*posse non peccare*), and full bestowal in the future life of glory of inability to sin (*non posse peccare*)—which for Augustine meant perfect freedom from all that is truly evil for all that is truly good. In the idiom of the English-speaking Reformed theology of the past four centuries, the denial of free will to the unregenerate is correlative to the assertion of total inability to merit, due to *total depravity* (total not in degree, as if all are as bad as they could be, but in extent, meaning that all human activity is morally and spiritually flawed at some point, so none are as good as they should be). This in turn is correlative to assertions that sin has dominion over fallen *humanity*, that *original sin* is the universal human condition, and that monergistic *regeneration* through sovereign grace is the necessary and sole source of such *faith, repentance,* and godliness as emerge under the Word.

Against this, Pelagianism ancient and modern holds that free will in the defined sense remains intact in all humanity despite the fall, and semi-Pelagianism sees it as diminished but not destroyed. Semi-Pelagianism, viewing humanity as essentially good though weak through sin rather than essentially bad but restrained by common grace, appears substantively, if not under that name, in Arminian and liberal Protestantism; in Eastern Orthodoxy, which follows the free will teaching of the Greek Fathers; and in pre- and post-Tridentine Roman Catholicism, which sees human merit as decisive for *salvation.*

The conception of free will throughout this debate is narrower than in the "free agency" (no. 1 above) view. Free will here means, quite precisely, being able to do what appears good, wise, right, and pleasing to God out of a heart that rejoices in it just because it has these qualities.

3. Metaphysical (ontological) indeterminism, that is, the state of not being fully controlled by one's insights (i.e., one's understanding of what is best to do), nor by one's character, nor (some would add) by God. Free will here signifies power to act irrationally and at random, which is certainly a fact of life; it is sometimes dignified with the name of liberty of indifference or the power of contrary choice.

Does this fact, which makes everyone's future acts unpredictable to a degree so far as humans are concerned, imply that God's predetermining *foreknowledge* of each person's future behavior is in any respect incomplete, so what is done is not always God's will? A spectrum of semi-Pelagian positions, from classical *Arminianism* with its concept of God's self-limitation to process theology with its *doctrine* of the finitude and relative impotence of God, say yes; Reformed theology, with the Bible, asserts that no future event is unknown or indeterminate to God and that contrary views err by conceiving God in humanity's image. There seems to be no need to buttress this scriptural position by claiming that the will (i.e., the agent) is always moved by the strongest motivational drive operative at that moment, as Edwards did. This claim seems to deny the reality of random action, which is implausible.

Augustine, *Enchiridion*; and *On Grace and Free Will*; D. and R. Basinger, eds., *Predestination and Free Will: Four Views of Divine Sovereignty and Human Freedom* (1986); J. Calvin, *Inst.* 2.1–4; J. Calvin, *The Bondage and Liberation of the Will* (1996); J. Edwards, *Freedom of the Will*, in *Works*, vol. 1 (1957); D. J. Hoitenga, Jr., *John Calvin and the Will: A Critique and Corrective* (1997); M. Luther, *The Bondage of the Will*, trans. J. I. Packer and O. R. Johnston (1967).

JAMES I. PACKER

Freedom   In the history of Christian *doctrine* and the Reformed *tradition,* freedom has three basic foci: the freedom of *God* in the work of *creation* and redemption; the basic freedom of willing and choosing with which human beings are endowed by nature, underlying all teaching concerning their responsibility before God and to their fellow human beings; and the Christian freedom that rests on the redemptive *grace* of God and follows as a corollary on the doctrine of *justification.*

Freedom of God. Freedom, like the various other attributes of God, stands both as a distinct attribute and as a major qualification and explanation of the other attributes. God is free in being and in action, in self and in relation to God's creatures; God's sovereignty is a sovereign freedom; and God's power is a free exercise, devoid of all constraint. The Reformed approach to divine freedom is nowhere more apparent than in the doctrine of the eternal decrees: God freely wills the existence and preservation of the created order and freely determines the eternal destiny of all creatures, solely on the ground of God's goodness and solely for the sake of God's ultimate glory. In creation and *providence,* God encounters no barriers to the exercise of God's will, and in the work of redemption God acts utterly graciously, apart from any merit belonging to the creature.

In the twentieth century, Karl Barth offered the most eloquent exposition of the freedom of God in his understanding of the *incarnation* as "God's freedom for man" and in his discussion of the divine perfections or attributes under the rubric of "the Being of God as the One who loves in freedom." The merit of Barth's discussion lies in his clear identification of the divine freedom as a positive freedom for relationship rather than as a negative freedom from restriction.

Freedom of human beings. Human freedom, unlike the freedom of God, is a relative freedom, bounded not only by our nature as given in the act of creation but also by the acts of other creatures, by the natural order around us, and by our sinfulness. Nonetheless, the Christian tradition has almost invariably assumed the fundamental freedom of the human will from external constraint and has tended to understand the boundaries of freedom in terms of the larger category of human nature or the more limited category of choice. *Reformed theology* has followed an Augustinian paradigm in its understanding of human freedom, noting distinctions between the capability of unfallen human beings and human beings after the fall, under grace, and in final fellowship with God. In their original condition, humans were capable of not sinning, because the freedom of choice (*liberum arbitrium*) remained whole. After the fall, though the will itself remained free, its capacity for choice was limited by the sinfulness of human nature. The issue is not the loss of freedom in the will itself, which, according to the older Reformed theology, remains uncoerced and under no externally imposed necessity, but the restriction of free choice by the pervasive sinfulness of fallen *humanity.* Human beings retain the capacity for choice, but all choosing occurs in the context of sin—so the defect belonging to human nature after the fall renders even the choice of good things sinful. The entrance of grace and *salvation* into human life restores the ability to do the good, but imperfectly, in and through the power of God's grace. Only in the next life, in union with Christ, is there a total restoration of goodness and, indeed, the ultimate removal of the ability to sin.

Christian freedom. Christian freedom in Reformed theology relates, on the one hand, to the Augustinian categories of human choice and, on the other, to the somewhat paradoxical relationship of Christians to the *law* in the light of their justification by grace through *faith* alone. The new relationship to Christ brought about by faith results in a free obedience unfettered by fears of the law. Luther summed up this freedom in two maxims: "A Christian is a perfectly free lord of all, subject to none" and "A Christian is a perfectly dutiful servant of all, subject to all." The paradox of this freedom arises from the fact that justification by faith opens the Christian life to a new obedience in which law no longer has the power to condemn.

Calvin, with considerably less paradox than Luther, brought this understanding of Christian freedom into the Reformed tradition: Christians, justified by faith, though still imperfect, are freed from slavery to *sin* for a new obedience. For Calvin, this free obedience is understood in terms of the third use of the law, the so-called normative use, where the law functions as a model for life rather than as a condemnation. This obedient life, rightly directed by God's grace, brings with it a freedom from the constraints of the law and, specifically, from "indifferent" regulations (*Inst.* 3.19.7; Gr. *adiaphora*) such as fasts, vestments, and outward ceremonies. In sum, Calvin understands Christian freedom as the peace of *conscience* that opens Christians to the use of God's gifts according to their true purposes. This understanding of Christian freedom also appears in the *Heidelberg Catechism,* where the Decalogue is treated, with the Lord's Prayer, under the rubric of "Thankfulness," and law is understood as a goal to be sought in faith rather than as a condemnation and burden.

In the twentieth century, the theme of Christian freedom has become the central focus of the ethics of Jacques Ellul. Christ, according to Ellul, offers us both the *revelation* of the freedom of God and the identification of true human freedom in the face of the choices pressed upon humanity by the sinful world—in God's choices to be incarnate, to fulfill the law, to live out the will of God, and to die. This freedom, as evidenced by Christ's temptations, is served not by the exercise of power but by seeking first and foremost the *kingdom of God.* In Christ and through the *Word of God,* this freedom becomes possible for Christians in service to God, in the *confession of faith,* and in right observance of the Sabbath, all of which point toward freedom in Christ from self, from our past, and from the world.

Augustine, *On Free Will,* in *Augustine: Earlier Writings,* LCC, vol. 6; Barth, *CD* I/2; II/1; Calvin, *Inst.* 3.19; J. Daane, *The Freedom of God* (1973); J. D. Douglass, *Women, Freedom, and Calvin* (1985); J. Ellul, *The Ethics of Freedom,* trans. G. W. Bromiley (1976); M. Luther, *The Freedom of a Christian* (1520), in *Luther's Works,* vol. 31, ed. H. J. Grimm (1957). W. R. Stevenson, Jr., *Sovereign Grace: The Place and Significance of Christian Freedom in John Calvin's Political Thought* (1999).

RICHARD A. MULLER

French Confession   Also called Gallican Confession and Confession of La Rochelle. Official confession of the French Reformed Church, adopted at the first National Synod (Paris, 1559), then more or less definitively ratified at the seventh National Synod (La Rochelle, 1571), though continuously revised by later national synods. (The controversial statement identifying the pope as the Antichrist adopted at the Synod of Gap [1603] shows the turn these revisions might take.) The confession was basically replaced by the Canons of the *Synod of Dort* when the National Synods of Alais

(1620) and Charenton (1623) accepted them and required subscription by all church officials.

Impetus for a confession came from a conflict over *predestination* in the Poitiers church (c. 1556). An appeal to the church of Paris led, after considerable discussion with the Parisian minister Antoine de la Roche Chandieu, to the decision to create a national organization and confession. John Calvin was consulted and, though not in accord with such formal structures, provided the resultant *synod* of Paris with a brief, thirty-five article confession. Under Chandieu's direction it was adopted by the synod, with revisions (principally the addition of five articles). Because both the thirty-five article confession and the forty article confession were subsequently published, the latter was reaffirmed at La Rochelle without change.

The structure and the content of the confession are very similar to Calvin's Confession (1537) and the *Geneva Catechism,* except for the first five articles (added by the synod), which present a scholastic definition of *God* (arts. 1–2) and a section on *scripture* (arts. 3–5). In addition, the confession attests the creating and preserving activity of the triune God (arts. 6–8); the disabling corruption of an originally pure human race (arts. 9–11); God's decision to call some to himself (art. 12); the incarnate Christ's redeeming work, which restores righteousness and eternal life to fallen *humanity* (arts. 13–14); *justification* through *faith* alone in God's free promises, which faith is engendered by the secret, regenerating work of the Spirit (arts. 18–22); Christ as the end of the *law* and only mediator (arts. 23–24); that the true *church* exists only where right *preaching* and proper administration of the *sacraments* is found (arts. 25–28); that it will be governed by pastors, *elders,* and *deacons* who have a true calling; that all pastors have equal *authority* and that all is done under Christ's authority and in subjection to one another (arts. 29–33); that the *sacraments* are two, are aids to faith and external signs of an inward *grace* that, through faith, unites us to Christ (arts. 34–38); and that God, having set up kingdoms and governments, would have us obey them, even if administered by unbelievers (arts. 39–40).

The confession was adhered to through seventeenth-century doctrinal disputes and "the church of the desert" of the eighteenth century, until a major revision (1872), which divided the French church into liberal and conservative factions.

A. C. Cochrane, ed., *Reformed Confessions of the 16th Century* (1966); H. Jahr, *Studien zur Überlieferungsgeschichte der Confession de foi von 1559* (1964); J. Pannier, *Les origines de la confession de la foi* (1936).

BRIAN G. ARMSTRONG

General Assembly The General Assembly (sometimes National Synod or Synod) is the highest governing body of Reformed denominations in a system of church government that traditionally consists of four levels of representative church courts—sessions (consistories), *presbyteries* (colloquies or classes), *synods* (provincial synods), and general assemblies (national synods). The system of ascending church governing bodies, characteristic of Reformed *polity*, combines the principles of local freedom and central unity. The French Reformed Church organized the first National Synod (1559) and adopted a book of *discipline* that laid the foundation for a more fully developed Presbyterianism than established by John Calvin in Geneva. The Scottish Kirk formed a General Assembly (1560), and other continental Reformed churches subsequently created similar provincial or national governing bodies. In 1789, the Presbyterian Church in the U.S.A., consisting of four synods and sixteen presbyteries, convened its first General Assembly in Philadelphia, with John Witherspoon as Moderator.

General Assemblies usually meet annually, with representatives being cler-ical and lay commissioners from each presbytery, the total number of which is proportional to the membership of the governing body. Although commissioners represent specific presbyteries, they are not instructed how to vote. A moderator who presides over the Assembly is elected for a one-year term. The chief executive officer of the General Assembly, the Stated Clerk, is elected for a designated term and eligible for reappointment. As the highest representative body in the Reformed system of government, the Assembly has authority to set denominational policies and supervise operations of various church boards and agencies. It also oversees and reviews decisions of lower governing bodies, which in turn overture or appeal to the General Assembly. The Assembly, however, has limited, defined, and delegated powers subject to the authority of the Constitution of the church. Changes in the Constitution and amendments to confessional standards can be implemented only after an affirmative vote (usually two-thirds) by presbyteries.

Among Reformed denominations, the precise authority of General Assemblies varied, often according to the historical circumstances under which they were constituted. In Scotland, where the Parliament officially adopted Presbyterianism and created the Assembly before lower governing bodies were established, the General Assembly has functioned with considerable autonomy. The moderatorial nominee is selected by a committee in advance of the annual meeting and after his or her year of service becomes a continuing member of the Assembly. Meetings are always held in Edinburgh and attended by representatives of the British monarchy. In the United States, where the lower governing bodies (presbyteries and synods) created the General Assembly, moderatorial candidates are nominated by presbyteries and the moderator is elected by the Assembly. Moderators do not become permanent commissioners, and annual meetings vary in location to acknowledge different regions of the national church. The American Reformed tradition has also emphasized the concept that undelegated powers remain in the presbyteries and not in the General Assemblies.

R. DOUGLAS BRACKENRIDGE

Geneva Catechism

Geneva Catechism   During his first Genevan period (1536), John Calvin prepared a short *catechism* to provide Christian instruction for the young and to secure greater unity in the Reformed faith. After his reluctant but dutiful return from a happy exile in Strassburg, he rewrote and expanded it.

In his introduction, Calvin mentions the universal concern that children be taught the basic *doctrines* of the Christian faith, done in former and better times by catechisms. Doubtless, he says, a single catechism for all the churches is desirable, but for many reasons each church is likely to use its own. This variety is acceptable to the extent "that we are all directed to the one Christ, by whose truth, if we be united in it, we may grow together into one body and one spirit, and with one mouth also proclaim whatever belongs to the sum of the faith" (Reid, 89).

The Geneva Catechism is divided into four (sometimes five) parts: the first, concerning *faith*, explains the Apostles' Creed; the second, concerning the *law*, deals with the Ten Commandments; the third, concerning *prayer*, expounds the Lord's Prayer. If the *Word of God* is considered the fourth division, then the fifth concerns the *sacraments.* Otherwise the sacraments are the fourth subject, with Calvin's exposition of the Word of God forming an introduction to them.

K. Barth, *The Faith of the Church: A Commentary on the Apostles' Creed according to Calvin's Catechism* (1958); I. J. Hesselink, *Calvin's First Catechism: A Commentary* (1997); J. K. S. Reid, trans., *Calvin: Theological Treatises* (1954), 83–139.

CHARLES PARTEE

God

God   The *doctrine* of God is the beginning of the early *creeds*, the foundation for all that follows. In the Reformed *confessions*, it is first in some, and follows immediately upon the issue of the source of our *knowledge of God* in some or our desperate need for God in others. Since it is so basic, one could incorporate much of Christian doctrine into this single issue. However, the doctrine of God has traditionally been subdivided into several others, including the Trinitarian nature of God, the *incarnation* of the Second Person of the *Trinity*, and the works of God in *creation, providence*, and redemption.

In the following sections, the specific issues of the understanding of God's oneness and attributes in the Reformed tradition will be discussed.

Background. Perhaps in this doctrine more than in almost any other, the Protestant *tradition* in general and the Reformed tradition in particular were dependent on the Hebrew tradition. The monotheistic belief was undeniable for Christians and had been maintained continuously. God is one; there is no other. Further, this God is the creator of all that is, not subject to preexistent matter or conditions. God is the ruler of all—the Almighty. Nothing is outside God's governance. This is the first and essential confession of faith.

The late-medieval period, immediately preceding the Reformation, had seen great interest in the nature of God. Was God to be thought of primarily as will, whose actions determined what was right and wrong rather than being subject to criteria external to the will of God? Was God to be thought of as supremely good and wise, whose goodness and wisdom were reflected, however dimly, in human understandings of goodness and wisdom? The Reformation discussions are best seen as continuations of this earlier debate. However, they were not a mere continuation. Particularly in Martin Luther, the issue of God's power was placed in the context of God's gracious love. The development of the Reformed tradition must be seen in this setting.

Huldrych Zwingli. The earliest representative of the Reformed tradition is Zwingli, who was far less dependent on Luther's work than later Calvin would be. Zwingli's reform began in Zurich (early 1519). Radical reform was in the air but was not yet very clearly defined. The Diet of Worms had not yet taken place; Luther's great treatises had not yet been written. Zwingli's work had different roots and outcomes from Luther's. G. W. Locher has written: "[B]oth reformers were awakened to their task through fear of the *judgment.* With Luther, this meant fear of being punished in *hell* for his sins; whereas with Zwingli, it was fear that the curse of God must fall upon Christendom, divided and betraying its Lord in bloody wars."

Zwingli is very important for the development of the Reformed understanding of God. For him, the holiness and majesty of God were paramount and were seen also in the Lordship of Christ. His basic concern was not *salvation* per se but the question of a holy God who chose a people and expected them to live under God's rule. *Sin* was real, and *forgiveness* was the gracious message of the gospel. Yet this *grace* should not be so interpreted that it lessened the need for holiness in God's people.

Zwingli shows clearly the tension always present in the Reformed understanding of God: between God's holiness and majesty on the one hand, and God's grace and love on the other. These cannot be arranged in a chronological order, that first we must know the holiness which puts us under judgment in order then to experience the grace that overcomes judgment. For the Reformed tradition, God's holiness and grace cannot in any way be played off against each other. Grace is to lead us to true holiness. Holiness has as its content not only *piety* but lives dedicated to living as God intends us to live, both as individuals and as a community.

Further, the incarnation tells us of God's nearness to us. But the astonishing majesty of God cannot be overlooked or made irrelevant by the incarnation. Not even in the Second Person can the divine majesty be overshadowed by *humanity.* God is One, Holy, Creator, Redeemer. Creatures are to *worship,* obey, and honor this One. Human rulers pale in comparison. *Idolatry* is the chief sin, for it denies this ultimate claim and results in disobedience. God is sovereign; there is nothing out of God's control and providence. From this the doctrines of divine *election* and *predestination* readily flow and are understood by Zwingli as directly derived from God's sovereignty over all creation.

Following Zwingli's death (1529), Heinrich Bullinger became leader of the Zurich church. His last confession of faith, put into the form of the *Second Helvetic Confession* (1566), stresses these elements: "We believe and teach that God is one in essence or nature, subsisting in himself, all sufficient in himself, invisible, incorporeal, immense, eternal, Creator of all things both visible and invisible, the greatest good, living, quickening and preserving all things, omnipotent and supremely wise, kind and merciful, just and true" (3.1).

John Calvin. Calvin is a second-generation reformer, building on the work of Zwingli, Luther, Bullinger, and many others. On the doctrine of God, he was strongly influenced by Luther, holding firmly to the primacy of grace, the astonishing act of the sovereign God who deigns to come among us with forgiveness and love. Yet this still must be placed within the framework that Zwingli provided: God's grace is for holiness; God's concern is for the creation of a holy and just people, visible as such in the world; God's love and condescension cannot be seen as lessening the awesome majesty of this One who by election and grace will create such a people. In Calvin, because of Luther's influence, there is a clear alteration, a softening of what can appear as harshness in Zwingli. However, it is not a compromise between the two positions; it is, rather, a new and creative structure that takes into account the emphases of both. In some of his writings, Zwingli has a more philosophical and speculative interest that also increases the starkness of his doctrine of God, particularly in the emphasis on God's sovereignty that governs all things. Calvin is less speculative and more concerned to interpret God's sovereignty in ways that leave room for secondary causes, including human wills.

By the end of the sixteenth century, when the Reformed tradition was increasingly delineated from both the Roman Catholic and the Lutheran traditions, the distinctive emphases would be in place: God's sovereignty, which governs all things; God's grace, which allows the faithful to trust that God's sovereign will works for our good; and *sanctification* as the goal of God's redemptive work in us, since we are to mirror God's holiness, both as individuals and as the community.

Calvinist scholasticism. The seventeenth century saw the development of detailed theological systems within confessional Protestantism, incorporating the use of Aristotelian logic and deducing the systems from scriptural statements. Within *Calvinism,* the results of this orthodoxy are recognized in various theologians and some confessional statements. For English-speaking Reformed churches, the classical formulation of this period is to be found in the *WCF.* In it, one finds the doctrine of God as the second chapter, immediately following the opening section on *scripture* as the source of all human knowledge of God and of God's will and intention.

In the doctrine of God, the attributes of sovereignty and righteousness of God are very strong, and the chapter leads immediately into the doctrine of election (WCF, ch. 3). The structure is more that of Zwingli than Calvin, and the softening aspects of sheer astonishment at the grace and love of such a God toward us are therefore far less than in Calvin. Yet the confession clearly maintains the reality of created wills and secondary causes, thus limiting the direct determination of all

things by God, as was more Zwingli's tendency. One needs to see the controversy around Arminius at least partly as a reaction to this stress on the sovereignty of God that appeared to lessen the gracious love, especially as manifested in the increasing prominence of the doctrine of predestination as directly derived from God's sovereign *omnipotence.*

Eighteenth century. The tension between the scholastic stress on the sovereignty of God and emphasis on the experience of God's graciousness—held together by Calvin—could not bear the strain under the pressure of the evangelical revivals of the eighteenth century. Particularly in the British colonies in America, and later in the young nation, the stress on the *experience* of God's gracious, forgiving love would become dominant and the orthodox stress on God's sovereign election would be challenged by an increasing *Arminianism* that fit the experience of surrendering to God's grace in the revivals. Jonathan Edwards was the major theologian who held together traditional emphasis on God's sovereignty seen in election and revivalist experiences of *conversion.* Others could not do so, and the splits in churches such as the Presbyterian—between New Lights and Old Lights, New Side and Old Side—institutionalized this division for decades.

These divisions—between the older scholastic forms of Calvinism and new, pietistic or evangelical forms—continued well into the nineteenth and twentieth centuries. The ongoing power of scholastic Calvinism is seen in the writings of Charles Hodge and the *Princeton Theology.* Especially in the United States and in churches founded through its missions, those who emphasized the conversion experience by God's grace vied with those who continued the orthodox emphasis on God's sovereignty. Both would maintain the traditional stress on God's holiness and the counterpart of human sanctification.

Nineteenth and twentieth centuries. There have been two very important systematic formulations of the Reformed tradition in the nineteenth and twentieth centuries. Both seek to retain the tension, present in Calvin, between God's character as absolute sovereign and God's gracious love, within the context of God's holiness. The first is that of Friedrich Schleiermacher; the second, that of Karl Barth. Both rejected the orthodox tendency to emphasize sovereignty or holiness at the expense of graciousness.

The structure of Schleiermacher's theology assumes the absolute dependence of the whole creation on the One who created it. Faith is the human creature's response to this One who is the Sovereign of all. This clearly parallels the traditional beginning point in Reformed dogmatics. In structuring his system in *The Christian Faith* (1821–22), however, Schleiermacher divides the experience of faith between consciousness of sin and consciousness of grace. The attributes of God paralleling the first are God's holiness and *justice*; those paralleling the second are God's love and wisdom. Both consciousness of sin and consciousness of grace continue in the person of faith, though the sense of guilt is always overcome by the sense of grace. The balance has returned, though in a form quite different from in Calvin. These attributes of God—holiness and love—are equally stressed in the human experience of *regeneration* and sanctification—where we see the Reformed emphases. In a unique and powerful way, Schleiermacher blends concern for the sovereignty of God and human appropriation of God's graciousness. Not accidentally, Schleiermacher places the doctrine of election within the experience of God's graciousness, as in Calvin, in contrast to being an aspect of God's sovereignty, as in Zwingli and Calvinist orthodoxy.

Barth long argued with Schleiermacher on both the method and the content of theology. But there are parallels in Barth's concern to preserve in balance the sovereign character of God, as the first and unalterable statement of theology, and the graciousness of God, which raises up to unimagined heights the human creature who has no claim upon such a creator. Barth also emphasizes sanctification as the goal of God's grace and states the Reformed tradition in a way that bypasses the harshness of orthodoxy on the doctrine of God. Though he stresses as unambiguously as possible human dependence on God's revelation and the sovereignty this dependence involves, the content of that *revelation* is gracious. Always the initiative is with God. Always the "yes" of God's graciousness involves a "no" against human waywardness. judgment is inevitable. Redemption is only because of God's initiative, not human choice. God's election is the election of Jesus Christ, in whom is found the new creation. Barth's understanding of God, combining graciousness and sovereignty, has led to his being accused of holding to universal salvation—a rare charge indeed against a Reformed theologian, and one he denied affirming explicitly.

Conclusions. Within the Reformed tradition, the doctrine of God tries to hold in balance the sovereignty of God, the holiness of God, and the gracious love of God. Where the balance is lost, historically it has usually been the graciousness that has received less emphasis. It would be difficult to recognize as authentically Reformed any doctrine of God that compromised the sovereign omnipotence of God, or lessened the emphasis of God's holiness, with the corresponding requirement of human sanctification. In the creative and comprehensive systems that have emerged in the Reformed tradition—notably in Calvin, Schleiermacher, and Barth—all three of these characteristics have been central to the systems, and God's love and grace have not been minimized. In lesser hands, the limitation of God's love often appears to be the simplest solution to combining sovereignty, holiness, and love. The strength of the tradition is that it clearly prevents a view of God as one who readily fulfills human wishes or one who fails to take sin with utmost seriousness and makes no demands. In much of contemporary church life, that in itself is a great contribution.

K. Barth, *CD* II; H. Bavinck, *The Doctrine of God* (ET 1951); D. G. Bloesch, *God the Almighty* (1995); J. O. Duke and R. F. Streetman, eds., *Barth and Schleiermacher: Beyond the Impasse?* (1988); Heppe, *RD*; G. W. Locher, *Zwingli's Thought* (1981); J. Rohls, *Reformed Confessions* (1999); W. P. Stephens, *The Theology of Huldrych Zwingli* (1986).

CATHERINE GUNSALUS GONZALEZ

Government, Church   *see* Polity

Government, Civil John Calvin's understandings of *church* and state took practical shape through his leadership of the Genevan church in relation to the city's governing body, the Council. The church and the Council were separate bodies and their duties did not ordinarily overlap. Together, Calvin held, church and state are responsible for fashioning a society where *justice* is done, where works of compassion are carried out, where the poor are maintained, and where civil stability allows citizens to live in peace. The Company of Pastors existed separately and it generally saw to the ordering of the church's life in the *ordination* and calling of pastors, catechetical instruction, and the like. The city's Small Council, which oversaw daily civic life, had no pastors as members, though it was occasionally visited by a pastor delegated to bring some matter to its attention. This separation of spheres of oversight between the Company of Pastors and the Small Council clearly illustrates the separation Calvin enjoined in the *Institutes.*

Cooperation took place through the Consistory. All Genevan pastors belonged to it as well as (theoretically) did those in the countryside under the city's control, though country ministers did not often attend meetings. A number of lay *elders* commissioned by the Council were members. The Consistory was moderated by one of the Council's four syndics (governing magistrates) elected yearly by the citizenry. Here issues of church and state sometimes became confused, such as when adulterers were admonished or excommunicated by the Consistory and then sent to the Council for sentencing—perhaps on bread and water for a few days in addition to an obligatory appearance before the worshiping congregation.

This "mixing of magistracy," which Calvin deplored but tended in practical moral matters to insist on, gave Reformed churches a reputation as meddlers in magistracy. This was the charge for which Calvin was discharged from his Genevan pastorate and exiled (1538). All the Protestant Reformers believed that "a government will use every effort that the pure Word of God be faithfully proclaimed" (First Helvetic Confession, 1536), that the church and its ministers should be maintained, and that both church and state cooperate in diaconal and educational matters.

The charge that Calvin was a "theocrat" or "clerocrat"—both terms used to describe a clergy-dominated political order—are not well founded. More accurately, in Geneva Calvin was able to imbue civic leaders with moral energy to perform their political work as "vicars and lieutenants of God" (Geneva Confession of Faith, 1537).

When Reformed churches were established in less friendly lands, insistence on obedience to the magistrate was maintained in *confessions of faith,* except where obedience meant disobedience to **God.** The **French Confession** (1559), written when many had suffered at the hands of the government, still contended that magistrates should "suppress crimes against the first as well as the second table of the Commandments of God." So, though a minority faith, the Reformed insisted (still living in the "shadow of Constantine"!) that government maintain the church and use the temporal sword to punish offenders against religion. Calvin's own insistence on obedience to rulers as God's servants was so complete that his counsel in the last chapter of the *Institutes* (4.20) gave persecuted Protestants almost no redress. They could neither rebel, nor participate in Roman Catholic *worship,* nor blame anyone else for their sad estate. It was God's punishment for their sins that placed such bad rulers over them.

The *Scots Confession* (1560) summarized Reformed churches' teachings on the role of government (*BC* 3.24): Governments are appointed and ordained by God and are to serve "for the good and well being" of all. Those who rebel against duly established civil powers are both enemies to *humanity* and rebels against God's will. Those in authority are lieutenants of God who use the sword for the defense of the good and the punishment of evildoers. Such magistrates, whether kings or city magistrates, are appointed also to maintain true religion and suppress all religion that is idolatrous. David, Josiah, and others are examples. There is only a hint that rulers might be resisted in the oblique statement that no rebellion is allowable "so long as princes and rulers vigilantly fulfill their office." No doubt Calvin's admonition that such rebellion must be led by notable persons and only after grave provocation (*Inst.* 4.20.31) was being followed in this and all other sixteenth-century Reformed confessional statements.

Why then do historians call the Reformed branch of the Reformation the "revolutionary" branch? Why was it the Reformed who contributed to the revolt of the Netherlands against Spain, to the internal wars of religion in France, to the Puritan revolt against Charles I in England, and who were the New England leaders in the revolt against England? There are at least two reasons. First, there is a strong *doctrine* of lay empowerment in the Reformed understanding of the role of leadership. This led minor civic and regional leaders to assume strong opposition roles when it appeared that heredi-tary rulers were not ruling well. For example, John Knox's friend James Stewart, later the Earl of Moray, bastard son of James V of Scotland, opposed his half-sister's mother and regent, Mary of Guise, on just such grounds and was supported in this by Knox and other ministers.

Second, while rebellion was almost unthinkable for Calvin, his high standards and expectations of rulers produced a nonquietistic relationship to government that contrasted with the subservient attitude inculcated in Luther's laity or in the clear Erastian position of Anglicans. The smaller sectarian Protestants, on the other hand, took almost no interest in political rulers— provided they were left to practice their *faith* in peace.

Finally, it should be noted that, with the exception of Huldrych Zwingli, all the great Reformed thinkers believed rulers were subject to the church in spiritual matters. The Second Book of Discipline (1578) of the Scots Kirk said, "As ministers and others of the ecclesiastical estate are subject to the civil magistrate, so also the person of the magistrate is subject to the kirk spiritually and in ecclesiastical government." This was not the same as Pope Gregory VII's claim that all rule resided in Christ's earthly vicar. But in a world where magistrates owned church properties and many of the boundaries between church and state to which we are accustomed did not exist, this was certain to exacerbate church-state tensions. In Scotland and England these aggravations grew, until the Reformed contribution to theories of political revolution may have been as great as the "rights of man" doctrines usually ascribed to the great revolutions at the end of the eighteenth century. Undoubtedly, the Reformed contributed to these theories.

E. Busch, "Church and Politics in the Reformed Tradition," in D. K. McKim, ed., *Major Themes in the Reformed Tradition* (repr. 1998), 180–95; W. F. Graham, *The Constructive Revolutionary* (1971); H. Höpfl, *The*

Christian Polity of John Calvin (1982); J. T. McNeill, ed., *On God and Political Duty,* 2nd ed. (1956); J. Rohls, *Reformed Confessions* (1999); W. R. Stevenson, Jr., *Sovereign Grace: The Place and Siginficance of Christian Freedom in John Calvin's Political Thought* (1999).

W. FRED GRAHAM

Grace   Most broadly, "grace" describes both the nature of the triune *God,* who is revealed in Jesus Christ as the sovereign Lord of all *creation* and thus God's activity in the world, and also what happens to the lives of those who receive God's grace—those called into God's *covenant,* who are baptized into the *death* and *resurrection* of Jesus Christ. Baptized people are, by the grace of God, a "new creation," and grace describes how they come to life in Christ as well as the process whereby they are becoming a new creation in him. In the grammar of Christian theology, it is appropriate to speak both of "the grace of God" and "the Christian life of grace." The experiential reality of the latter is rooted in the ontological reality of the former. Grace, therefore, describes the human *experience* of God's free, gratuitous, salvific activity.

The grace of God is at the heart and center of most Christian theologies, including the Reformed tradition. Because grace is a thread running through the whole fabric of Christian theology, it is not always clearly defined and often appears not as a single theological topic but as an implicit presupposition in several, if not all, doctrines.

History of Christian thought. Though the Greek word *charis* ("grace") is found frequently in the NT, it appears twice as often in the Pauline letters as in the rest of the NT. Paul writes frequently of the "grace of our God and the Lord Jesus Christ" (2 Thess. 1:12). For Paul, God's grace is God's special favor made known to the world in Jesus Christ. He sees God's grace made visible and tangible in the person of Jesus. It is not surprising, therefore, that Paul often closes his letters with words similar to these: "The grace of the

Lord Jesus Christ, the love of God, and the communion of the Holy Spirit be with all of you" (2 Cor. 13:13). Jesus Christ is God's grace for the world because he is Emmanuel—"God with us."

When the *church* has faced practical and theological issues similar to those which Paul confronted, it has returned to Paul's emphasis on God's grace. His distinction between the righteousness of the *law* and the righteousness of *faith* is based on his understanding of the nature of God's grace. Consequently, when the church has encountered those who emphasize the human capacity for goodness (and thus minimize the radical nature of human *sin*), it has often been the Pauline theme of God's grace and God's grace alone that has been the basis of its response.

Four church history events illustrate the centrality of God's grace for the understanding and proclamation of the gospel. The first was the dispute between the British monk Pelagius and *Augustine,* bishop of Hippo in the early fifth century. Pelagius apparently argued that God would not have commanded humans to do something not possible for them to do. Hence, every person must have some capacity to choose good and evil, even after Adam's sin. In response, Augustine developed a *doctrine* of *original sin,* which stated that sin is not simply a perverse act but also a state and condition into which all people are born. Humans are free, therefore, only to sin and by themselves can do nothing righteous. Nevertheless, they are responsible for the sin and deserve only God's *judgment* and wrath. Their only *hope* is God's grace, which clothes them in the righteousness of Christ.

A second event was the sixteenth-century Protestant Reformation. In Paul's letters to the Romans and the Galatians, the Augustinian monk Martin Luther discovered the true meaning of Christian *freedom* for a soul tormented by the demands of God's law and a corrupt church that seemed to have turned its back on the gospel. Deeply dependent on

Augustine and Luther, John Calvin also found God's grace to be the basis for the Christian life and the doctrine of *justification*, which he described as "the main hinge on which religion turns."

A third event was the debate between the followers of Jacob Arminius and other theologians of the Dutch Reformed Church in the early seventeenth century. Arminius and his followers rejected the notion that God saves some people and damns others, that Christ died only for the elect and not for the world, and that grace is irresistible. *Arminians* did not deny that God's grace was necessary so a person could be saved, but they described that grace as an "assisting" grace. The *Synod of Dort* (1618–19) declared that all people are conceived in sin and are children of wrath, "incapable of any saving good." God, however, "graciously softens the hearts of the elect . . . and inclines them to believe." But faith is not a human act God assists; rather, God "works in man both to will and to do, and indeed all things in all, produces both the will to believe and the act of believing also."

Finally, in Germany (1930s), a small group of Christians known as the Confessing Church rejected the claim by some "German Christians" that the life and history of the German people was a *revelation* of God's Word and, consequently, that there were areas of human life where the *authority* of the state superseded that of the church. In the *Theological Declaration of Barmen* (1934), the Confessing Church declared there are not many voices in life to which Christians must listen. Rather, "Jesus Christ, as he is attested for us in Holy Scripture, is the one Word of God which we have to hear and which we have to trust and obey in life and in death" (*BC*, 8.11). The freedom of the church "consists in delivering the message of the free grace of God to all people in Christ's stead" (*BC*, 8.26).

Grace of God. In most forms of *Reformed theology*, God's grace is understood as the foundation for all things. As Calvin put it, "We make the freely given

promise of God the foundation of faith because upon it faith properly rests. . . . Faith properly begins with the promise, rests in it, and ends in it" (*Inst.* 3.2.29). Calvin describes God's grace as "the divine benevolence." Literally, God's grace, for Calvin, is God's good will made known in Jesus Christ. This strong sense of God's good will at work in individual lives and in the affairs of nations is the basis of Calvin's doctrine of *election* and his claim that goodness, wherever found, can be understood only as a gift of God's sovereign grace. The *WCF* also interprets God's grace in terms of God's sovereign will, because God works "all things according to the counsel of his own immutable and most righteous will"(WCF, 2.1).

In contemporary Reformed theology, God's grace is understood not primarily as God's sovereign will but as God's suffering and sovereign love. The *Confession of 1967* does not describe the grace of our Lord Jesus Christ in terms of God's "immutable and most righteous will," as does the WCF, but in terms of "God's sovereign love." The *Brief Statement of Faith* declares that God created the world good "in sovereign love."

Christian life of grace. According to Calvin, those who partake of Jesus Christ, and by means of the power of the *Holy Spirit* have their life in him, "receive a double grace: namely, that being reconciled to God through Christ's blamelessness, we may have in *heaven* instead of a Judge a gracious Father; and secondly, that sanctified by Christ's spirit we may cultivate blamelessness and purity of life" (*Inst.* 3.11.1). The significance of that statement for the Reformed tradition is threefold. First, Reformed theology since Calvin has understood the whole of the Christian life (both justification and *sanctification*) to be a gift of God's grace in Jesus Christ. Second, there is no human goodness apart from God's grace; hence, all people are caught in a web of sin and estrangement from which they cannot extricate themselves. They live utterly in dependence on God's grace. Finally, the grace of God that saves them from their sin also compels those who live in Christ to express their gratitude to God in *worship*, thanksgiving, and service in the world. Reformed Christians understand the grace of God to be that which frees them to witness to God in the world and participate in God's transformation of it.

GEORGE W. STROUP

Half-Way Covenant   A modification of church membership requirements in seventeenth-century New England Puritanism. By 1636, Massachusetts Puritans had adopted the principle that only those persons who could testify to a *conversion* experience would be admitted as church members. These "visible saints" were eligible for *baptism* and admission to the *Lord's Supper* and had the right to vote in church matters.

Their children could also be baptized. But a problem arose when these children found themselves unable to narrate a conversion experience. They could not qualify for full membership, and sought baptism for their own children. The compromise, known as the Half-Way Covenant, allowed baptism of children of baptized but not fully confirmed parents if they acknowledged the *discipline* of the *church.* Neither the parents nor the children were allowed to partake of the Lord's Supper.

The compromise was forged in two actions (1657, 1662) by ministers attempting to solve a pastoral problem. But in practice it was opposed by conservative laity. As late as the 1730s, some churches refused to implement the policy, and it arose again as a controversy during the First Great Awakening.

E. S. Morgan, *Visible Saints* (1963); R. S. Pope, *The Half-Way Covenant* (1969).

JOHN M. MULDER

Healing Ministry   Healing was a prominent part of Jesus' ministry. He cured the sick in mind and body through a combination of divine power and natural means. The early church continued to heal in the name and power of Christ, through charisms of healing (1 Cor. 12) and/or sacramental ministry (James 5). After Augustine's time, manifestations of divine healing power were no longer expected except at shrines or through the saints. The rite of anointing the sick became "extreme unction" for the dying. Bodily suffering was to be patiently endured and healing ministry transmuted into the "cure of souls," focusing on relationship with *God.* The Reformed inherited these approaches. In Calvin's Geneva there was Christian care for the sick and pastoral cure of souls. The "visible grace" of healing gifts seemed to be inactive. Bodily healing came through medical interventions or, rarely, by special *providence* of God.

The split of healing ministry into medical care (physical) and *pastoral care* (spiritual) continued into the twentieth century. The dominant Reformed attitude is seen in "Of the Visitation of the Sick" in the Directories for Worship of the Presbyterian Church (1789–1960). Sickness was clearly the harbinger of *death.* It was time for the sick to improve their relationship with God, examine their *consciences,* repent, and receive *forgiveness* along with comforting words of *scripture* and *prayer* to sustain them in their affliction.

A more holistic ministry to the sick person has been advocated in this century through movements such as clinical pastoral education and individuals such as Paul Tournier and Granger Westberg. Charismatic gifts of healing were revived by Pentecostal groups and individuals such as Agnes Sanford. Alfred Price and the ecumenical Order of St. Luke restored services for healing to many churches.

The shift in Presbyterian thinking is reflected in the UPCUSA "Report on Relation of Christian Faith to Health" (1960). A whole person approach to health, sickness, and healing was embraced. A modern theology of healing ministry was sketched: (1) All healing is from God; (2) illness is an evil to be overcome; (3) *faith* is its own reward, not a means to an end; (4) prayer is efficacious for healing; (5) God has many therapies; and (6) human mortality points us to our relationship with God. Practical suggestions for *ministry* to the sick were outlined for pastors, church members, and physicians. A medical/pastoral team approach to healing was advocated, and fruits of psychological research were incorporated in a holistic understanding of pastoral ministry. Presbyterian Directory for Worship instructions for ministry to the sick changed to conform to these new views of ministry to the whole person, first after the merger to form the UPCUSA in 1958, then after the reunion to form the PC(USA) in 1983. The 1990 Directory includes a section on "Services for Wholeness." Increasingly, clergy and laypersons of the Reformed tradition are actively involved in either charismatic or liturgical forms of healing ministry today.

M. T. Kelsey, *Psychology, Medicine, and Christian Healing* (1988); Presbyterian Directories for Worship (compare pre-1958 with 1970s and 1990).

BARBARA A. PURSEY

Health and Medicine

Beliefs and values shape the understandings and decisions that individuals make regarding their sexuality, birth, suffering, *death,* health, sanity, and many other matters of bodily and mental life. Religious heritage and present *faith,* a primary source of beliefs and values, thus give rise to and sustain personal and communal commitments here. The Reformed tradition has been a powerful source of such individual and social values.

The sovereignty of *God,* the reality of *sin* and *forgiveness,* the *grace* of Christ, the gift and responsibility of life, the imperative to love and *justice,* and the Lordship of God over nature, history, and human destiny are themes that animate belief and value in the Reformed faith.

As the creating, sustaining, and consummating Being, God gives life, safeguards well-being, and receives death. Recognizing this dependence yields dispositions of respect, *stewardship,* and ultimate acquiescence to God's will as individuals live their lives, generate families, experience illness, and face death. Redeeming purpose and *providence* are qualities of God's character that imprint one's existence. To succeed in life is to discern and accede to that plan and goodwill. Virtue or health is to advance that kingdom in all of one's action. In concerns of health and medicine, the *doctrine* of sovereignty has generated throughout *history* a curious blend of scientific and technical efforts to ameliorate the human condition and its ills and serene resignation in the face of deleterious forces, all the while confident of overriding purpose.

The Puritan ethic, for example, a cultural phenomenon in part created by Reformed faith, first articulated and propelled the medical value of prolonging life. At the same time, it developed a most exquisite theology of death anticipation, even celebration.

The Lordship of God places parental and regal expectation on God's children, which expectation they have forsaken and from which possibility they have fallen short. By violating our designed nature and intended destiny, we have sullied our native well-being. Sin allows disease to fester in our being, alienation to scar our emotional and relational lives, and death to cloud the horizon of our future. The drama of sin and grace punctuates our being most poignantly in disease and health.

"What is your only comfort, in life and in death? . . . My faithful Savior, Jesus Christ" (HC, q. 1). With these words, a second motif of the Reformed faith bearing on health and disease is expressed. The grace of Christ overwhelms our boundedness to sin and death and renders possible the righteousness or health (*salvation*) of God. In Christ we are heirs to the grace of life—which is health, love, marriage, progeny, longevity, and the good *conscience* of his service.

These existential doctrines of *creation,* fall, and redemption, especially given the tenor they develop within Calvinist history, activate a high sense of responsibility for life, health, and general welfare. Along with Jewish, Catholic, Lutheran, and Anglican communions, Presbyterians and Baptists found hospitals, medical schools and clinics, and send sons and daughters into the ministries of physical, mental, and spiritual health. Commitment is also inspired within this community to social justice as equity. Concern for the disadvantaged and charity are encouraged.

Finally, the Reformed faith proclaims God as the beginning, the center, and the end of our existence. We die, not to oblivion, but to God's presence. Death is the announcement that our work is done; we have completed our earth-side *ministry.* Though fighting disease and premature death is noble, our faith asks us to receive death as if we are entering a new life established by God who is faithful. As with Judaism, Reformed Christians honor life, health, the body, and longevity. In Christ we also receive pain, suffering, and death as the Lord's chastening, cleansing, and culminating will.

J. H. Smylie, "The Reformed Tradition, Health and Healing," in *Health Care and Its Costs,* ed. W. Wiest (1988); K. Vaux, *Health and Medicine in the Reformed Tradition* (1984).

KENNETH VAUX

Heaven

Heaven in Reformed understanding is a definite place. As *God* is creator of "all things visible and invisible," so heaven is the invisible portion of *creation,* that which is inaccessible to human beings. Heaven is God's dwelling place within creation, the seat of the divine rule, that place in the created order where God's will is done. Because heaven is part of creation, however, God's presence transcends it; even the highest heavens cannot contain God. Heaven is also the dwelling place of God's "ministering spirits" (angels), the souls of the faithful departed, and the place from which the ascended Christ rules at the right hand of God.

The Reformed tradition consistently affirms that the souls of the faithful departed enter immediately into heaven to be with Christ. John Calvin wrote his first major theological work, the *Psychopannychia* (1534), against the Anabaptist belief that the soul at *death* enters into a state of unconscious slumber awaiting the final *resurrection.* In contrast to the Roman Catholic *doctrine* of purgatory, the Reformed affirm that departed souls enter immediately into a state of heavenly bliss, though this bliss is perfected and consummated only at the final resurrection, when souls will be reunited with their glorified bodies.

The bliss of souls in heaven is frequently associated with a final sabbath rest (cf. Heb. 4), though such rest is generally understood not as cessation from activity so much as relief from earthly burdens and afflictions and fullness of joy in the presence of God. The final resurrection will also be accompanied by establishment of the kingdom of heaven on earth. *Reformed theology* tends to view this establishment as restoration rather than replacement of the world as we now know it.

Separation of heaven from earth is an important theme in the Reformed polemic against *idolatry.* Because God's dwelling is a place apart, we are prevented from associating God with any earthly likeness or image. The separateness of heaven also figured prominently in debates with Lutherans over the presence of Christ's body in the *Eucharist.* Against the Lutheran doctrine of the *ubiquity* of Christ's body, the Reformed assert that Christ's human flesh remains in heaven, spatially removed from the sacramental elements.

Heaven also plays a central role in Reformed *piety.* Constant meditation upon the heavenly life to come frees believers from enslaving attachments to earthly things, helps them recognize thankfully the foretastes of divine glory given in this life, teaches them patiently to bear adversity, frees them from an immoderate fear of death, and spurs them to a life of *faith* and obedience. If this vision of the heavenly life "be taken away," says Calvin, "either our minds must become despondent or, to our destruction, be captivated with the empty solace of this world" (*Inst.* 3.9).

J. Baillie, *And the Life Everlasting* (1948); Barth, *CD* III/3, 369–76; H. Bavinck, *The Last Things,* (ET 1996); R. Baxter, *The Saints' Everlasting Rest* (1650).

P. MARK ACHTEMEIER

Heidelberg Catechism The catechism was occasioned by disputes among strict and moderate (followers of Philipp Melanchthon) Lutherans, Zwinglians, and Calvinists in the Palatinate (1550s), whose capital was Heidelberg. Elector Frederick III, the first German prince to accept the Reformed faith, commissioned Zacharias Ursinus and Caspar Olevianus, Reformed professors of theology at the University of Heidelberg, to write a standard of *doctrine* to bring peace and unite the regional churches. The work of these young second-generation reformers (both in their twenties) was adopted as a *confession of faith,* a guide to pastors and teachers, and a manual for the instruction of youth (1563). It became one of the most widely accepted and used of all confessional statements in Reformed churches throughout the world.

The catechism begins with two introductory questions announcing the three-part outline that follows the order of Paul's letter to the Romans. Part I (qq. 3–11) broadly describes human *sin* and misery. Part II (qq. 12–85) deals with the redemption accomplished by Christ, explaining it with a Trinitarian exposition of the Apostles' Creed and a theology of the *sacraments.* Part III (qq. 86–129) describes Christian life in response to God's *grace,* summarizing it with an expo-

sition of the Ten Commandments and the Lord's Prayer. Typically Reformed is its discussion of obedient Christian life under the title "Thankfulness."

The character and the tone of the catechism are revealed by its famous first question and answer:

Q. 1. What is your only comfort, in life and in death?

A. That I belong—body and soul, in life and in death—not to myself but to my faithful Savior, Jesus Christ, who at the cost of his own blood has fully paid for all my sins and has completely freed me from the dominion of the devil; that he protects me so well that without the will of my Father in heaven not a hair can fall from my head; indeed, that everything must fit his purpose for my salvation. Therefore, by his Holy Spirit, he also assures me of eternal life, and makes me wholeheartedly willing and ready from now on to live for him.

The catechism is a warm, personal, generally nonpolemical and ecumenical confession of evangelical faith, representing a moderate *Calvinism* (there is no doctrine of double *predestination*) that appeals to the heart as well as to the mind, is unique among classical Reformed *confessions* in being expressed subjectively in the first person singular, and confesses Reformed faith and life as joyful, thankful, and free response to God's grace. It has been said to combine the intimacy of Luther, the charity of Melanchthon, and the fire of Calvin.

K. Barth, *The Heidelberg Catechism for Today* (1964); J. B. Rogers, *Presbyterian Creeds: A Guide to the Book of Confessions* (1985); Schaff, *Creeds,* vol. 1.

SHIRLEY C. GUTHRIE

Hell The *doctrine* of hell in the Reformed tradition has rested on three theological tenets: God's *justice,* human depravity, and limited *atonement.* God's justice demands the eternal damnation of all human beings. Only the elect will benefit from the atoning work of Christ and escape the terrible fires of hell. All others will be punished eternally.

Calvin's understanding accords with this. He differs from later Reformed theologians on the nature of hell. Hell is real and terrible but a place of spiritual rather than physical torment. The biblical descriptions of bodily torture serve as metaphors for the sinner's *experience* of total abandonment by *God* and, further, divine displeasure.

Though sixteenth-century Reformed *confessions* assume eternal punishment, most mention the doctrine in passing. Early exceptions are the *Basel Confession* (1534), which devotes a short article (art. 10) to it, and the *First Helvetic Confession,* where *salvation* and damnation have a few sentences in a long paragraph on *Christology* (art. 11). Significant elaboration is found only in the *Belgic Confession* (1561; art. 37). Here eternal punishment is related to *election,* and the terrors of damnation and the delights of salvation are juxtaposed. No doubt the bloody persecution of the churches of the Lowlands influenced the Confession's teaching; it promises that the elect "shall see the terrible vengeance which God shall execute on the wicked, who most cruelly persecuted, oppressed, and tormented them in this world."

Most theologians of *Reformed orthodoxy* considered Calvin's passive spiritual view of eternal punishment inadequate. The *Westminster Confession* (1647) holds that God does not merely withdraw from the damned but actively punishes them, though it does not specify whether the torment is physical as well as spiritual (ch. 33). Scholastic theologians would insist on both, distinguishing between *poena damni,* suffering caused by eternal separation from God, and *poena sensus,* pain of body and soul registered through the senses. The latter could occur only if hell were a place and not merely a state. The incorruptibility of the body permitted unremitting and endless torment, graded, some taught, according to the

gravity of earthly sin. Both *repentance* and annihilation were rejected. Puritan preachers gave such teachings imaginative elaboration in sermons designed to convert people through vivid depictions of hell's terrors.

Nineteenth- and twentieth-century theologians present a variety of views of hell. Reformed orthodoxy has continued to defend the doctrine, though usually mitigating the harshness of earlier formulations. Friedrich Schleiermacher taught universal salvation (*universalism*), rejecting eternal punishment as inimical to Christianity. While many nineteenth-century Reformed thinkers followed his lead, neo-orthodox theologians, recognizing that *scripture* teaches both *judgment* and promise, found Schleiermacher's formulations unacceptable.

Perhaps the most creative reassessment has been made by Karl Barth, who taught that Jesus Christ alone bears the world's damnation. Others, such as Hendrikus Berkhof, have advanced a purgatorial view of hell. Of the doctrine of eternal punishment's three foundational tenets, modern *Reformed theology* has affirmed God's justice and the inability of *humanity* to save itself but has questioned the proposition that atonement must be limited.

PAUL R. FRIES

Helvetic Confession, First

The *Confessio Helvetica prior,* or *Confessio Basiliensis posterior* (1536), was the first formula uniting Swiss Reformed cantons in common confession. Earlier documents, including the First Confession of Basel (1534), were more local. Pope Paul III's call for a general council in Mantua (1537) persuaded the Swiss to gather their theologians and prepare a confession for the council. Theologians delegated by the magistrates of Zurich, Bern, Basel, Schaffhausen, St. Gall, Mühlhausen, and Biel gathered in Basel (February 1–4). Martin Bucer and Wolfgang Capito were present in their continuing effort to unite

Lutherans and Zwinglians, a contributing reason for the conference.

Heinrich Bullinger and Leo Jud of Zurich, Oswald Myconius and Johann Grynaeus of Basel, and Kaspar Megander of Bern were named to prepare the document. It was signed by all the delegates on February 4 and published in Latin. Jud prepared the German translation, which is fuller than the Latin but of equal authority. Delegates of the town councils assembled on March 27 and adopted the document; Strassburg and Constance refused—Capito apparently preferred the Tetrapolitan Confession as an instrument of reconciliation between Lutheran and Reformed.

Luther received a copy through Bucer and made favorable response in letters (1537) to the burgomaster of Basel and Swiss cantons, promising to promote harmony. Bucer's Wittenberg Concord (May 1536) seemed hopeful but failed when the Swiss refused to sign.

The confession consists of twenty-eight brief articles (twenty-seven in the German, which combines arts. 13 and 14). It is comparable in content with the *Second Helvetic Confession*, which Bullinger with Peter Martyr Vermigli prepared (1561; publ. 1566) and which superseded it. Bullinger and Jud wished to add a caution against the binding *authority* of this or any confession that might compromise that of *scripture* and Christian liberty, but their declaration was not included.

Arts. 1–5. The First Helvetic Confession begins with scripture (presenting the "most perfect and ancient Philosophy"), its interpretation (governing love and faith: Lat. *moderante*; Ger. *die Richtschnur*) and scope, or purpose (Lat. *scopus*; Ger. *Zweck*).

Arts. 6–11. **God, humanity, sin, free will, salvation,** and Christ. Christ is our brother (*victor duxque*) in whom we are joined to God. The theme of union will pervade the Second Helvetic Confession. Article 11 and that on the **Eucharist** (art. 23) are the longest.

Arts. 12–14. The scope of evangelical teaching, office of the Christian (*sanctifi-*

cation), and *faith,* which is *substantia* and *assertio.*

Arts. 15–20. **Church, ministry,** ecclesiastical power, election of ministers, true pastors (*Christus . . . caput ac pastor solus est*), and office of ministry. Public gathering signifies the exalted Christ and his discipline.

Arts. 21–23. The crucial section on **sacraments** is moderate and mediating: *signa* (Ger. *Zeichen*) are not nude or merely tokens (*tessera*) but symbols of divine **grace,** offering what they signify by analogy: the "mystic meal" is fruitful, nourishing. Natural union of signs with signified is rejected, as well as local inclusion and carnal presence; the theme is thanksgiving (*gratiarum actio; Danksagung*).

Arts. 24–28. Church ordinances include media (de mediis—to be expanded in the **Second Helvetic Confession),** heresy and schism, magistrates and marriage.

H. A. Niemeyer, *Collectio confessionum* (1840), 105–22; Schaff, *Creeds,* vol. 3; cf. Schaff, *HCC,* vol. 8.

JOSEPH C. MCLELLAND

Helvetic Confession, Second

Authored by Heinrich Bullinger, who succeeded Huldrych Zwingli at Zurich, the Second Helvetic Confession was adopted by the cantons of the Swiss Reformation (1566) and many other Reformed lands.

Bullinger studied in the Netherlands and at the University of Cologne. Trained in medieval **scholasticism,** he was attracted to the church fathers, then to Luther and Melanchthon, and was converted to the cause of reform (1522). He met Zwingli (1523) and they became fast friends. Bullinger taught the Bible as a lay professor in a Cistercian cloister, which he converted to the cause of reform. When Zwingli was killed on the battlefield of Kappel (1531), Bullinger (age twenty-seven) was called by the Council to take his place in Zurich.

Bullinger sought to unite the reforming parties of the Swiss cantons and the Germanies. With colleagues from Bern, Basel, Schaffhausen, St. Gall, Mühlhausen, and Strassburg he wrote the *First Helvetic Confession,* seeking to effect such a union (1536). Initially, Luther spoke favorably of the document, but with the failure of the Swiss to accept the Wittenberg Concord, effected by Martin Bucer, the First Helvetic Confession failed to have any lasting effect among Lutherans. It did, however, unify all German-speaking Switzerland and was the first Reformed creed of national authority.

The Second Helvetic Confession follows the first in its structure but was expanded, improved, and written solely by Bullinger. First composed when it received the personal approval of Bucer (1561), it was rewritten during a pestilence in which Bullinger expected to die (1562)—attaching the confession to his will as a final gift to Zurich.

This private testimony of *faith* became a public confession through the needs of the Swiss cantons and the Palatinate. Frederick III, elector of the Palatinate, who had only recently published the *Heidelberg Catechism* (1563) to try to bring religious peace to his land, was now under attack by Lutherans who were considering charging him with *heresy* at the Imperial Diet. Thus, Frederick requested a full exposition of the Reformed faith of Bullinger (1565), who replied with a manuscript of his own recently completed confession. The Elector had it printed in Latin and German prior to the noble defense of his faith before the Imperial Diet, at which all charges were dropped.

The Swiss felt the need for a more ample description of their faith, the First Helvetic Confession being deemed too brief. Bullinger's was considered suitable, with a few changes to which he readily consented. The Second Helvetic Confession was printed at public expense in Zurich (March 1566) with agreement of all the Reformed cantons except Basel, which subsequently also accepted it. The same year Scotland gave its assent; a year later the Hungarian Churches at the Synod of Debrecen (1567); four years later the French at the Synod of La Rochelle (1571). The Polish Reformed churches affirmed it in 1571 and again in 1578. It was also used, albeit not officially received, in England and the Netherlands. Only the Heidelberg Catechism was more widely adopted among the Reformed.

The confession begins with the primary issue of church reform: *authority. Scripture* is the source of authority. With Luther, the preached word is the *Word of God.* In ch. 2, against Rome, the Holy Fathers, councils, and *tradition* are accepted only as they conform to the Word of God. Against Anabaptists, ch. 2 contains a hermeneutical guide that rejects a private interior interpretation by the Spirit in favor of one that is informed by the sense of scripture, the original languages, and the testimony of the Fathers. In ch. 3, against the Socinians, the *Trinity* is affirmed.

The iconoclasm of Bullinger rests on the affirmation of Christ as our sole mediator for adoration, *worship,* and invocation (ch. 5). The doctrines of *providence, creation,* the fall, and *free will* follow (chs. 6–9). On free will (ch. 9), Bullinger is neither as optimistic as Erasmus nor as hyperbolic as Luther. The *imago,* mind, and will are still present, but their ability to do good requires *regeneration,* which is the gift of God.

If regeneration is necessary to *salvation* and is the gift of God, what determines that gift? Bullinger, with Paul, *Augustine,* and Calvin, posit the corollary of *grace: predestination.* Predestination is tightly tied to Christ as the means. At the same time, a holy life is to be proclaimed. Inquiry into one's *election* is only in the mirror of Christ: "By baptism we are ingrafted into the body of Christ, and we are often fed in his church with his flesh and blood unto life eternal" (ch. 10).

The Anselmic *doctrine* of the *atonement,* built on Chalcedon, is reaffirmed. *Law* and gospel, *justification* by faith, and the role of good works are set forth with clarity and moderation, so that both Germans and Swiss might see their theology therein (chs. 11–16).

In the *Lord's Supper* the faithful indeed receive the body and blood of Christ, yet not corporeally but spiritually, but nonetheless "the very body and blood of our Lord Jesus" (ch. 21). Public worship receives much attention, including admonitions against "overlong" and tedious public prayers, the role of singing (ch. 23), holy days (ch. 24), catechizing (ch. 25), burials and purgatory (ch. 26), as well as admonitions concerning the patrimony of the church (now largely in the hands of the magistracy—for in the Reformation almost everywhere the *civil government* assumed the assets of the *church* in exchange for its reform and subsequent maintenance). Similarly, admonitions to the magistracy are to be read with the understanding that the church is financially dependent on the godly action of the state (ch. 30).

The Second Helvetic Confession is unique in that it was written by a theologian whose career spanned the first and second generations of reformers, was the product of a single hand, and received the widest international reception of any Reformed confession. It is therefore the most authentic guide we have to the theological and pastoral ethos of the Swiss Reformation.

J. H. Leith, ed., *Creeds of the Churches*, 3rd ed. (1982); J. B. Rogers, *Presbyterian Creeds: A Guide to the Book of Confessions* (1985); Schaff, *Creeds*, vol. 3; Istvban Tnokbes, *A Mbasodik helvbet hitvallbas magyarbazata, Commentarium in confessionem Helveticam Posteriorem*, 2 vols. (1968); and *Glauben und Bekennen: 400 Jahre Confessio Helvetica posterior* (1966).

DONALD J. BRUGGINK

Helvetic Consensus Formula

Late seventeenth-century theologians J. H. Heidegger, Lukas Gernler, Hummel, Johann Heinrich Ott, and Francis Turretin wrote to each other of the need for a new confessional statement. Thus, the diet of the four evangelical cantons (Zurich, Basel, Bern, and Schaffhausen) instructed their pastors to begin official correspondence (1674).

As completed, the twenty-six canons of the Consensus primarily reject the French Saumur Academy's teachings. Canons 1–3 reject the views of Louis Cappel, who questioned the authenticity of the Hebrew OT text as passed on to us. Canons 10–12 oppose Joshua de Ia Place because he rejected the immediate imputation of Adam's sin. Canons 4–9 and 13–25 reject the view of Mose Amyraut on the universality of God's *grace.*

The diet of the evangelical cantons accepted the Consensus (1675) and urged eight cities to adopt it. Some, such as Neuchütel and Geneva after much delay and urging by other churches, adopted it as a sign of union with the other churches.

The Consensus was never widely used outside Switzerland. Since other statements dealt with the same theological controversies, and the theological climate soon shifted, its influence did not last long even in Swiss churches.

D. D. Grohman, "The Genevan Reactions to the Saumur Doctrine of Hypothetical Universalism: 1635–1685" (diss., Knox College, Toronto, 1971); J. H. Leith, ed., *Creeds of the Churches*, 3rd ed. (1982).

DONALD D. GROHMAN

Heresy

Heresy   The rejection or distortion of a major element of Christian *doctrine,* particularly as defined in the church's *creeds and confessions.* John Calvin cites Augustine's distinction: "Heretics corrupt the purity of the faith with false dogmas, but schismatics, while sometimes of the very same faith, break the bond of communion" (*Inst.* 4.2.5). Heresy most appropriately denotes the deliberate and persistent denial by a professing Christian (thus distinguished from unbelief and apostasy) of a fundamental of the faith, especially a denial judged to put *salvation* itself at risk.

Major sixteenth-century Reformed theologians endorsed the ancient creeds and regarded the heresies that rejected creedal teaching, especially on the *Trinity* and the person of Christ, as serious enough in some cases (cf. Michael Servetus in Geneva) to merit capital punishment. The Reformers' own condemnations of false medieval doctrines (e.g., transubstantiation) were less precisely formalized but found lasting expression in Protestant church confessions.

Today, theological pluralism has made the concept of heresy of less practical value. Heresy trials have often hastened the relaxation of the terms of the churches' subscription to their confessions. Nevertheless, the *Theological Declaration of Barmen* (1934) stigmatized the "false doctrines" of the "German Christians," and in the 1980s the WARC declared apartheid a heresy. If in earlier generations the persecution of heretics shamefully disfigured Christianity, today a laissez-faire relativism is no less serious a danger. *Universalism* may yet come to be seen as the distinctive twentieth-century heresy.

DAVID F. WRIGHT

History   The understanding of history articulated within the Reformed tradition agrees with the common Christian interpretation of history found in the church's ancient *creeds.* According to this view, the course of history begins with the divine *creation* of the world, continues with a human fall into *sin,* proceeds toward the *incarnation* of Jesus Christ as Savior, carries on with the *church,* and culminates in the return of Christ and the beginning of life everlasting. The Reformed view of history differs from this common *tradition* by giving interpretive priority to the events and results of the Protestant Reformation in sixteenth-century Europe. The view is summarized in the titles given to the tradition: "Reformed" (past tense) and "the churches of the Reformation."

The churches founded during the Reformation enunciated their view of history in numerous new creeds. The *French Confession* (1559), based on a draft by John Calvin, stated the view clearly, saying that "it has been necessary for God to raise men in an extraordinary manner to restore the Church which was in ruin and desolation." This period of restoration succeeded two earlier periods: the primitive period of the ancient church and a long period of degeneration under the reign of the papacy. The period of the ancient church was a normative moment when the three creeds were adopted that the churches of the Reformation accepted as faithful to the Holy Scriptures—the Apostles', the Nicene, and the Athanasian. The period of the papal church that followed was regarded as a destructive time when the pure *Word of God* was banished, the *sacraments* were corrupted, and the faith was perverted into superstitions and idolatries. The period of restoration in the sixteenth century was meant to achieve the abolition of unwarranted "innovations" introduced by the Roman church as well as the reconnection of the church with the usages and customs of the primitive church. Calvin proclaimed to the king of France, when presenting the first edition of his *Institutes of the Christian Religion* (1536), that he and other faithful believers professed no novelty and no new gospel but merely wished to reassert the true religion of the scriptures as supported by the primitive Fathers.

The Reformed view of history expressed by this triad of periods was both cyclical and linear. On the one hand, the Reformation brought the church full cycle to the primitive period, claiming to renew ancient fidelity to the scriptures. On the other, it moved the church onward in the course of history to what amounted to a new expression of the ancient faith. The Reformation creeds emerged from debates and struggles against what they took to be an awesome enemy unknown to the early church. In their linear expression, the new creeds, such as the *Belgic*

Confession (1561) and the *WCF* (1647), asserted the continuity of the one true church from the beginning of the world to the end of history. The creeds recited the history of the world from the creation and Adam, through Abraham and the prophets to Christ, onward to each national experience. The *Scots Confession* (1560), for example, ran the story from Adam, Abel, and Cain to the true Church of Scotland associated with John Knox. In their cyclic expression, these creeds identified a process of history punctuated by repeated reform, in which devout people would arise as needed to recall the world to the true religion of *God.* A Reformed church is always reforming.

A series of history books elaborated the Reformed interpretation of history found in the creeds. During the sixteenth century, Theodore Beza wrote on the church reforms in France (1580), John Knox on the Reformation in Scotland (1560s and 1570s), and John Foxe on the English martyrs produced by the conflicts of Protestants against Rome (1563). In the nineteenth century, Jean Henri Merle d'Aubigné enlightened a host of Reformed readers in Europe and North America about the Reformation of the sixteenth century, calling it the revolution that began the new world (5 vols.; 1838–53). A series of Reformed theological treatises from Calvin to Karl Barth in the twentieth century discussed the common Christian doctrines of *predestination* and *free will* as well as *providence.* These doctrines defined the interaction of divine, satanic, and human agency in history and depicted history as an ensuing struggle between the proponents and the enemies of the gospel. The Reformed tradition became widely associated with an emphasis on the acts of God who governs and directs all created things, disposes and ordains by a sovereign will all that happens in the course of history. In the twentieth century, this traditional Reformed stress on God was counterbalanced by a new appreciation of human action. The idea of the cultural mandate

given by God to *humanity* acknowledged that people were the actual caretakers of the creation and the makers of history. As an expression of this idea, Herman Dooyeweerd elaborated a Reformed philosophy of history that depicted history as the opening up of the creation by means of the ordinary re-creative acts of human beings (1953–57).

In the late twentieth century, Reformed churches still sought their identity in the events of the sixteenth century. The newer churches in Asia, Africa, and Latin America experienced some discomfort with the linkage. Reformed theological curricula and scholarship still treated the Reformation as definitive and emphasized in their historical studies the prime role of the early church and the sixteenth century. In a new wave of creed making in the 1960s, 1970s, and 1980s, Reformed churches perpetuated both the cyclic and the linear features of the traditional view of history. The WARC, in a message titled *Called to Witness to the Gospel Today* (1982), summarized the modern Reformed view of history. Reformed churches, the message affirmed, continued in the movement initiated by the sixteenth-century Reformers for the renewal of the church in their time, but they sought a new reform of the tradition by offering fresh responses to the scriptures in the light of new experiences and new situations.

C. T. McIntire, ed., *God, History, and Historians* (1977); R. Wells, ed., *History and the Christian Historian* (1998).

C. T. MCINTIRE

Holy Spirit The "third person" of the *Trinity* has been specially emphasized in various streams of *Reformed theology* since the sixteenth century. Fundamental for Reformed pneumatology is the witness of *scripture* to the presence and activity of the Spirit of God in the world and among human persons, especially the testimony of the NT to the gift of the Spirit by the risen and ascended Jesus

Christ and to the work of the Spirit as "the other Paraclete" who enables Christian *faith, worship,* witness, and service. Reformed theology also follows the consensus of the early *church* articulated in the Niceno-Constantinopolitan Creed (Nicene Creed): the Holy Spirit is "the Lord, the Life-Giver, who proceeds from the Father, who with the Father and the Son is worshiped and glorified, who spoke by the prophets."

The term "Holy Spirit" is used in only two OT passages (Ps. 139; Isa. 63). But there is frequent mention of God's *ruach* ("wind"); in later strands, human or divine "spirit." God's *ruach* is associated with *creation* and preservation of life, with outstanding gifts and capacities, with prophecy, and with the future *hope* of *judgment* and restoration. Several of these emphases are developed and modified in intertestamental literature—for example, in the messianic anticipations of Palestinian Judaism, in the "Two Spirits" dualism of Qumran, and in the association of *pneuma* (Gr.) with the divine wisdom in Hellenistic Judaism.

In the NT the Holy Spirit comes fully onstage as "the Spirit of your Father" (Matt. 10:20), "the Spirit of Christ" (Rom. 8:9), "the Spirit of life" (Rom. 8:2), "the other Paraclete" (John 14:16), and so forth. The Messiah has come; the age of the Spirit has dawned; the Spirit is the power of the divine purpose and activity centered in Jesus Christ. The Synoptic Gospels and Acts emphasize the connection between Jesus and the Spirit and the presence of the Spirit in the church as manifested by charismatic signs and prophecy. More profound theological reflection is offered by Paul (e.g., 1 Cor. 12—14; the whole of Galatians, Romans, and the Corinthian letters) and John (esp. the Farewell Discourse, John 14—16).

The early church dogmatic consensus expressed in the Niceno-Constantinopolitan Creed (A.D. 381) issued out of hard debate that was provoked by the Arian controversy and led to the final rejection of previously widespread notions of the Spirit as an angel, creature, subordinate divine energy, or impersonal power—or as a charismatic dynamic entitling its bearers to cut loose from the historic Christian tradition. This recognition has paradigmatic significance for all subsequent Christian theology, for the old issues and questions continually resurface in plausible forms that nevertheless represent "old heresy warmed up." However, the fourth-century dogmatic consensus left open the question of the relation between the Holy Spirit and Jesus Christ as the incarnate Son and *Word of God.* The Western church followed *Augustine* in closing this gap by affirming (an expansion of the creed of Constantinople) that the Spirit "proceeds from the Father *and the Son"* (filioque). The Eastern Orthodox Church has more or less consistently rejected the *filioque* as an unauthorized Western interpolation, while Reformed churches have until recently generally followed the line inherited from the Western medieval tradition.

In classical Reformed theology of the sixteenth and seventeenth centuries, the Holy Spirit's activity was emphasized in three main respects. Together they contribute a distinctive profile to the Reformed tradition.

The combination of humanist historical, philological, and exegetical learning with the Reformation emphasis on the Word of God as the sole guide of faith and life put the exegesis and *preaching* of the Bible in the center of the church's life. This led on the one hand to a tendency to make the Spirit the slave of the letter in the avowed interests of a high *doctrine* of the inspiration of scripture; on the other, to an opposed inclination to exalt the Spirit above the letter. The resulting tensions are already clearly diagnosed (*Inst.* 1.6–9) and have fermented in Reformed churches ever since.

The controversy between Zwingli and Luther over the real presence of the body and blood of Christ in the *Lord's Supper* turned on pneumatological as well as christological hinges. Reformed concern in the controversy was to emphasize the divinity of Christ, to block excessive adoration of the consecrated elements, and to insist that it is by the Holy Spirit that believers are united with Christ, not by any kind of transmutation of the physical elements or any "consubstantiation" of Christ's physical body and blood "in, with, and under" the bread and wine. In this, a proper concern to distinguish between "spiritual" and "material" realities is recognized. Sometimes in the Reformed tradition, however, this has led to a denigration of the material that owes more to Hellenistic dualism or post-Enlightenment rationalism than to the biblical witness.

Classical Reformed theology, especially during the post-Reformation "orthodoxy" period, came to be much exercised with tracing and defining the various actions of the Holy Spirit in individual lives along the lines of an "order of salvation" (*ordo salutis*). Thus, the **WCF** deals with effectual calling, *justification, adoption, sanctification,* saving faith, *repentance* unto life, good works, *perseverance of the saints,* and assurance of *grace* and *salvation.* While this interest in the ongoing work of the Holy Spirit has its proper place, it is open in this form to the charge of artificial schematization (Barth, *CD* IV/2, 499–511). It also paved the way for a psychologizing reduction of the work of the Holy Spirit.

Three seminal nineteenth-century theological thinkers contributed especially to renewed reflection on the person and work of the Holy Spirit in Protestant theology. Schleiermacher gave a new centrality to *human experience* in theology, distinguished faith alike from *scientific knowledge* and *ethical action,* and stressed "God-consciousness" as the core of religious self-awareness. So he defined the Spirit as "the union of the divine essence with human nature," which—fully realized in Jesus Christ—is now "the common Spirit which animates the corporate life of believers" (*CF*[2], sec. 123). In effect, this was a Protestant restatement of the classical Roman Catholic sense of the Holy Spirit as "the soul of the church" (*anima ecclesiae*).

Hegel's philosophical theology made *Geist* ("Spirit" or "Mind") its basic category and developed a vision of the entire history of the universe as the dialectical unfolding and return to itself of the divine Spirit: "Spirit" produces or posits "Nature" as its own opposite, through which it moves to return to itself, transfigured as "Absolute Spirit." While Hegel's system was virtually pantheistic, it represented a significant attempt to overcome deeply rooted dualisms in Western thinking—for example, between "spirit" and "matter" or "subject" and "object." It suggested new applications of Trinitarian and incarnational models for theological reflection on the history of **God** with the created universe, and it pointed the way to a fresh understanding of "spirit" as a key to the nature of human existence.

Søren Kierkegaard ridiculed Hegel's system, inverted its method, and stressed the loneliness of the existence of the time-caught individual human person confronted with the overwhelming otherness of the eternal God. However, he also brought the notion of "spirit" into direct connection with his diagnosis of what it means to be human and developed a *relational* model of the human person: "Man is spirit. But what is spirit? Spirit is the self. But what is the self? The self is a relation which relates to its own self. . . . Man is a synthesis of the infinite and the finite, of the temporal and the eternal, of freedom and necessity" (*The Sickness unto Death* [ET 1941], 17). Essential to this analysis is Kierkegaard's insistence that the self-relatedness constitutive of human existence is posited from without, by Another, that is, by God: "By relating itself to its own self and by willing to be itself the self is grounded transparently in the Power which posited it" (ibid., 19).

These three approaches—the romantic-ecclesiastical (Schleiermacher), the cosmic-pantheistic (Hegel), and the individual-existentialist (Kierkegaard)—have set the scene and defined terms of reference for much twentieth-century theological work on pneumatology. Fascinating and challenging though they are, however, they all reflect in one way or another a tendency to make ecclesial, cosmological, or anthropological reflection the basis of theology. In the process, the Spirit of God can all too easily be regarded merely as an institutional energy, a universal cosmic force, or a validator of human personality. That the Spirit has to do with all of these areas is not denied, but it is not reducible to any of them. It must be remembered that the Spirit is the *Spirit of God* and the *Spirit of Christ*: Only a Trinitarian and christologically focused doctrine of God can give these perspectives their proper place in the overall scheme.

Twentieth-century theological work has been marked by a concern to achieve this correction, albeit along various paths. The two greatest Protestant systematic theologies of the postliberal era, Barth's *Church Dogmatics* and Tillich's *Systematic Theology*, deserve special mention, as does the rise of Pentecostal movements worldwide. Additionally, the new ecumenical climate of this century has encouraged Western rethinking of the *filioque* problem. Finally, the development of both the human and natural sciences has opened new perspectives on the relation of God, humankind, and the natural order, which may be expected to yield further fruits in the coming decades.

Guidelines for further reflection on the person and work of the Holy Spirit include:

God is Spirit and the Holy Spirit is God, nothing less.

God's Spirit is creator, ground, and goal of the human spirit, but not reducible to it.

God's Spirit may appropriately be seen as the immanent presence and action of God in the world and among human persons and communities but is not to be identified with the individual or social *psychē*, or "soul," as such.

God's Spirit "inspires" all kinds of gifts and activities but is not demonic or violent. Nor is it too quickly to be assimilated to this or that moral, political, or social program or claimed as their justification.

The abiding criterion of the presence and activity of God's Spirit is Jesus Christ, the unique receiver and giver of the Holy Spirit. He alone is the Lord of the church and Savior of the world; the Spirit of God is *his* Spirit, and none other.

As the crucifixion and *resurrection* of Jesus Christ demonstrates, the Spirit of God is the fellow sufferer with all human sufferings and at the same time their Transfigurer and Transformer. This is promise and *hope* for all Christian people.

A. I. C. Heron, *The Holy Spirit* (1983); H. I. Lederle, *Treasures Old and New: Interpretations of "Spirit-Baptism" in the Charismatic Renewal Movement* (1988); H. W. Robinson, *The Christian Experience of the Holy Spirit* (1928); T. A. Smail, *Reflected Glory: The Spirit in Christ and Christians* (1975); J. V. Taylor, *The Go-Between God: The Holy Spirit and the Christian Mission* (1972); L. Vischer, ed., *Spirit of God, Spirit of Christ* (1981).
ALASDAIR I. C. HERON

Hope   Hope as the inspiration and direction of Calvin's faith has been seen as preeminently central, as it was with his great example **Augustine.** The eternal destiny of **humanity** and the world was a major element of Calvin's faith and reflection.

Immortality of the soul. Calvin's first theological writing, outlined before the **Institutes** (in 1534), was *Psychopannychia* ("the watchfulness of the soul"). It opposed Anabaptists, who believed the soul is sleeping during the intervening state between **death** and the final **resurrection.** For Calvin, this was incompatible with the continuity and progress of the soul toward the vision of God.

Calvin claimed the status of (bodiless) souls in the intermediate state to be "a provisional felicity" because "the progressive work of regeneration must in no way be suspended by death" (*Psychopannychia* [1534], 55, 197). This notion of suspension returns in the *Institutes* with a different meaning: not suspended but not yet perfected and therefore still suspended "where in glad expectation they await the enjoyment of promised glory, and so all things are held in suspense until Christ the Redeemer appear" (*Inst.* 3.25.6). This concept bridges the second focus of Calvin's eschatological ellipse.

Growth of the church and the world toward the end. For Calvin, not only does an individual go through different stages toward fulfillment (i.e., ethical progress; *Inst.* 3.6.5), but there is also "a sort of eschatological progress" (Quistorp, 84). Calvin brought close together secular history, church history, salvation history, and "the signs of the times" that announce the consummation. In contrast, Luther emphasized the discontinuity between this world and the eschaton. This eschatological tension between the "not yet" and the "already," between suspension and progress, proves that "the Kingdom of God through ongoing processes increases until the end of the world" (*Commentary on Matt.* 6:10; cf. sec. 12 on parables of growth). Or, "as the sun rises at heaven, so also the time of salvation progresses toward its goal" (Berger, 100).

The progress paradigm is found also when Calvin speaks of the spread of the gospel or the great revival of the Reformation. It reaches its apex at the end of *history*, where the signs of the millennium and the Antichrist are found. Calvin is less interested in the first than the second because such a sudden and limited period of perfection is incompatible with his ideas of preliminary stages of suspended *grace.* His refutation of chiliasm, however, is exegetically inaccurate.

On the Antichrist, Calvin mainly follows 2 Thess. 2:2–7 and sees the Antichrist as embracing several persons, groups, and generations. Many popes belong to those enemies of the Word, as does Muhammad. The promise of v. 9 does not describe a sudden and short moment but a period of history that includes events such as the revival and the Reformation, the mission of the *church,* and the victory over its enemies. For Calvin, the saving of souls and the victory in history are two sides of redemption.

H. Berger, *Calvins Geschichtsauffassung* (1955); H. Berkhof, *Well-founded Hope* (1969); I. J. Hesselink, "Calvin and Heilsgeschichte," *Oikonomia* (1967): 163–70; D. E. Holwerda, "Eschatology and History," in *Readings in Calvin's Theology,* ed. D. K. McKim (1984); J. Moltmann, *Theology of Hope* (1967); H. Quistorp, *Calvin's Doctrine of the Last Things* (1955); T. F. Torrance, *Kingdom and Church* (1956).

HENDRIKUS BERKHOF

Humanity   Traditionally the *doctrine* of humanity involves the nature of human being and the end or purpose (Gr. *telos*) of human life. These are articulated by humanity's status as created, fallen, and redeemed.

General. Two approaches to humanity characterize pre- and post-Enlightenment options in theological method. Classic Reformed faith from John Calvin until the nineteenth-century "turn to the subject" is characterized by views of "man," but only as entailed in the biblically warranted doctrines about *God* and the order of *salvation.* That the earliest form of Reformed faith most certainly *did* offer important contributions to an understanding of humanity is suggested by Calvin's famous dictum on the necessary connection between God-knowledge and self-knowledge in the *Institutes.* This was simply not an approach allowing beliefs about humanity to create critical issues for revealed doctrines about God.

Only with the impact of modernity on theological reflection and the rise of historical consciousness and other critical disciplines might we properly speak of theological anthropology and mean the task of relating traditional convictions about theocentric human being to other, sometimes conflicting, knowledges of the human species. With this expansion, questions arise over what it means to define human being as religious being and how a Christian understanding is affected by cultural pluralism, gender, race, and other features of human difference. These explorations, in distinction from pre-Enlightenment approaches, bring alterations and conflicts over how theological authorities function allowing the doctrine of humanity more force in constructing other doctrine and practice.

Regardless of the approach or degree of reformation of the doctrine, three themes regularly appear in Reformed portraits of humanity as distinctive themes: (1) appreciation for the theocentric, or God-centered, nature of human being; (2) the central role of a lively *piety* or account of religious affections evoked by a relation to the sovereign God who orders the world; and (3) a definition of that theocentric dependence which holds together the radical bondage of *sin* with an equally strong conviction of accountability and call to activism in the world, a world ordered by that sovereign God.

Early boundaries. The recuperation of salvation by *grace* through *faith* from dormancy in medieval Catholicism by the sixteenth-century Protestant Reformation created crucial definitional boundaries for Reformed thinking. The order of salvation (understood chronologically) was determinative of Calvin's and later Reformed understandings of humanity, providing categories of *creation,* fall/redemption, and future consummation from which to define the nature and *telos* of human life. It was the lived dilemma of the life of faith, however, that proved most instructive for generating the distinctive claims.

Calvin put his stamp on a soteriological and ethical dilemma. On the one hand, he agreed with Lutheran reformers that salvation by grace through faith required denial that human actions merit salvation. God alone saves through Jesus Christ. On the other hand, Calvin was as clear that Christian life post-justification was shaped by a disciplined piety expressed as the rightly ordered response to the sovereign rule of this saving God, a God whose sovereignty extended to the ordering of the entirety of existence—individual, corporate, and societal.

Important implications from these boundaries for the image of God and the nature of sin followed. Sharing with Luther the conviction that the late-medieval Catholic account of post-fall human capacities for good were false to the human plight *coram Deo* ("before God"), Calvin set a precedent in Reformed faith for a distinctive account of sin's damage. To protect the need for salvation, Calvin claimed that the image of God and the will to fulfill God's *law* were destroyed. Human nature could be described as totally corrupt, not merely engaged in sinful acts, for creatures exist in a state of *total depravity* as a result of the primal parents' sin.

This dynamic is Reformed thought at its most pessimistic but incomplete. The *Second Helvetic Confession* (1566) puts it correctly: "By sin we understand that innate corruption . . . by which we, immersed in perverse desires and averse to all good, are inclined to all evil" (ch. 8). This view alone, however, has given *Calvinism* a reputation for harshness not entirely deserved. The other side of the reality of salvation by grace through faith is the conviction that humanity is created *imago Dei* for a *vocation* of glorifying God (WLC, q. 1). Reformed faith has always included the view that humanity as the image of God is part of a world that reflected the glory of God. Thus, boundaries against denigration and passivity implied by depravity are there to be drawn upon. From the perspective of God as creator-redeemer, human being is not a fated lump. Proper description of theocentric humanity requires that bondage to sin must be held together with accountability and enjoyment. Otherwise the vital piety that becomes a virtual Reformed vocation to reform whole societies cannot be understood.

Second- and third-generation developments. Another attempt to claim the human contribution to the drama of salvation came in response to second-generation developments of Reformed thought itself. Reaction against the forbidding logic of Calvinist orthodoxy's double *predestination* created a controversy that culminated in the *Synod of Dort* (1618–19). Dutch Reformed theologian Jacobus Arminius (1560–1609) and his followers, the Remonstrants, resisted orthodox positions on double predestination from concern for a clearer preservation of *free will* along with the attribution of salvation to God alone. Their preferred position, called *Arminianism,* proposed that persons could resist grace, that Christ died for all—not simply for the elect—and that persons' actions influenced their eternal destiny.

While the Arminians cut the nerve of the paradox of a Reformed understanding of theocentric human existence, the unpalatable theoretical resolution of the debate encoded the logic of double predestination in the Canons of Dort (1619). Its effect was to rescue God's priority in everything. However, it appeared to be a rescue made at the cost of obscuring how human life mattered. How a vital piety could be the distinguishing mark of a theocentric existence flattened out by the control of omnipotent, omniscient, and mysterious divine will would remain unresolved in the canons. The later adoption of Arminianism by John Wesley (1703–91) distinguished the Reformed doctrine of humanity officially from Wesley's Methodist tradition.

A very different emphasis emerged in a context where other Reformed convictions gained ascendancy. In seventeenth-century Puritanism, convictions about the goodness of creation, that human being is the pinnacle of creation's reflection of God's glory, and the purpose of human life in that glorifying is "to enjoy him forever," directed a unique understanding of humanity and its rightly directed powers of agency (WLC, q. 1). By this time, the faith of two generations of Reformed believers had been tested in the continental persecutions, forging convictions of great mettle. That faith emerged in the broader context of the transition from feudalism to the modern age and created conditions ripe for new forms of participation in the creation of states and their alignments with religion.

In English Puritanism, ideas such as Calvinist notions of vocation to worldly activity converged with changing ideas, both about the hierarchical nature of the body politic and about limits to resistance to unjust arrangements, to create a new theory of activity. The events associated with this brand of Puritanism culminating with the Cromwellian Revolution represented first attempts of ordinary people to change government, to act out politically the desire to reform the entire social order. In view of this generation, the extension of reform to Calvin's Geneva was only the first indication of the move generated by Reformed faith away from the inward piety of Lutheranism.

The Reformed vision that emerged, though failing to establish Presbyterianism in England, was a profound example of the noncontradiction between theocentric dependence at the heart of its piety and the life of disciplined obedience. The dependence implied by the theocentric doctrine of humanity proved congruent, even conducive, to creation of the first group of organized political revolutionaries in the West. The powerful combination of impetus for active corporate pilgrimage of faith together with the conviction that God alone is Lord which characterized this period fills out the meaning of depravity. In a real sense, predestination itself underwrote this activism, for the elect acted to "mirror" God's order for the world and therefore became agents over against the present order as it contradicted God's will. The work of redemption could create, then, not a world-denying piety but a world-transformative religious faith (Wolterstorff).

This faith proved open to the use of far more complex knowledges of the social networks of human life than Calvin could imagine. However, these would be explored in the later generations to discover the anthropological conditions for reform of a very different social order.

Post-Enlightenment shifts. With the post-Kantian turn to the subject in nineteenth-century theology, the press of other knowledges of the human began to affect the writing of theology, creating a new way to focus on human being. Theological anthropology in the hands of Friedrich Schleiermacher was still constructed by a "grammar" of redemption, but the ground was laid for future challenges to traditional doctrine by his focus on the construction of the human self and its environs, environs that would eventually range from historical context to ideological and historical forces.

Schleiermacher, father of modern Protestantism, set theology to investigating the "Christian religious self-consciousness." He thus placed theocentric human being and religious affections or piety in the center of the theological task. Kant's challenge intended to protect religious faith by locating it in the moral or practical reason. Schleiermacher sought, importantly, to distinguish faith from scientific knowledge but refused to reduce it to morality. Reinvigorating the theocentric piety of the Reformed tradition, he developed an account of the religious affections as they were shaped by the order of salvation. Responding to historical criticism, however, Schleiermacher articulated the terms of salvation history in the modern form of structures of the religious self-consciousness rather than chronological moments in history. What he discovered in these affections was, true to his tradition, a radically theocentric human being, whose connection with God is one of "absolute dependence."

American theologian Jonathan Edwards a full generation before distinctively contributed to Reformed anthropology in a different way by focusing on experiential piety. Responding to the experiential religion of the early eighteenth-century Great Awakening and aided by John Locke's epistemological tools, Edwards underscored even as he redefined the centrality of the religious affections. He made important unifying connections between the emotions and rationality to reinfuse Puritan discipline into the emotional excess of revival religion. He also joined the emotions with rationality in profoundly new ways to resist dead piety. His conviction that the center of faith was a reasoning affectivity captured the unity of the self and the role of desire in the rightly ordered God-centered life.

Twentieth-century Reformed theologians continued to break new ground with familiar emphases. Karl Barth, working with a more "objectivist" notion of revelation, set himself as the antithesis of Schleiermacher but in fact reinforced theocentric dependence by a different route. Theologians of realism (H. Richard Niebuhr and, less explicitly Reformed, Reinhold Niebuhr) struggled with defining the structures of human life as historical, contingent, and yet ordered by God's *providence,* adding a more tragic dimension to the paradox that has sometimes worked to protect God from the dark side of human existence.

In a more recent contrast of Reformed options, James Gustafson's theocentric ethics grants the God-centered strand of Reformed views of humanity such prominence that not only the christological emphasis but also the humanocentrism of Calvin or Barth is contested. God's ordering of the cosmos, says Gustafson, cannot be centered around humanity, given late twentieth-century knowledge. Rightly ordered piety is, then, truly life lived to the glory of God. Whether these options will force difficult future choices is not clear. It may be that late modernity challenges Reformed piety to a new version of the call to be willing to be damned for the glory of God.

Additional future work for a Reformed understanding of humanity is created by the continued study of different cultures and effects of language and social location on the formation of persons. What began as a feminist concern with the power of language to contribute to the exclusion of women from church leadership has broadened into a major scholarly enterprise and issue of piety. Gender and the concepts that name and place persons in relation to sexual difference are now a significant analytical tool in the exploration of humanity, no longer conceivable as an undifferentiated "mankind." It is explored, along with race, class, and other variables of excluded and marginalized social groups, in its function in Christian teaching and practice. The century ends ironically—given modernity's turn to the subject—with a host of challenges to the very unity of something called human being.

Our Confessional Heritage (PCUS, 1978); J. Edwards, *Religious Affections* (repr. 1959); M. P. Engel, *John Calvin's Perspectival Anthropology* (1988); J. M. Gustafson, *Ethics from a Theocentric Perspective*, 2 vols. (1981–84); L. M. Russell, *Household of Freedom: Authority in Feminist Theology* (1987); Schleiermacher, *CF*; M. L. Walzer, *The Revolution of the Saints* (1965); N. Wolterstorff, *Until Justice and Peace Embrace* (1983).

MARY MCCLINTOCK FULKERSON

Hymnody For two centuries after the Reformation, followers of John Calvin sang only scriptural songs, mostly metrical versions of the psalms. Psalters began to be published in Geneva, at first incomplete (1542), with periodic updates, until a completed volume of 150 psalms and 125 tunes was published (1564). In England, faithful Calvinists produced *The Whole Booke of Psalmes, collected into Englysh metre* by Thomas Sternhold and John Hopkins (1562) and subsequently *A New Version of the Psalmes of David fitted to the Tunes used in Churches* compiled by Nahum Tate and Nicholas Brady (1696). These English psalters also contained a few "hymns of human composition." Americans were using the *Ainsworth Psalter* until the publication of the Bay Psalm Book (1640), the first book printed in North America. Entire volumes of hymns were published, including Wither's *Hymnes and Songs of the Church* (1623) and Thomas Ken's *Morning, Evening, and Midnight Hymns* (1674).

John and Charles Wesley's collection, *Hymns and Sacred Poems* (1739), was instrumental in beginning a revival of hymn singing. Wesleyan congregations became noted for their singing, while their bishops mourned the state of psalmody. The influence of the Wesleys went further than the Church of England. Nonconformists were split over the issues of hymnody and psalmody as were Congregationalists and Presbyterians in the Americas.

Isaac Watts, an English congregationalist, Christianized the psalms and wrote extensively on the need to modernize psalmody. He also challenged the strict use of psalms in *worship,* citing the need for the *church* to voice praise to *God* in human language rather than in the language of God's *revelation* to *humanity.* In *Hymns and Spiritual Songs* (1707), he employed scriptural language and imagery adapted to the "mind of the living church." Strongly influenced by Watts was the young Congregationalist minister and hymn writer Philip Doddridge, who was the first nonconformist to sympathize with the work of John Wesley and George Whitefield.

Other hymn writers of note were two Calvinists, William Cowper (1731–1800) and John Newton (1725–1807). Together they published *Olney Hymns* (1779). In addition, the English Baptist John Rippon's *Selection of Hymns from the Best Authors* (1787) was intended to supplement Watts's materials.

Though Anglo-Catholic, John Mason Neale (1818–66) exercised significant influence over Presbyterians and their hymnody. His translations, "Of the Father's Love Begotten," "O Come, O Come, Emmanuel," and "Christ Is Made the Sure Foundation," among others, are greatly revered within Reformed circles. Tractarians were encouraged to sing translations of Latin hymns to plainsong melodies, while others were singing from William Henry Havergal's *Old Church Psalmody* (1847) and Henry John Gauntlett's *Hymn and Tune Book* (1852). Peter Maurice introduced the German chorale in his *Choral Harmony* (1854).

These trends merged in *Hymns Ancient and Modern* (1861), which influenced European hymnody for the next forty years, though there were outcries about the inferior quality of some of the texts and tunes. Both *The English Hymnal* (1906) and *Songs of Praise* (1926) sought to correct the problems and provide less emotional fuel.

Joachim Neander (1650–80) was the pioneer of Reformed hymnody in Germany with his *Hymns of the Covenant* (1679). His hymns were intended for prayer meetings and home worship, not for the church. Catherine Winkworth's (1827–78) translation of his "Praise Ye the Lord, the Almighty, the King of Creation!" continues to be sung in churches today. Neander influenced not only the Reformed of Germany but also the Pietists and Lutherans.

Because of the political scene, the eighteenth-century Reformed people in Germany suffered terribly, as did their worship. The Swiss-born Caspar Zollikofer von Altenklingen (1707–79) became one of the first to reform German hymnody with his *Neues Gesangbuch* (1766). It contained some four hundred hymns and only twenty-seven psalms. In 1773, the General Synod commended a psalter with hymnal supplement to the German Reformed Church. The Dutch Synod authorized a hymnal (1807), and two years later a hymnal was approved for use in Basel.

In the United States, Lowell Mason (1792–1872), heavily influenced by William Henry Havergal (1793–1870), feared that gospel music and folk tunes (what he considered "lighter music") would too much dominate Reformed worship. He published *Spiritual Songs for Social Worship* (1832), a collection not for church worship but for religious gatherings.

During the nineteenth century, hymnody took a romantic turn and many texts had a mission emphasis. The twentieth century's **Social Gospel** movement brought a deeper concern for worship, social *conscience*, prayers for peace, world community, environmental issues, ecology, and a deep yearning for the **kingdom of God.** Henry van Dyke (1852–1933), Harry Emerson Fosdick (1878–1969), Washington Gladden (1836–1918), William Pierson Merrill (1867–1954), and Henry Hallam Tweedy (1868–1953) were among those influenced by the Social Gospel.

The earliest English-language psalm and hymnbook issued independently of the Lutherans by the German Reformed Church in the United States was *Psalms and Hymns* (1834), which went through thirty-nine editions in twenty years. Aside from the work of Philip Schaff, American German Reformed hymnody depended largely on English, Scottish, and New England translators after the mid-nineteenth century. Schaff heavily influenced German-speaking Americans with his *Deutsches Gesangbuch* (1859). He included Winkworth's work, Moravian hymns, and English translations, as well as German translations of English hymns.

Within most Reformed churches, "gospel hymns" were confined to informal worship settings, as were African-American spirituals and other ethnic hymns. The political and social climate of the latter half of the twentieth century has forced the church to recognize the need to be more inclusive in its hymnody. Virtually every hymnal produced by Reformed communities in recent years has incorporated a broad spectrum of hymns to emphasize the diversity of the contemporary church. There is also a movement toward including more psalms. This perhaps attempts to balance the extremes of former centuries while highlighting contributions that Reformed faith has made to Christian hymnody.

The task of updating hymnody has been regularly undertaken. Each time, editors have to prune while trying to preserve worthwhile old favorites. In classic hymns they struggle to update archaic words, discriminatory language, and battlefield imagery while maintaining the essence of the original text. Most contemporary hymn writers have embraced inclusive language for humanity, but the debate over God-language continues.

J. G. Davies, *The New Westminster Dictionary of Liturgy and Worship* (1986); H. Eskew and H. McElrath, *Sing with Understanding* (1980); L. McKim, *Presbyterian Hymnal Companion* (1993); J. Melton, *Presbyterian Worship in America* (1967); J. H. Nichols, *Corporate Worship in the Reformed Tradition* (1968); M. Patrick, *Four Centuries of Scottish Psalmody* (1949); D. G. Reid et al., eds., *Dictionary of Christianity in America* (1990); S. Sadie, ed., *The New Grove Dictionary of Music and Musicians*, 20 vols., 6th ed. (1980).

LINDAJO H. MCKIM

Hyper-Calvinism

Hyper-Calvinism An exaggerated, rationalist form of the Reformed faith that originated in English nonconformity in the eighteenth century and is still found among Strict and Particular Baptists as well as some Dutch-American Calvinist groups. It emphasizes the absolute sovereignty of *God* and God's eternal decrees. Further, it deduces the duty of sinners toward God from the immanent acts of God (the eternal *covenant* of *grace,* eternal *justification,* and *adoption*). Thus, the grace of God, as far as the elect are concerned, is irresistible, and there is truly no need to offer the gospel to anyone. Thus, there is no need for evangelism but only to declare the truth so the *Holy Spirit* can use it to convert the elect sinners. This system encourages introspection to find out whether or not the sinner is truly of the elect.

The major proponent of hyper-Calvinism in the eighteenth century was John Gill in his *A Body of Doctrinal Divinity* (1767). But he learned his system from Joseph Hussey of the Cambridge Congregational church. In modern times, Hussey's *God's Operations of Grace but No Offers of His Grace* (1707) has been reprinted in America. A modern theologian whose system is much like Gill's is Herman Hoeksema, whose *Reformed Dogmatics* (1966) placed excessive emphasis on the sovereign grace of God. The description of hyper-Calvinism is, of course, made from within central or classic *Calvinism/Reformed theology.* To people outside the Reformed faith it merely appears as a form of Calvinism, no better or worse than others.

C. D. Daniel, "Hyper Calvinism and John Gill" (diss., University of Edinburgh, 1983); D. Engelsma, *Hyper-Calvinism and the Call of the Gospel* (1980); P. Toon, *The Emergence of Hyper-Calvinism* (1967).

PETER TOON

Idolatry

Idolatry A distinctive trait of *Reformed theology* has been its conception of *God* as utterly transcendent and its eagerness to safeguard the spiritual dimension of *worship* against materialist encroachments. During much of the early history of the Reformed tradition, this was expressed in a passionate struggle against idolatry, or false worship. It can be argued that the word "idolatry" itself became the Reformed shibboleth in the sixteenth and seventeenth centuries, the password through which the Reformed could be identified. In fact, the very name "Reformed" alludes to how this tradition opposed Roman Catholic devotion and cleansed itself from all perceived traces of corruption in worship and *piety,* in contrast to the more moderate and traditionalist reforms of the Lutheran and Anglican churches.

"Idolatry" is a polemical term presupposing a definition of what is true and what is false in religion. Most narrowly, it refers to worship of images constructed by human hands, or of false deities. More broadly, it means not simply worship of physical objects but any form of devotion judged incorrect. Reformed concern with idolatry extended far beyond use of painted or carved images in worship, and even beyond liturgical settings, to any devotional gesture displayed in public or private perceived as contrary to God's commands.

The Protestant Reformed attack on Roman Catholic piety had been foreshadowed in the Christian past by diverse protest movements, from the iconoclasts of eighth-century Byzantium to Lollards and Hussites of the fourteenth and fifteenth centuries. But its most evident immediate cause was the biblically centered reformist Christian humanism impulse, principally through Erasmus. Two of the most influential exponents of the Reformed theology of idolatry, Andreas Bodenstein von Karlstadt (1480–1541) and Huldrych Zwingli, admitted their indebtedness to Erasmus.

Though Zwingli began publicly to criticize much of late-medieval piety in Zurich (1519), the Protestant attack on Roman Catholic "idolatry" began in earnest with Karlstadt in Wittenberg (1521), albeit abortively (Luther hurried home from his hiding place at the Wartburg to expel Karlstadt from Wittenberg and reverse his colleague's iconoclastic reforms). Karlstadt published the first Protestant treatise against idolatry, *On the Abolition of Images* (1522), a tract that made a substantial impact in Zwingli's Zurich.

It was in Zurich that the war against idolatry first triumphed (1524), when images were removed from all churches and the Roman Catholic Mass was replaced with a simplified (and "purified") *liturgy*. It was principally through a series of public challenges against images and the Mass that the Reformed movement managed to spread to Bern (1528), St. Gall (1528), Basel (1529), Neuchütel (1530), and Geneva (1536). The Reformed theology of idolatry was further developed and refined by Zwingli, especially in his *Answer to Valentin Compar* (1525) and his larger *On the True and False Religion* (1525). Zwingli's successor at Zurich, Heinrich Bullinger, would add a historical dimension to the Reformed argument against idolatry in his *On the Origin of Errors* (1528–29; rev. and enlarged, 1539). This inspired Martin Bucer in Strassburg to take a more decisive stand and publish *That Any Kind of Images May Not Be Permitted* (1530).

Reformed Protestant polemic against idolatry reached its fullest and most enduring expression in the work of John Calvin. He extended the struggle beyond Geneva to lands where Reformed congregations risked persecution, especially France, the Netherlands, and England. Unlike his predecessors, Calvin had to teach Protestants who did not have the power to overcome the "idolatrous" societies in which they lived. Though Calvin contributed much to the development of an anti-idolatrous theology in his *Institutes* and in lesser treatises such as *Inventory of Relics* (1543), it is principally in his struggle against the compromising attitude of the so-called Nicodemites that he further sharpened the edge of the Reformed attack on Catholic piety. In opposition to the Nicodemites, who thought it permissible to partake in idolatrous worship as long as one's interior disposition was anti-idolatrous, Calvin argued that there could never be any compromise where worship was concerned and that any participation in Roman Catholic worship was sinful. In those cases where an open rejection of compromise raised the threat of persecution, Calvin allowed only two alternatives: exile or martyrdom.

After Calvin, another alternative began to be seriously considered by Reformed leaders: armed resistance to idolatrous rulers. In varying degrees, resistance, and even revolution, would eventually be deemed proper and necessary. Important figures who argued in favor of resistance were Theodore Beza, Pierre Viret, Philippe Duplessis-Mornay (1549–1623), John Knox, Christopher Goodman (c. 1520–1603), and John Ponet (1514–56).

In England, Reformed opposition to the "Romish" Anglican church and its idolatrous worship would lead to significant developments, not the least of which was creation of a Puritan separatist colony in Massachusetts (1620). Two decades later, the English Puritan struggle against idolatry would lead to civil war, regicide, and Oliver Cromwell's Reformed commonwealth.

Since the end of the seventeenth-century religious wars, the word "idolatry" has gradually fallen into disuse among the Reformed; in our own ecumenically minded age, it is no longer part of religious discourse. Nonetheless, the concepts signified by the earlier struggle against idolatry remain an integral part of the Reformed heritage.

C. C. Christensen, *Art and the Reformation in Germany* (1980); C. M. N. Eire, *War against the Idols* (1986); C. A. Garside, Jr., *Zwingli and the Arts* (1966).

CARLOS M. N. EIRE

Incarnation The biblical *locus classicus* for the *doctrine* of the incarnation—that "the Word (Gr. *logos*) became flesh and dwelt among us"—is John 1:14. The doctrine gained new significance in the second century when Christian apologists such as Justin Martyr, influenced by Middle Platonic *philosophy*, used it to argue that Jesus was the manifestation of God's eternal *reason* (also *logos*). Irenaeus, writing against Gnostic *Christology*, stressed the reality of the union of human and divine natures in the one person of Christ and argued that Christ became human so that human beings could become like *God*. For this apotheosis of *humanity* to occur, Christ had to be truly human and truly divine.

These early attempts to define the meaning of the incarnation led to many christological debates about the relationship between Jesus Christ and God the Father, and the relationship between the divine and human natures in the person of Christ. The orthodox teaching was promulgated at the Councils of Nicaea (A.D. 325) and Chalcedon (A.D. 451). The Chalcedonian Definition asserted that two distinct natures—divine and human—were inseparably united in the one person of Christ. To grasp fully the meaning of the doctrine of the incarnation, it would be necessary to examine the doctrines of *creation*, *revelation*, Christology, and the *sacraments*.

The Reformation did little to alter traditional teaching on the person and work of Christ. The Lutherans and the Reformed, however, in the context of sacramental debates, did arrive at somewhat different conceptions of the meaning of the incarnation for Christian faith. Martin Luther argued that in the incarnation, the Second Person of the divine *Trinity* willingly bound himself to the limits of human nature; a wonderful exchange took place in which humanity received the blessedness of Christ's divine being while Christ took up into himself the sinfulness and weakness of human nature. Through the *communicatio idiomatum* ("communication of properties") Luther argued, the divine nature in Christ shared properties of the human nature and vice versa. Thus, the risen body of Christ is ubiquitous and can be received in, with, and under the sacraments in all times and places. Luther believed that God must be sought exclusively in the person of Jesus. His Christology is reminiscent of Cyril of Alexandria's emphasis on the unity of the divine and the human in the one person of Jesus Christ.

The views of John Calvin on the incarnation, on the other hand, tended to emphasize the distinction between the two natures in Christ. In the incarnation, Calvin argued, God was manifested in human flesh. However, because nothing finite can completely contain the infinite (*finitum non capax infiniti*), Christ is also active outside the flesh of Jesus. No less than Luther, Calvin insisted that God wills to be known only in Christ. But he did not believe this meant that God is revealed only in the incarnation; Christ, the eternal Word, also operates outside the work of Jesus. Lutheran critics of Calvin's Christology called this the *extra calvinisticum*. Calvin's emphasis on the distinction between the finite and the infinite had consequences for the way he conceived the relationship between the divine and the human nature in the person of Jesus. He understood the communication of properties as a figure of speech. The suggestion that there is an actual exchange of properties between the two natures sounded to Calvin dangerously like a mixture of the two, and any such mixture would compromise the reality of both natures of Christ. The body of Christ belongs to Christ's humanity and as such it cannot be ubiquitous. The union of the two natures is not so much a static union in the person as a dynamic union in the action of the Mediator—specifically in his threefold office (*munus triplex*) as prophet, priest, and king.

It would be misleading to overemphasize the distinction between Lutheran and *Reformed theology* on this point. As Karl Barth pointed out, even Luther himself acknowledged that human limits could not enclose the divine. Calvin was no less insistent than Luther that we have no *knowledge of God* apart from Christ. Nevertheless, the distinction is not illusory; it becomes significant when one compares Reformed and Lutheran views on the sacraments.

Friedrich Schleiermacher argued that John 1:14 is the basic text of all theology. Unlike Luther and Calvin, however, he conceived the incarnation not as the enfleshment of the Second Person of the divine Trinity but as the absolute immanence of God in the human consciousness of Jesus. Because Jesus' God-consciousness was without interruption and disturbance, it was a "veritable existence of God in him." Schleiermacher also understood a union of the divine and the human to be central to the meaning of *justification* and *sanctification.* In this sense, the process of redemption in individuals and the *church* as a community is a progressive incarnation of the life of Christ.

In recent years, the logical status of incarnation language has been debated. A prominent British Presbyterian theologian, John Hick, has argued that although incarnation is a fundamental theme in the Christian tradition, it is solely a metaphor and should not be converted to a metaphysical proposition or hypothesis. His criticisms of the traditional understanding, however, have themselves been debated.

Barth, *CD* I/2, 168–70; II/1, 487–90; Calvin, *Inst.* 2.12–14; M. Goulder, ed., *Incarnation and Myth: The Debate Continued* (1979); B. Hebblethwaite, *The Incarnation: Collected Essays in Christology* (1987); J. Hick, *The Myth of God Incarnate* (1976); Schleiermacher, *CF*, secs. 93–99; E. D. Willis, *Calvin's Catholic Christology: The Function of the So-called Extra Calvinisticum in Calvin's Theology* (1966).

DAWN DEVRIES

Infralapsarianism

After the death of John Calvin, Reformed theologians were concerned with "the order of the decrees of God." The two chief views of this order were infralapsarianism and *supralapsarianism.*

Both views agreed that *God* brought all things to pass according to God's eternal plans or *decrees.* They disagreed, however, on what precisely went on in the divine mind as God formulated these eternal plans. In the supralapsarian view, God's highest purpose was to glorify God in the *salvation* of certain human beings. To do this, God determined to create these people and permit them to fall into *sin.* The eternal divine thought process was this ordered list of decrees: election-salvation, *creation,* and permission of the fall.

The infralapsarians objected that this order made the fall an upward step to fulfilling God's redemptive purposes; thus, it compromised the evil of sin. They posited a rival order rejecting attempts to explain the fall. This was: creation, permission of the fall, and election-salvation. In this view, *election* is more clearly an election of fallen human beings.

Most Reformed theologians have been infralapsarian. Reformed *confessions* generally express themselves in infralapsarian ways without condemning the other position. More recently, some theologians, such as Herman Bavinck, have refused to endorse either position. In this regard, it may be argued that both views exaggerated their competence to read the divine mind and the most to be learned from *scripture* is that each of God's thoughts takes each of the others into account. That is, God's purposes form a unity. Granted this premise, many "orders" are possible: God may do A for the sake of B and also B for the sake of A. Thus, there may be truth in many suggested orders, and these may be mutually exclusive less often than theologians have thought.

J. M. Frame, *Doctrine of the Knowledge of God* (1987); R. A. Muller, *Christ and the Decree* (1986); B. B. Warfield, *The Plan of Salvation* (1942).

JOHN M. FRAME

Institutes of the Christian Religion

John Calvin's *Institutes of the Christian Religion* is a summary of the Protestant approach to Christianity as understood by a French scholar of the sixteenth century.

First addressed to the French king, Francis I, Calvin's work was intended to win a favorable hearing for Protestantism at the French court. The first edition (Basel, 1536) was brief, clear, and scholarly. Claiming the *authority* of the *Word of God* and support of the ancient *church*, it explained the Ten Commandments, the Apostles' Creed, the Lord's Prayer, and the *sacraments*, emphasizing a simple, classical approach not only to the doctrinal but also to the moral and liturgical aspects of Christianity. It was not intended primarily for theologians, yet it gave a masterful presentation of *justification* by *faith* and its significance for the Christian life. While it did not win over the French king, it made clear that Protestantism was an international religious movement rather than merely a religious expression of German nationalism.

The second edition of the *Institutes* (1539), published during Calvin's Strassburg pastorate, took a very different character. It was enlarged to serve as a textbook for theological students. Here Calvin began to give a full treatment of many traditional theological themes such as *Trinity, incarnation,* and *atonement.* Though these subjects were not at issue for the Reformers, Petrus Caroli had denounced Calvin for a defective *Christology* (1537). This led Calvin to a meticulous study of both Greek and Latin Fathers. Calvin was a devoted classicist and always returned "to the sources." From then on, his Christology had a distinctly patristic cast. With this edition, the *doctrine* of *predestination* was fully thought out. Here as always, Calvin was, above all, concerned with being faithful to *scripture,* yet the influence of patristic authors is also found. Calvin's predestination doctrine is both Pauline and Augustinian. The matter was important, because ever since Luther and Erasmus debated the subject, it was clear that this was the issue that divided classical Protestantism from Renaissance humanism.

Another feature of the 1539 edition is the section on the Christian life. Today this would be called a treatise on *spirituality.* But Calvin preferred the word "piety." The Latin word *pietas* means a way of life that respects authority. Calvin presented the Christian life as a humble and disciplined following of Christ. He rejected asceticism, teaching that God's gifts are to be appreciated and, with a sense of stewardship, employed for the ends God intended. In the *Institutes, piety* is a primary theological concern.

After reorganizing the Genevan church, Calvin produced a third Latin edition (1543) and wrote into it large sections on the doctrine of the church and the *ministry.* As a trained lawyer, Calvin was interested in questions of church government and administration, which in the Middle Ages were handled by canon lawyers rather than systematic theologians. Part of the genius of the *Institutes* is that it handles both. Several editions followed in which minor changes were made. But in 1559, Calvin produced an expanded final edition in which he completely rearranged the work, intending to make it a comprehensive statement of the Christian religion.

The 1559 *Institutes* is arranged in four books. Book 1 deals with our *knowledge of God* the Creator. Here Calvin works out his doctrine of *revelation*, showing the authority of scripture both for a knowledge of God and of ourselves. He treats the doctrine of the Trinity, adding a considerable amount of polemical material against Michael Servetus. The doctrine of *creation* is addressed and finally the doctrine of *providence* as the logical continuation of creation. Calvin carefully distinguishes the biblical understanding of providence from the philosophical concept of determinism.

Book 2 treats our knowledge of God the Redeemer. In Christ, crucified and risen, God is known as redeemer. While Book 2 speaks at length of the objective divine work of redemption, Book 3 treats the subjective *experience*. Now Calvin talks about *salvation* through *election*, justification, *sanctification*, and glorification. Election is discussed in terms of the subjective experience of salvation. The point of this doctrine is that salvation is a divine gift rather than a human accomplishment. In Book 3, Calvin underlines the work of the *Holy Spirit* in the human heart. While his emphasis on the Spirit only becomes clear in the 1559 edition, the doctrine of the Spirit had always been fundamental to his understanding of scripture, *prayer, ordination,* and the sacraments. The *Institutes* is characterized by an equal emphasis on the subjective and objective aspects of religion.

Book 4 is devoted to the external means by which God invites us into the society of Christ. Here too the doctrine of the Holy Spirit is prominent as Calvin discusses the church, the ministry, and sacraments. The *Institutes* presents a strong doctrine of church and ministry. For Calvin, the ministerial structure of the church is not indifferent but important to the church's faithfulness. These chapters are as theological as the earlier ones, even if they treat the more objective problems of *polity* and *worship.*

Calvin's treatment of the *Lord's Supper* is an example. First, he aimed at an approach that avoided making the sacrament into a sacrifice and thus compromising the unique sacrifice of Christ. For Calvin as for Luther, the chief problem with the Roman Mass was that it had been made a sacrifice. Second, Calvin wanted to recognize our union with Christ at the Supper and yet avoid the scholastic doctrine of transubstantiation. As Calvin saw it, Christ is present by means of the Spirit. The Spirit unites us to Christ in his death and *resurrection* through sharing the covenant meal. Calvin's approach was guided by the biblical concept of *covenant* as well as the wisdom theology of John's Gospel which emphasized the real presence of the Word.

***

J. Calvin, *Institutes of the Christian Religion* (1559 ed.), ed. J. T. McNeill and trans. F. L. Battles (1960); *Institutes* (1536 ed.), trans. F. L. Battles (1986); D. K. McKim, ed., *Calvin's Institutes: Abridged Edition* (2000).

HUGHES OLIPHANT OLD

Irish Articles of Religion

Irish Articles of Religion One hundred and four theological points adopted by the Irish Episcopal Church (1615) that incorporated the *Calvinism* of the *Lambeth Articles.* The Irish Articles were the church's doctrinal standard until 1635 when the Church of England's *Thirty-nine Articles,* to which these are similar, were adopted. The Irish Articles were written by James Ussher (1581–1656), professor of divinity in Dublin, and were a major influence on the *WCF,* which adopted the same order of topics, chapter headings, and phrasings at many points.

The articles cite the Nicene, Athanasian, and Apostles' Creeds as scriptural (art. 7) while declaring that "the holy Scriptures contain all things necessary to salvation, and are able to instruct sufficiently in all points of faith that we are bound to believe, and all good duties that we are bound to practice" (art. 6). Only the "good pleasure of God" is the basis for *predestination* (art. 14) where-by *God* ordained "whatsoever in time should come to pass" (art. 11) and "some unto life, and reprobated some unto death" (art. 12). *Election* in Christ is to be "full of sweet, pleasant, and unspeakable comfort to godly persons" (art. 16). The articles maintain that God is not "the author of sin" (art. 28), and that "a true, lively, justifying faith and the sanctifying spirit of God is not extinguished nor vanished away in the regenerate, either finally or totally" (art. 38). The articles declare that it is lawful for Christians "at the commandment of the magistrate, to bear arms and to serve in just wars" (art. 62). General councils of the *church* "may err, and sometimes have erred, even in things pertaining to the rule of piety" (art. 76). The *sacraments* are "not only badges or tokens" of Christian profession "but rather certain sure witnesses and effectual or powerful signs of grace and God's good will towards us" (art. 85).

Schaff, *Creeds*, 3:526–44.

DONALD K. MCKIM

Irresistible Grace *see* **Dort, Synod of**

Jesus Christ *see* **Christology**

Judgment *see* **Hell**

Justice Justice has a special place in Reformed understanding, particularly in Anglo-American Calvinist traditions. Calvin emphasized justice by adding a third use to Luther's two uses of the *law*. For Luther, law convicted of *sin* and, second, sought to limit human action and force. For Calvin, law could have a positive third role as teacher of the will of *God* in human matters. Calvin learned from Plato and Aristotle, *Augustine,* and Aquinas that justice is central to human interaction. Law can be a chief instrument for justice.

Plato and Aristotle posited justice as the virtue that gave content as well as form to human interactions wherein the other virtues of courage, prudence, and temperance could be evidenced. Augustine built his views of religion and society on two sorts of law and justice—the temporal (emphasizing love of self) and the eternal (characterized by love of God). He argued that justice is a universal norm. To do justice is to render proper due to each. Our duty to God is to love God. Hence, justice can summarize Christian as well as more general ethics.

Calvinism emphasized the continuing validity and normativity of the Hebrew Scriptures for Christians. Old Testament emphases on justice and godly societal relations thus received important attention in *Reformed theology.*

A Renaissance scholar and trained lawyer before he became a pastor and a reformer, Calvin retained and practiced high regard for the magistrate's office as it seeks to govern justly. Subsequent Calvinists, such as the Rhinelanders, the Dutch, and John Knox, continued this emphasis. The Puritan "revolution of the saints" (Michael Walzer) was centrally a Reformed movement. It brought parliamentary government to Anglo-Saxon lands. The Puritans developed nascent bourgeois and contractual justice and society to replace the declining medieval order. That Reformed contribution continues to provide a major foundation for modern Western democratic social, political, and economic relations.

Biblical emphases. Biblical concerns for justice and society were reemphasized in twentieth-century Reformed thinking. Before mid-century, Christian realism (cf. Reinhold Niebuhr) utilized biblical understandings of *humanity* and society to remind the *church* that human possibility for good makes democratic justice possible and that human proclivity for evil makes democracy necessary. The power of structures and systems caused realism to insist that Christian virtue and discipleship must have concrete expression in political and economic justice. In

Europe, neo-orthodox resistance to Nazism was similarly grounded (cf. Karl Barth).

After mid-century, *liberation theology* reminded the church that both the Hebrew and early church scriptures have social justice as a central emphasis. The Hebrew exodus from Egypt is seen as determinative for OT understanding. Not only the book of Exodus and the Prophets but the entire corpus was read in terms of God's overriding concern for justice in society and *creation* (cf. black and Latin American theology, José Miranda, Phyllis Trible, Walter Brueggemann, Paul Hanson). Where the KJV has usually read the Hebrew *mishpat* as (God's) "judgment," the better perspective sees God as creatively involved with and working for "justice."

Interpretation of early church *scripture* was more mixed. In the early twentieth century, Walter Rauschenbusch and others saw Jesus as particularly concerned with social justice. After mid-century, the Lukan narrative became a seminal source for justice, since Jesus proclaims his *ministry* precisely as the establishment of justice in a broad social context (esp. Luke 4).

Attention to social settings of both the Hebrew and early church scriptures proposes that social arrangements and the implied issues and norms of justice are central to NT understanding. Attention to justice and social context are important ways in which contemporary theological inquiry engages pressing contemporary concerns.

Senses of justice. "Justice" is used in various ways. Four senses are often distinguished.

1. The Bible depicts God as *just and righteous.* These emphases have recently dominated. God's *mishpat* is viewed as justice rather than as *judgment.* That is, God works positively for just relationships rather than as one who principally chastises evil. Second, a strong emphasis on God as special friend of the poor and weak has emerged in the past decade (African-American and third-world liberation theology). Third, the link between God's justice and human activity is seen especially as a call for godly people to do social justice with special regard for the poor and weak.

2. *Justice and society.* Biblical justice is thus closely linked to justice in the broader society and the political community. From Calvin and the Puritans to contemporary churches, a particular strength of Reformed Christians has been their emphasis on the interrelationship between Christian and general social norms. H. Richard Niebuhr (*Christ and Culture* [1951]) termed this the "transformational" pattern. It has dominated expressions of Reformed theology in the United States and elsewhere, thus profoundly influencing U.S. and other history and theology.

Reflection on justice in the United States since Reinhold Niebuhr has been led by such social thinkers as John Rawls (*A Theory of Justice* [1971]) and Michael Walzer (*The Spheres of Justice* [1983]). They both view justice as the "first virtue" of social arrangements. Both are committed to egalitarian principles and approve inequality only when it benefits the weak and needy.

For Rawls, justice in Western democracies preeminently requires *procedures* by which self-interest can be set aside in social decision making. For Walzer, justice requires communities that self-consciously and with sophisticated insight work to treat persons with respect in complex and differentiated social roles.

Given their histories and theologies, it is no accident that Reformed Christians and Jews are overrepresented in U.S. legislatures and in the legal profession. Like Calvin, Knox, the Puritans, and Barth, contemporary Reformed persons have unusual resources and opportunities to engage the broader culture.

In these roles, Christians participate in the authoritative allocation of values and address critical questions of social distributive and commutative justice. *Distributive justice* aims to distribute fairly a community's benefits and burdens (e.g., wealth, taxation, health care). Distributive justice is a seminal subject whether in liberation theologies or in works of Rawls ("Justice as Fairness") or Walzer (and a more social tradition). *Commutative justice* focuses more on direct interpersonal relations and thus deals with contracts (consent) and interpersonal crime and punishment. The great size, complexity, and pluralism of U.S. society make commutative justice much more perplexing than in earlier, simpler times.

3. *Justice and love.* Some Christian traditions separate and contrast justice and love. Such separation is easiest when both love and justice are caricatured: love is private, perfectionist, self-sacrificing, subjective, and so forth; justice is public, realistic, and objective.

If "justice" is a difficult and complicated concept, "love" has even more numerous and less precise meanings. The word "love" is often debased in contemporary thinking. The Greek word *agapē* (God's self-giving love) surely includes justice and no doubt goes beyond formal human justice categories. But justice often challenges and structures erotic love (*erōs*) and neighbor/brotherly love (*philia*). Justice requires higher standards than "All is fair in love and war."

A useful criterion is: "It is not Christian to get to love too soon." A danger of U.S. Protestant ethics is that of locating morality in the individual and one's subjective understanding. Love is particularly susceptible in this regard. When we interpret love from this perspective, we easily justify much in terms of self-interest. With love a debased concept, even married partners would do well to ask how to live justly with each other. That is, in order to know what it is to love, we must first understand what is just.

4. *Justice and character.* "Justice" is used to describe the character of a moral agent. God is preeminently the just One. It matters greatly, however, whether the emphasis is on God doing and bringing justice or whether God's justice is primarily ontological in God's self. Similarly, our overall theological and biblical understandings will control whether *mishpat* is rendered as God judging or God doing justice.

Some recent Protestant thought has emphasized the church as character-shaping community rather than as centrally concerned with teleology or public policy. Through the *Holy Spirit* and by our living in the Christian community, our character will be shaped toward virtues such as justice. Among the four classical virtues (justice, courage, prudence, and temperance), justice was supreme, ordering the others. To the classical virtues in Aristotle, Thomas Aquinas added the (higher, if more unusual) theological virtues of *faith, hope,* and love. In these terms, Christian character will be marked by justice ordering the virtues. Christian *spirituality* will result in justice as well as in courage, prudence, temperance, faith, hope, and love.

Disappointment at the failures of policies and actions that seek justice is partly offset by contemporary emphases on community and character. The disappearance of a U.S. Protestant moral consensus and the emergence not only of pluralism but of sharp cleavages over moral issues lead communities to emphasize the shaping of character (education and socialization). There is an easier and closer relationship between character shaping and current theologies of rhetoric or narrative than between the latter and policy ethics. It is easier for Reformed church folks to think about "shaping Christian character" than to work for justice in the complexities of pluralistic public policy. Recent studies suggest that genotype plays a major role in what we often term "character." Culture plays a major role in the definition and evaluation of virtue (bravery, prudence, temperance, justice). Character ethics and policy ethics are thus perhaps best linked in such phrases as "By their fruits you shall know them."

FRED O. BONKOVSKY

Justification   The *doctrine* of justification by *grace* through *faith* alone is central to the teaching of the Reformation. It stood as a key to Martin Luther's own exegetical insight at the beginning and wellspring of the Reformation.

The importance of this biblical and doctrinal insight to both Lutheran and Calvinist forms of Protestantism can easily obscure the fact that the Reformation view of justification was not always the doctrinal view of the *church* and that neither the early church nor the medieval church recognized the principle of justification *sola fide*. Additionally, the patristic and medieval tradition, together with several of the first Reformers—notably Luther and Martin Bucer—did not make an absolute distinction between justification and **sanctification**. Bucer spoke of a double justification according to which believers were both counted and made righteous. Nonetheless, it is the *"sola,"* by faith *alone*, to the utter exclusion of works, that is the distinctive characteristic of the Protestant and Reformed teaching and the reason Luther, Calvin, and the later Protestant **tradition** affirmed categorically that justification is the *articulus stantis et cadentis ecclesiae*, the "article of the standing or falling of the church."

Luther's doctrine of justification by grace alone through faith rests on a view of faith as trusting or faithful apprehension of divine things, an utter trust in the grace of **God** that sets aside all trust in worldly things and in **salvation** attainable by human means. This faith itself is unattainable by human means and must be brought about by the work of the **Holy Spirit** on the human heart. It is this faith alone that justifies. Luther insisted that the correct understanding of Rom. 3:28 requires the addition of *sola* to the translation. **Forgiveness** and righteousness are graciously imputed by God on the ground of this faith. Indeed, for Luther, faith itself justifies inasmuch as it is faith that apprehends Christ and appropriates his righteousness. This is not to say, however, that justification can be grounded even in part on Christian love or on works, as if faith were an act or choice of the individual. **Sin** remains in the justified who, on the basis of their own acts, can never be worthy before God; and faith is an inward openness to God, a setting aside of our own merit, a negation of our insufficient moral striving. For Luther, as for all subsequent Lutheran and Reformed thinkers, the believer is *simul iustus et peccator*, "at once justified and a sinner."

Philipp Melanchthon's early systematization of Protestant theology was crucial to the development not only of Lutheran but also of Reformed doctrine. With Luther, he identified justification as the chief article of the Christian faith. Perhaps more consistently than Luther, Melanchthon regarded justification as a forensic act, but very much in the spirit of Luther he also insisted justification was intimately connected with the regenerative work of the Holy Spirit. The initial order of salvation proposed early on by Melanchthon moved from contrition or sorrow for sin to faith and, on the basis of faith, to the forgiveness of sins, understood forensically as justification, and the **regeneration** of the believer. Faith, therefore, provides the ground both for the counting righteous and for the making righteous of believers—and it precedes both justification and regeneration or sanctification.

Calvin offers a clarification and codification of his predecessors' teachings. Like them, he was concerned to separate justification from any notion of works-righteousness but also to retain the connection between justification and the new life in Christ. He therefore spoke of a twofold grace (*duplex gratia*), by which believers are both reckoned righteous in Christ and sanctified by his Spirit (*Inst.* 3.11.1). Calvin insisted on the parallel and connection between the divine acts of counting the believer righteous and making the believer righteous; justification and sanctification are grasped together. But Calvin equally clearly removed all consideration of works and of personal righteousness from the basic calculus of justification, which is entirely forensic. A person is justified when counted righteous—"who, excluded from the righteousness of works, grasps the righteousness of Christ through faith" (*Inst.* 3.11.2). Faith therefore is not merely knowledge and assent. It is also a profound heartfelt or volitional acceptance of Christ that grounds the application of God's grace to believers.

Calvin's emphasis on faithful acceptance of Christ and his benefits as the basis of justification points toward the profound connection in his theology between justification and the substitutionary *atonement* effected by Christ. Believers are counted righteous because of the righteousness of Christ who stands in their place and fulfills the righteousness and obedience required by God of human beings. Since individuals remain sinful after they are counted righteous through faith, Calvin can also argue a double justification—first of the sinner and then of the works of the justified sinner, which now are counted righteous insofar as they are offered to God in and through the grace of Christ.

Just as Calvin had offered a still clearer view of the utterly forensic character of justification than any of his predecessors, so the later Reformed tradition continued to sharpen the distinction between justification and sanctification. The development of *Reformed orthodoxy* in the late sixteenth century saw the formulation of a more strict view of the order of salvation in which calling, regeneration, faith, justification, sanctification, and glorification were understood not only as distinct moments in the order but also as strictly separate in significance and, to a somewhat greater degree than had been typical of the Reformers, were explained in terms of the fourfold Aristotelian causality. Nonetheless, Reformed orthodox dogmatics, notably the *Leiden Synopsis* (1626), continued to follow Luther and Calvin in identifying justification as a "foremost" and genuinely foundational

doctrine of Protestantism. Justification is not, therefore, an infusion of righteousness but a judicial act of God that declares a believer righteous by grace apart from any personal merit. The orthodox declared that in this act God sits as a judge, but on "the throne of grace" rather than on "the throne of righteousness," inasmuch as the divine righteousness no longer stands over against human unworthiness as a ground of *judgment.*

Unlike Luther, but quite in the tradition of Calvin, the orthodox indicated it is not, strictly, faith that justifies but grace in Christ. Faith, defined as consisting not only in knowledge and assent but also and primarily as a faithful apprehension of Christ and of Christian truth by the whole person, provides the inward means of receiving God's grace. Since, moreover, faith itself is a gift of God's grace and not something initiated by the believer, there can be no confusion of faith with works. The efficient cause of justification is the grace of God, while the material cause is neither faith nor works but the righteousness of Christ applied against the case of the faithful but still sinful person. Righteousness remains inherent only in Christ and belongs to the believer by imputation.

Protestant orthodox writers also drew lines of connection between justification and other doctrines somewhat more clearly and pointedly than the Reformers. Thus, justification, as well as the faith on which it is grounded, is identified as a result of *election* and, in the theology of strict predestinarians like Samuel Maresius (1599–1673), as an eternal forensic act executed in time. Similarly, the idea of double justification is connected more clearly and fully by the orthodox with the inward working of grace and the Spirit in believers, with the inherent but imperfect righteousness brought about in believers in their regeneration and sanctification, and with the freely given obedience of believers to the *law* considered according to its third use.

After the orthodox codification of Reformed doctrine, the most notable discussion of the doctrine of justification in the Reformed tradition is Karl Barth's. Barth attempted both to sum up the Reformed insights and to refashion them in the light of his own highly Christocentric model of theology. Barth's teaching builds on a conception of justification as a totally gracious temporal act of God in Christ rooted eternally in "God's freedom for man" as it is expressed in Jesus Christ. For Barth, justification must be understood as God's eternal decision for *humanity* in Christ who, in the cross and *resurrection,* is himself both elect and reprobate. Justification, therefore, remains a justification of the unrighteous, an acquittal by God opening for the sinner a new future grounded in faith. Thus, in his basic definition of the believer as "at once justified and a sinner" and in his insistence on justification as occurring by faith alone apart from all works, Barth remains faithful to the Reformed tradition. What is original to Barth is the way justification binds together time and eternity in Christ's own election and *reprobation*—granting that earlier Reformed theology understood election, but not reprobation, as being in Christ, and viewed both decrees as directed toward human beings as individuals.

Barth, *CD* IV/1–2; G. C. Berkouwer, *Faith and Justification,* trans. L. B. Smedes (1954); J. Calvin, *Inst.* 3.1–4, 14–16; W. Dantine, *Justification of the Ungodly,* trans. E. W. and R. C. Gritsch (1968); H. Küng, *Justification: The Doctrine of Karl Barth and a Catholic Reflection* (1981); A. E. McGrath, *Iustitia Dei: A History of the Christian Doctrine of Justification,* 2 vols. (1986); A. Ritschl, *A Critical History of the Christian Doctrine of Justification and Reconciliation,* trans. J. S. Black (1872).

RICHARD A. MULLER

Kairos Document *The Kairos Document: Challenge to the Church (KD)* was first published in South Africa (September 1985), with a revised second edition following a year later. The title indicates that the *KD* is a theological witness to reading "the signs of the times" in South Africa. It was drafted and signed by pastors and theologians, mainly but not exclusively black, seeking theological direction amidst the current South African political crisis. A significant number of the persons involved were members of denominations that belong to the Reformed family of churches, and the *KD* reflects several recurrent themes in the history of *Reformed theology* and confession.

The *KD* distinguishes between and critically examines three types of theology. "State theology" supports and legitimates an unjust status quo on the basis of a false reading of Rom. 13:1–7, a confusion of *justice* with law and order, as well as a conflation of Christianity and patriotism.

"Church theology" proposes reconciliation as the solution to apartheid and advocates nonviolence as the only Christian means to social change. While both reconciliation and nonviolent action are grounded in the gospel, the way they are understood is based on faulty social analysis. The reconciliation proposed does not require justice as a condition, and the advocacy of nonviolence fails to deal with the violence of state and its structures of oppression.

"Prophetic theology" begins by analyzing the South African conflict in terms of the suffering of those who are oppressed. It proclaims that *God* is on the side of the oppressed and against the tyranny of the oppressors. On the basis of the biblical message of God's liberation, it provided grounds for hope, and in the light of that hope, it advocates concrete ways in which Christians and the *church* can participate in the struggle for justice in South Africa.

The *KD* is clearly influenced by *liberation theology.* However, its critique of the *idolatry* of "state theology" and of the inadequacy of "church theology" to deal with the harsh reality of political oppression, and its espousal of a "prophetic theology" that is both iconoclastic and socially transformative, resonate well with prophetic trajectories within the Reformed tradition. Indeed, bringing together liberation and Reformed insights is indicative of a major contribution being made by South African theology to the ecumenical church and especially its social witness. This is seen in the worldwide responses to the *KD* and the subsequent *The Road to Damascus: Kairos and Conversion* (1989), prepared and signed by third-world Christians.

W. H. Logan, *The Kairos Covenant* (1988); and "Kairos Documentation," *Journal of Theology for Southern Africa,* nos. 55–60.

JOHN W. DE GRUCHY

Kingdom of God   The biblical symbol of the kingdom is closely linked with God's dominion over nature, *history,* and every dimension of human life in the past, present, and future (Ps. 93:1; 97:1; 99:1; 1 Chron. 29:11; Dan. 4:3, 34–35). Many of the prophets look for the future consummation of God's reign in *judgment* and righteousness or a new age when nations shall be peaceably united by their willing obedience to the one true *God* of Israel (Isa. 2:1–5; 18:7; 59:20; Zeph. 3:9ff.; Zech. 14:9).

In the NT, Jesus proclaims and embodies the new age: "The time is fulfilled, and the kingdom of God has come near; repent, and believe in the good news" (Mark 1:15; Matt. 4:12–25; Luke 17:21; 21:31). The Sermon on the Mount may be read as proclamation of the possibility for a complete obedience that exemplifies what it means when God's kingdom breaks in. In John's Gospel, those who hear Jesus' words and have *faith* already possess *salvation* and eternal life, though the full gift comes only after Jesus' *ministry* through the *resurrection* (John 20:31). The Revelation to John envisions the future culmination of the kingdom in a new *heaven* and a new earth where nations walk by the light of God's glory and the lamp of Christ, the Lamb (Rev. 21).

Reformed theology typically under-

stands the kingdom as God's sovereign and transformative reign of righteousness and truth in contest with the forces of Satan, chaos, and *sin.* John Calvin says that *humanity* withdraws from God's kingdom in the fall and is therewith deprived of spiritual gifts, including faith, love of God, and charity toward the neighbor—qualities restored only through the *grace* of *regeneration.* In Christ, God forgives our sins, corrects our inordinate desires, reshapes our obedience, and overcomes those powers and persons who stubbornly resist. Nevertheless, those who are thus returned to God's kingdom continue as pilgrims on earth until God is all in all. In the meantime, ecclesiastical constitutions are to order the *church* under God alone, without entangling regenerate consciences in human inventions, encroachments, and ceremonies. Civil *authority* is not to command anything against God's law, and it provides for a public manifestation of true religion at the same time that it establishes civil *justice* and outward morality (*Inst.* 1.14.15; 2.2.12; 3.19.15; 3.20.42; 4.10; 4.20.1, 32).

English Puritans, such as Thomas Cartwright and William Perkins, were more optimistic about the extent to which a new order might be realized here and now. They discussed an order where church patterns based on God's Word became the standard for social and political life. Puritans in New England such as Robert Winthrop and John Cotton consciously attempted to fashion a new society under God's reign by framing constitutions and covenants based on revelation, upholding the independence of the church in determining its own organization and discipline and supporting the limitation of human powers in every aspect of life (David Little, *Religion, Order, and Law* [1969], 77, 81–131).

Albrecht Ritschl, a nineteenth-century Lutheran, understood the kingdom as the perfect moral fellowship or divinely ordained highest good. This final end, he said, is actualized in Jesus Christ and reflected Christian character; it also comprises the true motive for moral action and for the Christian's *vocation* in society (*The Christian Doctrine of Justification and Reconciliation*, vol. 3 [1874; ET 1900, repr. 1966], 284–326). For Walter Rauschenbusch, an American Baptist who espoused the **Social Gospel**, the kingdom is both present and future, task and gift, and it invites immediate action aimed at the redemptive transformation of society (*A Theology for the Social Gospel* [1917], 131–45).

More recently, Wolfhart Pannenberg has argued that the coming kingdom, though now hidden, will fulfill the social destiny of humanity. Sharing in Christ's mission, the church provisionally anticipates the kingdom and calls present society to attend to God's promised future (*Jesus—God and Man* [ET 1968], 373–75). The **Confession of 1967** notes that the kingdom's final triumph cannot be identified with partial earthly achievements; yet it also insists that "with an urgency born of this hope the church applies itself to present tasks and strives for a better world" (*BC* 9.55–56; cf. 4.123; 7.102; 7.301).

H. R. Niebuhr, *The Kingdom of God in America* (1937).

DOUGLAS F. OTTATI

King's Confession

An appendix to the *Scots Confession* (1560). It was also called the Second Scots Confession or Negative Confession. James VI of Scotland commissioned Rev. John Craig, a previous catechism writer, to compose it.

The Scots Confession is a Calvinist document portraying the faith of the Scottish reformers. From its publication to the production of the King's Confession (1581), there was great national fear of a resurgence of the Roman faith. It was believed the Scots Confession was signed by many secret papists, not because they agreed with its articles of faith, but with deceit in their hearts and perhaps even with a papal dispensation. There was a felt need for an appendix to the Scots

Confession to root out hidden papists. With the king's signature and power for ecclesiastical authorities to prosecute all who refused to sign the King's Confession, it was widely circulated and all university graduates were required to subscribe to it. The King's Confession is a strongly worded litany of all that the Scottish Protestants detested about the teachings and practices of the Roman Church.

G. D. Henderson, ed., *The Scots Confession, 1560* (1960).

RICHARD C. GAMBLE

Knowledge of God

The category of knowledge functions as a major motif in *Reformed theology*. **God** is viewed as the revealer and the human being as the knower. Accordingly, Reformed theology is preeminently a "theology of the Word," a theology that, following Calvin, speaks of a twofold knowledge of God as creator and redeemer.

The exaltation of the category of knowledge is evident in the opening question and answer of the **Geneva Catechism** (1541): "*Teacher*: What is the principal end of human life? *Student*: It is to know God." Appropriately, the first two books of Calvin's **Institutes** (1559) are titled "The Knowledge of God the Creator" and "The Knowledge of God the Redeemer."

Normally the words for "knowledge" are the Latin *cognitio* and *notitia* and the Old French *cognoissance*. These terms do not denote a purely objective knowledge of God, a knowledge *that* (that God exists or that the gospel history is true) but a knowledge intensely personal in nature. Objectivity and personalism are held closely together, particularly in Calvin's theology (cf. Torrance).

Reformed theology has often been accused of overintellectualizing the Christian faith, and while admittedly the works of **Reformed orthodoxy** betray this tendency, for Calvin knowledge was not simply a matter of the intellect but also of the heart and will. Calvin described *faith* as a kind of knowledge, not something that "flits about in our brains" without touching our hearts. It is "a firm and certain knowledge of God's benevolence toward us," which is "both revealed to our minds and sealed upon our hearts through the Holy Spirit" (*Inst.* 3.2.7). Moreover, it is intimately connected with the doing of God's will: "All right knowledge of God is born of obedience" (*Inst.* 1.6.2). Perhaps the closest modern equivalent of what Calvin meant by knowledge is "existential apprehension" (J. T. McNeill).

The Reformed understanding of the knowledge of God may be summarized:

1. Knowledge of God is the gift of God's *grace*. All our knowledge of God arises because of God's gracious action. The prior act of all human knowing and speaking of God is God's gracious self-revelation. If God had not freely chosen to be revealed, *humanity* would know nothing at all about God. Knowledge of God is not of "what God is," that is, of God's essence, which remains incomprehensible to us, but only "of what sort God is," that is, of God's gracious giving of God's self to us.

2. Knowledge of God is accommodated knowledge. In God's revelation, God accommodates himself to our weak human capacities. "God cannot be comprehended by us," says Calvin, "except as far as He accommodates (*attemperat*) Himself to our standards" (*Commentary* on Ezek. 9:3, 4; *CO* 40, col. 196). God walks with a mother step, prattles to us as to a baby, and "lisps" in speaking so we may understand. This *accommodation* is necessary for two reasons: first, because of the gap between creator and creature; second, because of the separation between a holy God and a sinful humanity. The twofold accommodation is seen supremely in Christ. As truly divine and truly human, Christ bridges the gulf between God and humanity and achieves our reconciliation "by the whole course of his obedience" (*Inst.* 2.16.5).

3. Knowledge of God is correlative knowledge. Calvin's opening sentence in the *Institutes* describes the bipolar character of knowledge: "Nearly all the wisdom we possess, that is to say, true and sound wisdom, consists of two parts: the knowledge of God and of ourselves" (*Inst.* 1.1.1). For Calvin, this was a fundamental principle: to know God is to know ourselves and to know ourselves aright is to be driven to look to God. Knowledge of God and knowledge of ourselves are so intimately related that all theological statements have their anthropological correlates and all anthropological statements their theological correlates.

4. Knowledge of God is twofold in character. Calvin also spoke, as did those who followed him, of a twofold knowledge of God (*duplex cognitio Dei*): the knowledge of God as creator and the knowledge of God as redeemer in and through Christ.

The sources of the knowledge of God as creator are:

a. Humanity itself. "There is within the human mind, and indeed by natural instinct, an awareness of divinity. . . . God himself has implanted in all men a certain understanding of his divine majesty" (*Inst.* 1.3.1). "Knowledge of God is naturally innate in the minds of all" (Vermigli, *Loci communes*, preface). This knowledge, however, is suppressed or corrupted by *sin*. In Calvin's judgment, scarcely one person in a hundred acts on it rightly and there is not one in whom it grows to maturity. Humanity does not apprehend God aright. The human mind under the condition of sin is a veritable "factory of idols."

b. The fashioning of the universe and God's government of it. According to Calvin, God "daily discloses himself in the whole workmanship of the universe." Indeed, the universe is "a sort of mirror in which we can contemplate God, who is otherwise invisible" (*Inst.* 1.5.1). Calvin at times is lyrical in speaking of God's *revelation* in *creation,* which he describes as "a dazzling theater" of God's glory. Though sufficient to render humanity inexcusable, because of human sinfulness the knowledge of God gained from creation is woefully inadequate: "If men were taught only by nature, they would hold to nothing certain or solid or clear-cut, but would be so tied to confused principles as to worship an unknown god" (*Inst.* 1.5.12). Interpreters of Calvin, however, have diverged sharply regarding the role and usefulness of *natural theology* in Calvin's teachings.

On the basis of God's inward and outward revelation, Reformed orthodoxy distinguished between the natural knowledge of God, drawn discursively from the *conscience* and created things, and revealed or saving knowledge, which was the result of God's special revelation. While asserting the truth and usefulness of natural theology in rendering humanity inexcusable before God, Reformed theologians were virtually unanimous in asserting that natural knowledge is not saving knowledge.

Since the "seed of religion" in the human mind and the revelation in creation failed for their proper effect, God provided a self-revelation in the written Word as well as an inner testimony of the *Holy Spirit* in the heart enabling sinful humanity to receive this revelation. By this conjoint divine action, objective and subjective, a true saving knowledge of God is communicated to sinful humanity. Calvin's formula is Word and Spirit. The work of the Spirit is not to supplement the revelation in *scripture* but to authenticate it in our hearts.

The knowledge of God as redeemer has only one source: *God's revelation in Jesus Christ embodied in scripture and testified to by the Holy Spirit.*

The Enlightenment resulted in a fundamental shift in sensibility regarding the matter of the knowledge of God. Since Locke and Kant, modern theology has been faced with the question of justifying claims to the knowledge of God. Some Reformed theologians, such as Friedrich Schleiermacher, adopted a foundational epistemological theory to justify the possibility of God's knowability. Schleiermacher understood revelation as supernatural and suprarational but believed it actualized a universal human possibility. Abraham Kuyper and Herman Bavinck strongly emphasized general revelation and common grace. Karl Barth forcefully rejected the search for a foundational epistemological theory and every notion of a natural theology. According to him, there is no real knowledge of God apart from God's self-revelation in Jesus Christ. While denying the idea of a general revelation in nature and history, Barth granted, in the context of discussing the prophetic office of Christ, that there may be in creation and *history* "parables of the kingdom," lesser lights that reflect Jesus Christ, the Light of life (*CD*).

T. F. Torrance has sought to establish both the uniqueness and the rationality of revelation in the intuitive self-evident nature of revelatory *experience*. Ronald Thiemann has given primacy to the paradigm of promise rather than knowledge. He believes we can still speak of revelation, not as a matter of God's knowability, but as narrated promise in which the *doctrine* of revelation is an account of God's identifiability.

E. A. Dowey, Jr., *The Knowledge of God in Calvin's Theology* (1952; repr. 1964); Heppe, *RD*; T. H. L. Parker, *Calvin's Doctrine of the Knowledge of God* (1959); R. F. Thiemann, *Revelation and Theology* (1985); T. F. Torrance, "Knowledge of God and Speech about Him according to John Calvin," in *Theology and Reconstruction* (1965); B. B. Warfield, "Calvin's Doctrine of the Knowledge of God," in *Calvin and Augustine* (1956); Weber, *FD*.

WILLIAM KLEMPA

Lambeth Articles   Originally composed by William Whitaker to oppose William Barrett's theology at Cambridge University, the Lambeth Articles (1595) were modified by Archbishop John Whitgift to reflect the scholastic Calvinist view of *predestination*. Approved by Whitgift and ecclesiastical commissioners whom Whitgift had gathered were nine articles affirming: (1) predestination of some to life; *reprobation* of some to death; (2) predestination to life is caused by God, not by foreseen *faith* or good works; (3) predestination of a certain number; (4) condemnation is based on sins; (5) justifying faith "is not lost nor does it pass away either totally or finally in the elect"; (6) true faith is accompanied by full assurance of *salvation* through Christ; (7) saving *grace* is not made available to all people; (8) only those drawn to *God* by Christ actually come; and (9) "It is not in the will or the power of each and every man to be saved."

The Lambeth Articles reflect opposition not only in Barrett but to Reformed and Lutheran theologians who viewed saving grace as applied to all people, gave a role in salvation to good works, made reprobation conditional, and temporized the idea that salvation was fixed eternally. At Cambridge, the French Reformed thinker Peter Baro asserted many of the above ideas, and the issues became hotly contested in the Dutch Calvinist struggles over *Arminianism.* Though the scholastic Calvinist view became the orthodox standard under Whitgift, the Elizabethan bishops, and the Heads of Cambridge's colleges, the Articles were not universally approved in England. In spite of Calvinist urgings, the Articles never became part of official Anglican church *doctrine.*

This failure was due to political opposition within the Elizabethan government and anti-Calvinism under James I (d. 1625) and Charles I (d. 1649). Politically, William Cecil and the queen opposed divisive public discussion of predestination. They also opposed the independent way Whitgift, the ecclesiastical commissioners, and Cambridge Heads had acted, for it seemed to imply an ecclesiastical freedom the Elizabethan state would not allow. Theologically, Baro and his followers immediately began to debate the Articles, largely from the viewpoint that people were created for salvation but lost it by rejecting God. Baro claimed that his views were identical with Augustine's before the conflict with Pelagius, many early church fathers, Philipp Melanchthon, and the Danish theologian Niels Hemmingson. In spite of his claims, Baro was forced to flee Cambridge.

After 1595, the Lambeth Articles remained the standard expression of English Calvinist orthodoxy; some, such as Archbishop Ussher, wanted to give the Articles confessional status. Others, such as Richard Neile and William Laud, attacked Calvinist orthodoxy and advanced notions of grace based on sacramental observances and on good works.

P. Lake, *Moderate Puritans and the Elizabethan Church* (1982); H. C. Porter, *Reformation and Reaction in Tudor Cambridge* (1958); N. Tyacke, *Anti-Calvinists* (1987).
RONALD J. VANDERMOLEN

Larger Catechism   *see* Westminster Confession of Faith

Law   *Third use of the law.* A distinctive characteristic of the Reformed view of the law is its emphasis on the third use of the law. For John Calvin, this function of the law as a norm and guide for the believer is its "proper and principal" use. Since Martin Luther used the same words to describe the second use of the law (Lat. *usus elenchticus*)—for Calvin the first—whereby sinners come to know their sinfulness and need for *grace,* it is assumed by some scholars (e.g., W. Elert) that this represents a polemic against Luther. This is doubtful, however, since Calvin nowhere alludes to Luther when treating this theme (*Inst.* 2.2.7ff.), and in their respective expositions of the Decalogue, Luther is even more extravagant than Calvin in praising the usefulness of God's commandments for the believer.

Yet it is true that Luther never formally taught a third use of the law. Calvin and he were one in their understandings of the first two uses of the law, the other being the political or civil use. They were also one in their views of grace, *justification,* and Christian *freedom,* as well as in their opposition to any form of works-righteousness on the one hand, or antinomianism on the other. Their exegesis of key passages in their commentaries on Romans and Galatians is fundamentally the same.

Nevertheless, dogmatically, as over against exegetically, there is a basic difference between Luther and Calvin in approaching the law. For Luther it generally connotes something negative and hostile; hence his listing the law along with *sin, death,* and the devil. For Calvin, the law was viewed primarily as a positive expression of the will of *God* whereby God restores the image of God in *humanity* and order in the fallen *creation.* Calvin's view could be called Deuteronomic, for to him law and love are not antithetical but are correlates. Another way of describing the differing approaches of Luther and Calvin is to designate their exegetical understandings "denotative" and their broader, more dogmatic usage "connotative." Denotatively, Luther and Calvin were basically agreed; connotatively, they were worlds apart, due largely to their differing backgrounds and faith experiences. Accordingly, "for all the agreement on various designations of the law in these two theologies, and even that it is the law that curses and kills, there is a very different fundamental apprehension of law in Calvin that controls his usage and creates a very different connotative field of force whenever the law is mentioned with reference to the life of the believer" (Dowey, 151).

Outside the Lutheran-Reformed context, some form of the third use is generally recognized except by situationalist ethicists who recognize no rules or norms at all. Here Calvin and the Reformed tradition are closer to Wesley with his emphasis on *sanctification* and the role of the law in that process.

Law and gospel or gospel and law? The question of the relation of law and gospel came to the forefront on the Continent again when Karl Barth published his controversial "Gospel and Law" (1935). As a result of nineteenth-century Luther research, the order law-gospel had become a veritable dogma in Lutheran theology. By reversing the order and declaring that the gospel precedes the law, Barth was attacking a sacrosanct pillar of Lutheranism. Barth recognized a certain validity in the Lutheran approach, but fundamentally, he maintained, we must begin with the promise (Gal. 3:17) and recognize that the law is "enclosed in the ark of the Covenant" (Barth, 71). The law is first of all a gift, an expression of God's grace, not a demand. Through sin, which deceives us, the law is seen and experienced as something hostile and negative and becomes "the law of sin and of death" (Rom. 8:2). In short, the law, according to its original purpose, is simply a form of the gospel.

Yet Barth recognized that law and gospel are not the same and must not be confused. "The gospel is not the law, just as the law is not the gospel; but because the law is in the gospel, comes from the gospel, and points to the gospel, we must first of all know about the gospel in order to know about the law, and not vice versa" (Barth, 72).

Many Lutherans assumed that this was simply an updated and radicalized variation of Calvin's position. There are similarities: Calvin, too, stressed the unity of the *Word of God* and the covenantal character of law. He also portrayed the law as a gift to God's chosen people and charter of their liberty subsequent to their redemption from bondage. However, the differences are significant. For example, contrary to Barth, Calvin also allowed for a significant role for the law of nature, however inadequate, prior to the clearer version of God's will given to Moses and the Israelites in the Decalogue. Calvin also recognized that though the accusing, killing function of the law is "accidental," because of the fall, there is nevertheless something inherent in the law that results in an antithesis between law and gospel, narrowly conceived (*Commentary* on Gal. 3:10; 2 Cor. 3:7–8). Ultimately, the difference here goes back to their differing views of *election* and their different anthropologies.

Ethic of gratitude. One of Barth's concerns was to make *theological ethics* a part of dogmatics. A corollary is an ethic of gratitude. The believer strives to follow God's law not simply as an act of obedience but as a response of gratitude. This approach was already inherent in the classic answer to question 1 of the *HC*: "What is your only comfort, in life and in death?" The answer includes not only the pellucid statement of the gospel: "That I belong—body and soul, in life and in death—not to myself but to my faithful Savior, Jesus Christ." It also includes its ethical corollary: "Therefore, by his Holy Spirit, . . . he makes me wholeheartedly willing and ready from now on to live for him." Here we have "an ethics in embryo" (Niesel, 194). More precisely, we have in the HC an ethics of gratitude, for the Decalogue is treated in part III: "Thankfulness" (cf. WLC, q. 97). The first use of the law (*usus elenchticus*) is also there, but in the first part of the catechism, which deals with human misery and sin, and in here, the form of the law is the two great commandments. The Decalogue, however, provides the basis for "the praise of works," which are done out of gratitude in response to the grace of God in Jesus Christ.

Barth, *CD* II/2, ch. 8; and "Gospel and Law," in *Community, State, and Church* (1960); Calvin, *Inst.* 2.7–11; 3.6–7; 4.20; E. A. Dowey, Jr., "Law in Luther and Calvin," *Theology Today* 41, no. 2 (1984): 146–53; I. J. Hesselink, *Calvin's Concept of the Law* (1991); W. Niesel, *The Gospel and the Churches* (1962); Weber, *FD* 2:362ff.

I. JOHN HESSELINK

Leiden Synopsis   The *Synopsis purioris theologiae* (1625), composed by Polyander, Walaeus, Thysius, and Rivetus, is an apologetic and polemic manual (880 pages) of Reformed *doctrine* as defined by the *Synod of Dort*. With *scripture* as its criterion, it surveys the history of doctrine. While it rejects idle speculation, traces of medieval *scholasticism* abound. Its physics is still pre-Copernican. *Socinianism*, Anabaptism, Catholicism, and Lutheranism, but also Manichaeism, Pelagianism, Epicureanism, and anthropomorphism are rejected.

H. Bavinck, ed., *Synopsis purioris theologiae* (1881); G. Itterzon, "De Synopsis Purioris Theologiae," *Nederlands Archief voor Kerkgeschiedenis* 23 (1930): 225–59.

DERK VISSER

Liberation Theology   A term applied to theologies that read the Bible and theological *tradition* from the perspective of poor and oppressed people and make liberation the central focus of Christian faith and life. Often used to refer to black, feminist, and third-world theologies, it refers more specifically to the Latin American theology that developed from an awakening of *conscience* to the poverty and suffering of the poor majority.

A Protestant movement, Church and Society in Latin America (ISAL), which began in the late 1950s, made a major contribution during the first stage of liberation theology's development. Led largely by Presbyterians and Methodists, it broke new ground in church circles by analyzing societal structures and patterns of dependency dominant in Latin America and emphasizing the need for systemic or revolutionary change. It dealt with social revolution as a theological problem, gradually moving from neo-orthodox theological categories to a theology of God's transforming action in *history*. A Brazilian Presbyterian, Rubem Alves, gave creative expression to this approach in *A Theology of Human Hope* (1969).

Under the impact of Vatican II and the Medellín Conference of Latin American Bishops (1968), many Catholic priests, women religious, and laypersons moved toward the poor and began to read the Bible and rethink their *faith* in dialogue with them. This led them to use a new theological method and articulate a new theological paradigm.

Gustavo Gutiérrez, a Peruvian priest, laid out the main lines in *A Theology of Liberation* (1971). Authentic theological reflection must be grounded in faith and commitment to the struggle of the poor. It is "critical reflection on praxis in the light of the Word of God," reflection about *God* rising out of a shared experience of oppression, tested and transformed in effective participation in the struggle for *justice.*

Biblical faith is primarily concerned with liberation, which integrates three elements into one salvific process: liberation of the poor from oppressive economic, social, and political conditions; the ongoing historical process of creation of new human beings in a new society; and Christ's liberation of each person from *sin,* the ultimate root of all injustice and oppression, for communion with God.

In the last several decades, growing numbers of theologians and biblical scholars, including a significant number of Protestants, have contributed to liberation theology's further development. Biblical study occupies a central place, giving particular attention to the centrality of the exodus in the Hebrew Scriptures, the focus of the prophets on social justice, and Jesus' message about the reign of God. Scholars emphasize the role of the poor as legitimate interpreters of the biblical message. They also use the "hermeneutical circle" in which interpretation is an ongoing process moving from *experience* to text and back again to experience. Many christological studies give greater importance to the historical Jesus and insist that following Jesus is a precondition for knowing Jesus. More recently, the *spirituality* of liberation has come to occupy a central place.

Liberation theology has a strong pastoral orientation, calling on the *church* to make a "preferential option for the poor" and working toward developing a new model of church, the Christian Base Communities. Focused on the transformation of human life in history, it uses the social sciences and categories of social analysis provided by Marxism. It also envisions a new economic order that responds to the needs of the poor majority.

In developing their theology, Latin Americans have drawn on the work of European biblical scholars and theologians of the Reformed tradition. As Protestant participation grows, there is increasing recognition of elements in the Reformed heritage that are essentially liberationist or point in that direction: affirmation that truth is in order to goodness; the emphasis of John Calvin on the sovereignty of God over all of life and history; his concern for the poor in Geneva and efforts to order the city's life by the *Word of God.* Moreover, as liberation theology contributes to a new reformation today, it challenges Reformed churches to recover their vision of the *ecclesia reformata semper reformanda* ("the church reformed and always being reformed"), thus creating conditions for more dynamic ecumenical relationships.

M. RICHARD SHAULL

Liberty, Religious

Generally, the condition in which individuals or groups are permitted to adopt and, within limits, express and act upon beliefs concerning religious matters, free of interference or penalties imposed by outsiders, including the state. Leading members of the Reformed tradition have differed widely on the degree of latitude within which religious beliefs may permissibly be expressed or acted upon without the interference or restriction of human authorities. They have also differed over whether the *church* or the state ought properly to decide the limits of religious expression and action.

For John Calvin, the liberty or *freedom* to adhere to and put into practice the central tenets of religious *faith* is an essential implication of authentic belief. Just as compelled belief is no belief at all, human interference with legitimate belief is a grievous offense. This concern is focused particularly in Calvin's *doctrine* of the freedom of *conscience*. The conscience is a special point of contact between human beings and God. As such, it is "higher than all human judgments" and therefore not finally bound by any human laws, "whether made by magistrate or by church" (*Inst.* 4.10.5). By the same token, it is exempt from the coercive control of human authorities, "because [the power of the sword] is not exercised over consciences" (*Inst.* 4.11.8).

In addition, Calvin's preoccupation with organizational questions for both church and state is related to his concern for religious liberty. For example, his consistent opposition to monarchy, especially in church organization, and his preference for a "polyarchic" *polity*—a system combining aristocracy and democracy—was aimed at institutionalizing a greater opportunity for the free exercise of conscience on the part of believers.

There are grounds in Calvin's thinking, then, for a strongly libertarian theory of religious freedom, in which the state plays a very restricted role in regard to religious expression and practice. Such a theory eventually did emerge among radical seventeenth-century Reformed thinkers, particularly in England and America. At the same time, there are certain emphases in Calvin's thought that worked to inhibit that development. Having stressed that the inner forum of conscience and the outer forum of *civil government* are presided over by "different kings and different laws" (*Inst.* 3.19.15), and must therefore be considered separately, Calvin proceeded to assert that the civil government must nevertheless "cherish and protect the outward worship of God" and "defend sound doctrine of piety and the position of the church" (*Inst.* 4.20.2). His apprehension, too, that democracy in church and state be tightly limited, lest it degenerate into anarchy and chaos, is an additional indication of the less radical side of Calvin's thought.

Whereas the reflections on freedom of conscience drive in the direction of sharply differentiating church and state, the concern civilly to establish uniform *piety* and *worship* modifies the distinction between the two spheres and considerably narrows the range within which religious beliefs may be expressed and practiced free of coercive restraint by civil authorities. Calvin's own practical policies in sixteenth-century Geneva were not notably libertarian. Expressions of *idolatry* or blasphemy or attacks against what were regarded as "the essentials of the faith" were subject to civil punishment.

The ambiguity and the instability in Calvin's thought on religious liberty are reflected in the deep and complex tensions and conflicts within Reformed thinking, more broadly considered. For example, though Zwingli, like Calvin, in practice favored the establishment of a uniform orthodoxy, he argued that it is the civil *authority* that is responsible to determine and supervise the "outward" aspects of religious life, namely, matters of ecclesiastical organization and discipline. Calvin, on the contrary, believed that such decisions were properly under the church's jurisdiction.

Some of Calvin's followers, such as John Knox in Scotland, Christopher Goodman and John Ponet in England, and Philippe Duplessis-Mornay and other Huguenots in France, agreed with him that the church was ultimately responsible to impose authentic religious discipline and worship by means of civil enforcement. But in attempting "to rescue consciences from the tyranny of men," as Calvin said (*Inst.* 4.10.5), and thereby to implement their version of religious liberty, they went farther than Calvin was usually willing to go. To his annoyance, they frequently called for open and armed rebellion against those whom they regarded as illicit rulers. The campaign against idolatry by people such as these inspired the revolutionary movements in northern Europe in the sixteenth century that are associated with Reformed Christianity.

However, in English and American Puritanism in the late sixteenth and the seventeenth century the full range of ambiguities and tensions in Reformed thinking about religious liberty were most evident. In Elizabethan England, the Presbyterians, featuring the uniformist, establishmentarian side of Calvin's thought, were opposed by a "free church" separatist form of Congregationalism. Inferring a more radical lesson from the Calvinist teachings of the Presbyterians, the separatist Congregationalists endeavored to widen substantially the range for the exercise of conscience by liberating religious expression and practice from "the civil forcing of men," in the words of Robert Browne, father of the movement.

These same struggles within Puritanism were manifested again in the seventeenth century, both in England and in America. The question of religious liberty was at the center of the Puritan Revolution in England (1640–49). Once more, the Presbyterians sought to impose a uniform, civilly controlled religious system but were resisted by more moderate and radical Puritans who favored varying degrees of religious freedom. In colonial New England, conflicts between Reformed leaders such as John Cotton and the radical Calvinist Roger Williams were, at bottom, but another reformulation of the same contradictory religious liberty impulses.

In 1789, American Presbyterianism reversed its attachment to the uniformist, establishmentarian side of the Reformed tradition in favor of a much more libertarian doctrine of religious liberty. Declaring that "God alone is Lord of the conscience," the church rejected the authority of the civil magistrate to punish *heresy* or convene a church *synod* or, "in the least, [to] interfere in matters of faith."

———————

DAVID LITTLE

Liturgy, Reformed Reformed *worship* glorifies *God*, the holy God, whose gracious *salvation* is a free, undeserved gift. Therefore, Reformed worship can be described as "objective"; with awe it glorifies the sovereign God, yet it is essentially thankful.

If medieval worship had become an "office," a propitiatory work offered to God securing mercy, Reformation worship was responsive—like the biblical tenth leper who, healed, turned back to praise God. Thus, Reformed liturgy is dialogic—we hear of God's graceful saving goodness and respond in gratitude, *charis* and *eucharistia.* Worship is neither a transactional sacrifice nor an awareness of religious *experience.* God acts and, empty-handed, we respond to God's goodness in a "sacrifice of praise and thanksgiving."

The Reformers were scarcely innovative in liturgy. They inherited worship from Catholicism and, for the most part, retained the traditional shape of the liturgy. They were more concerned with theology. So they corrected theology, simplified forms, and restored proper congregational participation. But the basic movement of the Mass, from confessional rite to readings of *scripture* to prayers of the faithful to eucharistic celebration, was preserved.

Origins of Reformed worship. The history of Reformed liturgy is a tale of three cities: Strassburg, Geneva, and Zurich.

In 1524, Reformed worship began in Strassburg with the German mass of Diebold Schwartz. Within a few years, Schwartz's vernacular Mass included a "common confession," psalms for congregational singing, and sermons preached *lectio continua* from scripture. *Eucharist* was celebrated by ministers behind the table, facing the people. Martin Bucer further modified the service, adding intercessions and a didactic exhortation prior to the Supper. His *Grund und Ursach* (1524) became a "textbook" for worship in the Reformed tradition. He argued that worship must be founded on "clear and plain declarations of Holy Scripture" and should not attend the physical but be led by the Spirit who impresses God's Word on our hearts, urges prayers, and provides gifts for mutual service.

In 1524, Zurich was in turmoil. Huldrych Zwingli had written *An Attack on the Canon of the Mass*. He considered the sacrificial Mass "full of Godlessness." Nevertheless, Zwingli was liturgically conservative; he retained Latin, much ceremony, vestments, and the like. He did, however, add additional Latin prayers to the Canon. While conservatives in Zurich were uneasy, radical "Anabaptists" were appalled. Under pressure, Zwingli stripped churches of statuary, relics, and ornamentation. Walls were whitewashed and organs silenced so that worshipers could revere the **Word of God** alone. A year later, Zwingli urged abolition of the Mass in his *Commentary on True and False Religion* (1525). During Holy Week, a new service was introduced based on a medieval "Prone" that included *prayer*, scripture, and *preaching*. Peculiarly, the service retained sung Ave Marias and a Commemoration of the Dead, and it concluded with Confession of Sins.

Zwingli shaped a radical understanding of the **Lord's Supper**: Christians do *not* receive the substantial body and blood of Christ. Instead, the **Holy Spirit** nourishes common *faith* as congregations, aided only by symbols ("The flesh profiteth nothing"), recall redemption on Calvary. Zwingli's quarterly Communion was starkly simple; after Words of Institution, people passed wooden plates around in silence while portions of the Gospel of John were read. Through preaching, scripture, and the action of the Supper, Christians realized and reaffirmed unity in the body of Christ.

Zwinglian *tradition* reached Geneva by way of the evangelical *ministry* of William Farel. Farel prepared *La manière et fasson* (1524), a worship manual, based on Basel and Zurich practices. In Zwinglian fashion, he exalted the sermon and treated the Supper as a disconnected adjunct. Farel regarded the Eucharist as a testimony of faith and fellowship in the body of Christ. His service involved recital of the promises from God, an invitation to table, a call for self-examination, excommunication of the unworthy, the words of institution, plus an injunction to regard the risen Christ by faith rather than through "visible signs." Such was worship in Geneva when Calvin visited (1536).

Under the influence of Calvin, "Articles Concerning the Organization of the Church and of Worship at Geneva" were drafted. The document called for a celebration of the Supper every Sunday and church discipline to excommunicate those who manifestly did not belong to Christ. Calvin had to compromise, accepting monthly celebrations of the sacrament, because Genevan officials bridled at the notion of weekly Eucharists. Reaction to discipline was sharper; Calvin was chased from the city.

Calvin served a French congregation in Strassburg (1538) and became acquainted with the liturgical revisions of Bucer. As a result, Calvin drew on Strassburg tradition in preparing liturgy and a metrical Psalter for his congregation. Thus, Calvin's new liturgy incorporated the basic shape of the Mass, Word and Sacrament, rather than the stark "preachiness" of Farel's *La manière*. When the Eucharist was omitted, Calvin's service was an obvious Ante-Communion.

Calvin returned to Geneva bringing with him the Strassburg liturgy, published as *The Form of Prayers*. Once more Calvin urged a weekly Lord's Supper instead of annual communication ("an invention of the devil"). Calvin was rebuffed when magistrates rejected his proposals, opting for quarterly celebrations. Until his death, Calvin pleaded for weekly observance of the Supper.

Ordering of worship. The structure of Calvin's Strassburg service was as follows:

Call to Worship: Psalm 124:8
Confession of Sin
Declaration of Pardon
Commandments Sung with Kyrie Eleison
Prayer of Illumination
Scripture and Sermon
Offering

Intercessions
Paraphrased Lord's Prayer (omitted with Communion)
(When the Supper was omitted, a psalm was sung and people were dismissed with a Blessing.)
Apostles' Creed during Preparation of Elements
Eucharistic Prayer
Words of Institution
Fencing the Table
Recital of Promises
Sursum Corda
Communion
Psalm 138
Thanksgiving Prayer
Nunc Dimittis
Aaronic Blessing

In Geneva, the rite was abbreviated when people questioned a Declaration of Pardon and the Commandments. Initially the service was conducted at table except for the reading of scripture and sermon.

Distinctive features of Calvin's order often found in Reformed liturgies may be noted. (1) The Confessional featured acknowledgment of corporate sinfulness, a bold Declaration of Pardon, and a recital of Commandments *following* absolution, expressing Calvin's "third use" of the *law*. (2) Before the reading of scripture, there was a Prayer of Illumination, dove-tailing with Calvin's notion that scripture is interpreted and applied by the Holy Spirit. (3) Eucharist was preceded by a fencing of the table, a reading of the Words of Institution as warrant for celebration, and an acknowledgment of the risen Christ joined to the "Lift up your hearts" of the Sursum Corda.

Character of Reformed liturgy. "No meeting of the church should take place without the Word, prayers, partaking of the Supper, and almsgiving" (*Inst.* 4.17.44). Preaching, prayers, Eucharist, and offering—the terms are an outline of Reformed worship.

Preaching. Reformed liturgy involved biblical preaching. In most congregations there were several Sunday sermons and weekday preaching as well. The Reform-ers did not separate scripture and sermon in their thinking; together they were "The Word." They affirmed a "transubstantiation of the word," sure that when scripture came into contemporary voice, human words became Christ's own word of mercy and command. Preachers often met for group scripture study and sermon preparation.

Prayers. To Calvin, prayers were said *and* sung. The true choir in worship *is* the congregation, he observed. So the people's part in worship was sung in melodies not unlike plain song. In particular, metrical psalms were used that Calvin understood as typologically related to Christ and appropriate for Christian praise. In addition, congregations sang Commandments, the Creed, and the Song of Simeon after Communion.

Other prayers in the service were prayers of the people—the Confession, Prayer of Illumination, Intercessions, and a usual Prayer of Thanksgiving.

Eucharist. For Calvin, Eucharist was union with Christ, specifically with the glorified *humanity* of the risen Christ. In Communion, by Christ's choice we are joined to one another and to him by the mysterious bonding of the Holy Spirit. With Zwingli, Calvin affirmed that Christ is risen and therefore cannot be locally present in bread and wine. Likewise, with Zwingli, he saw the Supper as a public witness and rehearsal of the Christian life. But Calvin rejected Zwingli's "symbolic" understanding of the sacrament. Like *Augustine,* Calvin used realist language for the Eucharist, but he was a "virtual-ist," affirming that through the Supper we receive saving benefits of Christ's sacrificial death, which, in a way, *is* Christ himself for us. Thus, Calvinists have repeatedly denounced the notion that Eucharistic elements are "bare and naked signs." Since he understood the Supper as union in faith with the risen Christ, Calvin installed preparation for the Lord's Supper, a time of self-examination and instruction, prior to Communions.

Offering. Though there was no presentation of offerings, lest propitiatory meanings attach to giving alms, offerings for the *church* and the poor were not slighted. Thanksgiving leads us into the world of neighbors in need—hungry, naked, and imprisoned. Offering was part of *eucharistia*—thanksgiving prompted by the self-giving of God in Christ.

J. J. von Allmen, *Worship, Its Theology and Practice* (1965); Y. T. Brilioth, *Eucharistic Faith and Practice* (1931); H. G. Hageman, *Pulpit and Table* (1962); A. I. C. Heron, *Table and Tradition* (1983); W. D. Maxwell, *An Outline of Christian Worship* (1936), *John Knox's Genevan Service Book* (1931), and *History of Worship in the Church of Scotland* (1955); K. McDonnell, *John Calvin, the Church, and the Eucharist* (1967); J. Melton, *Presbyterian Worship in America* (1967); J. H. Nichols, *Corporate Worship in the Reformed Tradition* (1968); H. O. Old, *Worship That Is Reformed according to Scripture* (1984); F. Schmidt-Clausing, *Zwingli als Liturgiker* (1952); G. J. van de Poll, *Martin Bucer's Liturgical Ideas* (1954); R. S. Wallace, *Calvin's Doctrine of the Word and Sacrament* (1953).

DAVID G. BUTTRICK

Lord's Supper *Definition.* The preferred Reformation term for the sacrament or ordinance that Jesus instituted at the last supper. The Latin is *coena Domini*; the French, *sainte cène*; and the German, *(Heiliges) Abendmahl* or *Herrenmahl.* Zwingli also liked "Eucharist" (the title of the *First Helvetic Confession* art. 23 in Lat.), which expresses the element of gratitude (Gr. *eucharistia*) in response to *grace* (*charis*). As another meaningful alternative, the Anglican *Book of Common Prayer* and the *Scots Confession* (art. 21; cf. *French Confession,* art. 36) use "Holy Communion," that is, communion with Christ's body and blood (WCF, 29.1) and also the communion of believers in Christ. The Reformers unanimously abandoned the medieval term "Mass" because of its intrinsic meaninglessness and dubious theological and practical associations.

The Supper is the second of the two dominical or evangelical *sacraments,* that is, sacraments that the Lord appointed and that have a sign, word, and gospel promise. The command "Do this" constitutes the appointment, the repeated "This is" forms the basic word, and the promise is that "with his crucified body and shed blood" Christ "feeds and nourishes my soul to everlasting life" (HC, q. 75). The five observances that the medieval church added to produce seven sacraments are not in this sense "sacraments of the Gospel" (*Thirty-nine Articles,* art. 25), that is, "actions ordained by God himself . . . whereby he seals up his promises" (*Second Helvetic Confession,* ch. 19). They may serve a profitable purpose, but they lack the features that give *Baptism* and the Supper this distinctive rank.

Covenant. As Zwingli (see *Zwingli and Bullinger,* ed. G. W. Bromiley, LCC 24:131) and Calvin (*Inst.* 4.14.6) both say, the sacraments are covenant signs. They resemble the covenant signs of the OT (LCC 24:138ff.). When *God* covenanted with Abraham and Israel, God gave them the symbolic actions of circumcision and the passover as perpetual pledges. The *covenant* contained both a promise and a command: "I will be your God and you shall be my people." The covenant signs thus testify to God's self-giving to his people and to his people's self-giving to God. Jesus fulfilled the covenant on both sides. The NT covenant is thus the same in substance, but the administration changes, and two new signs replace the old (WCF, 7.5ff.).

The NT itself supports the equation of the covenants. In Colossians 2, the thing signified in circumcision and baptism is the same, and Jesus instituted the Supper in a passover setting. The most obvious difference explains the change. The OT signs involve blood-shedding, prefiguring Christ's death. The NT signs are bloodless, representing the blood that was shed once for all. "With the shedding of the precious blood of Christ the shedding of physical blood ceased." We now have "most friendly elements and signs" (LCC 24:132), "more firm and durable," but also "more simple, nothing so painful" (*Second Helvetic Confession*, ch. 19). The substance, however, remains unchanged.

Reformed theology in the seventeenth century at times advocated an original covenant of works in Eden (WCF, 7.2). In some versions this also had two sacraments, the two trees. When disobedience annulled it, God set up the covenant of grace (WCF, 7.3). For the most part, however, churches have not pressed this speculative concept. The covenant of grace is the biblical covenant, promulgated in the OT and fulfilled in the NT. The common substance, as the Second Helvetic Confession perspicaciously observes, is Christ himself, "the only Mediator and Savior of the faithful" (ch. 19). The covenant is no abstraction. God fulfilled it in Christ. In token, God gave the prophetic signs of circumcision and the passover and the corresponding apostolic signs of Baptism and the Lord's Supper.

Visible Word. Word and Sacrament are two aspects of the one proclamation of the gospel. In Augustine's phrase, the sacrament is a "visible word." It supplements the audible word as a sign and action that vividly illustrates what the spoken or written word proclaims.

As a visible word, the Supper is a divine *accommodation* to human weakness. Zwingli called it a bridle to check the senses from dashing off in pursuit of their own desires (LCC 24:264). Calvin, who called the Word itself "God's baby talk," says that "because we are of flesh" we have it "under things of flesh . . . to instruct us according to our dull capacity" (*Inst.* 4.14.6). It is given "the better to present to our senses" what God "signifies to us by his word" and "works inwardly in our hearts" (*Belgic Confession*, art. 33).

The Supper engages all the senses, not hearing alone. Calvin stressed the visual side, a painted picture or reflection in a mirror (*Inst.* 4.14.6). Zwingli saw a larger involvement. We hear God's voice in the sacramental word, see the broken body and the shed blood in bread and wine, touch as we take in our hands, smell and taste as we receive. The Supper claims all the senses for the work of faith (LCC 24:263–64). Indeed, we do more than perceive. We are caught up in an action. We enact our reception and self-commitment to God.

The visible and audible words belong together. Addition of the word makes the sacrament (Augustine). But the word must be more than mumbled and unintelligible repetition (*Inst.* 4.17.39). It must be clear and understandable proclamation that declares the meaning. By word and sign God gives himself objectivity in the sensory world to solve the problem of knowing divine things. If word and sign conceal, they also reveal, communicating the supersensory by the sensory.

Stress on the audible word and a learned *ministry* might seem to entail disparagement of the Supper, or its observance only for hallowed associations. Calvin, for all his Renaissance learning, disagreed. "So great is our native inability to know God," he stated, that by the sacraments God "attests his good will and love toward us more expressly than by word" (*Inst.* 4.14.6).

Sacrifice. The Supper graphically depicts Christ's self-offering for us. Bread and wine symbolize for Zwingli the reconciliation of God and the human race in and through Christ (LCC 24:263). The body was broken and the blood shed "as certainly as I see . . . the bread of the Lord broken for me, and the cup communicated to me" (HC, q. 75). The Supper is a seal "that the very body of the Lord was given up for us, and his blood shed for the remission of our sins" (*Second Helvetic Confession*, ch. 19). Its function is to "offer and set forth Christ to us" (*Inst.* 4.14.17).

Exhibiting the unique self-sacrifice of Christ for *sin*, the Supper is not itself an expiatory sacrifice (WCF, 29.2). The elements are not immolated, as medieval theology proposed, to remit the temporal penalties of postbaptismal sin. Christ's offering is the "perfect redemption, propitiation, and satisfaction, for all the sins of the whole world" (*Thirty-nine Articles*, art. 31). Priests are not "Mediators betwixt Christ and his Kirk" (*Scots Confession*, ch. 22). This belief, said Calvin, dishonors Christ, suppresses his cross and passion, and brings forgetfulness of his death and its benefits (*Inst.* 4.18.2–6).

The Supper, if it does not specifically represent or plead Christ's sacrifice to God, undoubtedly represents it to us. It is also our own sacrifice of the praise and thanksgiving that we "both owe and render" to God (*Inst.* 4.18.13). It is "a spiritual oblation of all possible praise unto God" (WCF, 29.2). We thus pray God to "accept this our sacrifice of praise and thanksgiving." In so doing, we offer ourselves to God as "a reasonable, holy and living sacrifice," which is in fact our "bounden duty and service" (*BCP*; cf. *Inst.* 4.18.16).

Presence. Beneath the medieval concept of a eucharistic sacrifice lay belief in the real presence of Christ in the elements. By consecration, it was held, the bread is substantially the body of Christ and the wine his blood. Naturally we still see, touch, taste, and smell bread and wine, for the so-called accidents remain intact. But the substance has supposedly changed (transubstantiation). Hence the priest offers Christ's body and blood on the altar, and communicants receive them by receiving the elements.

Luther attempted a mediating view, rejecting a change of substance but stating that Christ is substantially present in, with, and under the bread and wine. The Reformed, in contrast, rejected both those forms of presence. As Zwingli insisted, Christ in his *humanity* is now at the Father's right hand and will return only in his eschatological glory (LCC 24:214ff., 256ff.). Even at the first institution, when still present on earth, Jesus obviously was not present simultaneously both in person and in bread and wine.

This rejection does not imply Christ's absence from the Supper. The disagreement concerns only the mode. There is no need for a sham miracle by differentiation of substance and accidents. As

Zwingli noted, Christ is present according to his omnipresent deity, which includes the humanity in virtue of the unity of the person (LCC 24:256ff.). More boldly, the **Belgic Confession** (art. 35) speaks of a partaking of "the proper natural body." The Scots Confession, too, refers to an eating and drinking of Christ's "flesh and blood" (art. 21), and the **WCF** states that Christ is "really, but spiritually present" (WCF, 29.7).

The secret lies in "the operation of the Holy Ghost" (*Belgic Confession*, art. 35). As Calvin said, the power of the Spirit "towers above all our senses" (*Inst.* 4.14.10). The Spirit unites things separated in space, raising us up to Christ, and making bread and wine our spiritual food and drink. The mode of the presence is not that of the *incarnation, resurrection,* or return. It is that of presence by the Spirit. Himself in *heaven,* Christ feeds us "by the secret and incomprehensible power of his Spirit" (*French Confession,* art. 36).

The senses do not perceive the presence. It defies clear conceptualization. No one, said Calvin, "should measure its sublimity by the little measure of my childishness." We can only "break forth in wonder at this mystery, which plainly neither the mind is able to conceive nor the tongue to express" (*Inst.* 4.17.7). Yet the presence is real. It is the presence of the whole Christ, proclaiming his sacrifice, proffering fellowship with himself, and providing nourishment to eternal life.

Benefits. As a visible word, the Supper testifies to the historicity of Christ's crucifixion and resurrection (Zwingli; LCC 24:262). The material nature of the elements rules out false spiritualizing. Here is sensory historicity. The Word was made flesh. The Word takes bread and wine and hands them to us in attestation of the facticity of his saving person and work.

As this testimony, the Supper confirms and augments *faith.* Zwingli amended his initial rejection of this benefit (LCC 24:138, 263ff.). The *confessions* agreed that the sacraments are "sure witnesses . . . by the which" God "doth . . .

strengthen and confirm our Faith in him" (*Thirty-nine Articles*, art. 25). For Calvin, it was the office of the sacraments to "sustain, nourish, confirm, and increase our faith" (*Inst.* 4.14.7). Does the Supper also "quicken faith" (*Thirty-nine Articles*, art. 25)? Is it a converting ordinance? Why not? Calvin stated that it might "beget faith" so long as the word is preached (4.14.4). Communion seasons can be great evangelistic occasions, as in the Scottish Highlands in the nineteenth century.

The Supper also grants fellowship with Christ. "Christ communicates himself with all his benefits to us" (*Belgic Confession*, art. 35). In it we have "conjunction with Christ Jesus" (*Scots Confession*, art. 21). Union with Christ is the "special fruit" of the Supper (*Inst.* 4.17.2). There we are "one with Christ and Christ with us" (*BCP*).

This fellowship embraces spiritual nourishment, as the symbolism indicates. The *HC* expresses this beautifully: "With his crucified body and shed blood he himself feeds and nourishes my soul to everlasting life as certainly as I receive . . . and taste . . . the bread and cup of the Lord" (HC, q. 75). Christ is in fact the "substance" of the sacrament, so this is a "substantial eating" (*Inst.* 4.14.16). The nourishment is real, for "Christ himself . . . delivered up for us . . . is that special thing and substance of the Supper" (*Second Helvetic Confession*, ch. 21).

Mutual Christian fellowship is a final benefit. "Godly souls" have here a "witness of our growth into one body with Christ" (*Inst.* 4.17.2). Distinctions vanish at the Lord's Table. Old and young, rich and poor, men and women, believers of all nations, races, or classes—all gather at the one table as members of the one body. Assured of God's *forgiveness* and forgiving one another, they go out to live and work together as the one fellowship of reconciliation, anticipating the consummated fellowship of God's eternal kingdom.

Efficacy. Medieval teaching deduced from Christ's presence by transubstantia-

tion an automatic efficacy. In a valid celebration, all who receive the elements receive Christ, whether to blessing or, in the case of unabsolved mortal sin, to condemnation.

The Reformers did not deny sacramental efficacy. "God gives us really and in fact that which he there sets forth to us" (*French Confession*, art. 37; cf. *Belgic Confession*, art. 35). But they rejected automatic efficacy. All receive the sign, not all the thing signified (*Belgic Confession*, art. 35). Christ proffers himself to all, but he is received only to *salvation.* If some miss the benefits, it is because they do not receive Christ. Condemnation comes, not by receiving Christ unworthily, but by despising him (*Inst.* 4.17.33).

The efficacy of the Supper relates to the Word. As there is no Supper apart from the Word, "whatever benefit may come to us from the Supper requires the Word" (*Inst.* 4.17.39). Nor is the Word merely the word of institution (WCF, 37.3). It is the "living preaching" that "reveals its effectiveness in the fulfillment of what it promises" (*Inst.* 4.17.39).

The efficacy relates to the Spirit (*French Confession*, art. 37). Partaking is dependent on the "power of the Spirit" (*Belgic Confession*, art. 35). We are partakers "through the working of the Holy Ghost" (HC, q. 79). Sacramental efficacy implies the "inner grace of the Spirit" (*Inst.* 4.14.17). We seriously wrong the Spirit if we do not attribute partaking of Christ to his "incomprehensible power" (4.17.33).

Efficacy relates finally to faith. Christ offers spiritual food to all, but only "the faithful, in the right use of the Table," have fellowship with him (*Scots Confession*, art. 31). Those who are "void of a lively faith" "press with their teeth" but "in no wise are they partakers of Christ" (*Thirty-nine Articles*, art. 29). Faith need not be perfect. It needs confirming and augmenting. The Supper is "medicine for the sick, solace for sinners" (*Inst.* 4.17.42). Yet without faith, we receive no more than the sign, doing "despite unto the

Death of Christ" (*Second Helvetic Confession*, ch. 21).

In sum, the Lord's Supper means efficacious union with Christ when it includes proclamation of the Word, is administered in the power of the Spirit, and is received with the faith of humility and obedience.

Administration. As a visible word, the Supper demands clear administration with open actions and in an understandable language. Elaborate ceremonial, though impressive, can hinder rather than help by obscuring the central event, which is simple. As a meal and not a sacrifice, the Supper calls for a table rather than an altar. Bread and wine are the essentials, served in appropriate but not necessarily costly vessels. Essential too is rehearsal of the words of institution and proclamation of the associated gospel promises. A prayer of consecration and thanksgiving, a hymn or psalm, and a common confession of faith, also of sin, all belong suitably to the administration. Adoration and reservation of the consecrated elements, and their being carried in procession, have wrong theological implications and easily nurture superstition (*Thirty-nine Articles*, art. 28).

Properly, the Supper should be administered "very often, and at least once a week" (*Inst.* 4.17.43). Unhappily, the medieval practice of weekly Mass but infrequent Communion still exerts a lingering influence. Noncommunicating attendance makes no sense, nor does the private Mass that supposedly reduces purgatorial pains (*Thirty-nine Articles*, art. 31; WCF, 29.4). It is a denial of communion (*Inst.* 4.18.8) and encourages cupidity (*Second Helvetic Confession*, ch. 21) and error. By Christ's institution, all communicants receive the cup as well as the bread. Reasons given for its denial to the nonordained are flimsy (*Scots Confession*, art. 21; *Inst.* 4.17.47ff.). Matters such as the time of administration may be arranged as is most convenient, and rules should not be imposed to cover personal practices, for example, the rule of fasting communion.

Since Christ himself is the host and true minister, the unworthiness of a human minister, though reprehensible, does not affect the sacrament's validity (*Thirty-nine Articles*, art. 26). Nevertheless, since faith is a prerequisite of efficacy, communicants should examine themselves, and obvious unbelievers and flagrant and impenitent offenders may be debarred (*Scots Confession*, art. 23). Yet "fencing of the tables" must not be pressed too far in relation to either self or others. To wait until fully worthy, or to exclude for every offense, is to deprive the Supper of its evangelical purpose (*Inst.* 4.17.41–42). The Supper is not primarily a disciplinary tool. It is a means of grace. God has instituted it in grace, not **judgment.** In the power of God's Spirit, God uses it to build up the people of God in their new life in Christ and in a solidarity of fellowship and service.

B. A. Gerrish, *Grace and Gratitude* (1993).
GEOFFREY W. BROMILEY

Marburg Colloquy A conference between Luther, Zwingli, and other Reformation leaders to promote political unity and theological consensus among various Protestant parties. Convened by Landgrave Philip of Hesse at his castle in Marburg (1529), the meeting included Luther, Philipp Melanchthon, Justus Jonas, Johann Brenz, Kaspar Cruciger, and Andreas Osiander on the Lutheran side, and John Oecolampadius, Wolfgang Capito, Martin Bucer, and Johannes Sturm who, together with Zwingli, emphasized the symbolic significance of the **Lord's Supper.** The two sides agreed on fourteen of the fifteen Marburg articles, embracing such cardinal tenets as the **Trinity,** person of Christ, *justification* by **faith,** and rejection of transubstantiation. On the nature of Christ's presence in the Supper, however, Luther and Zwingli sharply disagreed.

The breakdown at Marburg led to a widening rift between the Lutheran and

Reformed churches. Luther continued to oppose any confessional alliance with "sacramentarians," as he called those who opposed his eucharistic theology. Zwingli defended his view that the controverted words of institution, *Hoc est corpus meum*, should be understood as "This signifies my body," since the literal body of Christ was in *heaven* at the right hand of the Father. Bucer, and later Calvin, proposed a mediating position between the Lutheran and Zwinglian alternatives. Still, differences in eucharistic theology and practice remained a serious obstacle to Protestant unity long past the Reformation era.

T. George, *Theology of the Reformers* (1988); W. Köhler, *Zwingli und Luther: Ihr Streit über das Abendmahl nach seinen politischen und religiösen Beziehungen*, 2 vols. (1924–53); G. W. Locher, *Zwingli's Thought* (1981).

TIMOTHY GEORGE

Marriage, Theology of Reformed Christians have typically agreed that marriage is a life partnership analogous to the *covenant* relationship between *God* and God's people in *scripture*. They have disagreed about the implications of this analogy.

Following John Calvin, Reformed Christians have traditionally believed that marriage faithful to the biblical norm is the relationship between the superior man, whose role is to rule, and the inferior woman, whose role is to obey. However, they have also insisted that the husband is not to be a domineering tyrant or the wife a subservient slave but that marriage should be true companionship in which there is mutual giving and receiving, helping and being helped, caring and being cared for. Further developing the theology of Karl Barth that began to move in this direction, many contemporary Reformed Christians reject the traditional hierarchical-patriarchal view and defend the full equality and mutual responsibility of husband and wife, each created in the image of God and called to love and serve the other.

Since the sixteenth century, *Reformed theology* has increasingly emphasized that Christian marriage is a partnership in which both parties freely and gladly decide to marry in order to establish a relationship that is good in itself and exists for its own sake, not just to "remedy sinful lust," produce children, or serve other personal, social, or economic goals.

There has also generally been increasing acknowledgment that though the full committed partnership of marriage is more than a relationship based on romantic-erotic love, such love is also included in it as the good gift of God who created us male and female, thus not only legitimating but blessing the physical-emotional-sexual side of marriage.

The Reformed tradition has consistently believed that marriage is ordained by God to be a permanent relationship. However, most Reformed Christians today acknowledge that divorce can be the legitimate recognition that human error and/or *sin* may prevent a marriage from becoming a true life partnership. When a marriage ends in divorce—as when it begins and continues—Christians count on the *grace* of God that both forgives sinful people and enables them to make fresh starts (including the possibility of new marriage for divorced persons).

Rejecting the idea that marriage is a purely private arrangement between isolated individuals, the Reformed tradition has always insisted on the importance of an official wedding ceremony as the public confirmation of the broadening of two family circles, the couple's acceptance of their rights and responsibilities as members of a larger society, and (in the case of Christians) their desire for the blessing of God and declaration of their intention to live as members of the Christian community.

While Reformed Christians recognize marriage as a good gift of God, they realize too that those who never marry and those who lose their partner through divorce or *death* may also live fully human lives as single people who have their own particular gifts and tasks from God.

Barth, *CD* III/4, 116ff.; E. Brunner, *The Divine Imperative* (1932; ET 1937); R. S. Wallace, *Calvin's Doctrine of the Christian Life* (1959).

SHIRLEY C. GUTHRIE

Mercersburg Theology

Mercersburg Theology A gentle movement (1840–60) stressing the centrality of Jesus Christ and his presence in the **Lord's Supper** that sought to correct perceived individualism and revival excesses of Edwardsean "new theology." From the Theological Seminary of the German Reformed Church and its Marshall College in Mercersburg, Pennsylvania, John W. Nevin, a Presbyterian, led the movement with books such as *The History and Genius of the Heidelberg Catechism* (1841–42), *The Anxious Bench* (1843), and *The Mystical Presence* (1846). His faculty collaborator, Philip Schaff, came to teach at Mercersburg from the University of Berlin, eager to share the richness of continental Reformed Christianity with American Christians.

In debates with other leaders of the German and Dutch Reformed, Lutheran, and Presbyterian Christians, Nevin and Schaff argued for a sense of the *church* that emphasized the catholic affirmations of the Nicene and the Apostles' Creeds. They stressed the importance of the Christian church through the ages and appreciated some Roman Catholic contributions to *doctrine* and *ethics.* They looked forward to Christian development in the future.

Drawing on contemporary German theology, Nevin and Schaff criticized American sectarianism, loss of a sense of *providence* in American dependence on revival techniques, and any Protestant "jump" straight from the Bible to the current situation. They urged on Reformed Christians especially a deep Christocentric *piety,* dependence on the *sacraments,* and an irenic disposition toward the rest of the Christian family.

J. H. Nichols, ed., *The Mercersburg Theology* (1966).

LOUIS B. WEEKS

Millennialism

Millennialism Millennialism (Lat.), or chiliasm (Gr.), refers to a type of Christian *eschatology* organized around the notion of a thousand-year reign of Christ at the close of *history.* The idea is derived from Rev. 20:2–7, the only biblical occurrence of the expression.

Premillennialism holds that Christ's second coming is forewarned by biblically identified "signs of the times": catastrophes, widespread apostasy, appearance of the Antichrist, and a great tribulation for God's people. Upon his appearing, Christ will inaugurate his thousand-year reign, either in person or through his faithful. Deceased saints will be raised. Peace, general blessing, prosperity, and many *conversions,* especially of Jewish people, will follow. At the close of the millennium, Satan will be briefly unleashed but then destroyed, the unbelieving dead raised and condemned eternally, and the saints welcomed into the new *heaven* and new earth. Irenaeus, Justin Martyr, and Tertullian advocated variations of this view. A few medieval thinkers and many modern evangelicals do.

A version of premillennialism is *dispensationalism.* It teaches that *salvation* comes in different modes and periods during history, notably in the crucified and risen Christ during the era of the *church,* and especially in the reigning Christ during the millennium. As taught by John Nelson Darby (1800–1882), it defends a secret rapture of the church before the tribulation and return of Christ with his saints to establish his millennial rule. Cyrus Ingerson Scofield (1843–1921) spread dispensationalism through the notes of his widely used *Scofield Reference Bible.*

Reformed theologians occasionally proposed premillennialism, particularly during times of political and social turmoil. Johann Heinrich Alsted (1588–1638) and Edward Irving are examples.

Reformed emphases on the historical continuity of God's redemptive work, the unity of the Bible's two Testaments, God's *covenant* of *grace* with *humanity*, the symbolic nature of apocalyptic and prophetic literature, and God's use of the means of grace have yielded a different eschatology. Through great outpourings of his Spirit, effective *preaching*, and his people's faithful service, Christ establishes his rule, converts the nations, and bestows spiritual and material blessings. Christ will visibly return, amidst such signs as the appearance of Antichrist, conversion of the Gentiles, and the regrafting of Israel into God's vine (Rom. 11:25–32). When he comes, the dead will be raised and the last *judgment* will occur.

The postmillennial variation within Reformed eschatology holds that the gospel's success rather than Christ's visible intervention will yield the millennium. Daniel Whitby (1638–1726) and Jonathan Edwards were two proponents. A late twentieth-century mutant known as "theonomy" sees the substantial reintroduction of OT standards as essential to this era.

Many Reformed theologians, however, emphasize the continuous, simultaneous flourishing of God's kingdom and the kingdom of darkness until the end of history. Known as amillennialism, their position rejects the notion of a millennium since it does not interpret this text literally. "The thousand years" of Revelation 20 represents the entire period between Christ's *resurrection* and his return, between Satan's defeat and his destruction.

H. Bavinck, *The Last Things*, ed. J. Bolt, trans. J. Vriend (1996); G. C. Berkouwer, *The Return of Christ* (1972); R. Clouse, ed., *The Meaning of the Millennium* (1977); S. Grenz, ed., *The Millennial Maze* (1992); A.

Hoekema, *The Bible and the Future* (1979).

JAMES A. DE JONG

Ministry

Ministry   The service of *God* within the *church* and by the church to the world, which has its source, inspiration, and model in Jesus Christ, the suffering servant of God. He who came from *heaven* to be the Word incarnate did not come to be served by people but rather to minister to *humanity* in its abject need and give his life sacrificially for all. He entered wholly into the pitiful and perverse condition of the human race as it exists before God, sharing its pain and estrangement; and he did so in order, by meek and personal service in doing good and offering healing and liberation, to bring reconciliation and *peace* between humanity and God. Thus, as the climax of his diaconal ministry, he offered himself as an *atonement* for *sin* at Calvary's cross to bring to a conclusion on earth his ministry. Now in heaven he ministers as priest through his intercession for his people.

In his earthly ministry, Jesus created a community of the new *covenant*: that is, a people called to minister by sharing in his ministry, which began on earth and continues at the right hand of the Father in heaven. Each Christian finds the *freedom* to minister in the reality of being a slave/servant of Jesus Christ, who is both the Servant/Minister and the Lord and Master to his disciples. Ministry is therefore for the household of faith the humble service of God the Father and also in God's name and love the serving of fellow human beings in their sin, anxiety, degradation, need, and rebellion against God. Thus, each and every baptized believer in his own situation is called to share daily in the diaconal ministry of Christ, yet is to do so not individualistically but rather as a member of the one body in fellowship with others.

Though ministry is primarily the *vocation* of the whole people of God of the new covenant as it lives in fellowship with and in obedience to Jesus, some members are set apart as ordained ministers in order to facilitate the ministry of the whole. In the spirit of the NT, the offices are those of *elder* (or presbyter) and *deacon.* The historic threefold ministry of bishop, presbyter, and deacon was thereby reduced to two in the sixteenth-century Reformed churches. Of these, the presbyterial ministry is in essence that by which the Word and sacraments are dispensed to the people of God: Presbyters act in the name of Christ as sent by him to proclaim his word of *grace.* As servants of Jesus, they are never to cease from administering the teaching and leading and from sharing wholly in the caring ministry of the whole people of God.

The diaconal ministry is that activity by and through which the responses of the people of God to God's saving grace are facilitated. Deacons set an example of what is involved in being servants of God and together with teaching assist the congregations in the exercise of true *diakonia* (Gr.; ministry). In no other area have modern churches so failed as in the effective use of deacons to ensure the true *diakonia* of the whole body of Christ to the world. Deacons, female or male, are called to minister the mercy of God toward God's creatures. In particular they are to inspire and assist the intercessory **prayers** of churches for the world so that their prayers are united to those of Christ, the heavenly intercessor. Then also they are to lead the churches in witnessing for Christ by imitating him in his compassionate concern for humanity in its varying needs. This is not merely social service but concern for the whole person's relation to God as well as for relations with fellow humans. Such witness will usually involve suffering, for it will entail encountering the true face of evil and sin in the world. Then, also, they will seek to ensure that there is reconciliation and true unity both in the congregation and between congregations, so the people of the new covenant may exhibit to the world God's reconciliation in Christ.

The essential characteristic of all *diakonia* is that while it is to be undertaken in and by the love of Christ, it is also a service commanded by Christ and laid by him upon each and every member of the household of faith. There are no exceptions to this rule.

R. S. Anderson, ed., *Theological Foundations for Ministry* (1979); Barth, *CD* IV/3; R. S. Paul, *Ministry* (1965).

PETER TOON

Munus triplex   In *Reformed theology,* Jesus Christ is often described as mediator, explicated by the *munus triplex*—the threefold office of prophet, priest, and king.

Though John Calvin was not the first Christian theologian to use the *munus triplex* to describe Christ, his discussion (*Inst.* 2.15) is the basis for frequent use of the formula in many sixteenth- and seventeenth-century Reformed *confessions.* Martin Luther and others had described Christ by the twofold office of priest and king; Calvin added the third office of prophet to interpret Christ's work as mediator.

In describing Christ as prophet, Calvin did not apparently think of Christ's announcement and enactment of the **kingdom of God.** Rather, Christ is a teacher of "the perfect doctrine." The description of the mediator as king refers to the eternal, spiritual reign of Christ over the *church* and each individual in the church, a reign promising the church's perpetuity and protection. Because Christ is king, we pass through this miserable world "content with this one thing: that our King will never leave us destitute, but will provide for our needs until, our warfare ended, we are called to triumph" (*Inst.* 2.15.4). When he describes Christ as priest, Calvin refers to an everlasting intercessor who, by his death on the cross, "washed away our sins, sanctifies us and obtains for us that grace from which the uncleanness of our transgressions and vices debars us" (*Inst.* 2.15.6).

The *munus triplex* is in many classical Reformed confessions, such as the *HC* (q. 31) and the *WCF* (ch. 8). The *Larger Catechism* asks, "Why was our Mediator called Christ?" The answer is that Christ is the mediator because he was anointed by the *Holy Spirit* and set apart "to execute the office of prophet, priest, and king of his Church, in the estate both of his humiliation and exaltation" (q. 42).

The *munus triplex* is not prominent in contemporary Reformed theology, though Karl Barth and Emil Brunner continued to discuss it in their interpretations of *Christology.* Contemporary theologians worry that the *munus triplex* represents the imposition of a dogmatic structure on the biblical text and that Calvin's interpretation of the threefold office may not stand up under careful exegesis. Those who continue to use the *munus triplex* do so because it reflects the conviction that Jesus cannot be understood as Christ and mediator apart from the history of Israel's *covenant* with God.

Barth, *CD* IV/3, pt. 1, 3–38; Heppe, *RD*; J. F. Jansen, *Calvin's Doctrine of the Work of Christ* (1956).

GEORGE W. STROUP

Mystical Union   *see* Union with Christ

Narrative Theology   A loosely knit body of literature that first appeared in the last third of the twentieth century. The literature is "loosely knit" in that it spreads across both confessional boundaries and theological disciplines, and there is no consensus among those contributing to the literature concerning program or method. The one theme running throughout is the category of narrative. But there is little agreement on what genre narrative refers to and how it functions in theological reflection. Theologians, biblical scholars, ethicists, homileticians, Christian educators, and pastoral counselors have all used some

form of narrative to rethink the nature and tasks of their disciplines.

Some theologians have asked how the *doctrine* of the *Trinity* might be reinterpreted if it were understood not in terms of the metaphysics of being but as God's narrative history. Others have tried to reinterpret *Christology* by turning from the formulae of classical Christology and giving closer attention to the ways in which Jesus is described in the Gospels. Many biblical scholars have asked whether the theological voice in the Bible has not been muted in recent generations by an exclusive use of historical-critical methods and have turned to literary-critical methods of interpretation. Some Protestant ethicists have asked whether their discipline has emphasized principles, rules, and norms at the expense of equally important topics such as character, disposition, virtue, and vision.

Though the literature on narrative theology is relatively new, the role of narrative has long been present in Christian life and thought. Israel recites its *history* in its scriptures by means of a story, and the *church* proclaims its message about Jesus as the Christ by means of Gospels, which are, after all, stories about Jesus. Further, some of the most important theological documents in Western Christianity either make use of some form of narrative or presuppose it. The first nine books of Augustine's *Confessions* are a reinterpretation of his life story from the perspective of Christian faith. Though Calvin's *Institutes* are not written in narrative form, the opening sentences make clear that Christian theology begins with the relation between *knowledge of God* and knowledge of self. Christian narrative, therefore, might be understood as the result of an individual's or a community's interpretation of history by means of the knowledge of God derived from biblical narrative.

Many important problems remain unanswered in narrative theology, such as the relation between narrative and history, the role of imagination in reading and interpreting narrative, and whether narrative is simply a useful introduction to theology or whether some form of it can and should be used to reinterpret Christian doctrine.

Barth, *CD* IV/2, 154–264; H. Frei, *The Eclipse of Biblical Narrative* (1974); H. R. Niebuhr, *The Meaning of Revelation* (1941); G. W. Stroup, *The Promise of Narrative Theology* (1981).

GEORGE W. STROUP

Natural Theology The attempt to know *God* by *reason* and *experience* apart from any special *revelation*. The Reformed view is basically that of *Augustine,* who taught that there is no unaided true *knowledge of God.* In the Reformed tradition, the closest that one gets to natural theology is with such concepts as general revelation and common *grace.* In the seventeenth century, Reformed theologians occasionally spoke of natural theology in contrast to revealed theology. But here natural theology at best served as a prolegomenon to revealed theology. An aspect of natural theology taught by John Calvin and later Reformed theologians is natural law, but again with different presuppositions from those of advocates of natural theology.

The idea of a natural theology originated with Plato and the Stoics and received its classical formulation in Thomas Aquinas, who distinguished natural and revealed theology, giving a significant place to the former. This is illustrated in Aquinas's five proofs for the existence of God. The official Roman Catholic position was stated at Vatican I (1870): "The Holy Mother Church holds and teaches that God . . . may certainly be known by the natural light of human reason, by means of created things." In Roman Catholicism, however, natural theology never suffices for a knowledge of the divine mysteries and hence must be augmented by divine revelation.

This is not so in the Enlightenment, where German scholars such as H. S. Reimarus and G. E. Lessing preferred reason and natural theology to *faith* and revealed theology. Deists John Toland and Matthew Tindal also totally rejected special revelation. Thus understood, natural theology does not exist in *Reformed theology.* However, in a modified sense, certain related concepts have played a minor role in the Reformed tradition beginning with the Swiss reformers.

John Calvin. One might begin with Huldrych Zwingli, who, despite his clear views of the holiness of God, human sinfulness, and *sola gratia,* made a few exceptions with his favorite Greek philosophers. Despite the inability of sinful *humanity* to know God aright, Zwingli believed that these philosophers were granted a sufficient, albeit dim, knowledge of God, which allowed them to join the saints in glory.

Zwingli never developed this notion, however, whereas the whole first book of Calvin's **Institutes** is devoted to the knowledge of God the creator. Here are echoes of what might appear to be traces of a natural theology with Calvin's appeal to a natural "awareness of divinity" (*sensus divinitatis*) and a "seed of religion" (*semen religionis*) in all people. He also follows the Roman Catholic understanding of Rom. 1:20–21 that in all humans the conviction of God's existence is "naturally inborn in all, and is fixed deep within [us], as it were in the very marrow" (*Inst.* 1.3.1; 3.4.1).

However, Calvin proceeds to declare "this knowledge is either smothered or corrupted, partly by ignorance, partly by malice" (*Inst.,* title of ch. 4). He is only trying to establish humanity's responsibility. In fact, this "primal and simple knowledge" of God was effectively lost in Adam's fall (*Inst.* 1.2.1). Like the Stoics and Aquinas, Calvin can appeal to the light of nature, "for even in man's perverted and degenerate nature some sparks still gleam" (*Inst.* 2.2.12). Moreover, in the realm of "earthly things," which do not pertain to the *kingdom of God,* humans are by nature endowed with many natural gifts. However, when it comes to knowing God aright and the things that pertain to our *salvation,* "the greatest geniuses are blinder than moles" (*Inst.* 2.2.18).

The idea that God endows all people with certain natural gifts has given rise to concepts of common grace or general revelation. Calvin used the former phrase only once (*Inst.* 2.2.17), the latter not at all. But it came to be a key concept in Dutch and Dutch-American *Calvinism* in the late nineteenth and early twentieth centuries.

Reformed confessions. A trace of what has been labeled natural theology is found in certain Reformed *confessions.* In the opening articles of the *French Confession, Belgic Confession,* and Hungarian Confession, and in the *WCF,* God is said to be known "first, in his works," and "secondly, and more clearly in his Word" (*French Confession,* art. 2). The Belgic Confession repeats this affirmation almost verbatim, whereas the WCF surprisingly is closer to Calvin: "Although the light of nature, and the works of creation and providence, do so far manifest the goodness, wisdom, and power of God, as to leave men inexcusable; yet they are not sufficient to give that Knowledge of God, and of his will, which is necessary unto salvation" (WCF, 1.1).

Arthur Cochrane, following Barth, lamented: "Having gained admission in the French Confession, the virus of natural theology quickly spread to the Belgic Confession of 1561, and thence to the Westminster Confession of Faith of 1643. Not until the Barmen Theological Declaration of 1934 was natural theology categorically rejected in its first articles, and the original witness of the Reformed Confessions of the 16th century reaffirmed" (*Reformed Confessions of the 16th Century* [1966], 139). The question is, which sixteenth-century confessions? Moreover, this "virus of natural theology" has hardly had the destructive effects in the churches adhering to those confessions that Cochrane suggested. If there is a problem in these confessions, it is not the positing of a revelation in *creation* and the Word but rather the danger of assuming that one can appreciate God's revelation in creation and *providence* apart from the Word, a point Calvin stresses more clearly.

Neo-Calvinists and common grace. The two great theologians of the reform movement in the latter part of the nineteenth century in the Netherlands, Abraham Kuyper and Herman Bavinck, devoted much attention to the concept of common grace (*algemeene genade* or *gemeene gratie*). This concept, with slight variations, was also taught by Charles Hodge and A. A. Hodge of Princeton Seminary. As over against special grace, which relates to salvation, common grace is extended to all people, believers and unbelievers, and is responsible for restraining evil and making life tolerable. Moreover, it also accounts for the natural gifts of humanity, social and civic *justice,* and makes possible the fruits of culture. As common grace is understood in Dutch Reformed theology, however, it does not mitigate human depravity or compromise the radical need for the special grace of God manifest in Jesus Christ. The goal, rather, is a world and life view (Ger. *Weltanschauung*) that acknowledges God's presence and activity in every sphere of creation. Though the Dutch neo-Calvinists would subordinate creation to redemption in order to fulfill their vision of the "cultural mandate," in the case of Kuyper it was combined with the idea of an antithesis between the *church* and the world. This "left Neo-Calvinism with ominous ideological strains" (J. D. Bratt, *Dutch Calvinism in Modern America* [1984], 18), but in no way did it result in a natural theology, for, similar to Calvin, whatever good non-Christians could accomplish was attributed not to human effort but to divine grace.

Barth-Brunner debate. In the 1930s, the question of natural theology came to a head in the famous dispute between Karl Barth and Emil Brunner. A key issue was whether there is a point of contact (Ger. *Anknüpfungspunkt*) for the gospel in so-called natural man. Brunner challenged Barth's thoroughgoing Christocentrism and accused him of an unbiblical discontinuity between creation and grace. Barth replied with his sharp *Nein!* and attacked Brunner's use of the term *Offenbarungsmächtigkeit* (capacity for revelation). Brunner, no less than Barth, believed that God is truly known only by God's self-revelation in Jesus Christ as witnessed in **scripture**. At the same time, however, Brunner taught that God's general revelation could be seen in the creation, especially in orders (Ger. *Ordnungen*) of creation such as **marriage** and the state, and in God's image in humanity, though defaced by the fall. "Its *form*, if not its *content*, remains our essential humanity, our personhood, our reason and our ethical responsibility" (A. I. C. Heron, *A Century of Protestant Theology* [1980], 87). Brunner appealed to the traditional interpretation of Rom. 1:19–20 and maintained that this interpretation was Calvin's. Barth also claimed Calvin for his position and was later defended in this regard by his brother Peter. Brunner, it is generally agreed, could lay better claim to having Calvin on his side, but various of his misleading statements made it possible for Barth, with some justification, to claim victory in this dispute.

For Barth this issue was more than academic. He regarded Brunner's "compromise" as a stab in the back in the midst of a life-and-death struggle against the "German Christians" who had succumbed to the wiles of Nazi ideology. Out of this struggle came the **Barmen Declaration** (1934) with its forthright attack on the position of the "German Christians": "Jesus Christ, as he is attested for us in Holy Scripture, is the one Word of God which we have to hear and which we have to trust and obey in life and in death." This declaration was adopted as one of the confessions of the UPCUSA (1967).

Conclusions. The threat of subtle forms of natural theology did not end with the demise of the German Christians at the end of World War II. Reformed churches are also susceptible to the temptation to let other gods in the form of false ideologies undermine "the faith once for all delivered to the saints." The unresolved question is whether there can be a legitimate understanding of creation, nature, or culture apart from a specific reference to Jesus Christ. Now that we are concerned about a theology of creation, which is quite different from a natural theology, it may be possible to praise the God of creation who is none other than the God and Father of our Lord Jesus Christ.

Barth, *CD* II/1, 10ff., 88ff.; K. Barth and E. Brunner, *Natural Theology* (1934); G. C. Berkouwer, *General Revelation* (1958); E. Brunner, *Revelation and Reason* (1946); Calvin, *Inst.* 1.1–8; 2.1–4.

I. JOHN HESSELINK

Neo-Orthodoxy The term "neo-orthodoxy" describes the work of several twentieth-century European and North American theologians and, specifically, their approach to the task and substance of Christian theology. Neo-orthodoxy is a term of categorization that usually refers to Karl Barth, Emil Brunner, the early Rudolf Bultmann, and Friedrich Gogarten in Europe, and Reinhold Niebuhr and H. Richard Niebuhr in North America. Donald Baillie, John Baillie, and T. F. Torrance of Scotland, as well as the early Paul Tillich, are also cited as neo-orthodox.

None of these theologians referred to their work by this term, which originated in the English-speaking world, nor by other terms like it: "theology of crisis," "Barthianism," "dialectical theology," and, in relation specifically to Reinhold Niebuhr, "Christian realism." The term, invented by critics, was never quite free of denigrative connotation. Though novel aspects were present in those theologies, such as the critical study of **scripture**, openness to other sciences, and aversion to metaphysics or **natural theology**, thereby justifying the appellation "neo," critics meant to score what they believed to be the repristination of classic dogmatic loci of the Protestant Reformation. From this view, neo-orthodoxy reinstituted an orthodoxy that modern Christian theology in the West had long believed itself to have left behind.

The theologies to which neo-orthodoxy refers were worked out between the end of World War I and the height of the Cold War. This dating is not accidental. Many critics of neo-orthodoxy associate its rise with the disillusionment of a *humanity* failing its highest aspirations. In such times, the critics held, longing for firm ground turns to transcendentally legitimated *authority*, like that of scripture in traditional Protestantism. Coupled with it is a pessimism about the potential of the spirit, will, and mind of humankind; the affirmation of *God* breeds an abnegation of the human and vice versa.

Neo-orthodox theologies share a strong repudiation of Western confidence in the abilities of goodwill and historical progress. Experiences of massive political and religious support of World War I (Barth), the actual fighting and its huge cost in human life (Tillich), the murderous exploitation of workers by the acquirers of capital (Reinhold Niebuhr and Barth), and the like led to a loss of faith in social and cultural progress. Gone was confidence that the gospel proclaims God's reign as an optimistic and moral entity that can and ought to be realized by human beings, and this had shaken trust in the place and talk of *church* and theology. The reconstruction that neo-orthodoxy undertook sought to renew theology and church in continuity with the Reformation and its reliance on the Bible, the sole "authoritative" witness to the *Word of God.* As this Word, the gospel tells the truth about the world, namely, that it is powerless to redeem itself and that every self-generated liberation leads eventually to new *idolatry* and oppression.

Neo-orthodoxy is marked by Christocentricity. For example, Calvin's teaching that the *grace* of God's *incarnation* in Christ granted to humans *knowledge of God* gave structure to Barth's critique of liberal theology; Luther's teaching on the

work of Christ relating to *sin* and *justification* informed Reinhold Niebuhr's searing assessment of liberalism, particularly its efforts to "Christianize the social order." Their positive theological projects drew on the Reformation's incarnational Christologies in contradistinction from the liberal preoccupation with the "historical" Jesus. While the Christologies of neo-orthodoxy are not identical, they fueled discussion about *Christology* "from above" and "from below," the "human Jesus" and the "divine Christ." Neo-orthodoxy spoke decisively about the "Christ above us" who exceeds the liberal "Christ within us."

An antiliberal stance appeared in other features of neo-orthodox theology, accounting for much of its critics' reactions, both then and now. Neo-orthodox theologians stressed the otherness of God, the discontinuity between the divine and the human. They replaced human religious *experience* with divine self-revelation as the source of human knowledge of God. They interpreted God's reign and the meaning of *history* in the light of biblical *eschatology*, grounding it in God's action rather than in the progressive labors of humankind. They rejected the view that sin was human ignorance and unwillingness to transcend what belongs to nature and that it was overcome by sound education. Sin was, rather, the desire to be godlike, a perversion of *freedom,* which is undone entirely by God's *forgiveness* alone.

Neo-orthodoxy held that God's truth is never direct and transparent but always indirect and dialectical, found in the tension between one truth and another. Because *revelation* brings together eternity and time, revelation needs to be spoken of in terms of paradox, supremely in the paradox that Jesus Christ is both human and divine.

It was said that neo-orthodoxy succeeded in replacing the anthropocentrism of modernity with a theocentrism bordering on a supernaturalism that "bids us go back at a time when, if ever, we must go forward" (Edwin Lewis,

Christian Century, March 22, 1933). The perduring issue of critique is the "otherness of God," the insistence that God is wholly other and, as such, breaks in on the world from above. More often than not, this is taken to be a metaphysical assertion about God's being. Rather, it was a claim that the human experience of the God of whom the Bible speaks is wholly other from that of the God of whom modern theology spoke. For this reason, the language of neo-orthodoxy about revelation sounded so different from liberalism.

Neo-orthodoxy has relatively little influence now in Europe and North America. Yet it is no mere stage in the history of theology. Its criticism of liberalism was valid and creative and responsive to the changing context. The theologies of Reformation churches and their ecumenical partners were influenced significantly by neo-orthodoxy, as is the thought of churches that are bearers of their people's liberation struggles; the work of A. A. Boesak in South Africa and J. M. Bonino in South America come to mind. Neo-orthodoxy was ignored by theologians and churches at their peril, whether they understand it or not.

J. D. Godsey, "Neoorthodoxy," *The Encyclopedia of Religion,* vol. 10 (1987); P. L. Lehmann, "Crisis, The Theology of," *NSH Sup* 1:309–312.

H. MARTIN RUMSCHEIDT

New England Theology   A rather standard Calvinistic theology came to New England with John Cotton, Thomas Hooker, Thomas Shepard, and Peter Bulkeley. The *Half-Way covenant,* a distinct departure from traditional *Calvinism* (which permitted *baptism* only for infants of communicant members), was adopted (1662). This led to Solomon Stoddard's opening of the Communion itself to persons with "historical faith" but not claiming *conversion.* Jonathan Edwards's objection to this led to his dismissal from the Northampton pastorate (1750).

Charles Hodge contended that the senior Edwards deviated from Calvinism only on mediate imputation and metaphysical idealism, though he was disappointed also with Edwards's qualifications for admission to the Lord's Table.

What came to be called New England Theology was a more profound departure that could not call Edwards father, though his son, Jonathan Jr., Joseph Bellamy, Samuel Hopkins, and many others did so claim until its end with Andover Seminary and Edwards Amasa Park (1808–1900). B. B. Warfield contended that Edwards, in spite of his activism, delayed the triumph of *Arminianism* in New England a hundred years.

It is generally agreed that the *Concio ad Clerum* (1828) of N. W. Taylor represented a clear break with Calvinism and Edwards, though this was not generally admitted by Yale's "New Divinity" or Taylorism. By 1837, a split in the Presbyterian Church between New School and Old School occurred.

At least six doctrines are commonly associated with the New England Theology: the unconverted are by "natural ability" able to choose virtue but never do so of themselves; the governmental theory of the *atonement;* inability does limit responsibility; disinterested benevolence; *God* in *creation* aims at humanity's happiness; and "seeking" *evangelism.*

JOHN H. GERSTNER

New Haven Theology   Initially propounded by Timothy Dwight, this Reformed perspective made more room for the revivals that had been God's "surprising work" in colonial America. As Dwight, his student N. W. Taylor, and others developed it, the New Haven Theology accentuated human agency more than had Jonathan Edwards's theology. *Original sin* here was seen as inevitable but not determined genetically. Humans are responsible for their *sin* and can overcome sinning. God's special care for the redeemed was accented over God's care for the whole *creation.* Christian life was largely a reasonable configuration of "duties."

In the New Haven Theology, Scottish *common sense philosophy* prevailed over Edwards's Lockean grounding. It also "worked," as Dwight led a revival among Yale students (1818). Other New Haven revivalists joined in the prolonged Second Great Awakening. Thus, the theology provided a vehicle in the reconstruction of *Calvinism* to appeal to a democratic American culture.

LOUIS B. WEEKS

Omnipotence

The affirmation that *God* is omnipotent has traditionally been taken to mean that God can do all things. While widely held that God is omnipotent, there is considerable disagreement on what this really entails. For John Calvin, omnipotence was a central conviction understood to mean the effectual exercise of the divine personal will in accomplishing divine purposes. Closer study will reveal that Calvin's conception was complex, nuanced, and formed by diverse influences. He formed his view in conversation with (and over against) other perspectives available on his theological horizon.

In the medieval conversation about the scope of divine omnipotence, certain intractable problems were addressed. Does omnipotence mean that God can change the past? Can God create a square circle? Two significant limitations on the scope of omnipotence were proposed as a way of resolving such difficulties. In the interest of affirming the primacy and *freedom* of the divine will, Calvin refused both limitations.

The first limitation was to define omnipotence in terms of what is logically possible. The standard meaning came to be, "God can do whatever is doable." Calvin countered that it is in the freedom of the divine will to "determine" what is possible. The possibilities that are open to God are not limited by metaphysical necessities. God's personal will is what defines God's power. Therefore, no exter-

nal, metaphysical limitations can be placed upon divine power.

The second limitation employed in the Middle Ages involved a distinction between God's "absolute power" (divine power in itself) and God's "ordained power" (divine power in connection with divine willing). Calvin refused this distinction as well, saying that the concept of absolute power was an empty abstraction. God's power is not independent of God's moral character; rather, it expresses it. This power is not a neutral blind force of nature; it is the power of a free, personal will. Like the will of any person, God's will has a certain character—namely, the character of goodness that is part of the divine nature. While external, metaphysical limitations are to be refused, internal, moral limitations are to be admitted. God's power may be unlimited, but it is not arbitrary. Thus, any abstract definition of omnipotence as "absolute power"—a definition that Duns Scotus was supporting—is to be rejected. This omnipotent power is displayed in the *creation*, governance, and final disposition of the world. The nature of its operation is as personal and particular care that works universally and continuously. By describing the operation of divine power in this way, Calvin found a middle way between the *necessitas* of the Stoics and the *fortuna* of the Epicureans.

Calvin vehemently and explicitly denied the accusation that he was a determinist. He saw two difficulties in the Stoic determinism of his day. First, a thoroughgoing determinism bound even God in its "fate," thereby denying God's freedom. Second, determinism had the effect of denying human freedom and responsibility. His insistence on omnipotence as expressed in personal and particular care excluded *necessitas* or "blind fate."

Calvin's quarrel with the Epicureans was that their system left things to chance. While he would admit it appears that some things are left to chance, this is only because God's purpose in them is hidden from our view (*Inst.* 1.16.9). God's power operates universally and continuously;

nothing is outside its operation. Therefore nothing—not even the smallest detail—is left to chance. This is not just a general ordering in which God governs immanently through neutral laws of nature set up and left to function independently. God governs personally and directly. "Law of nature" is only a descriptive phrase connoting God's self-consistency in exercising power. What we call a "miracle" is not a special display of omnipotent power suspending "laws of nature." It is only one more example of God's unceasing (continuous) intervening activity. To multiply loaves and fishes is not qualitatively different from providing daily bread; it is just more calculated to strike the eye (Hunter, 57).

As Calvin articulated his understanding of the operation of divine omnipotence, his insistence on God's personal and particular care excluded necessity. His insistence that God's power is exercised universally and continuously excluded chance as well.

A. M. Hunter, *The Teaching of Calvin* (1950); C. B. Partee, *Calvin and Classical Philosophy* (1977); T. Rudavsky, ed., *Divine Omniscience and Omnipotence in Medieval Philosophy* (1985); A. Verhey, "Calvin's Treatise 'Against the Libertines,'" *CTJ* (1980): 190–219; A. Case-Winters, *God's Power* (1991).
ANNA CASE-WINTERS

Ordination   Ordination is an act of the *church* whereby persons are commissioned to a public *ministry.* It intends to establish them in ministries of service and leadership by the *authority* of Jesus Christ. Reformed churches generally recognize three offices: ministry of the Word and *sacraments* (pastor), governance (*elder*), and service (*deacon*). Terms used by other Christian bodies are variously appropriated to these three offices, for example, bishop to pastor. The ideals of a parity of ministry (no hierarchical order) and collegiality of ministry are reflected in the idea of calling and the language of the rite itself. Recently many Reformed

churches have been reshaping their rites to reflect more faithfully the general call to ministry that all Christians receive at their *baptism.* This sets the particular ministry of leadership and service, for which ordination is the public sign, in the context of the universal ministry of the church. "We have gifts that differ according to the grace given to us" (Rom. 12:6).

Ordination to the ministry is enacted as part of the common *worship* of the church: the proclamation of the *Word of God,* celebration of the gospel sacraments, and the prayers of the people. The distinctive action is "the laying on of hands of the presbytery," a valuable precedent from the earliest Christian communities, and invocation of the Spirit of *God* by whose effectual power the ministry will be carried forth. By this act, the gift of God is recognized and received, a link to the historic ordained ministry of the whole church is forged, and persons are established in the special ministries to which they have been called by inward persuasion, outward gifts, and public election. Additional practices, such as vesting the newly ordained, are optional.

Ordination is not a sacrament of the gospel; it is a matter of good order for the health and fidelity of the churches. According to John Calvin, God does not need ministers to do the work of the Spirit, but we do. God shows high regard for us by calling some among us to represent the divine will to the rest of us. We learn humility by being taught by another fallible human being and thus are nourished in a bond of love. The ordinand is set apart for this particular service within the company of the faithful. The ordained ministry depends on the ministry of the whole church, not the other way around. Although ordination is for life, it is not assumed that ordination conveys an "indelible character." The emphasis is on special responsibility for a lifetime of leadership and service.

Calvin, *Inst.* 4.3; T. F. Torrance, *Conflict and Agreement in the Church* (1960); H. J.

Wotherspoon and J. M. Kirkpatrick, *A Manual of Church Doctrine according to the Church of Scotland* (1960).

THOMAS D. PARKER

Original Sin The good *creation* fell into *sin*. This is the story of original sin. We confess it but cannot explain it. We must start where the Bible starts. It reveals the historical beginning of sin and evil but not its behind-the-scenes origin. Yet Christian thinkers struggle with this problem.

Two biblical presuppositions must govern such theological reflection. First, *scripture* affirms creation's pristine goodness. Sin and evil cannot claim creaturely status. They are not ontic realities. The Maker's handiwork was "very good" (Gen. 1:31). Second, is the creator responsible for this downfall? No, for "in him is no darkness at all" (1 John 1:5). Reformation *creeds* echo this note: *God* is "by no means" and "in no sense" its cause. No third possibility exists. The originating sin remains an unfathomable mystery. This is the end of the matter. But no.

Three major theories have emerged, "explaining" original sin as the effect of some prior, deeper cause. Monist theories trace it back to the divine decrees. As God acts "right-handedly" to do good, God is also involved "left-handedly" in evil. Both arise from an ultimate divine principle. Dualist theories trace it to two deities—the God of light and an anti-god of darkness. World *history* is a power struggle between them. Demonic theories point an accusing finger at the devil. The devil becomes our "scapegoat."

All such "explanations" are exercises in futility. They only push the problem a step back into the hidden unknown. Every theodicy of sin ends in speculation. The biblical account is our only starting point: "In Adam's fall we sinned all" (*New England Primer*; Rom. 5:12–21).

The momentous event in Genesis 3 is our ultimate witness to the sin behind all sins. There Adam, with Eve, acting vicariously as covenant head of *humanity*, failed the probationary test, broke the *covenant*, and brought God's *judgment* down upon every creature. We fell from the state of uprightness into condemnation. Our sinfulness is a settled issue. Adam's decision was also ours, made for us but not apart from us. This is our existential predicament.

The transmission of guilt addresses the question, How are we implicated in that original sin? By imitation, Pelagius and his followers answer. Adam's act of disobedience set a bad example, which all persons habitually emulate. By propagation, according to Augustinians. Sin is transmitted by heredity from generation to generation. By imputation, Calvinists hold. Adam acted representatively for us. We now share vicariously in the righteousness of the last Adam as an *atonement* for our vicarious participation in the unrighteousness of the first Adam. Contemporary views appeal to the theory of evolution, viewing sin and evil as remnants of a primitive stage in our development.

The effects of original sin are evident in personal and corporate rebellion against God, broken human relations, and abuse of the cosmos. As to legal status, we are guilty; as to condition, polluted. Our sinful nature issues in actual sins. Only in Christ is there now "no condemnation" (Rom. 8:1).

H. Berkhof, *CFI*; L. Berkhof, *Systematic Theology*, 4th rev. and enl. ed. (1949); G. C. Berkouwer, *Sin* (1971); Weber, *FD*, vol. 1.

GORDON J. SPYKMAN

Orthodoxy, Reformed The terms "orthodoxy," "scholasticism," "scholastic orthodoxy," and "confessional orthodoxy" refer to the post-Reformation theological development in the Reformed churches. It began in the late sixteenth century following the work of second-generation codifiers of the Reformation such as John Calvin, Heinrich Bullinger, Wolfgang Musculus, and Peter Martyr Vermigli and extended into the eighteenth century. This theology is identified as orthodox or confessional because it attempted to codify and systematize "right teaching" within the bounds created by the great Reformed *confessions* of the sixteenth century. It is termed "scholastic" primarily because of the theological method it used in formulating its systems of *doctrine*. The *scholasticism* of the late sixteenth and seventeenth centuries was facilitated by the increased openness of Protestant theology to the use of *reason* and *philosophy*, specifically to the revised Aristotelianism of the late Renaissance. In their attempt to create a genuinely Protestant, but also orthodox and essentially catholic or churchly, theological system, the Reformed thinkers of the post-Reformation era had recourse both to traditional models for theology, including the great medieval systems of Peter Lombard, Thomas Aquinas, Duns Scotus, Durandus, and others, and to the ongoing philosophical tradition, notably the thought of Francesco Zabarella and Francisco Suárez, that linked them to those systems. Granting the developments in logic, rhetoric, and metaphysics that had taken place in the fifteenth and sixteenth centuries, neither the method nor the philosophy of the Protestant scholastics was identical to that of the medieval thinkers.

The development of Reformed orthodoxy was paralleled by a similar development in the Lutheran church. This orthodox or scholastic Protestantism would be the dominant form of Protestant theology for nearly two hundred years. Within that two-century span, we can identify roughly four phases: early orthodoxy, high orthodoxy, the pietist and "transitional" phase, and the increasingly rationalistic phase of late orthodoxy and rational supernaturalism.

Origins of Protestant scholasticism and the early orthodox codification of system (c. 1565–1640). The initial codification of the theology of the Reformation in the era of Calvin, Bullinger, and the great national confessions of the Reformed churches was a major theological development in itself. A transformation in style and method equally as profound as that witnessed in the transition from the writings of the first Reformers to the works of Calvin, Bullinger, Musculus, and Vermigli occurred in the years following 1560. Of these four representatives of the first great doctrinal formulation of Protestantism, only one, Bullinger, lived past 1564, and his greatest systematic efforts had been completed by that date.

Several factors account for the transition from the theology of the Reformers to that of orthodoxy, not the least being the polemic with Rome. In the canons and decrees of the Council of Trent, called in December 1545 by Pope Paul III, the Reformation was answered and condemned by the best theological minds of the Roman Catholic Church; at the same time, the diverse strains of medieval theology, with the exception of the radical *Augustinianism* that fed into the Reformation, were reconciled into a single, overarching confessional statement. After Trent, Protestant theology was subjected to the searching criticism of Cardinal Robert Bellarmine. Trent elicited several detailed Protestant rebuttals, notably from Calvin and the Lutheran theologian Martin Chemnitz (1522–86), and Bellarmine's polemic was answered in detail by a considerable number of early orthodox writers such as William Ames (1576–1633) and Festus Hommius (1576–1642). In the course of this polemic, Protestantism developed a more detailed synthesis of its own theological position.

A second factor was the demise of the first- and second-generation Protestant leaders and the third generation's need to state for themselves the meaning of the Reformation. This factor, together with a third, the interest among the successors of the Reformers in maintaining and emphasizing the catholicity of the Reformation in the light of the Christian tradition, may be viewed as a positive, internal impetus toward orthodox system. Also, the attempt to formulate a theological system for Protestantism on a large scale—far beyond that offered by the second-generation Reformers—necessitated the reintroduction of philosophical categories and, indeed, of metaphysical discussion, particularly in such areas of doctrine as the essence and attributes of God, *creation,* and *providence.*

The early orthodox era, extending roughly from 1565 to 1640, is characterized by a certain newness and freshness of formulation and, in the cases of major formulators such as Theodore Beza (1519–1605), Zacharias Ursinus (1534–83), Caspar Olevianus (1536–87), Girolamo Zanchi (1516–90), and Franciscus Junius (1545–1641), a consistent wrestling with the problems of the organization and definition of theology in the light of the interplay between exegesis, *tradition,* and confessional synthesis. Zanchi was particularly important to the development, since he had been trained in Thomist theology at Padua before his *conversion* to the Protestant cause and provided the model of a fully developed scholasticism for the next generation of Reformed theologians.

This was the age of the *Heidelberg Catechism* (1563) and its exposition as system, of the Swiss Harmony of Reformed Confessions (1581), the *Irish Articles of Religion* (1615), and the *Synod of Dort* (1618–19). The combined effect of well-defined dogmatic presuppositions on the confessional level, the need for more detailed positive doctrine and for a self-conscious theological methodology, and the ever-escalating polemic between Roman, Reformed, Lutheran, and the various sectarian theologies was to produce a more traditionally "scholastic" theology among Protestants, a theology open on the one side to the medieval tradition with its use of Aristotelian philosophy but on the other side ever aware of the Reformation mandate to allow no norm for doctrine equal to or higher than *scripture.*

The continuation of an "early orthodox" style can be identified well into the seventeenth century in the theologies of Amandus Polanus (1561–1610), William Perkins (1558–1602), Bartholomäus Keck-ermann (1571–1609), Johann Heinrich Alsted (1588–1638), Franciscus Gomarus (1563–1641), Johannes Maccovius (1588–1644), John Downame, and James Ussher (1581–1656). Though the era of confessional formulation came to a close at Dort, at the very same time that the Thirty Years' War was breaking out in Bohemia and the Palatinate, it was only after 1640 that the scholastic style of theology moved beyond that of writers such as Polanus and Alsted, the great codifiers of the early orthodox system.

Corresponding roughly to the period of the Thirty Years' War (1618–48), there is a phase of polemical formulation in which the various theological perspectives were still more clearly defined and full-scale polemical summa were written by theologians such as Johannes Cloppenburg (1592–1654) and Johannes Hoornbeek (1617–66). These theologians waged their own intellectual warfare, analyzing in purely polemical compendia the various doctrinal options—and, ultimately, by the end of the war, standardizing the attack, formalizing their victory, to the point that the "high orthodox" of the generation following the Peace of Westphalia could concentrate all the more on the internal elaboration of system.

High orthodoxy in the seventeenth century (c. 1640–1700). The era of "high orthodoxy" is by all accounts the great age of theological system, in which the theological task receives final definition down to the smallest, finest distinction at the hands of theologians such as Markus Friedrich Wendelin (1584–1652) and Gisbert Voetius (1589–1676). It was an age of considerable intellectual activity and genuine development in the fields of theology, linguistic study, and exegesis, the most notable achievement in the latter two fields being the great London Polyglot Bible (1654–57), edited by Brian Walton (1600–61), and its companion, the Lexicon heptaglotton (1669), by Walton's colleague, Edmund Castell (1606–85).

The internal Reformed controversies of the era, notably the debate over

Cocceian federalism and the several controversies generated by the theologians of Saumur, were all debates over highly technical theological questions. Granting that the two theological systems of Johannes Cocceius manifest all the organizational, logical, and indeed, metaphysical concerns typical of the works of his contemporaries and that the theology of his most bitter adversary, Voetius, manifests as much concern for *piety* and praxis as Cocceius's, the debate ought not to be viewed as often portrayed—as a debate between a biblical, covenantal theology and a predestinarian scholasticism. Rather, it was a debate between Reformed scholastics over the hermeneutical implications of the covenant concept and particularly over the implications of Cocceius's notion of a gradually abrogated *covenant* of works and a gradually inaugurated covenant of *grace.*

The debate over the theology of Saumur extended from the end of the early orthodox era through the era of high orthodoxy and placed the theologians of that eminent French academy— Louis Cappel (1585–1658), Moïse Amyraut (1596–1664), Claude Pajon (1626–85), and Joshua de la Place (Placaeus; 1606–55)—against a considerable array of French, German, and Swiss Reformed orthodox, including Pierre DuMoulin (1568–1658), Johannes Buxtorf Sr. (1564–1629), Johannes Buxtorf Jr. (1599–1664), Frédéric Spanheim (1600–48), Francis Turretin (1623–87), and J. H. Heidegger (1633–98). Each of the debates manifests the difficulty experienced by orthodoxy in maintaining doctrinal continuity with the Reformation while also formulating a full theological system in an era of scholastic method, changing patterns in textual criticism and exegesis, and genuinely revolutionary development in *science* and philosophy. Cappel argued, against the elder Buxtorf, that the vowel points of the Hebrew text of the OT were invented by the Masoretes some six or seven centuries after Christ. This philological question was, at that time, inextricably linked with the doctrine of

the *authority* of scripture in its original languages. Since Cappel's views could be used to support Roman Catholic claims of the prior authority of the Vulgate, the orthodox opposed his findings. La Place held that the imputation of Adam's *sin* to the human race was founded on the actual sinfulness of human beings and was therefore "mediate" or mediated by the facts of heredity. Against this, orthodoxy held an "immediate imputation of sin" on the grounds of no foreseen demerit in the progeny of Adam in order to maintain a strict parallel with the totally gratuitous imputation of Christ's righteousness to the faithful. In both cases, fine points of argument became tests of orthodoxy.

More important to the development and change of theology in the high orthodox era was the loss of the traditional Aristotelian synthesis of theology, philosophy, and science. Not only was the Aristotelian metaphysic now met by an equally powerful rationalist metaphysic but the Ptolemaic geocentric universe, to which the Aristotelian metaphysic and its theory of causes were bound, had been replaced by a new worldview, the Copernican. Orthodoxy began to feel the impact of Cartesian rationalism and, in England, of the *natural theology* of early Deism. Toward the end of the era, the rationalistic systems of Spinoza, Leibniz, and Locke manifested even more clearly the changed philosophical climate. Spinoza and Leibniz, for all their positive interest in theology, constructed metaphysical systems inimical to orthodox dogmatics. At the same time, Arminian theology proved to be far more open to rationalism than the Reformed, moving first toward Cartesianism and then, in the thought of Philipp van Limborch (1633–1712), toward the Lockean epistemology and ethics.

Late orthodoxy and rationalism (c. 1700–1790). During the final decades of the seventeenth and throughout the eighteenth century, the phenomenon of theological orthodoxy and the companion phenomenon of a Protestant scholasticism entered an era of decline and stagnation. The spirit that produced a living orthodoxy and an energetically formulated scholasticism at the end of the sixteenth century and in the early decades of the seventeenth had long since dissipated, and even the essential intellectual strength of that initial formulation, which had carried Protestant orthodoxy in its several forms through the better part of the seventeenth century, had begun to wither. Orthodoxy and scholasticism such as remained after 1700 were transformed by the forces of pietism, doctrinal indifferentism, and rationalism into forms radically different from those that dominated the seventeenth century.

Pietism offered a critique of scholastic theology from the perspective of the life of religion and the practical application of doctrine. Together with the so-called indifferentist theologians, the pietists were able to argue that orthodoxy had substituted detailed formulae for piety and conviction and had lost touch with the needs of the *church.* The impact of "indifferentism" to the fine doctrinal distinctions made by scholastic orthodoxy, or, as it is sometimes called, latitudinarianism, can be seen already in the ecumenical efforts and writings of William Chillingworth (1602–44), John Dury (d. c. 1675), and the Lutheran theologian Georg Calixtus (1586–1656), in the middle of the seventeenth century. These theologians tired of internecine Protestant polemic and searched for Protestant unity in the common affirmation of biblical truth beyond particularistic confessions. The impulse became stronger at the end of the century in the writings of continental theologians such as Jean-Alphonse Turrettini (1671–1737) and Jean Frédéric Ostervald (1663–1747), who experienced, far more than any of their predecessors, the difficulty of maintaining a scholastic and strictly confessional orthodoxy in the face of changing patterns of hermeneutics, philosophy, and science.

The late orthodox era, roughly from 1740 to 1790, begins with the victorious return of Christian von Wolff to the University of Halle, by imperial order, over the protest of the pietist theologians. After 1740, under the tutelage of the prolific Wolff, scholastic orthodoxy found its new philosophy, replacing Aristotle and ridding itself of the questionable Cartesian alternative by adopting as its intellectual underpinning the rationalism of Wolff and his associates. Among the Reformed theologians influenced by Wolffian philosophy were Daniel Wyttenbach (1706–79) and Johann Friedrich Stapfer (1708–75). Both systems assume that reason is the initial and necessary foundation for theology and that the truths of *revelation* ought to be grounded on a foundation of natural theology. By 1790, this rationalist phase of Protestant scholasticism had come to a close under the impact of Kant's critique of rationalist metaphysics.

The Age of Reason in England and France was as rationalist as the German Enlightenment but not nearly so congenial to traditional Christianity or to theological system. The Deists were particularly critical of the supernaturalistic assumptions of orthodoxy, and in England the development of a more or less *Reformed theology* was further complicated by the confessional and political disunity of the dissenting churches. Thus, John Gill defended the older orthodoxy in the name of a fully developed supralapsarian determinism, while at the same time losing sight of the confessional bounds of the older Reformed theology. Thomas Ridgley's (1667–1734) massive exposition of the WLC manifests both the inroads of rationalism and, particularly in its modal approach to the doctrine of the *Trinity,* the problem of adapting orthodox theological language to the new age. The theological system of the Anglican Thomas Stackhouse (1680–1752) evidences not only a rational supernaturalism in its approach to religion and revelation but also a willingness to accommodate theology to the findings of science in its doctrine of creation and to rehearse the niceties of the debate with *Arminianism* over *predestination* in an almost objective style.

This "decline of orthodoxy" was not, of course, the end of the historical phenomenon of orthodox dogmatics. Orthodox Protestantism did not disappear under the critique of pietism and rationalism any more than in an earlier time did Thomism vanish under assaults of Scotism and nominalism or, in a slightly later time, did rationalism pass out of existence following the critiques of Kant and the dawn of romanticism. Throughout the eighteenth and even the nineteenth and twentieth centuries, Protestant orthodoxy and Protestant scholasticism have remained alive in the theological work of writers such as Heinrich Heppe, Charles Hodge, and Louis Berkhof. It is also clear, however, that during the early eighteenth century, orthodoxy ceased to say anything new either to the culture or to itself. The eighteenth century, viewed as a positive age of intellectual growth, moved religious thought and the discipline of theology away from traditional orthodoxy and mounted a critique of facile dogmatism, such as the older orthodoxy had ultimately become.

B. G. Armstrong, *Calvinism and the Amyraut Heresy* (1969); I. A. Dorner, *History of Protestant Theology Particularly in Germany*, 2 vols. (ET 1871); Heppe, *RD*; R. A. Muller, *Christ and the Decree* (1986); and *Post-Reformation Reformed Dogmatics*, vol. 1: *Prolegomena to Theology* (1987); O. Ritschl, *Dogmengeschichte des Protestantismus: Grundlagen und Grundzüge der theologischen Gedanken und Lehrbildung in den protestantischen Kirchen*, 4 vols. (1908–27); H. E. Weber, *Die philosophische Scholastik des deutschen Protestantismus im Zeitalter der Orthodoxie* (1907); and *Reformation, Orthodoxie, und Rationalismus*, 2 vols. (1937–51).

RICHARD A. MULLER

Pastoral Care   In the Reformed tradition, pastoral care is one of the church's structured expressions of the means of *grace*. Exercised by both clergy and laity, this care includes traditional tasks of general visitation, comfort of the grieving, help for the sick and needy, *forgiveness* for the guilty, and the "cure of souls" through discipline and forgiveness. Pastoral care is also a *ministry* of the *church* to bring comfort and redirection to persons in need of renewal.

Pastoral care is not limited to theology and ecclesiology for its content. From the Reformed belief that *God* is active and present in all the world, there is a willingness to use knowledge from the human sciences of psychology, sociology, and anthropology. Informed by these multiple perspectives on God and human nature, pastoral care seeks the most effective means to carry out its tasks both for the sake of the recipients of the care and for the church.

The Reformed awareness of human finitude and *sin* recognizes that special initiatives are often needed in the midst of life's difficulties. When *death* occurs, for example, family members may become so bereft or angry with God that they fall away from the structured life and care of the congregation. The ministry of pastoral care takes the initiative to extend comfort, not only to offer sympathy but also to keep the deceased's family involved in the church's life, working actively to claim and affirm God's grace for them in times of suffering. Pastoral care in the Reformed tradition, then, consists of those acts designed and carried out by pastor and congregation that help persons interpret the significant events in their lives and that invite persons into involvement and growth in the life of the community of faith.

Historically there has been a disciplinary dimension to Reformed pastoral care as well. To persons who have "fallen away," care has been extended aggressively to return them to the community of faith, where God's grace is openly acknowledged.

Pastoral care in the Reformed tradition is a ministry of nurture and support. Its forms of expression vary over time. Sometimes the reaching out has been done from a dogmatic, or authoritarian, posture; at other times with more gentleness and winsomeness. But whatever the form, the integrity of pastoral care in the Reformed tradition hinges on its purpose of maintaining an awareness of God's presence and activity in the world and interpreting that presence in people's lives. This in turn strengthens them to continue the pilgrimage to which God has called them in the world.

R. Baxter, *The Reformed Pastor* (1656; repr. 1963); D. S. Browning, *The Moral Context of Pastoral Care* (1983); W. A. Clebsch and C. A. Jaekle, *Pastoral Care in Historical Perspective* (1964; repr. 1983); E. B. Holifield, *A History of Pastoral Care in America* (1983); T. C. Oden, *Pastoral Theology* (1983).

WILLIAM V. ARNOLD

Pastoral Theology As a special branch of practical theology concerned with the practice of *ministry,* pastoral theology exists alongside historical and systematic theology, distinguished yet inseparable from them, with a particular responsibility for explaining the actual relationships between the *Word of God* and the lives of God's people.

The discipline of pastoral theology today is difficult to define. Often associated with various psychological perspectives and psychotherapeutic techniques, *pastoral care* has been cut adrift from clear theological foundations. Pastoral theology continues to be associated with the practical end of the curriculum, having acquired a functionalist and professionalized character. Much has been learned, but at the cost of a lost identity. Contemporary pastoral theology within the Reformed churches is not exempt from this condition.

Within Reformed faith, pastoral care has its place within theology and the *church.* Pastoral care is ordered first of all by clear theological principle. John T. McNeill suggests that Calvin's approach to pastoral care was ordered by his understanding of the *doctrine* of *repentance.* What Calvin had in mind was

regeneration or *sanctification,* the process by which a person grows in the obedience, holiness, and goodness that mark the restoration of the image of God. For Eduard Thurneysen, the theological heart of pastoral care is the proclamation of the *forgiveness* of sins. In short, the theological focus of pastoral care within Reformed faith is the reconciliation of the believer with *God.*

Pastoral care is, second, a discipline of the church. The marks of the church are the *preaching* and hearing of the Word of God and proper celebration of the *sacraments.* Early in the history of Reformed faith, however, *church discipline* was added (*Scots Confession,* art. 18). Today we would see this pastoral care, not, however, as a third mark of the church but the means of expression to the individual of the same gospel preached in sermon and celebrated in sacrament. Calvin wrote: "Christ did not ordain pastors on the principle that they only teach the Church in a general way on the public platform, but that they care for the individual sheep, bring back the wandering and scattered to the fold, bind up the broken and crippled, heal the sick, support the frail and weak" (*Commentary* on Acts 20:20). But note: Under no circumstances could pastoral care have a content different from the content of sermon and sacrament.

Reformed pastoral theology is focused on the objectivity of God's *grace* in Jesus Christ. "We have taught," wrote Calvin, "that the sinner does not dwell upon his own compunction or tears, but fixes both eyes upon the Lord's mercy alone" (*Inst.* 3.4.3). Like Luther, Calvin was concerned to get people to look away from themselves to a gracious *God* who alone could bring them *salvation,* healing, and peace. But one cannot look to God unless one first hears the voice of God. Therefore, the Word of God is the center of all ministry. As Calvin noted, "It would not be sufficient for God to determine with himself what he would do for our safety, if he did not speak to us expressly by name. It is only when God makes us understand, by his own voice, that he will be gracious to us, that we can entertain the hope of salvation" (*Commentary on Ps.* 12:5).

It is uncertain yet whether we will see a significant recovery of a Reformed pastoral theology of the Word of God. Richard Baxter's *The Reformed Pastor* (1656) is rarely read today, yet it remains a text awaiting rediscovery. Thurneysen's *A Theology of Pastoral Care* (ET 1962) is a modern classic of Reformed pastoral theology that deserves wider recognition and more careful study than it has received in recent years.

J. Firet, *Dynamics in Pastoring* (1986); J. T. McNeill, *A History of the Cure of Souls* (1951); E. H. Peterson, *Five Smooth Stones for Pastoral Work* (1980); E. Thurneysen, *A Theology of Pastoral Care* (ET 1962); R. S. Wallace, *Calvin, Geneva, and the Reformation* (1988).

ANDREW PURVES

Peace   Historically there are few discussions of peace in the Reformed tradition. An almost unanimous assumption of the just war theory has existed from John Calvin to the present; only since World War II has there been a shift in the treatment of the subject.

Christian thought on the relationship of the Christian to *war* has been dominated by Augustine's just war theory. Many refinements have been made. For any war to be considered just and valid for Christian participation, it must be entered upon only after all other means of resolution are exhausted, be purely self-defensive, take measures to protect noncombatants, ensure the benefits of victory to outweigh the horror of war, and be declared by proper authorities. Just war theory assumes that war is wrong and forbidden to the believer until the conditions that justify the carnage are proven.

The Protestant Reformers embraced that *tradition* of the *church.* Calvin argued against the pacifism of the Anabaptists and asserted the government's call to "defend by war the dominions entrusted to their safekeeping, if at any time they are under enemy attack." *Scripture* "declares such wars to be lawful" (*Inst.* 4.20.11). In the same vein, the *WCF* declares that the civil magistracy has the right to "wage war upon just and necessary occasions" (ch. 23).

Adherence to the just war theory has produced two major results: support for efforts to promote peace (short of pacifism) and acquiescence to the justness of wars once a nation engages in them. Reformed bodies in the United States display both tendencies. Individuals, particularly Presbyterians and Congregationalists who held the **New England Theology,** were early supporters of the American Peace Society (1828). The movement that caught the imagination of many, however, was the drive for international arbitration of disputes between nations. The PCUS mounted a campaign for arbitration beginning in 1890. By 1898, 145 churches had signed petitions addressed to the governments of thirty-one nations. Reformed denominations supported the Presbyterian President Wilson's call for a League of Nations at the end of World War I.

While seeking peace, Presbyterians went to war. In 1898, the UPCNA *General Assembly* argued that Spanish cruelty "justifies the interference of our government in the cause of humanity" in the Spanish-American War. The Allied cause in World War I was held to be God's cause, and prayers for the enemy's defeat were repeatedly invoked. Disillusioned with the results of the war and the failure of the peace, Presbyterians in the United States joined calls for disarmament (1920s and 1930s) and passed resolutions never again to "bless" war. Between world wars, a pacifist witness against all war emerged within the Presbyterian Church in the U.S.A. in the form of the Presbyterian Peace Fellowship. The PCUS saw the formation of the Southern Presbyterian Peace Fellowship (1949). These bodies federated (1978) and were merged with reunion of the PCUS and UPCUSA (1983).

But the churches again "presented arms" with the onset of World War II, though in a more penitential and reserved spirit than during World War I. With the end of the war, Presbyterians again supported an international body for mediation of claims. Fearing communism, churches called for a strong defense and containment policy overseas but resisted efforts to militarize the nation (through universal military training and a peacetime draft) and abridgment of freedom in the form of McCarthyism. The PCUS said: "Communists often . . . make a strong appeal where inequalities, injustices and hunger prevail. But this does not mean that we have become communistic when we also speak out boldly for justice, equality and social welfare, for these are the basic standards of our Faith" ("The Christian Faith and Communism," General Assembly *Minutes* [1954]).

The Vietnam War proved to be a turning point in Presbyterian thought on peace and war. The churches, like the nation, were divided by the conflict. General Assemblies of the UPCUSA and PCUS questioned the war's morality, eventually declared it unjust, and called for U.S. withdrawal. At the same time, emphasis on whether war could be justified shifted to a positive theology of peace. This is seen in a number of General Assembly declarations and agency papers, perhaps most clearly in the UPCUSA's *Confession of 1967* and the PCUS's A Declaration of Faith. Both stressed the horror of war, God's call to reconciliation and justice, and those efforts that make for peace. There was no mention of a just war.

This trend resulted in the paper "Peacemaking: The Believer's Calling" (UPCUSA, 1980; PCUS, 1981) and the establishment of the Presbyterian Peacemaking Program. Peace was defined as the biblical *shalom* (wholeness, harmony, right relations). Far more than the absence of conflict, peace was held to entail active work to create *justice* for all

people, understanding and reconciliation between communities and nations, and a mutual upbuilding at all levels of society. "We know that peace cannot be achieved by ending the arms race unless there is economic and political justice in the human family," the paper declared. The reconciling character of peacemaking made it central to discipleship. Though not embracing pacifism, the emphasis no longer fell on the right to war but on the necessity—indeed, the call of God—for true peace.

R. Abrams, *Preachers Present Arms* (1933); J. L. Brooks, "In Behalf of a Just and Durable Peace: The Attitudes of American Protestantism toward War and Military-Related Affairs Involving the United States, 1949–1953" (diss., Tulane University, 1977); A. C. Cochrane, *The Mystery of Peace* (1985); U. Mauser, "Peacemaking in a Militaristic Society," *JPH* 61 (Spring 1983): 118–26; R. Nutt, "To Witness for Christ as They Saw Him: The Southern Presbyterian Peace Fellowship and Peace Work in the Presbyterian Church in the United States, 1949–1983" (diss., Vanderbilt University, 1986); R. Smylie, "A Presbyterian Witness on War and Peace: An Historical Interpretation" *JPH* 59 (Winter 1981): 498–516; "Peacemaking: The Believer's Calling," UPCUSA General Assembly *Minutes* (1980), PCUS (1981).

RICK NUTT

Perseverance of the Saints The fifth of the so-called five points of *Calvinism,* also known as preservation, eternal security, and the "once saved, always saved" *doctrine,* it is more properly designated as "perseverance of God with the saints." It asserts that whomever *God* regenerates will surely not be permitted to fall back into perdition but will be kept by the power of God unto eventual *salvation.* This does not preclude the possibility of serious setbacks that may necessitate severe chastisements by God, as with David's monstrous *sin* "in the case of Uriah the Hittite" (1 Kings 15:5). This view is supported by many biblical passages, such as Matt. 24:24; John 5:24; 6:37, 39, 40, 44, 47, 51, 54, 56, 58; 10:3–5, 14, 27–29; 17:6, 9, 12, 24; Rom. 5:9–10; 6:4, 8; 8:11, 15–17, 30, 33, 35–39; 11:29; 14:4; 1 Cor. 1:8, 9; 2 Cor. 1:21–22; Eph. 1:13–14; 4:30; Phil. 1:6; Col. 3:3; 2 Thess. 3:3–4; 2 Tim. 1:12; 2:13; 4:18; Heb. 5:9; 6:9, 17–20; 7:25; 10:19–23; 1 Peter 1:3–5; 5:6–10; 1 John 2:19; 3:6–9; 5:18; and Jude 24. Since these emphasize God's action in safeguarding God's own children rather than human steadfastness in remaining attached to God, it is apposite to speak of God's perseverance with the saints rather than use the other terms. Perhaps the strongest of all passages is John 10:28, where it is clear that the hand of the shepherd will prevent anyone from snatching out any sheep and will not permit any sheep from withdrawing (they shall never perish!). A shepherd who would explain the loss of some sheep by the excuse, "They left of their own will," would be adjudged seriously delinquent!

Throughout the history of theology and interpretation, there have been strong objections to this view, however, both because of the many scriptures that warn against apostasy and because some people who had given strong evidence of being born again turned away and appeared to close their lives without *repentance. Augustine* tied perseverance with *election,* not with *regeneration,* no doubt because his view of baptismal regeneration multiplied enormously the number of nonpersevering regenerates! The Remonstrants indicated that the matter should be investigated anew, and Arminians of all stripes have denied that regeneration ensures ultimate salvation. They have advanced in the main four arguments against this doctrine.

1. The warnings of *scripture* against turning away from the path of life (Ezek. 33:12, 13, 18; Matt. 10:22; 18:32–34; 1 Cor. 9:27; 10:11–12; 15:2; 2 Cor. 11:3–4; 13:5; 1 Thess. 3:5; 1 Tim. 2:15; 4:15–16; 5:8; 6:11; Heb. 3:6, 14; 4:1, 11; 6:4–8; 10:26–29, 36, 38; James 1:12; 2 Peter 1:9–10; 2 John 8–9; Jude 20–21; Rev. 2:5, 16; 3:5, 11; 22:19).

These passages are interpreted by supporters of perseverance as providing the kind of exhortation by which God implements perseverance with those who also by God's *grace* do persevere. Hebrews 6:4–9 and 10:26–29 are seen as describing an external profession without an actual regeneration.

2. The examples of people such as King Saul, Judas, Hymenaeus, and Alexander who, after being apparently renewed, turned away and "shipwrecked their faith" (cf. further Matt. 7:21–23; 18:32–34; 24:12; 25:12–13, 28–30; John 15:2, 6; Rom. 14:15; Gal. 5:4; Col. 2:19; 1 Tim. 1:6, 19–20; 4:1; 5:15; 6:9–10, 21; 2 Tim. 2:18; Heb. 10:29; 2 Peter 2:1; Rev. 3:16).

Such cases may be shown to be in harmony with perseverance by showing either that the people in view were never regenerated (Judas; John 15:2, 6) or that after a period of decline they returned to the faith.

3. God's certain safeguarding of God's own regenerate children is thought to be in conflict with the reality of human *free will,* which demands that obedience or apostasy continue to be real possibilities.

Holders of perseverance indicate that this is a misunderstanding of the relation between the sovereign will of God and the reality of the power of decision in rational agents. The Arminian logic would destroy either free will in *heaven* or the security of those who are redeemed in heaven and the holy angels.

4. A very harmful use of this doctrine is made by people who count firmly on their salvation while engaged in a course of willful disobedience to God. They say, "Once saved, always saved, so I can do whatever I please without endangering my salvation."

This is a drastic distortion of the doctrine, and if this type of reasoning is presented as one's life program, there is good reason to question that this person is at all regenerate. To invoke God's grace as an excuse for sinning is Satanic rather than regenerate (Rom. 6:1).

The doctrine of perseverance associated with the glorious assurance of salvation for obedient Christians was one of the great factors of strength in the whole Reformation movement (Lutheran, Anglican, and Reformed). The doctrine of *assurance* separated from perseverance leaves the child of God subject to the constant fear that one's weakness may yet forfeit everything Christ has done for us!

Augustine, "On the Gift of Perseverance," *Post-Nicene Fathers,* 1st series, vol. 5; G. C. Berkouwer, *Faith and Perseverance* (1958); J. Owen, *The Doctrine of the Saints' Perseverance: Works of John Owen,* ed. W. Goold, vol. 11.

Against perseverance: I. H. Marshall, *Kept by the Power of God* (1969); R. L. Shank, *Life in the Son* (1960).

ROGER NICOLE

Philosophy   Literally (Gr. and Lat.) "the love of wisdom and/or knowledge" (*philia-sophia*), philosophy crystallizes the supreme ambition of *reason* and symbolizes the worthiest mode of existence. In Plato's *Republic,* dialectic or philosophy is called knowledge of beauty and goodness. In the heyday of *scholasticism,* Thomas Aquinas, like Aristotle, characterized philosophy as knowledge of things through their causes (*Summa contra gentiles* [1258–60]). At the apogee of idealism, Hegel argued that philosophy was absolute *science* and true *worship* because it conceptually fathomed the true nature of things.

The contemplation of the totality of reality is the primary concern of philosophy. According to Francis Bacon, reality embraces God, nature, and *humanity* (*Advancement of Learning* [1603]). As *sapientia humana,* philosophy investigates the essence of all things and addresses the fundamental issues regarding nature, humanity, and society. To define pure positions, draw general principles, frame a consistent, comprehensive, and meaningful system, and prescribe a way of living—together these constitute the philosophical task. As encyclopedic knowledge and rigorous quest for the highest truth, philosophy lays claim to universal science (*philosophia perennis*).

Ordinarily its method of procedure is logical and rational. Despite topical affinities with religion and methodological congruences with the sciences, philosophy is irreducible to either. Exclusively dependent on reason and *experience,* philosophy as discipline repudiates the *authority* of supernatural *revelation* and ecclesiastical *tradition.* Unlike any particular science, philosophy does not confine its concern to one particular area of reality.

Western philosophy was born in Greece in the sixth century B.C. At the crossroads of Euro-Asian trade, the confluence of Hellenic cosmogony with Middle Eastern wisdom, geometry, and astronomy created a psychocultural cradle in which philosophy and science (physics, mathematics) arose from religion concomitantly. Henceforward both remained closely related until the advent of nineteenth-century positivism (Auguste Comte) that sealed their divorce. The Milesian school initiated the crucial shift from mythological account (*mythos*) to conceptual-argumentative and universally verifiable explanation (*logos*), and the Eleatic school inaugurated metaphysics by differentiating the world of truth from the world of seeming.

The standard divisions of philosophy are logic, epistemology, anthropology, natural philosophy, metaphysics, ethics, and *politics.* There are three historical models of classification: hierarchical, symbiotic, and pedagogical.

In the hierarchical classification, Aristotle's *Prior Analytics* distributes the sciences into speculative (theology, mathematics, dialectic) and practical (mechanical arts, ethics). Descartes, the founder of modern metaphysics, compared philosophy to a tree whose roots are metaphysics and whose trunk and branches are the sciences (*Principia philosophiae* [1644]). Christian von Wolff, the rationalist, subsumed logic and metaphysics (theology, psychology, *cosmology*) under theoretical science, and ethics and politics under practical science (*Rational Thoughts* [1719–21]).

The symbiotic and pedagogical classifications were introduced by the Stoics, Platonists, and Neoplatonists and adopted by the Alexandrian school (Clement's *Stromateis* [A.D. 214]), Eusebius of Caesarea, *Augustine* (*The City of God* [A.D. 411]), and the Jesuits (*Ratio studiorum* [1580]). Their tripartite classification—physics, ethics, logic, or ethics, physics, epoptic—was associated with the triadic virtues, logos theology, and the *Trinity*. Similarly, in Hegel's *Phenomenology of the Spirit* (1807), the Absolute Idea's dialectic triad unfolds into logic, philosophy of nature, and philosophy of the Spirit.

In modern times, the following were prominent schools: rationalism, empiricism, criticism, idealism, romanticism, positivism, evolutionism, materialism, philosophy of existence, dialectical materialism, pragmatism, vitalism, neoempiricism, neo-Kantianism, neo-Thomism, and phenomenology, whose epistemology treats the essences as acts of consciousness (Husserl's *Ideas* [1913]). Anchored in the belief in progress and in human rationality and sociability, one century, the eighteenth, earned the title "the philosophic age." The developing natural sciences and birth of the human and social sciences, which gradually disrupted the unity of philosophy, generated a wealth of topical theories: the philosophies of history, education, religion, art, science, and *economics.*

Generally, philosophy confronts Christian faith in matters of metaphysics and ethics, whereas Christian dogmatics needs philosophy either as propaedeutic or for its epistemology, anthropology, and rational elucidation. *Natural theology* traditionally is where reason encounters *faith.* Historically, relations between philosophy and Christian theology took four patterns: (1) mutual noninterference, as recommended by Descartes and Pascal; (2) unrestricted belligerency to achieve complete supremacy, as advocated by irreligionists such as Spinoza, d'Holbach (*System of Nature* [1770]), and Nietzsche, as well as by foes of reason such as Tatian, Bernard of Clairvaux, Luther (*Conclusiones contra scholasticam theologiam* [1517]), and Barth; (3) radical

transformation by which either Christianity is reduced to a religion of humanity (Ludwig Feuerbach) or philosophy turned into a theology of the *Word of God,* the *philosophia christiana* of Rupert of Deutz, Erasmus, and Calvin (*Christianae religionis institutio* [1536]); and (4) expedient alliance either to Christianize natural reason (Kierkegaard) or enslave philosophy as the handmaiden of revealed theology (scholasticism, Schleiermacher, and neo-Protestantism).

After World War I, the philosophical scene was dominated by existentialism, analytical philosophy, logical positivism, language philosophy, Frankfurt social theorism, and neo-Marxism, and recently by structuralism and deconstructionism. Ludwig Wittgenstein reduced the philosophical labor to the clarification of thoughts in his *Tractatus logicophilosophicus* (1921). It was as much the dawning of a new era as the pronouncement of a death sentence upon the perennial ambition of the *sapientia humana.*

D. Allen, *Philosophy for Understanding Theology* (1989).

JEAN-LOUP SEBAN

Piety Throughout the history of the Reformed faith, "piety" (often in the biblical phrase "practice of piety"), along with "devotion," "pilgrimage of the soul," "spiritual warfare," and "godly conversation," has denoted qualities and exercise of the Christian life today often associated with "spirituality." While in the nineteenth century the word tended to become debased to suggest merely "doing good," its broader meaning includes the cultivation of *faith* and godly knowledge, religious experiences both intensely mystical and more routine, and the varieties of personal devotional and corporate worship exercises that foster experiences of the divine.

Reformed piety has been characteristically evangelical, rooted in the biblical mandate to confess one's sinfulness and in the gospel promise of *forgiveness* and *grace.* While in the thought of Martin Luther the *doctrine* of *justification* was paramount, Calvinists have stressed the experience of *conversion* and growth in grace (*sanctification*). From Huldrych Zwingli and John Calvin onward, Reformed *spirituality* has been characterized by its activism, both in family and church-centered religious life and in the world. The Reformed tradition embraced the concept of the *covenant* developed by Calvin, Heinrich Bullinger, Martin Bucer, and other early theologians. Reforms of individuals, *church,* state, and society in general have been equal priorities. Outward effort directed toward godly ends has been deemed spiritual activity. This fusion of individual and social spiritual ideals in the Reformed tradition helped nurture the development of national identity, for weal or woe, in such places as Scotland, the United States, and South Africa.

Church organization, based on *federal theology* and scrutiny of NT models, became an expression of Reformed piety's concern for fellowship (as in Congregationalism) and orthodoxy (as in Presbyterianism). Unlike more radical groups related to (as with Baptists) or just outside (as with Quakers) the Reformed tradition, it has always identified the church and its *ministry* as indispensable "means of grace." This stance has at times opened Reformed pastors and theologians to the charge of "formalism" or "scholasticism" by more "Spirit-led" detractors. But personal piety, a yearning for a more immediate, powerful experience of Christ or the *Holy Spirit,* continually resurfaces among the Reformed faithful.

Calvin's lifelong personal anxiety was shared by many of his heirs. The quest for "assurance of salvation," exacerbated by the doctrine of *predestination* of the elect and the damned, became a hallmark in the experience of Puritans and other later Calvinists. Puritan spiritual writers analyzed the conversion process biblically and psychologically, with an extremely detailed, empirical approach. Individuals were urged to examine their lives against the standard of this *ordo salutis* laid down in sermons and theological tracts. This is not to say that those in the Reformed tradition did not find spiritual satisfaction. Spiritual "pilgrims" were expected to make "progress" on their way to *heaven.* The first question of the *Heidelberg Catechism* (1563), for example, exudes personal assurance: "What is your only comfort, in life and in death? That I belong—body and soul, in life and in death—not to myself but to my faithful Savior, Jesus Christ." This text was revered next to the Bible by German and Dutch Calvinists on both sides of the Atlantic. English and American Puritans sought assurance through devotional Bible-reading, meditation, and "closet" *prayer;* family prayers and catechetical training; pastoral visitation; neighborhood devotional meetings; and in public worship. Devotional manuals (including directions for meditation and sample prayers), spiritual diary keeping, meditative poetry, and spiritual biography were widely used aids to the spiritual life. Many methods of meditation and prayer found in the Reformed tradition were quite similar to those characteristic of medieval and early-modern Catholicism. The personal writings of representative figures reveal that believers within the Reformed tradition were indeed blessed with powerful spiritual experiences. Despite Calvinism's tough-minded theology, many experienced *God* as gracious and Christ as bridegroom of the soul.

Reformed worship has traditionally centered on the reading of *scripture,* prayers (often freely conceived by the pastor), the singing of psalms (and, by the eighteenth century, hymns), and, most especially, the sermon. Reformed piety is intensely Bible-centered. The *sacraments,* nevertheless, are also an integral part of this spiritual tradition. A doctrine of personal and corporate encounter with the real presence of Christ achieved high expression in America in seventeenth-century Puritanism and in the nineteenth-century German Reformed Church's

Mercersburg movement. Presbyterians in Scotland and in America's middle colonies participated in "sacramental seasons," in which thousands of members from many far-flung churches camped together for up to a week, devoting themselves to countless sermons, arduous prayer, Bible study, and self-scrutiny in preparation for massive and joyful celebrations of the *Lord's Supper.* These traditional exercises, central to the spiritual and social lives of whole communities of people, issued in the revivalism of the Great Awakenings.

Reformed piety is distinctive among the various other families of Christian spirituality in its understanding that the personal experience of grace and *salvation* is inseparable from the corporate relationships of church, community, and world.

L. Bouyer, *Orthodox Spirituality and Protestant and Anglican Spirituality* (1965; vol. 3 of *A History of Christian Spirituality*); L. Dupré and D. E. Saliers, eds., *Christian Spirituality: Post-Reformation and Modern* (1989); C. E. Hambrick-Stowe, *The Practice of Piety: Puritan Devotional Disciplines in Seventeenth-Century New England* (1982); J. Riatt et al., eds., *Christian Spirituality: High Middle Ages and Reformation* (1987), 300–33, 454–63; H. Rice, *Reformed Spirituality* (1991); L. E. Schmidt, *Holy Fairs: Scottish Communions and American Revivals in the Early Modern Period* (1989); D. D. Wallace, Jr., ed., *The Spirituality of the Later English Puritans* (1987); M. J. Westerkamp, *Triumph of the Laity: Scots-Irish Piety and the Great Awakening, 1625–1760* (1988).

CHARLES E. HAMBRICK-STOWE

Politics Politics is the process by which groups of people make choices of their leaders and the use of their collective resources. Thus, John Calvin was among the most political of theologians, for he relied for reformation of *church* and society not upon individuals, "however high their social status or great their inspiration. He relied above all on orga-

nizations, and imparted to his followers an extraordinary organizational initiative and stamina. There have been few men in history who loved meetings more" (Walzer, 29).

Calvinists have paid extraordinary attention to politics in two spheres: church and state. They have often influenced the second while trying chiefly to change the organization of the first. Yet in neither arena did they assume they could appeal to their own knowledge of absolute principles of how humans should organize themselves. Nothing was to rival the absoluteness—the sovereignty—of *God* in Calvinist faith, *worship*, and social life. All human *authority* and wisdom gets cut down to merely human size in this vision of God: kings such as Charles I, forms of church government, particular human claimants to church leadership, one political party or another. The Calvinist vision of God was only indirectly "political," but images of power, rule, order, and change dominate it. Sweeping political change emerged from those willing to live by those images.

As a people "astonished by the mercy of God" (J. T. McNeill), they were not easily astonished—or intimidated—by human politicians. This was a theology that "dignified the concrete, historical lives of ordinary people with the purposes of God" (Leith, 205). Puritans, nerved by such belief, identified with John Knox's public defiance of a queen, Parliament's decision to execute a sovereign in the name of *the* Sovereign (God), new balances of power between parliament and kings, and a revolt of American colonists against all kings whatsoever.

If the political power of *Calvinism* stemmed from its vision of God, the political *practice* of the Calvinists was regularly shaped in the deliberations of their churches. For many, the congregation was "the school of democracy" (A. D. Lindsay). There, "the humblest member might hear, and join in, the debate, witness the discovery of the natural leader, and might participate in that curious process by which there emerges from the clash of many minds a vision clearer and a determination wiser than any single mind could achieve" (Woodhouse, 76). In the structure and processes of its church government, modern Presbyterianism reflects these same political instincts.

The history of the influence of Reformed church politics on public secular politics is complex; historians will continue to argue over how much Calvinism aided or hindered the rise of Western democracy. Virtually all agree, however, that this theological tradition—from John Calvin to Jonathan Edwards to Reinhold Niebuhr—sought with peculiar intensity to hold together in one system of thought and action a huge array of opposing human social ideas: liberty and equality, individual *conscience* and social restraint, church witness to society alongside separation of church and state, the universal sway of God and the limited local *vocation* of humans, sinful church and sinful society, holy church and holy community.

The Calvinist as righteous politician has been satirized, and modern disciples of "that Frenchman" of Geneva have to admit that the Calvinist concern for "liberty" has frequently conflicted with a "passionate zeal for positive reform, with the will, if necessary, to dragoon men into righteousness" (Woodhouse, 51). This phenomenon prompts a comparison of the spirit of Calvinism to the political spirit of Marxism, with the latter's tendency to dragoon whole societies into "justice" (Walzer, 230). Ernst Troeltsch concluded that Calvinists, as rigorously as any Christian movement in history, embraced a vision of a "Holy Community," a church and an entire secular order reformed according to the will of God revealed in *scripture.* That the reach of this political-theological vision exceeded its historical grasp surprises no one, including Calvinists. That ever they had the courage thus to reach is the surprise.

The advantage of Calvinism over other politically minded faiths continues to be its capacity for recourse to the Tran-

scendent, including new understandings of that Transcendent. "Perpetual revolution" in Calvinist political rhetoric entails perpetual *repentance*: intellectual, moral, and political repentance. Modern Calvinists may even need Karl Marx to enable them to remember, with modern theologies of liberation, Calvin's own skepticism of wealth and power, his sense of the equality of all humans before God, and his expectation that God has no commitments to the defense of established human orders. The God who raised Jesus from the dead is sovereign over everything. Those with this *faith* can stand up when nations rage, human kingdoms totter, and God devises new political things for the world.

E. Busch, "Church and Politics in the Reformed Tradition," in D. K. McKim, ed., *Major Themes in the Reformed Tradition* (repr. 1998): 180–95; J. H. Leith, *An Introduction to the Reformed Tradition,* rev. ed. (1981); R. H. Stone, *Reformed Faith and Politics* (1983); M. Walzer, *The Revolution of the Saints* (1965); A. S. P. Woodhouse, *Puritanism and Liberty* (1951).

DONALD W. SHRIVER JR.

Polity   A particular form of government. The Latin and Greek roots of the word carry connotations of community, organization, and citizenship. There are three distinct types of church polity: episcopal, congregational, and presbyterian, each with distinguishing characteristics. Episcopal polity can be recognized by the presence of a singular leader (or bishop) as in Lutheran, Methodist, or Roman Catholic communions. Congregational polity is characterized by the principle of one person, one vote of a pure democracy, as in Baptist polity. Presbyterian polity may be characterized as a representative democracy and is found in such communions as the Church of Scotland, the Presbyterian Church (U.S.A.), or the Reformed Church of Hungary. The origins of presbyterian polity are in the Reformation and Calvin's understanding of church governance developed in his *Institutes* and practiced in Geneva.

Characteristics of Reformed polity.

Scriptural: Those who practice a presbyterian form of polity perceive its order to be derived from *scripture,* as understood by **Reformed theology** and expressed in the **confessions** of the Reformed faith. It expresses the principle that those of the Reformed faith must order their life together in accord with their faith and as a witness to the demands of scripture. Accordingly, the *ministry* practiced in presbyterian polity preserves NT forms of ministry and is shared according to the gifts of its members: proclamation (ministers of Word and Sacrament), governance (*elders*), sympathy and service (*deacons*).

The foundation stone of Reformed polity is the conviction that the *church* is "the body of Christ" (1 Cor. 12) and that all *authority* in the church belongs to Jesus Christ, head of the church.

Corporate: Decision making in presbyterian polity is always corporate, never individual. Decisions concerning the welfare of the church and all matters of theology and mission are made in governing bodies led by "moderators" and composed of elders and ministers of Word and Sacrament sitting in parity. At least two courts are always present in a Reformed polity. The most fundamental court of the church is the session. It governs the local church, is moderated by the pastor, and is comprised of elders elected by the congregation. Overseeing the session is the presbytery, in which the membership of all ministers of Word and Sacrament is lodged. The presbytery has oversight of its ministers, congregations, and sessions and is responsible for the *ordination* of all ministers of Word and Sacrament.

Representative: Reformed polity is characterized by a representative form of government in which ministers of Word and Sacrament sit in deliberative assemblies with elders. The Greek word *presbyteros,* from which the polity derives its name, means "elder"—governance by elders who are representatives of the people.

Characteristics of American Reformed polity. The American Presbyterian church has developed distinctive characteristics of its own because of its historical development in a frontier society and in a society that insists on the separation of church and state. The clearest exposition of the polity of the Presbyterian Church (U.S.A.) is in ch. 1 of the *Book of Order,* part of which, "The Historic Principles of Church Order," is believed to have been written by John Witherspoon and adopted by the founding **General Assembly** of the church (1789).

Constitutional: The polity of the PC(USA) is expressed in its Constitution, which consists of four parts. The *Book of Confessions,* the first and determinative part, contains theological statements of churches of the Reformed faith. The remaining three parts of the Constitution are derived from, and express, these confessions. The Form of Government and the Directory for Worship detail how the members of the church shall live together, make their decisions, and *worship.* The Rules of Discipline make up the fourth part of the Constitution, which outlines procedures for discipline and judicial process within the church in a manner that emphasizes fairness, redemption, and mercy rather than retribution and punishment.

Ordered: The PC(USA) is governed by four interrelated governing bodies: session, presbytery, synod, and General Assembly. Each governing body makes its decisions by majority vote, the representatives of the larger part of the church having the power of review over governing bodies representing a smaller part of the church. The powers of each governing body are limited by the Constitution. They have no civil power. In the American church, the synod is a geographical entity composed of presbyteries under its jurisdiction. Its responsibilities are related primarily to enabling its presbyteries and to organizing mission within its geographic area. The synods also perform a crucial role in the judicial process of the church as a court of appeal. The

General Assembly is the highest court of appeal in the church. It is responsible for national and international mission. The General Assembly, when it meets annually, speaks as prophet to the church, with no legislative power over the lower governing bodies; but, like the other governing bodies, it may legislate for itself.

Reformed and reforming: The PC(USA) claims not only to be a church in the "Reformed tradition" but to be a church that is constantly reforming. Reformation of the church's polity is continual and accomplished through amendment of the Constitution. The amendment process is illustrative of the interrelated nature of the governing bodies: any member of the Presbyterian Church may propose an amendment to the Constitution through the session; and the session, through the presbytery. Either a presbytery or a synod may propose an amendment directly to the General Assembly, which, by majority vote, may choose to recommend the amendment to the presbyteries. A majority of the presbyteries is required for a successful amendment to the Constitution. A two-thirds majority vote is necessary for an amendment to be made to the *Book of Confessions*, since the effect of such an amendment might be to change the theological foundations upon which all of the polity of the church rests.

H. Höpfl, *The Christian Polity of John Calvin* (1982).

MARIANNE L. WOLFE

Prayer, Practice of

Prayer, Practice of　The Reformation brought radical changes in the way Christians prayed. Yet it was in the century following that prayer disciplines of the Reformed church matured.

The Reformers' perception that the prayer life of the Middle Ages had broken down led to a thorough study of the scriptural disciplines of prayer. Rather than emphasizing the mental prayer that developed out of the Neoplatonism of late antiquity and monastic asceticism, the Reformers sought *God* in the frailties of the human condition. They understood Jesus to teach that we are creatures of need and in our hungering and thirsting we have communion with God (Matt. 5—7). Jesus, therefore, taught his disciples to pray about their common needs: relieving poverty and sickness, guidance in uncertainty, and patience to bear adversity. The Protestant catechisms in explaining the Lord's Prayer all taught that daily prayer was essential to living by *faith*.

The Puritans developed a rich literature to guide Christians in the practice of prayer. Classics are John Preston's *The Saint's Daily Exercise* (1629); Thomas Watson's *The Lord's Prayer* (repr. 1960); Matthew Henry's *Beginning and Ending the Day in Prayer*; and John Flavel's *The Mystery of Divine Providence* (1678). Because of their strong belief in *providence*, seventeenth-century Calvinists were particularly concerned in prayer to seek out their destiny from God's own hand.

Three characteristics of prayer in the Reformed tradition stand out.

Prayers of intercession. Early Reformed liturgies all devoted a large portion of public *worship* to intercessory prayer. It was understood as the priestly function of the assembled people of God to pray for the unity, sanctity, and apostolicity of the *church* (1 Peter 2:4–10; John 14—17). The church was to pray for the needs of *humanity* in general, the civil *authority*, the *ministry* of the church, the propagation of the gospel, and persons suffering various trials (1 Tim. 2:1–8; Eph. 6:18–20; Col. 4:2–4; Acts 4:23–31). This ministry of intercession regularly followed the *preaching* of the Word because in the hearing of the Word the church was guided to ever-new intercessory concerns.

Praying the Psalter. Early in the Reformation, the Strassburg Psalter set the precedent for translating the Hebrew psalms into metrical poetry so they could be sung by the common people. Clément Marot and Theodore Beza provided the Genevan Psalter with superb metrical psalms, which the Huguenots have sung for centuries. The same was true in the Netherlands, Scotland, and New England. The psalms are prayers of the *Holy Spirit*, the songs God has given us to cry out in time of need, to assure us of the covenant promises, and to give us an intimation of our future (Ps. 42:8; 137:4; Acts 4:25). For Christians, to pray the psalms is to pray with Christ. When Jesus prayed the psalms in his passion, he offered up the sorrows and the hopes that God's people have expressed through history. In this priestly ministry, he fulfilled the psalms; therefore, Reformed psalmodists, such as Isaac Watts, have often paraphrased the psalms in a Christian sense.

Family prayer. While the tradition of daily prayer was maintained by the Reformation, it soon became most frequently observed in the home rather than in the church. The Church of Scotland added a chapter to the Westminster Directory for Worship that distinguished family prayer from public worship on the one hand and "secret" or private prayer on the other (1646). Family prayer consisted of singing psalms, reading a chapter of *scripture*, and offering a full and comprehensive prayer including praise, confession, petition, intercession, and thanksgiving. It was to be held morning and evening each day. As Richard Baxter put it, the family is a little church and therefore has the sacred privilege and duty to offer regular worship to God (*Christian Directory* [1673]).

C. E. Hambrick-Stowe, *The Practice of Piety: Puritan Devotional Disciplines in Seventeenth-Century New England* (1982); F. Heiler, *Prayer* (ET 1932); H. O. Old, "Daily Prayer in the Reformed Church of Strasbourg, 1523–1530," *Worship* 52 (1978): 121–38.

HUGHES OLIPHANT OLD

Prayer, Theology of   Prayer is human speech addressed to *God*. It arises from a consciousness of the relation in which one stands to God and expresses the emotions, desires, and needs stemming from that consciousness. It includes adoration, thanksgiving, confession of *sin*, submission, commitment, and petition. Within the Reformed tradition, there has been general agreement that petition is the central focus of prayer.

John Knox defined prayer as "an earnest and familiar talking with God, to whom we declare our miseries, whose support and help we implore and desire in our adversities, and whom we laud and praise for our benefits received" (*Declaration of the True Nature and Object of Prayer* [1554]).

Prayer in the Reformed confessions. In the Reformed *confessions*, statements about prayer are generally brief and address Roman Catholic beliefs and practices that are being rejected. Prayer is to be made through the intercession of Christ as the only mediator, so invocation of saints is forbidden. Prayers are not meritorious but express thankfulness for free *grace*. In place of formality, there should be an orderly freedom. Prayer should be in the language of the people, not in an unknown tongue, so that it may be intelligible.

The *Second Helvetic Confession* (1566), alone of the major confessions, devotes a separate chapter to prayer. It advocates brevity in public prayer, lest the people be wearied and so think the sermon to be overlong. The *WCF* and the *Confession of 1967* contain brief positive statements about prayer within the context of *worship*.

The Reformed catechisms on prayer. Since the early *church*, expositions of the Lord's Prayer have formed the basis of catechetical instruction. The catechisms of the Reformation and post-Reformation eras follow the same procedure.

The *HC* (1563) devotes questions 116–129 to prayer. Question 116 calls prayer "the chief part of the gratitude which God requires of us" as well as the means by which God gives his grace and Spirit. The WLC and the WSC (1648) treat prayer, along with the Word and *sacra-*

ments, as a means of grace. A classic Reformed definition of prayer is obtained by collating the statements from the two catechisms: "Prayer is an offering up of our desires unto God, for things agreeable to his will, in the name of Christ, by the help of his Spirit, with confession of our sins, and thankful acknowledgment of his mercies" (WSC, q. 98; WLC, q. 178). The Larger Catechism asserts that the Lord's Prayer may be used as a form of prayer in public worship as well as a framework for the composition of other prayers.

Prayer and Reformed theology. It is surprising that systematic theologians within the Reformed tradition do not give more attention to prayer. Heppe's *RD* has no section on prayer. Calvin is one exception. He treats prayer fully as "the chief exercise of faith, and by which we daily receive God's benefits" (*Inst.* 3.20.1). Calvin defends the necessity of prayer in relation to God's sovereignty. For proper prayer, one must have reverence, a sense of need, penitence, confidence that God will answer, and reliance on Jesus alone. Public prayer is to avoid ostentation and formality and be in the common language. While church buildings are not holy places, Christians are to pray in the appointed assemblies. When answers to prayer are delayed, perseverance is needed. Calvin includes a full exposition of the Lord's Prayer.

Charles Hodge discusses prayer briefly as one of the means of grace (*Systematic Theology,* 3.20.20). He seeks to vindicate prayer by appealing to God's personhood and arguing for the occurrence of "spontaneous action" not limited by natural law.

Karl Barth included prayer under ethics in his *CD* (III/4, sec. 53, par. 3). For Barth, the basis of prayer is human *freedom* before God, which is also God's gracious command. Since prayer is essentially petition, it is not meritorious. Those who pray do so as united with Jesus Christ and pray as representatives of the whole world. Barth repeats the Reformers' emphasis that true prayer is

surely heard by God. In practical matters, prayer should be vocal, not silent; spontaneous, even though formulated; offered at regular times; and short.

The revitalization of prayer within the Reformed tradition would be furthered by recapturing Calvin's emphasis on true prayer as a response of faith to the *Word of God* found in *scripture.*

D. G. Bloesch, *The Struggle of Prayer* (1980); B. M. Palmer, *Theology of Prayer* (1894); W. R. Spear, *Theology of Prayer* (1979).
WAYNE R. SPEAR

Preaching, Theology of

The Reformation did not invent preaching. Before Martin Luther there were centuries of preaching: Clement and Origen, John Chrysostom, *Augustine,* and Bernard of Clairvaux, not to mention preaching orders, namely, Dominicans and Franciscans. Prior to the Reformation, preaching may have lost track of *scripture* and was sometimes given to droll rhetorical excess, but there were still faithful preachers: Wycliffe and the Lollards were both biblical and bold. In the late medieval world, preaching may have become calculating, frivolous, or neglected, but it never died.

The Reformation ushered in a new era of biblical preaching, both in quality and in quantity. Most of the Reformers preached many times each week. Luther's sermons fill twenty volumes; Calvin's forty; and Bullinger, the successor of Zwingli, preached the entire Bible in a little more than fifteen years. Most Reformers preached *lectio continua,* working their way through scripture passage by passage. Though their sermons were biblical, they were, above all, gospel; according to the Reformers, they were preaching the *Word of God.*

The major Reformers (except for Philipp Melanchthon) were preachers, yet their understandings of preaching were scarcely monolithic. Luther, Zwingli, and Calvin differed in sacramental theology; they differed similarly over preaching as the Word of God. If consubstantiation allowed Luther to affirm that bread and wine in **Eucharist** *are* Christ for us, so he insisted that when preachers preach, their voices *are* the voice of God! Luther's tendency toward Eutychian **Christology** shows up analogously in his treatment of Word and sacrament. Similar parallels are in Zwingli and Calvin; they deal with Word and sacrament in much the same way that they approach Christology. Luther and Zwingli represent somewhat antithetical positions on preaching, while Calvin, coming later, is often seen as a *via media.*

"The preaching of the Word of God is the Word of God." The issue dividing Luther and Zwingli was the relationship between Word and Spirit. In contrast to enthusiasts (*Schwärmer*), who supposed the Spirit was an immediate gift to the human soul quite independent of Word and sacrament, Luther insisted that the Spirit was given by means of the Word: "The Word, I say, and only the Word is the vehicle of God's grace." Fearful of **idolatry,** Zwingli demurred, rejecting Luther's binding of Word and Spirit. He edges close to the enthusiasts by insisting that preaching was a human witness to Christ, intended to prompt us to seek the true inner Word of God, given by the Spirit. Thus, Zwingli sharply distinguishes between the *verbum Dei externum,* which is human preaching, and the *verbum Dei internum,* which is the **Holy Spirit.** He quotes the Gospel of John with approval: "No one can come to me unless the Father who sent me draws him" (John 6:44). Preaching might point to Christ, but only the Spirit draws.

Luther and Zwingli also differed in their view of scripture. Luther appears to equate preaching and scripture as "Word of God"; God's voice is heard in both. For Luther, the Word of God is the gospel, the free, soul-consoling message of *justification* from pulpit or biblical page. In Zwingli's thought, scripture is elevated above any human testimony. **God** the Spirit is the author of the Bible and the only true interpreter of scriptural texts.

The man in the middle. Calvin's position may seem to occupy a middle ground. With Luther, Calvin affirms a kind of "transubstantiation of the Word." Though preachers are human, nevertheless preaching is the will of God for the **church** and, *instigated by the Spirit,* is the mouth of God addressing us: "[God] deigns to consecrate to himself the mouths and tongues of men in order that his voice may resound in them" (*Inst.* 4.1.5). Of course, preaching is nothing apart from the Spirit who illumines our minds to hear. With Zwingli, Calvin stresses the biblical origin of preaching and the inward testimony of the Holy Spirit, but he insists that the Holy Spirit is given *in* preaching and is not waiting hidden in the heart.

The high and holy task of preaching. Calvin's confidence in the power of the Word is awesome: God's Word, never fruitless, does what it declares. Thus, if preaching declares absolution, then those who hear are truly absolved. In his *Commentary* on Isaiah, Calvin announces, "Nothing that has come out of God's holy mouth can fail in its effect." Of course, we must be quick to add that the power of preaching is by the Holy Spirit. If the Spirit is not with the Word, then sermons, no matter how eloquent, will be empty and altogether ineffective. Preaching is a human act having no intrinsic efficacy: Sometimes God connects with preaching and sometimes separates from preaching. But when God chooses preaching, then it is surely the power of *salvation.* Notice that Calvin links preaching to the purposes of God, namely, salvation.

Even when preaching is rejected, it is nonetheless efficacious. Preaching will either soften or harden the heart, save or condemn. The proper office of the gospel is salvific, but, because of human depravity, in an "accidental" way the gospel can harden and destroy. Though Calvin is blunt about the two-sided sword of the Word, preachers may not excuse themselves if the gospel is rejected; they must examine themselves and their preaching. Of course, ultimately Calvin links the acceptance or the rejection of the Word to God's *election*.

Preaching is crucial because Christ with all his saving graces comes to us through preaching. The means of our union with Christ is the Word. So preaching is *revealing* and *saving* and *commanding*.

1. Though Calvin would insist there can be no further **revelation** beyond God's self-disclosure in Christ Jesus, yet when preaching brings Christ to us in a contemporary context, revelation is "new" in its applications. Calvin's own preaching was never past-tense Bible study but was *doctrine* applied to life.

2. Calvin stresses the gracious benefits we receive through preaching. Union with Christ is both our justification and our **sanctification**. Forgiveness is conferred through preaching, and holiness is shaped by preaching.

3. Preaching is the means by which Jesus Christ exercises *authority*. The sovereign Lord claims rule in the church through preaching and, as the gospel is spoken evangelically by the church, claims Lordship in the world. Preaching establishes the *kingdom of God* wherever the gospel is announced.

The mode of our union with Christ is *faith,* and faith is the product of the Holy Spirit. Though Calvin, with Luther, is fond of quoting Rom. 10:17, "Faith comes from hearing," and insists that without the Word faith is impossible, nevertheless faith is a gift of the Spirit who opens our ears truly to hear the promises of God. Faith, for Calvin, is not passive; faith is active obedience. Through preaching, Christ establishes his rule, and therefore congregations must receive the Word with humble obedience. Among the Reformers, Calvin had more to say about a congregation's active, intelligent responsibility in attending sermons, even though hearing was a gift: "[Our Lord] will open our eyes and ears, and will not only give us intelligence but will also so form our hearts that we shall follow Him when He calls us" (CR 54, col. 114).

Preaching and scripture. Calvin insisted that preaching is properly an explication and application of scripture. Preachers should be schooled in the Bible, for scripture is the Word of God provided by the Holy Spirit. Therefore, scripture is the source of the Word we preach and the norm by which we judge our gospel message. Yet the Holy Spirit is the true interpreter of scripture and forms inner testimony of the Bible's truth. At times Calvin will speak of the "dictation" of the Spirit in the writing of scripture, but he does not espouse a rigid theory of inspiration; he has an eye for error. Nevertheless, Calvin is sure the message of scripture is the saving truth of God and thus the source of proclamation. In many ways, Calvin's understanding of scripture seems to parallel his theology of preaching.

The preacher. What of the preacher? For Calvin, preachers are chosen by God to be ambassadors of the Word. Preachers ought to be holy, insightful, scholarly, and, above all, able teachers. Yet *the* qualification for the preaching office is God's choice and inner assurance of God's call formed by the Holy Spirit. The dignity of the preaching office is not based on character or position but on speaking the Word of God. While sinlessness is scarcely a criterion for *ministry,* preachers should seek to bring their lives under the Word they speak. All that preachers can do is to serve God as "ministers of the divine Word," praying, "Come, Holy Spirit!"

K. Barth, *Homiletics* (1991); D. G. Buttrick, *Homiletic* (1987); H. J. Forstman, *Word and Spirit: Calvin's Doctrine of Biblical Authority* (1962); P. T. Forsyth, *Positive Preaching and the Modern Mind* (repr. 1964); G. W. Locher, *Zwingli's Thought* (1981); T. H. L. Parker, *The Oracles of God: An Introduction to the Preaching of John Calvin* (1947) and *Calvin's Preaching* (1992); R. Stauffer, *Dieu, la création et la providence dans la prédication de Calvin* (1978); W. P. Stephens, *The Theology of Huldrych Zwingli* (1986); R. S. Wallace, *Calvin's Doctrine of the Word and Sacrament* (1953).

DAVID G. BUTTRICK

Predestination Predestination, or election, is the belief or *doctrine* that *God* has chosen some persons for the gift of *salvation*. It is not to be confused with *providence*, that is, God's governance of all things, nor with fate or philosophical determinism. An important teaching in Western Christianity, it has been especially emphasized in *Reformed theology*.

Predestination is rooted in the OT theme of God's choice of Israel and is based on many NT passages, especially in Paul (e.g., Rom. 8:29–30; 9:6–33). It was developed doctrinally by *Augustine* against Pelagius, whom Augustine accused of teaching salvation by human effort. Augustine believed that out of the mass of sinful *humanity* God had chosen some to illustrate God's *grace*, while passing by the remainder to illustrate God's *justice*. For Augustine, this was compatible with the will's *freedom*, understood not as choice but as free and willing assent to God's will (voluntary necessity). Moreover, since God was in eternity, not time, there was for God neither past nor future, so predestination was outside time. Augustine's teaching reappeared in such medieval anti-Pelagians as Thomas Bradwardine and John Wycliffe. Wycliffe used the doctrine to spiritualize the divine-human relationship and undermine priestly authority.

During the Reformation, Martin Luther asserted predestination against Erasmus, whom he accused of Pelagianism. But Lutheran theology eventually minimized it. Reformed church leaders, however, emphasized predestination to glorify God, instill humility and gratitude, insist against Roman Catholicism that salvation was by God's grace alone and did not entail human merit, and to affirm that it was God's purpose to elect and sanctify a people to fulfill God's will in the world. Thus, Huldrych Zwingli taught predestination as part of the sovereignty and providence of God. His Zurich successor, Heinrich Bullinger, described it as God's gracious choice of the undeserving. Martin Bucer related predestination to the doctrine of salvation (it was "in Christ") and stressed election to holiness of life.

John Calvin carried on Bucer's approach and also followed Augustine. He did not make predestination the center of his theology, nor did he treat it abstractly as an aspect of the doctrine of God, but he considered it in relation to soteriology and the Christian life: Believers humbly and thankfully look back to their election as solely a gift of saving grace. Especially in later controversy, however, Calvin affirmed double predestination, or the *reprobation* of those not elected, though this was only because of their own sins. Like Augustine, he thought predestination harmonized with the will's freedom, since God never forced the will. The approach of Bucer and Calvin is reflected in the early Reformed *confessions*.

The growth of scholastic method in Reformed theology gave predestination more precise definition and more central theological placement than in Zwingli's programmatic writings and Calvin's exegetical ones. The Italian exile theologians Peter Martyr Vermigli and Girolamo Zanchi were significant in this process as they brought the logic of Aristotle and familiarity with medieval *scholasticism* to their versions of Reformed teaching. Zanchi followed medieval theologians in connecting predestination with the doctrine of God. Scholastic method is also apparent in Calvin's Genevan successor, Theodore Beza, who put God's decrees at the beginning of his system. Beza was also a supralapsarian, holding that God's decrees of election and reprobation preceded God's decree of *creation* and permission of the fall. The doctrine of the earlier Reformed theologians had generally been infralapsarian, with predestination subsequent to these things, but some later Reformed theologians further developed Beza's approach. In spite of these scholastic refinements, there remained an experiential core to belief in predestination, especially apparent among Puritan theologians such as

William Perkins, who emphasized its uses in giving *hope* and assurance to believers and stimulating good works. Those who trust in Christ and strive to lead a holy life should consider themselves among the elect.

There was resistance to such a prominent, sharply defined, and sometimes supralapsarian doctrine of the double decree, often deriving from the Erasmian and humanist elements of the early Reformation. Among the early Reformed, Theodor Bibliander was cautious about predestination. The seventeenth-century French theologian Mose Amyraut taught hypothetical *universalism,* which he said had been Calvin's view: The death of Christ was on behalf of all, even if effective only for the elect. This view became widespread among French Calvinists and was adopted by some of the English Presbyterians, including Richard Baxter. More radically, Jacobus Arminius in the Netherlands maintained that God predestined on the basis of *foreknowledge* of who would believe. After bitter conflict, the *Synod of Dort* (1618–19) condemned Arminius's opinion and affirmed unconditional election as necessary for the preservation of salvation by grace. The *Westminster Confession* (1646) reflected the scholastic and anti-Arminian form of the doctrine but stopped short of *supralapsarianism.* In the following decades, Reformed scholastics such as John Owen and Francis Turretin continued to refute *Arminians.*

The evangelical movements of the eighteenth century stressed God's grace, giving the doctrine of predestination renewed life, as in its defense by Jonathan Edwards in New England. However, evangelicalism eventually led to a simplification of theology that eroded predestination, especially after its rejection by Wesleyan Methodism; the nineteenth-century American evangelist Charles G. Finney denounced it as an impediment to revivals. Thereafter, revivalism tended to be Arminian, and many Presbyterians and Congregationalists in the United States abandoned belief in predestination, a process also abetted by the growth of theological liberalism. The Presbyterian Church in the U.S.A. added to the Westminster Confession a section stating it was God's desire that all be saved (1903). But scholastic predestinarian theology continued at Princeton Seminary with Charles Hodge.

Liberals among continental Reformed theologians emphasized predestination. Friedrich Schleiermacher, who said the essence of religion was the feeling of absolute dependence upon God, defended predestination as necessary for affirming that essence, though he rejected reprobation. Alexander Schweizer argued that Schleiermacher had revitalized Reformed theology by emphasizing predestination, which Schweizer thought was the primary motif of Reformed theology. But Schweizer felt that the doctrine could be replaced by its distilled essence: dependence upon God.

The *neo-orthodoxy* of the early twentieth century revived much in Reformation theology in reacting against liberalism. Emil Brunner, however, criticized Zwingli for determinism and Calvin for the double decree. He held that election assures believers that a personal God calls from eternity those who, in the world of time, believe; there is no before or after, only grace.

Karl Barth performed a more drastic recasting. For him, Jesus Christ is the object of predestination, and humanity is elected in him. Thus, the grace of God as the sole cause of salvation is preserved at the same time that the universality of this election removes the greatest obstacle to the doctrine: its invidious distinction of elect and non-elect.

Predestination is a difficult point for modern Christians. Yet it is an important guarantee of the gratuitousness of salvation, surely a central intention of Reformed theology. Also, when one considers that doctrinal formulations are human ways of understanding the mysteries of divine revelation, it may well be best to accept the intention of the doctrine—affirmation of God's gracious favor bestowed upon the undeserving, and set aside its negative implications as unbiblical. Further, it should be remembered that predestination rules out human merit, not freedom; God's will is exercised through secondary causes and does not compel the human will to any end to which it has not freely assented.

B. G. Armstrong, *Calvinism and the Amyraut Heresy* (1969); Barth, *CD* II/2; B. A. Gerrish, *Tradition and the Modern World* (1978); P. K. Jewett, *Election and Predestination* (1986); R. A. Muller, *Christ and the Decree* (1986); D. D. Wallace, Jr., *Puritans and Predestination* (1982).

DEWEY D. WALLACE JR.

real priesthood of the whole people of God into a meaningful and workable reality.

This doctrine was clearly expounded by Luther and Calvin. But while Luther made some exaggerated claims and statements, Calvin's teaching is clear and balanced. Whether it has ever been truly grasped and put into full operation by a local church is doubtful. It remains that toward which the people of God are to move.

C. Eastwood, *The Priesthood of All Believers* (1960); J. H. Elliott, *The Elect and the Holy* (1966).

PETER TOON

Presbytery *see* **Polity**

Priesthood of Believers The *doctrine* (based on 1 Peter 2:9–10; Rev. 1:6; 5:10) that the whole people of *God* of the new *covenant* is a priesthood because it is in, with, and through Jesus Christ, the true and only priest (Heb. 3:1). This is a royal and holy priesthood with a corporate *vocation.*

The doctrine has often been explained in popular teaching as pointing to the right of every individual believer to act in a priestly way—to pray to God for self and others and to teach God's ways to others. As such, it has been coupled with *justification* by *faith*—being "put right with God"—so that one may act as a priest. A better approach is to link the concept of priesthood with covenant (as in the OT; Ex. 19:5–6) and see this doctrine as highlighting the corporate privilege and responsibility of the believing people of God of the new covenant. As a body, they offer spiritual sacrifice and prayers to God and commend God in Christ to the world. Thus, each congregation of faithful believers is to act as a priesthood, being a microcosm of the whole *church.*

There is no specific priesthood of the ordained minister, but ordained ministers do have the vocation of making the

Princeton Theology An American expression of the Reformed Protestant tradition that emanated from a group of nineteenth-century Presbyterian theologians from Princeton Seminary. Three generations of scholars attuned to the *WCF* shaped many of the theological discourses in America's Reformed communities. The first generation was comprised of Archibald Alexander (1772–1851) of Virginia, Samuel Miller (1769–1850) of Delaware and New York, and Charles Hodge (1797–1878) of Philadelphia and Princeton. The second generation included Joseph Addison Alexander (1809–59), James Waddell Alexander (1804–59), Albert B. Dod (1805–45), and William Henry Green (1825–1900), while a third generation involved Archibald Alexander Hodge (1823–86), B. B. Warfield (1851–1921), Francis L. Patton (1843–1932), and J. Gresham Machen (1881–1937).

Like sentinels, two major works stand at the front and back entrances in the theological territory occupied by these Old School Presbyterian theologians. At the beginning was Miller's influential *A Brief Retrospect of the Eighteenth Century* (2 vols.; 1803), which scrutinized encyclopedically the promises and perils of *science, history, philosophy,* literature, and religion. Charles Hodge's *Systematic Theology* (3 vols.; 1871–73) stands at the other end. It structured and summarized a vast array of theological issues from the "Didactic Enlightenment" to the waning impulses of romanticism. These multivolume works addressed an unusual breadth of issues confronting Reformed communities in the emerging nation and simultaneously revealed reasoned, confessional discourses amidst the fluid commitments of nineteenth-century Protestantism.

Most of the Princeton theologians wrote voluminously. Among their most notable works were Archibald Alexander's *Thoughts on Religious Experience* (1841), Hodge's popular *The Way of Life* (1841), J. A. Alexander's internationally acclaimed commentary on Isaiah (2 vols; 1846–47), W. H. Green's *The Pentateuch Vindicated* (1863), and Warfield's *The Westminster Assembly and Its Work* (1931). From 1825 to 1871 these theologians published a journal usually called the *Biblical Repertory and Princeton Review,* which emerged as one of the premier Protestant journals in nineteenth-century America. Few issues of theology, philosophy, science, Protestant churches, or national *politics* escaped its comment. Hodge's masterful essays on the ecumenicity of the *church,* slavery, and the Civil War are only hints of these efforts to interpret the Reformed heritage to a splintered Protestantism, a divided nation, and an increasingly pluralistic culture.

Most estimates of these Princeton theologians are too narrow and polemical. A few recent historians, however, have noted an amalgam of commitments that characterized these Presbyterians' style and stance while doing *Reformed theology.* These include an unswerving commitment to the classical Calvinistic theism and the Westminster Standards; an informed commitment to the Bible's inspiration and *authority* and a skeptical response to German biblical criticism; the generous employment of Scottish *common sense realism* and a revulsion for German idealism; an evangelical *piety* articulated in both personal and social terms; a sympathy for American Whig (and later Republican) political perspectives; a quest for credibility among the nation's scientific community; and an irenic ecclesiology both within Presbyterianism and the wider Christian church.

With the advent of historical scholarship about the Bible, the impact of European liberal theology, the growing imperialism of scientific claims, and the faltering Protestant consensus in a pragmatic and democratized nation, the third generation of Princeton theologians narrowed their agendas. A. A. Hodge's *Outlines of Theology* (1878) operated safely within his father's orbit. Warfield and A. A. Hodge published a pivotal article on the Bible's inerrancy (1881), and Warfield's Inaugural Address at the seminary (1887) insisted that theology was essentially scientific. Two scholarly tasks—a quest to substantiate the tenets of the Princeton Theology by referencing the church's dogmatic heritage (see especially the essays by Warfield in his *Calvin and Augustine* [repr. 1956]) and an aggressive apologetical effort—displaced earlier emphases on religious *experience,* a breadth of societal interests, and an encounter with the frontier theological issues of the nineteenth century.

By the end of the century, however, the "golden days" of the old Princeton Theology had waned. Faced with an exhaustion of philosophical underpinnings, denominational conflict about biblical authority, and an increasingly secularized society, the heirs of the earlier Princeton theologians were confronted with at least two options. Either they could broaden their understanding of the Reformed heritage to include newer scholarship about the Bible, science, and the church's mission or they could regroup behind older formulae. Actually, the progeny of Miller, Alexander, and Hodge did both. But by the opening decade of the twentieth century, the original Princeton theologians' vision appeared blurred and their earlier inner cohesion, community, and accountability deteriorated.

A few historians have tried to show a linkage, however inadvertent, between the Princeton Theology and the emerging fundamentalism of the twentieth century, while other students have noted the Princeton pedigree in various Reformed orthodox movements during the modern era. Most scholars of nineteenth-century American religious history agree, however, that the Princeton theologians were without peer in their efforts to communicate a Reformed confessionalism to the mind and manners of Victorian America.

A. A. Hodge, *The Life of Charles Hodge* (1880); A. Hoffecker, *Piety and the Princeton Theologians* (1981); L. A. Loetscher, *The Broadening Church* (1954); G. M. Marsden, *Fundamentalism and American Culture* (1980); M. Noll, ed., *The Princeton Theology, 1812–1921* (1983); A. Schorsch, "Samuel Miller, Renaissance Man," *AP* 66 (1988): 71–87; n.a., *Theological Essays: From the Princeton Review* (1846).

JOHN W. STEWART

Protestant Ethic   The term is associated with Max Weber's *The Protestant Ethic and the Spirit of Capitalism* (1904–5; ET 1930; repr. 1958). Weber's thesis was that the teachings of John Calvin contributed to the rise of capitalism. While this continues to be debated, evidence supports Weber's thesis among later Calvinists rather than in Calvin himself.

The seed for the "Protestant ethic" is lodged in Calvin's insistence that *God* calls us to a life of holy living, exhibiting self-denial and seeking God's will and destiny. Calvin emphasized strict adherence to the Ten Commandments and an uncompromised stance to follow God's will, not the will of the world. The Christian life was a struggle in the world, not a monastic separation from the world. Calvin's intraworldly quasi-asceticism was based on his theological convictions that (1) God holds absolute sovereignty over the totality of life, (2) humans are helpless and lost without the commandments to guide and exhort them, and (3) the reality of human sinfulness is overcome by God's *grace* for our *salvation* and *forgiveness* of sins.

The *ethics* derived from these convictions leads to a life of reverence and awe before God and to maintenance of chastity, sobriety, and frugality. Human life is a *stewardship* and sacred trust before God. For Calvin, the "Protestant ethic" is characterized by a life of gratitude to God, the pursuit of the divine will in all things, and a lifestyle of discipline and productivity without conspicuous consumption. It also means giving to the poor and confronting wisely the sins of society through regulations, while never forgetting as good stewards to labor to God's glory.

A. Biéler, *The Social Humanism of Calvin* (1964); R. W. Green, ed., *Protestantism, Capitalism, and Social Science*, 2nd ed. (1973); R. H. Stone, "The Reformed Economic Ethics of John Calvin," in *Reformed Faith and Economics*, ed. R. L. Stivers (1989), 33–48.

CARNEGIE SAMUEL CALIAN

Protestant Principle   A phrase popularized by Paul Tillich. It is a commentary on the first commandment ("You shall have no other gods before me"), a protest against *idolatry*, or the *worship* of "false gods." The human temptation is always to worship as absolute that which is only relative (political party, nation, *church*, etc.), thus rendering it a rival "god" to the true God.

The principle is likewise embedded in the Hebrew prophets who inveighed consistently against the creation of idols or false gods. It is behind the rallying cry of the Protestant Reformers, *ecclesia semper reformanda* (the church always in process of being reformed), and it fueled their charge that the church of the time was demanding uncritical allegiance to its institutional forms and beliefs, thus substituting itself for the God it should have been proclaiming.

The Protestant principle, then, "contains the divine and human protest against any absolute claim made for a relative reality. . . . It is the prophetic judgment against religious pride, ecclesiastical arrogance, and secular self-sufficiency and their destructive consequences" (Tillich, *The Protestant Era*, 163).

But the principle is not exclusively negative. Tillich insists on wedding the Protestant principle to "Catholic substance," that is, affirming the basic Christian **tradition** in its wholeness or "catholicity" but always taking account of the dangers of idolatry.

P. Tillich, *Systematic Theology*, vol. 3 (1963); and *The Protestant Era* (1948).

ROBERT MCAFEE BROWN

Providence of God *Reformed theology* has traditionally understood the providence of God to embrace a threefold work: God's preservation of **creation**, God's cooperation with all created entities, and God's guidance of all things toward God's ultimate purposes and their highest good. What this **doctrine** emphasizes is that the triune God, in goodness and power, preserves, accompanies, and directs God's entire universe. No facet of God's work is excluded from divine care.

This concept had been advanced and defended by many Reformed writers. Johannes Braunius notes: "The acts of the providence of God are three: (1) He preserves all things in their being and duration; (2) He moves all things to their action by concurrence, in fact by precurrence; (3) He steers and guides all things to the desired end to which they were appointed from eternity" *(Doctrina foederum* 1.12.2, in Heppe, *RD*, 256). Louis Berkhof observed that "providence may be defined as that continued exercise of the divine energy whereby the Creator preserves all His creatures, is operative in all that comes to pass in the world, and directs all things to their appointed end" *(Systematic Theology*, 166). Similarly, Karl Barth writes: "By `providence' is meant the superior dealings of the Creator with His creation, the wisdom, omnipotence

and goodness with which He maintains and governs in time this distinct reality according to the counsel of His own will" *(CD* III/3, 3).

Reformed theologians further maintain that this doctrine is explicitly taught in *scripture*, where *God* is portrayed as fulfilling this threefold activity, as outlined above. It is not a doctrine derived from general revelation; rather, it is a doctrine preserved and taught in scripture.

First, the Reformed tradition understands the providence of God to be a work of *conservatio, sustentatio,* and *preservatio,* God actively preserves and upholds what God has created. God continues to see that the creation is maintained, that order prevails, and that life is sustained through, over, and above each species' divinely given power to propagate itself. As Calvin explained: "We see the presence of divine power shining as much in the continuing state of the universe as in its inception" *(Inst.* 1.16.1).

God's preserving activity is a divine work in which the Son also participates. It exists for his glory (Rom. 11:36; Col. 1:17; Heb. 1:3). Christ is its principle of cohesion.

For Charles Hodge, *preservatio* means (1) "that the universe as a whole does not continue in being of itself" and that (2) "all creatures, whether plants or animals, . . . are continued in existence not by any inherent principle of life, but by the will of God" *(Systematic Theology*, 1:575). For L. Berkhof, preservation entails "that continuous work of God by which He maintains the things which He created, together with the properties and powers with which He endowed them." For Emil Brunner, God's conserving work is to be seen in the "constancy" of the "orders and forms of nature," which are expressions both of the divine will and of God's faithfulness to God's creation.

For Reformed theologians, however, it is not merely the preservation of the cosmos, or its orders, that scripture emphasizes. God the Father through Christ the Son also preserves and upholds human life. This is accomplished both through

God's commandment to the original couple (Gen. 1:28) and through the ineffable working of God's Spirit and God's divine loyalty to God's servants.

The Hebrew word *shamar* is central. It means "to keep, to preserve, to protect." It is the primary verb used to describe God's faithfulness to God's servants and is used in numerous passages (Gen. 28:15; Ex. 23:20; Num. 6:24; Josh. 24:17; Job 29:2; Ps. 16:1; 121:5).

Above all, the preserving activity of God is a divine work whose purpose is to sustain and uphold God's servant Israel and the church. God's work of preservation cannot be separated from the *covenant* and God's purposes of *election* in Jesus Christ. Neither the cosmos nor humankind possesses absolute value per se. The universe and human life exist for higher purposes than mere self-continuance, or self-affirmation, or propagation of the species. Both have been created and are sustained for the glory of God, who, in Jesus Christ, has resolved from eternity "to unite all things in him" (Eph. 1:10).

Second, Reformed theology has understood God's providential work as a divine cooperation with all creatures, or as a divine operation that accompanies the activity of all creatures. Orthodox dogmatics refers to this function as *concursus*. In L. Berkhof's view, *concursus* involves "the co-operation of the divine power with all subordinate powers, according to the preestablished laws of their operation, causing them to act and to act precisely as they do" (*Systematic Theology*, 170). Consequently, created powers do not act by themselves. Equally important, each power, as a second cause, is real and acts in accordance with its created powers. As such, it is accountable for its actions. Furthermore, second causes are voluntary, and not merely passive or involuntary instruments of God's will.

This distinction between active and passive, or between God's immanent accompaniment yet transcendent Lordliness, is viewed as a necessary qualification against pantheism on the one hand and Deism on the other. Nothing occurs aside from God's will. All things are allowed, foreseen, or caused by God. Yet second causes, in themselves, are accountable for their choices and actions.

As Calvin explained: "There is no random power, or agency, or motion in the creatures, who are so governed by the secret counsel of God that nothing happens but what he has knowingly and willingly decreed" (*Inst.* 1.16.3). Yet God cannot be blamed for human *sin*. Rather, "in this way, while acting wickedly, we serve his righteous ordination, since in his boundless wisdom he will know how to use bad instruments for good purposes" (1.17.5).

Etienne Gilson identified two further qualifications that are necessary to avoid extremes of "extrinsicism" and "intrinsicism." In "extrinsicism," God does it all by forcing God's will upon entities from without. In "intrinsicism," God does little or nothing, abandoning created beings to operate on their own. Neither extreme can be accepted without violating God's Lordship or humankind's uniqueness. Hence, God acts as a "total cause," conferring upon each being its unique capacities, while constituting the principal cause of all its interactions in the world.

Barth enthusiastically accepted the terminology of *cause* and *second causes* and believed it is a legitimate language for the theologian to use. He wrote, "The divine *causare* takes place in and with [our] *causare*."

Brunner is suspicious of such a doctrine. He considers it a "danger-zone" and warns that the church must renounce attempts to understand how human *freedom* and God's activity are interwoven. Barth, however, contends that if it is an error, it is an error meant to uphold the *maior Dei gloria* along with the scripture's affirmation of the *minor gloria creaturae*.

Third, Reformed theology recognizes that the entire universe belongs to God and belongs to God to direct, both toward its immediate and its highest ends. This element is known as *gubernatio*, or steering. It has to do with the direction, purpose, and goal that God assigns to each entity as God directs the whole toward the accomplishment of God's divine purpose.

The Reformed tradition understands this work of *gubernatio* to pertain to nature, to all its sentient creatures, above all to humankind, and to *history* itself. Intelligent creatures and voluntary things especially come under God's guidance. So too do nations and history. All is in God's hands, and God knows the ends toward which God steers it (Eph. 1:9–12; Phil. 2:9–11).

Modern theologians from Friedrich Schleiermacher to the present (Rudolf Bultmann, Gordon Kaufman, and Langdon Gilkey) are quick to point up the inseparability of the nature-history nexus and the extent to which all things are caught up in a web of sociopolitical interconnections. Nonetheless, for Reformed theology, none of this erodes the central biblical conviction that the triune God, in goodness and power, is present preserving, accompanying, and guiding the entire universe toward God's highest will for it. Whatever aspects of self-determination God has conferred on voluntary creatures in no way detracts from God's power to forgive sin or to call forth believers to participate in God's providential ordering of the world.

Barth, *CD* III; L. Berkhof, *Systematic Theology*, 4th rev. and enl. ed. (1949); E. Brunner, *Dogmatics*, vol. 2 (1952); B. W. Farley, *The Providence of God* (1988); L. Gilkey, *Reaping the Whirlwind* (1976); E. Gilson, *The Christian Philosophy of St. Thomas Aquinas* (1961); Heppe, *RD*; C. Hodge, *Systematic Theology*, vol. 1 (1871).

BENJAMIN WIRT FARLEY

Racism *Calvinism*, or the Reformed faith, is closely associated in origin and development with the modern world. It is not surprising therefore that it is intertwined with modern racism, a pattern of relation among groups and individuals that asserts that one group and its members are by divine **creation** and nature superior to another and therefore deserving of greater power, privilege, and status. Modern racism had its beginning in the fifteenth century with European industrialization, conquest, and colonization of much of Africa and the Americas and its incursions into Asia. Modern racism consisted of doctrines of white supremacy rooted in beliefs about the divine creation and natural superiority of white groups and individuals and practices of discrimination and prejudice against nonwhite people because they were not white. The doctrines' function was to explain and justify the military, technological, and cultural dominance of white people. Calvinism contributed both to the achievements of European people and to their discrimination and prejudice against nonwhite people. The *doctrine* of God's total sovereignty, equal creation of all people, and investment of persons with a special calling or *vocation* not only motivated people to perceive themselves as sacred and their vocation as divinely given but also permitted them to see differences among people as divinely sanctioned. Whiteness gave birth to political, social, and economic superiority. Nonwhiteness was responsible for the absence of the Christian religion, civilization, and a just state. While the doctrine of God's total sovereignty and equal creation of all people suggested the oneness of the human family, the idea of different divinely approved vocations permitted Calvinism to understand social hierarchy and inequalities as God-ordained. Some people were destined by God's will to be slaves, to be incapable of participation in civil society and high culture, and to be without vote or representation in gvernment. Calvinism in the Americas, in the West and East Indies, and in South Africa affirmed these forms of racism. Within and without slavery they supported conceptions of white supremacy. Conception of stewardship or duties owed slaves by masters mitigated but did not remove the idea and practice of white supremacy.

In North America, this paternalistic idea of stewardship was widespread and sanctioned by an official statement (1787) by the forerunner of the *General Assembly*, the Synod of New York and Philadelphia:

> The Synod of New York and Philadelphia do highly approve of the general principles in favor of universal liberty that prevail in America, and the interest which many of the States have taken in promoting the abolition of Slavery; yet, inasmuch as men, introduced from a servile state, to a participation of all the privileges of civil society without a proper education, and without previous habits of industry, may be in many respects dangerous to the community; therefore they earnestly recommend to all the members belonging to their communion to give those persons who are at present held in servitude, such good education as to prepare them for the better enjoyment of freedom; and they moreover recommend that masters, whenever they find servants disposed to make a just improvement of the privilege, would give them *a peculium,* or grant them sufficient time and sufficient means of procuring their own liberty, at a moderate rate; that thereby they may be brought into society with those habits of industry that may render them useful citizens and finally, they recommend it to all their people to use the most prudent measures consistent with the interests and the state of civil society, in the countries where they live, to procure eventually the final abolition of slavery in America.

The pattern outlined in the statement came to dominate American Calvinism whether or not the denomination favored the abolition of slavery, and it persisted until the 1960s. Under its influence, Calvinism established racially separate denominations, congregations, and units of governance and mission. They were as a *church* passive in respect to social, political, and economic programs that advocated racial equality.

In the period following World War II and characterized by the demise of colonialism and the success of the civil rights revolution under the leadership of the Reverend Martin Luther King Jr., and the Southern Christian Leadership Conference, these teachings and practices were changed. The *Confession of 1967* recognized these changes:

> God has created the peoples of the earth to be one universal family. In his reconciling love he overcomes the barriers between brothers and breaks down every form of discrimination based on racial or ethnic difference, real or imaginary. The church is called to bring all men to receive and uphold one another as persons in all relationships of life: in employment, housing, education, leisure, marriage, family, church, and the exercise of political rights. Therefore the church labors for the abolition of all racial discrimination and ministers to those injured by it. Congregations, individuals, or groups of Christians who exclude, dominate, or patronize their fellowmen however subtly, resist the Spirit of God and bring contempt on the faith which they profess. (*BC* 9.44)

Following the adoption of the Confession of 1967, the church acted to define itself and its society in nonracial ways. In 1990, the Dutch Reformed Church of South Africa became the last Calvinist body to accept these teachings as doctrine. The abandonment of white supremacy as an official Calvinist teaching was due not only to cultural and political changes in western Europe and the United States but also to the initiatives of African, Asian, African American, and Latin American Calvinists who provided a new understanding of the temporal implications of the doctrines of God's total sovereignty and creation and the human person's obligations in respect to stewardship and covenantal community.

Having acknowledged their complicity in racism, Calvinistic people and churches are now pledged to rid themselves and their societies of racism. Racism has been defined as *heresy,* because it denies the fundamental tenets of Christianity and the conceptions of human dignity and worth. The *Brief Statement of Faith* of the Presbyterian Church (U.S.A.) says:

> We trust in God,
> whom Jesus called Abba, Father.
> In sovereign love God created the

world good
and makes everyone
    equally in God's image,
      male and female, of every race
      and people,
to live as one community.

Differences among human people are no longer seen simply in terms of superior and inferior. Calvinism does not deny inequalities or social hierarchy. But it does assert that God employs differences among persons and groups to enrich human flourishing and community. God is to be obeyed in all domains of life and by all persons. God has not willed the superiority of any group or individual. God desires and enables all groups and individuals to live together without conflict, coercion, or violence. Relations among men and women of all groups are to embody mutuality and respect. Superior power where it exists, if it is just, is to be used in the interests of the common good and, where it is unjust, destroyed. Determination of human relationships on the basis of race is sinful and a violation of God's love for every human person. God's covenantal community is bonded by the image of God in persons and not language, culture, gender, and race. These natural bonds of association are to be transformed by one's loyalty to the totally sovereign Lord of creation and the universe.

W. D. Jordan, *White over Black: American Attitudes toward the Negro 1550–1812* (1968); A. Murray, *Presbyterians and the Negro: A History* (1966); A. J. Raboteau, *Slave Religion* (1978).

PRESTON N. WILLIAMS

Reason   The capacity in human beings by which universal judgments are made. "Reason" is sometimes used interchangeably with "understanding." It is the means by which one knows oneself and the surrounding world. But its principal use is to know *God*, a goal it could attain before, but not after, the fall.

Rejecting the complex discussions of the philosophers, John Calvin held that the human soul is an incorporeal substance, set in the body. It has two faculties, understanding and will, to which every other faculty is related. Understanding, "the leader and governor of the soul" (*Inst.* 1.15.7), distinguishes between things. The five senses, common sense, and the imagination supply materials about which reason forms universal judgments. What reason considers in a step-by-step analysis, understanding contemplates. The will strives toward those things that the understanding and reason present as good. According to Calvin, this simple account of these faculties suffices for godliness; those who desire more detail may study the philosophers.

Before the fall, the light of reason was sufficient, so that "his [humanity's] reason, understanding, prudence, and judgment not only sufficed for the direction of his earthly life, but by them men mounted up even to God and eternal bliss" (*Inst.* 1.15.8). The principal use of human understanding was to seek happiness, which consists in being united with God.

After the fall, a true ***knowledge of God*** is not possible through reason alone, for "his [humanity's] supernatural gifts were stripped from him" (*Inst.* 2.2.12). ***Faith***, love of God, love of neighbor, and desire for holiness and righteousness were lost. There remains a natural instinct, an awareness of divinity (*divinitatis sensum*), which results in every person having the conviction that there is some God. This is the "seed of religion," but it now leads to superstition, denial of God, and false religion.

In the fall, the "natural gifts" were corrupted. Reason's ability to understand was weakened, so it tends to focus on empty and worthless things, while paying too little attention to important matters. Still, with regard to its understanding "earthly things," such as government, household management, mechanical skills, and the liberal arts, the natural reason manifests considerable aptitude. Ability in the liberal and manual arts is a natural gift found among believers and unbelievers alike. The competence of secular writers, jurists, mathematicians, and natural scientists is praised by Calvin and seen as evidence that the minds of fallen persons are "sharp and penetrating in their investigation of inferior things" (*Inst.* 2.2.15). Though the truth in them is not complete, it comes from the Spirit of God, who is the source of all truth and so is not to be rejected or despised.

Human reason after the fall lacks spiritual insight, which is based on knowing God, God's way of *salvation,* and how to live according to God's *law.* On these matters, the philosophers grasp only an occasional truth but remain filled with error. True spiritual knowledge can be gained only through faith.

Faith is a knowledge of God that is "revealed to our minds and sealed upon our hearts through the Holy Spirit" (*Inst.* 3.2.7). In faith, the understanding is raised beyond itself. In reasoning about ordinary things, the mind attains a comprehension that results in certitude about them. With faith, however, the mind becomes persuaded of what it does not comprehend. It has certitude even where it does not understand, because the knowledge of faith is founded on love. So believers are more "strengthened by the persuasion of divine truth than instructed by rational proof" (*Inst.* 3.2.14). Faith is like the certitude of a child who knows its parent's love but cannot explain it.

Because Calvin was only one among several theologians whose ideas gained acceptance in the Reformed churches, his conception of human reason was not the only one found in the Reformed tradition. Also, because Calvin gave a simplified account of reason and other faculties of the soul, Reformed thinkers have repeatedly found it necessary to supplement his ideas. Consequently, there has been no definitive Reformed view of the nature of reason. Calvinist views of reason have tended to reflect the influence of their age. Some Calvinists have been influenced by Cartesian, Lockean, Reidian, Hegelian, neo-Kantian, and other positions. Many debates in the Reformed tradition on the nature and capacity of reason have had their origins in the divergences among these perspectives.

D. J. Hoitenga, *Faith and Reason from Plato to Plantinga: An Introduction to Reformed Epistemology* (1991); A. Plantinga and N. Wolsterorff, eds., *Faith and Rationality: Reason and Belief in God* (1984).

ARVIN VOS

Reformed Scholasticism   *see* Orthodoxy, Reformed

Regeneration   While sometimes used of the cosmic renewal at the end of the age (Matt. 19:28; Acts 3:21), regeneration is more often used of the inner renewal of individuals by the *Holy Spirit* (Titus 3:5). In this latter sense, it is a "new birth," or a "birth from above," caused by the sovereign action of the Spirit of God (John 3:3–5), and entry into God's kingdom is dependent on this inner transformation within the soul.

This action of the Spirit was promised by the prophets (Jer. 31:31; 32:40) as belonging to entry into the new *covenant.* Paul expounds it both in relation to the Spirit and to being "in Christ"—a coresurrection with Christ (Eph. 2:5; Col. 2:13) and a new *creation* in Christ (2 Cor. 5:17; Gal. 6:15). Peter and James set out its connection with the gospel, for *God* "begets anew" (1 Peter 1:23) and "brings to birth" by the living word (James 1:18). While the duty of sinners is to receive the gospel by repenting of *sin,* believing the promises of God and obeying the divine word, the work of God is to regenerate the soul so that the sinner can truly respond to the gospel.

In church history, regeneration as the act of God has been closely connected with the sacrament of *Baptism* because of the intimate NT relation of *conversion* to God and baptism ("of water and the Spirit," John 3:5). Most baptismal liturgies of the early and medieval *church* proclaim an inseparable connection, so that regeneration is believed to occur at the time of baptism and God is thanked for having caused it. In fact, baptism was seen as conveying *ex opere operato* regeneration to all who did not obstruct the work of the Spirit. In Anglican and Lutheran baptismal liturgies, this close connection (with some ambiguity) is continued, so that baptismal regeneration can be claimed to be, in a minimal way, a Protestant as well as a Roman Catholic and an Orthodox *doctrine.*

In *Reformed theology,* the close connection of the dominical sacrament of Baptism and the sovereign act of regeneration by the Spirit have been maintained but without any hint of *ex opere operato* teaching. This is because the Reformed doctrine of regeneration has emphasized that God implants a divine "seed" of life in the soul and, from this, true *repentance* and *faith* spring and grow. Thus, God may or may not implant this divine seed when an infant is baptized. An adult believer being baptized is presumed to be regenerate because he or she now believes the gospel and baptism is a sign and seal of this faith.

In Reformed theology, the doctrine of regeneration is linked to other doctrines such as divine *election* (God only regenerates the elect), human sinfulness (God implants new life in a sinful soul), *sanctification* (God provides internal renewal to produce holiness), and mortification (God gives strength to mortify the old nature). However, unlike other systems of theology, Reformed thought will not allow for any cooperation in the new birth by the Spirit. Regeneration is not caused by human effort or human cooperation. As God alone created the cosmos, so God alone is making the new creation, and each act of regeneration in the human soul is totally and wholly the act of God. Yet by this act, God unites the recipient not only with God in Christ but also to all others who are in Christ. So it is the beginning of everlasting life, holiness, and fellowship.

H. Burkhardt, *The Biblical Doctrine of Regeneration* (1978); B. Citron, *The New Birth* (1951); P. Toon, *Born Again: A Biblical and Theological Study of Regeneration* (1987).
PETER TOON

Repentance

The distinguishing characteristic of the *doctrine* of repentance in early *Reformed theology* is that true repentance is possible only through the work of the *Holy Spirit* in a person's heart.

John Calvin defined repentance as "the true turning of our life to God . . . and it consists in the mortification of our flesh . . . and in the vivification of the Spirit" (*Inst.* 3.3.5). He was explicit that repentance is not the cause of *salvation* but "a singular gift of God" (*Inst.* 3.3.21).

The seventeenth-century theologian William Ames stressed that repentance is not only a turning from evil but a "firm purpose to follow good." However, Ames says that insofar as repentance refers to the terror aroused by the *law,* it precedes *faith* and is found in the unregenerate. But repentance that is a true turning from *sin* depends on faith. So far, this accords with Calvin's thought. Then, however, Ames modifies Calvin's view when he speculates that repentance is likely to be known before faith, because one cannot be convinced that one is reconciled to *God* unless one turns from sin (*Marrow,* 1.26.31–34).

Friedrich Schleiermacher's concern to give proper attention to the human, subjective dimension of repentance led him initially to distinguish repentance and faith. Maintaining this separation would be to abandon the distinctive element of the Reformed view. However, he does eventually affirm the inseparable relationship between them when he writes that "true conversion-regret must always eventually arise out of the vision of the perfection of Christ." This means that the "beginning of regeneration must be due to Christ's redeeming activity. It is only on this view of repentance and faith that their interconnexion is clear, their origin thus being the same" (*CF*, sec. 108).

Karl Barth devoted considerable attention to the themes of *conversion*, awakening, and repentance in his *Church Dogmatics* (ET 1936–69). He is faithful to the Reformed insight that repentance is the work of God, but he goes to great lengths to affirm that repentance involves the human heart, soul, and mind. A person's awakening is "both wholly creaturely and wholly divine." Barth is dependent on Calvin for many of his ideas but criticizes Calvin's treatment of repentance for neglecting the importance of "vivification" in the vivification-mortification distinction. Calvin dwells on mortification, while Barth wants to stress that repentance is liberation. "Vivification is God's proper work in repentance; mortification is God's alien work."

The distinction between remorse and repentance allowed Reinhold Niebuhr to maintain the Reformed understanding of repentance. If one recognizes only *judgment*, one will experience remorse. Niebuhr preserved one of Calvin's essential insights into the psychology of repentance when he wrote that "without the knowledge of divine love, remorse cannot be transmuted into repentance." This is true because only the person who knows of God's love will rigorously examine one's self and be fully aware of sin's depths. In other words, the awareness of guilt in the repentant person is more profound than in the merely remorseful.

W. Ames, *Medulla Theologiae* (1623 and 1627; ET *The Marrow of Sacred Divinity* [1643]); Barth, *CD IV/2, 553ff.;* Reinhold Niebuhr, *The Nature and Destiny of Man*, 2 vols. (1941–43), 1:241ff.

DAVID FOXGROVER

Reprobation   *see* Hell

Resistance, Right of   Group of theories employed by Calvinist groups in the early modern period to justify their use of

force against European rulers. Calvin himself was initially extremely reluctant to sanction resistance to constituted authority either in theory or in practice. The final paragraph of the *Institutes* ambiguously commended the Spartan ephors' function of restraining the king. Toward the end of his life, the threatening civil war in France led Calvin to become more sympathetic to the constitutional justification for resistance, and he permitted the princes of the blood to act against the French monarch. Such caution had already been abandoned by the exiles from Marian England in their revolutionary tracts: John Ponet, *Short Treatise of Politic Power* (1556), Christopher Goodman, *How Superior Powers Ought to Be Obeyed* (1558), John Knox, *The First Blast of the Trumpet against the Monstrous Regiment of Women* (1558), and others. Later, George Buchanan in *De jure regni apud Scotos* (1579) produced the most radical but least religious theory of resistance to explain the removal of Mary Queen of Scots from her throne. French Calvinists Theodore Beza, *Du droit des magistrats* (1573), François Hotman, *Franco-gallia* (1573), and the author of *Vindiciae contra tyrannos* (1579), followed by their Dutch coreligionists such as Philipp Marnix de Sainte-Aldegonde, *Letter to William of Orange* (1580), argued for resistance to the ruler by the people's representatives. These ideas were also employed in seventeenth-century Britain, notably by the Scottish Covenanters, by Charles I's English opponents, and in the Glorious Revolution (1688–89).

Calvinist theorists drew heavily upon two types of Lutheran argument developed during the Schmalkaldic Wars: the religious and the legal/constitutional. The Calvinists expanded the idea of a religious duty to establish and defend the "true church" by force, especially against the agents of Antichrist (the papacy). They also adapted the legal/constitutional justification of resistance to the Holy Roman Emperor to fit circumstances elsewhere in Europe. The concept of "inferior magistrates" was broadened to include all the nobility and government officials. Greater emphasis was placed upon the historical/traditional theme of "liberties" and "Ancient Constitution" so strong in medieval thought. Roman law precedents were combined with covenant and contract ideas to explain the derivation and exercise of political authority. The resulting mix of arguments, strongly medieval and nontheological, was used to justify a right of resistance. This right, however, was not universal but confined to "public persons." Revolutionary in its own time and in its implications, it was eclipsed by the subsequent development of democratic thought.

J. Franklin, *Constitutionalism and Resistance in the Sixteenth Century* (1969); D. Kelley, *The Beginning of Ideology* (1981); Q. Skinner, *The Foundations of Modern Political Thought*, vol. 2 (1978); M. L. Walzer, *The Revolution of the Saints* (1965).

JANE DAWSON

Resurrection   No tenet of Christianity is more central than "the resurrection of the dead" (Apostles' Creed). Resurrection is at once the foundation of Christian *faith* and the focus of Christian *hope.*

While the notion of resurrection is certainly not foreign to the OT, explicit references are few (e.g., Isa. 26:19; Dan. 12:2). These, however, reflect the much more pervasive conviction that Yahweh is the *God* of the living and, as the creator and source of life, will prevail over the power of death/Sheol (e.g., Ps. 16:10–11; 49:15). This conviction becomes dominant in the NT, now that Jesus has been raised from the dead. Inseparably connected with his death, such that the one is a "synecdoche" for the other (*Inst.* 2.16.13), Christ's resurrection is at the heart of the gospel (e.g., Rom. 10:9; 1 Cor. 15:3–5). Along with the promised restoration of the entire *creation,* the believer's own resurrection is the dominant hope of the gospel (e.g., Rom. 8:21–25; 1 Cor. 15).

In the history of *doctrine,* the resurrection of Jesus has been relatively eclipsed—in Eastern Orthodoxy, where the accent has been on the *incarnation* (*salvation* as deification) and in Western Christianity (both Roman Catholic and Protestant), where attention has been largely focused on the significance of the cross (the nature of the *atonement*). The resurrection has been considered primarily for its apologetic worth, as the crowning evidence for Christ's deity and the truth of Christianity in general. In the modern period, especially since the Enlightenment, this apologetic value has been rendered increasingly problematic as the historicity of the resurrection has been questioned or denied. But for the NT, the gospel plainly stands or falls with the reality of the resurrection, understood, despite its uniqueness, as lying on the same plane of historical occurrence as his death.

Although a cardinal belief for all Christians, the resurrection has been given a distinctive emphasis in the Reformed tradition. For instance, in the Reformed tradition's christological differences with Lutheranism, the resurrection (not, in part, the descent into *hell*) begins the state of exaltation. Similarly, rejecting the Lutheran notion of a ubiquitous human nature (the *extra calvinisticum*), the accent has been on the glorified human nature that Christ does not possess until his resurrection.

Based on NT teaching, *Reformed theology* has seen the significance of the resurrection along several interrelated lines. The resurrection of Jesus is the pivotal *eschatological* event. The resurrected Christ is "the first fruits of those who have fallen asleep" (1 Cor. 15:20, 23); his resurrection is the actual beginning of the general resurrection ("harvest" of believers). It is not simply a miracle, however stupendous, isolated in the past, but it forms an unbreakable unity with the resurrection of believers. It belongs to the future and anticipates the consummation of *history*; it (together with the *ascension* and Pentecost as a single event-complex) inaugurates the eschatological "age to come."

This eschatological dimension serves to reveal the *christological* and *pneumatological* and so the *soteriological* importance of the resurrection. At his resurrection, Christ received a glorified, "spiritual" body (1 Cor. 15:42ff) and was constituted the glory image of God (2 Cor. 3:18; 4:4). This climactic transformation of his person, however, is not simply personal but corporate. All those united to Christ by faith "have been raised with Christ" (Col. 2:12; 3:1); they share with him in the benefits of his resurrection. For them, resurrection is not only a future hope but a present *experience.* As resurrected, he is their *sanctification* (1 Cor. 1:30), the image into which they are already being transformed (2 Cor. 3:18) and to which they will finally be conformed completely in their bodily resurrection (1 Cor. 15:49; Phil. 3:21). That will be as well the full realization of their *adoption* (Rom. 8:23), so he might be "firstborn among many brothers" (v. 29). At the same time, the resurrection is the vindication of Christ in his suffering (1 Tim. 3:16). It reveals and seals the efficacy of his death for the *forgiveness* of sins (1 Cor. 15:14, 17); he "was raised for our justification" (Rom. 4:25).

At his resurrection, Christ, as "the last Adam," became "life-giving spirit" (1 Cor. 15:45). As resurrected, Christ is in such total and final possession of the *Holy Spirit* that the two, without confusion or the obliteration of personal Trinitarian distinction, are one (cf. 2 Cor. 3:17) in the work of communicating eschatological, resurrection life; the activity of the Spirit in the *church* is the activity of the resurrected Christ (Rom. 8:9–10). Primarily with Pentecost in view, the resurrected Christ tells his disciples, "I am with you always, to the end of the age" (Matt. 28:20). This forms the background for the Reformed understanding of the real, "spiritual" presence of Christ in the sacrament.

The pneumatic factor also sheds light, with all the mystery that remains, on the much-discussed question of the nature of the resurrection body. What God has done for Christ, in raising him from the dead through the Spirit, God will also do for believers (Rom. 8:11). Their bodies, like Christ's, will be "spiritual" (1 Cor. 15:44), not in the sense of being adapted to the human spirit or composed of an ethereal, immaterial substance, but as transformed and made immortal by the power of the Holy Spirit.

The resurrection of unbelievers for final *judgment* and eternal condemnation, though less prominent in *scripture* (e.g., Dan. 12:2; John 5:28–29; Acts 24:15), has received confessional status in both mainstreams of the Reformed tradition (e.g., *Belgic Confession,* art. 37; *Westminster Confession,* 32.2–3; 33.1–2).

G. C. Berkouwer, *The Work of Christ* (1965); Heppe, *RD*; J. F. Jansen, *The Resurrection of Jesus Christ in New Testament Theology* (1980); G. Vos, *The Pauline Eschatology* (1930).

RICHARD B. GAFFIN JR.

Revelation   *Sources.* Christian theology teaches that we have access to God's nature and purposes only through God's willful deeds of revelation, of which Jesus Christ is the center. These acts are not all we can say of *God* but are the basic ones on which other actions such as guidance, inspiration, and *providence* are founded. In every Christian theology, revelation is fundamental. While apparently there are many similarities among traditions, there are also essential differences. The Roman Catholic concept of revelation, formulated mainly by Thomas Aquinas, centers around the duality of nature and *grace;* the Reformation concept centers around *sin* and grace, the Lutheran more specifically around *law* and gospel, whereas Calvin and his followers prefer to summarize God's revelation as a "twofold grace" (*duplex gratia*), that is, *justification* and *sanctification.* These seemingly minor differences create a different view of God, *humanity,* sin, revelation, and redemption but also affect social and political matters.

For Calvin and the other Reformers, the center of revelation is Jesus Christ, who is himself the center of the *Word of God* as incorporated in *scripture*. In his 1559 *Institutes*, Calvin does not start with the law or in classical medieval subjects and doctrines but with the believing subject (*Inst.* 1.2.2: "Knowledge of God involves trust and reverence"). Following, however, is a chapter titled "The knowledge of God has been naturally implanted in the minds of men" (*Inst.* 1.3; cf. 1.4, 5). These deal with "natural religion" or "natural theology," beginning with: "There is within the human mind, and indeed by natural instinct, an awareness of divinity." This is supported by quotations from Cicero and Plato. In *Inst.* 1.2.2, the person of Jesus Christ and his reconciling work is no more than superficially mentioned. Calvin wrote:

I do not yet touch upon the sort of knowledge with which men, in themselves lost and accursed, apprehend God the Redeemer in Christ the Mediator; but I speak only of the primal and simple knowledge to which the very order of nature would have led us if Adam had remained upright. . . . It is one thing to feel that God as our Maker supports us by his power, governs us by his providence, nourishes us by his goodness, and attends us with all sorts of blessings—and another thing to embrace the grace of reconciliation offered to us in Christ. First, in the fashioning of the universe and in the general teaching of Scripture the Lord shows himself to be the Creator. . . . Of the resulting twofold knowledge of God we shall now discuss the first aspect; the second will be dealt with in its proper place. (*Inst.* 1.2.1)

Twofold knowledge of God (duplex cognitio Dei). This expression was added in the last edition of the *Institutes* and is "basic to the structure of the completed work" (LCC ed., 40n3). The sharp division of the two kinds of knowledge, in spite of Calvin's repeated methodological warnings, often created confusions and misunderstandings. Calvin spoke of the "naturally implanted knowledge of God" with so much ardor (*Inst.* 1.2, 3), in words

like "fatherly care," "benefits," "love," "mercy," and so forth, that many who were acquainted with his earlier editions and catechisms must have been puzzled, if not shocked, by the novelty of a reasoning in which the door to the true God is opened not by notions such as Christ, scripture, or reconciliation but by quotations from pagan philosophers.

This turn becomes more complicated because now the *authority* of scripture itself functions in a twofold way: Sometimes it means the message of God's salvation and reconciliation in Christ; at other times it testifies to God's work in *creation*, preservation, providence in nature and history, and in common blessings and judgments for humanity. On top of all, Calvin suddenly uses a conditional by-sentence about "the primal and simple knowledge to which the very order of nature would have led us if Adam had remained upright" (*si integer stetisset Adam; Inst.* 1.2.1). This seems to overthrow the whole preceding argument. One group of interpreters have seen it as a loose remark in a wrong context, others as the cornerstone in the whole argument, which removes almost all that is said before. Calvin seemed to have wanted to express too many thoughts in too few words. *Institutes* 1.4 tries to bring them into a larger and more convincing cohesion (see Dowey). Calvin's wrestlings here are symptoms of his endeavor to combine what cannot be synthesized into a divine unity. This is why in Calvin so often there are ambiguities, tensions, or ambivalences. But these reflect the multicolored truth of God. Wilhelm Niesel characterized Calvin's method as *complexio oppositorum* ("composition of opposite viewpoints").

What, then, is the relation between the first and the second order, between God's work of redemption and that of God's action? Calvin deals with this (*Inst.* 1.6–18) through the famous image of the spectacles that people of limited visual faculty need for reading a book distinctly: "So Scripture, gathering up the otherwise confused knowledge of God, . . . shows us the true God" (*Inst.* 1.6.1). Even the OT patriarchs had to pass first through the general knowledge before that other inner knowledge was added (*Inst.* 1.6.1). Calvin passes from biblical and dogmatical arguments for the authority of Scripture to other revelatory sources: the witness of the Spirit, function of reason, and "marks" to distinguish the true God from the idols. These arguments are not of equal weight and approach. The testimony of the Spirit is a major and indispensable source of revelation; the others are more secondary but must not be neglected if we seek true and pure knowledge about God.

Witness of the Holy Spirit (testimonium Spiritus Sancti). The first half of the title of *Inst.* 1.7 reads: "Scripture must be confirmed by the witness of the Spirit. Thus may its authority be established as certain." We are used to concentrating, if not limiting, revelation in the Reformed tradition to scripture alone (*sola scriptura*). But Calvin says the authority of scripture does not suffice in itself (*Inst.* 1.7.5; often overlooked). The Spirit points away from the Spirit to Jesus Christ and to scripture. Inner and outer authority presuppose each other (cf. *Inst.* 3.1–24—a long description of the Spirit's work). Calvin is even characterized as "the theologian of the Holy Spirit" (B. B. Warfield). Calvin saw Word and Spirit as each other's presuppositions and instruments in the process of revelation.

Revelatory function of reason (fides quarens intellectum). Institutes 1.8 is titled: "So far as human **reason** goes, sufficiently firm proofs are at hand to establish the credibility of Scripture." Yet this holds only when one begins with the authority of scripture, not vice versa. The arguments of reason—"not strong enough before to engraft and fix the certainty of Scripture in our minds—become very useful aids" (*Inst.* 1.8.1). Calvin thought of comparisons between the Bible and Greco-Roman literature, the profundity of Greek **philosophy,** or the antiquity of Egyptian culture. Ancient achievements in the arts and sciences Calvin called

"most excellent benefits of the divine Spirit." If "the Lord has willed that we be helped in physics, dialectic, mathematics, and other like disciplines, by the work and ministry of the ungodly, let us use this assistance. For if we neglect God's gift freely offered in these arts, we ought to suffer just punishment for our sloths" (*Inst.* 2.2.16). Reason helps maintain and develop *justice,* law, and welfare for individual and societal benefit. All this is summarized as "general" or "common grace" (*Inst.* 2.2.12–17; LCC ed., 276n63).

Calvin called all these blessings of the Spirit "earthly," separating them sharply from the "heavenly" ones. The first preserve and protect our temporal lives; the second pertain to the mysteries of the heavenly kingdom and the blessedness of future life (*Inst.* 2.2.13). Earthly blessings are strictly limited and in many respects corrupted by sin. Both the blessings of common grace and their limitations by creation and by sin must be kept clearly in mind.

"Reason" is Calvin's general word for cultural gifts and achievements worked by the divine Spirit. As such, it is a great but ambivalent reality. It must constantly be judged according to the standards of God's creation as revealed in scripture. While reason is a source of revelation, it is a secondary one.

Negative revelatory function of idolatry ("You shall not make yourself a graven image"). Ample space in these apologetic sections is reserved for the "antiquated" subject of polytheism (*Inst.* 1.9–14). Calvin taught that "every figurative representation of God contradicts his being" (*Inst.* 1.11.2). The starting point for Calvin's doctrine of revelation is God's transcendence, sovereignty, and uncomparability. Yet how can this God really be revealed to human creatures? Or, in reverse, how can God create man and woman "in his own image, after his own likeness" (Gen. 1:26)? For Calvin, *accommodation* is important.

Condescendent revelatory principle of accommodation ("I dwell in the high and holy place, and also with those who are contrite and humble in spirit" [Isa. 57:15]). Accommodation can be considered the "central feature of the entire range of Calvin's theological work" (a "working principle," not as the topic of a separate locus; see Battles). Accommodation is the reverse of God's transcendent nature, and "at the center of God's accommodating Himself to human capacity however is His supreme act of condescension, the giving of His only Son to reconcile a fallen world to Himself" (Battles, 24). Calvin sees that, in order to bridge the gap of our ignorance and disobedience, God has accommodated God's self to the limits of human capacity and relates to humanity as a parent, teacher, and physician. These metaphors enable Calvin to introduce a flexibility in God's relations to human creatures in their advancing toward spiritual maturity.

Divine authority of the Bible (Dei loquentis persona). The main feature of the Reformed faith is the central position of the Bible as source, standard, and court of appeal of all divine truth. Nearly every page of Calvin's works testifies to this fact and function. His commentaries exhibit this, and his exegesis is still valuable today. But Calvin, like Luther, practiced the authority of the Bible in a rather "free" manner. Luther concentrated on justification by faith alone; Calvin, on the general and practical meaning of the text, without much interest in real or seeming contradictions within a passage or between several books. Many Calvin scholars interpret Calvin's words such as "dictate," "inspiration," "amanuensis," or "notary" as pointing to verbal inspiration. But, for Calvin, this would have contradicted his concept of accommodation or created an anachronism because the concept of literal dictation by mechanical means came up in the seventeenth century, the period of Reformed *scholasticism.* Calvin used synonymously mechanical, organical, and personal images. His pointed definition said: "The highest proof of Scripture derives in general from the fact that God in person speaks in it" (Lat. *Summa Scripturae probatio passim a Dei loquentis persona sumitur;* Inst. 1.7.4). By the mechanical images, Calvin wanted to stress the instrumentality and irresistibility of the process; by the personal images, the character of a person-to-person encounter or *free will.* The Reformed concept did not feel an either/or contrast but two language fields that complemented each other, until new paradigms required a more precise and less analogous terminology, as later happened in the doctrine of "organic inspiration."

Barth, *CD* I/1; I/2; F. L. Battles, "God Was Accommodating Himself to Human Capacity," *Interpretation* 31, no. 1 (January 1977): 19–38; Berkhof, *CF*; E. A. Dowey, Jr., *The Knowledge of God in Calvin's Theology* (1952; repr. 1964); D. K. McKim, "Calvin's View of Scripture," in *Readings in Calvin's Theology* (1984); H. R. Niebuhr, *The Meaning of Revelation* (1941); Rogers and McKim, *AIB.*

HENDRIKUS BERKHOF

Sacraments Visible holy signs and seals instituted by *God* so that by their use God may make us understand more clearly the promise of the gospel and put God's seal on that promise. This is to grant us *forgiveness* of sins and eternal life, by *grace* alone, because of the one sacrifice of Jesus Christ on the cross (HC, q. 66).

The two sacraments set forth in the NT—*Baptism* (Matt. 28:19; Acts 2:38) and the *Lord's Supper* (Matt. 26:26–29)—were prefigured in the OT rites of circumcision (Gen. 17:11; Col. 2:11–12) and the passover (Ex. 12:7–8, 13; 23:14–17; 1 Cor. 5:7). All were intended to function as means of grace within the covenant community, bringing its members into a closer walk with God. Baptism and the Lord's Supper had particular reference to redemption in Christ and communion with him through the *Holy Spirit* (Acts 2:38; Rom. 6:3–5; Titus 3:5; 1 Cor. 11:23–27; John 6:53–58, 63; Col. 2:11–12). That the early *church* understood them this way seems clear (Mark 10:38–39; 1 Cor.

10:1–5). To the first Christians, the sacraments were not mere memorials of Christ's saving work but a representation of that work, which became a means of grace through *faith* and the power of the Holy Spirit. Baptism and the Lord's Supper, then, are dramatizations of the Word that is proclaimed, appealing to sight, touch, and taste as well as sound. It is possible to hear the **Word of God** without the sacraments, but there are no sacraments apart from the Word that gives them meaning. It can even be said, with Luther, that the Word is the one sacrament and that Baptism and the Lord's Supper are pictorial representations of it. By extended usage, a contemporary theologian, Edward Schillebeeckx, has called Christ "the sacrament of the encounter with God" in a book with that title (1963).

"Sacrament" derives from a Latin word that classically meant something sacred. In a lawsuit, money deposited by contending parties was *sacramentum*, for when forfeited it was used for a sacred purpose. The word was also used judicially and militarily; *sacramentum dicere* meant to swear an oath.

In the early church, *sacramentum* came to apply to many things sacred and to rites that had a hidden meaning. Thus, it was used to describe religious ceremonies and was brought into connection with *mystērion* (Gr.), meaning "secret." In the Latin Vulgate, *sacramentum* is translated for *mystērion* (Eph. 1:9; 3:9; 5:32; Col. 1:27; 1 Tim. 3:16; Rev. 1:20; 17:7). Whereas Tertullian was the first theologian to use *sacramentum* with clear religious meaning, two centuries later *Augustine* wrote that signs which "pertain to divine things are called sacraments." That broad meaning of the word continued into the Middle Ages. The sign of the cross, palms, ashes, anointing with oil, *preaching, prayer,* and visitation of the sick were all included. With sacrament conceived as a "sign of a sacred thing" (Peter Lombard), some theologians listed thirty. However, these "sacraments" were divided into classes, with

Baptism and the Lord's Supper given prominence. In the thirteenth century, the number was set at seven.

The meaning given to sacraments was also an important development. Whereas Augustine had said they were visible signs of an invisible grace, they were later said to contain and confer grace. No mere channels, they were declared to be "efficient causes" of grace by a virtue inherent in themselves when properly administered. Thus, Baptism regenerated, and the Lord's Supper, by conversion of the bread and wine into the body, blood, soul, and divinity of Christ, was conceived as a propitiatory sacrifice to God for the remission of sins. The elements consecrated in transubstantiation could be reserved for later use and adored even as Christ himself (Council of Trent, Sess. 13, 22).

The Reformers swept aside these accretions to biblical teaching but disagreed among themselves as to the meaning and efficacy of the two sacraments they accepted. All rejected transubstantiation and the Mass as a propitiatory sacrifice, but Luther insisted on the real physical presence of Christ in the Supper. Acknowledging the mystery, he took literally Christ's words, "This is my body," and said that if we cannot believe *scripture* here, we cannot believe it anywhere and are on the way to "the virtual denial of Christ, God, and everything" (*Works*, 37:29, 53).

Luther was protesting Zwingli's view that denied any physical presence of Christ in the Supper and separated the sign from that which it signified to such an extent that he said we *worship* an "absent" Christ. Zwingli thought dualistically: The Word is both inward and outward, the church is visible and invisible, grace has an external form and is inward. No physical element can affect the soul but only God in sovereign grace. There must be no identification of the sign and that which it signifies; through the use of the sign we rise above the world of sense to God and the grace signified. By contrast, Luther held that God comes to us in the physical signs that sense apprehends.

Zwingli held that the word "is" in the words of institution meant "signifies"; the bread signifies Christ's body. Thus, Zwingli believed that in this instance "is" is similar to the other "I am" statements of Jesus. Luther's notion of the physical eating of Christ's body, which was held to be "in, under, and with" the elements, was repugnant to Zwingli, and he believed that Luther's *doctrine* of the *ubiquity* was nonsense.

Calvin agreed with Zwingli in the latter's rejection of Luther's positions but denied Zwingli's claim that we worship an absent Christ. For then, Calvin reasoned, there would be no real communion, no real feeding on Christ in the Supper, and no reception of him. But communion with the crucified and risen Savior is what the Lord's Supper is all about. Thus, Calvin took a position midway between the extremes of Luther and Zwingli. Learning from both, he held a doctrine truly his own.

The key to Calvin's understanding is his view of the Holy Spirit's role in communicating the benefits of Christ to believers. With Luther, he held that there is a reception of the body and blood of the Lord Jesus in the Supper but that it occurs in a spiritual manner. The ascended Christ, in *heaven* with his body, gives himself to the faithful through the Holy Spirit. Nothing should be taken from Christ's "heavenly glory—as happens when he is brought under the corruptible elements of this world, or bound to any earthly creatures. . . . Nothing inappropriate to human nature [should] be ascribed to his body, as happens when it is said either to be infinite or to be put in a number of places at once" (*Inst.* 4.17, 19). Luther's "monstrous notion of ubiquity" (4.17.30) and the associated idea that Christ is corporeally (physically) received in the Supper were thus rejected along with Zwingli's mere "memorialism," in which the signs were conceived as representing that which is absent.

Reformation teaching on Baptism was less disputatious than on the Eucharist but followed similar lines of thought. In place of the baptismal *regeneration* of Rome, there was explicit emphasis on the Word, faith, and the Holy Spirit. Within Protestantism there were those who saw baptism as little more than a badge indicating belief or sign of the *covenant.* But most Reformed people, including the Church of England, believed that baptism was a real means of grace with multiple significance: the acknowledgment of sin, of cleansing through Christ, union with Christ, the gift of the Holy Spirit, and baptism as a sign of covenantal status. As a covenantal sign, it was seen as replacing circumcision (Col. 2:11–12). Because of Christ's redemption, it has a richer meaning than the OT ordinance. There was debate about the candidates for baptism and the amount of water that was proper to use. But there was nothing like the acrimony that attended the "sacramentarian controversies" over the Lord's Supper.

The Reformed church generally followed Calvin in its confessional teaching about Baptism and the Lord's Supper. The sacraments are not "bare signs" (*signa nuda*) but are described as real means of grace with which the Holy Spirit nourishes believers. Signs and seals of God's promise of *salvation,* they are made effective by God's Spirit, who quickens and nourishes those within the covenant community who are united to Jesus Christ.

Thus, the Reformed tradition, with most of the Christian church, believes it pleases God to use earthy materials—water, bread, the fruit of the vine—in the reconciliation of the world to God. Those Christians who depreciate the sacraments through disuse or by giving them minimum meaning because of their material nature, if consistent, might seek a word from God beyond the paper and ink of scripture or adopt a docetic *Christology,* in which the *humanity* of Christ, an earthy reality, is denied. In denigrating the sacraments, they reject a gift that God has given to God's people for the enrichment of their spiritual life and the strengthening of their faith.

There is also a "sacramental principle" discernible in life and universally utilized in natural religion. Though this is by no means the reason the church administers its divinely ordained sacraments, the presence of that principle is relevant to Christian theology as a witness to the reality of God's interaction with all people.

G. W. Bromiley, ed., *Zwingli and Bullinger,* LCC, vol. 24 (1953); J. Calvin, *Tracts Relating to the Reformation,* trans. H. Beveridge, 3 vols. (1844–51); O. Cullmann, *Baptism in the New Testament* (ET 1950); W. F. Flemington, *The New Testament Doctrine of Baptism* (1948); J. C. McLelland, *The Visible Words of God: An Exposition of the Sacramental Theology of Peter Martyr Vermigli* A.D. 1500–1562 (1957).

M. EUGENE OSTERHAVEN

Salvation   The NT Greek terms translated "to save" and "salvation" are *sōzō* and *sōtēria.* They connote snatching others by force from serious peril. They may also mean saving from judicial condemnation or from an illness, hence curing. The Hebrew *yeshu'ah* has the sense of "deliverance." Fundamentally, the root means "to be broad" or "spacious." Thus, to deliver is to set free from constraint, confinement, or oppression so the one delivered can develop unhindered. The OT story of Israel tells of God's mighty acts of deliverance and salvation. God's righteousness is manifest in saving the humble who cannot save themselves, the poor and the dispirited (Isa. 40:18–20; 44:9–20; 46:6–7). The phrase "God saves" could almost be likened to a primitive creed. The proper name "Jesus" has its root in this affirmation.

Christian *tradition* has many ways of imaging how our salvation is brought about in the work of Christ. All these NT images stand with no attempt to harmonize them, and the *church* has not found it necessary to sanction exclusively any one view. The pluriform richness of these images may say there is more here than

one model for understanding can carry. Each view in its own way sheds a light on what remains a profound mystery.

One view sees our predicament as a subjective sense of *guilt* for our *sin* that causes us to turn from *God* and hide in shame. Salvation happens as God's love, which has *already forgiven,* is manifest in Christ. Our hearts are stirred to *repentance* and a response of love. Christ's life, which reveals both who God is and who we are (essentially, in union with God), becomes an "example" or "moral influence" for us. Abelard's view is of this type.

A second model draws upon images from the ancient Jewish sacrificial system. Here the priest is seen as the *mediator* between God and *humanity,* offering sacrifices to atone for sin. Blood is shed— in expiation, not propitiation—as a sign of the people's sorrow for their sin. In this model, Christ is presented as our great high priest (Hebrews), who lays down his own life as sacrifice in our behalf.

A third model draws upon military images. God and the devil are pictured as locked in combat over the destiny of humankind. Christ is the warrior of God who, after having been apparently defeated on the cross, by his *death* invades the realm of the evil one and does battle with sin and death and the devil. In the *resurrection,* Christ shows himself victorious (Christus Victor) and leads out of captivity those who had been carried off (Mark 3:23–27; 1 Cor. 15:24–28).

A financial image gives yet another angle of vision. Here the human condition is compared to slavery or imprisonment. We are in bondage or are held captive by the forces of evil. Christ offers his own life as our ransom. We are "redeemed" at great cost.

Yet another model, which has perhaps been the most prominent for Western Christianity, is the juridical model. In its early presentation, which was developed in a feudal context (Anselm, *Cur Deus Homo?*), it portrayed God as an overlord against whom a vassal had committed a crime. The seriousness of a crime in feudal culture depended upon whom it was committed against. Since the crime was against God, an infinite guilt was incurred. Only an infinite restitution—which only God could provide—could satisfy the demands of *justice*. But it is the offender who must pay. Therefore, only a human being could make restitution. Thus, the only resolution possible would be restitution offered by one who was fully human and fully divine.

This "satisfaction" model was modified somewhat by Calvin's day to a courtroom drama with God as the judge and human beings as lawbreakers. The verdict is "guilty," and the sentence is "death," but a righteous person stands in defense and offers "substitution," taking the punishment due to the offenders upon himself.

Calvin made use of all these images, even the subjective "Christ as example" model. "Christ . . . has been set before us as an example, whose pattern we ought to express in our life" (*Inst.* 3.6.3). Calvin draws most frequently upon the mediator image (*Inst.* 3.11.9) as a way of thinking about Christ's reconciling work. Our primary predicament is alienation from God. We need one who can mediate and bring reconciliation. In this model, as all others, Calvin wants to show that the reconciling is God's work in Christ. He opposes and avoids any bifurcation that pictures God as wrathful and desirous of our destruction and Christ as merciful and desirous of our salvation—Christ over against God. "God was in Christ, reconciling the world" (2 Cor. 5:19).

The juridical model is also frequently employed by Calvin. It provides a way of articulating *justification* and *forgiveness* of sins, which are central to Calvin's understanding of salvation. So prominent in the Reformation, this view of salvation was cast in the Pauline, juridical terms of "justification by grace through faith." Calvin follows Paul, but with interesting nuances.

For Calvin, the original sin was unbelief—not believing in God, turning to our own resources. We are, in Augustine's words, *incurvatus in se*. That fundamental disorientation led to a corruption of our true relation to God and consequently a corruption of our true nature. This in turn is manifest in the multitude of "sins" imaged as "lawbreaking." The fundamental need is for reconciliation to God—a renewal of our relationship with God—and forgiveness of sins (which were the consequences of our disorientation from God).

If unbelief is the root sin, then it follows that *faith* is the locus of God's saving activity. This faith is God's gift to us. For Calvin, faith is engendered in us by God's Word (*Inst.* 3.2.6) and Spirit (*Inst.* 3.1.4), and it works to renew our relationship to God. Reversing the order that Luther proposed, Calvin insists that faith precedes repentance, that repentance is in fact a consequence of faith (*Inst.* 3.3.1). Because we have received *grace* and the promise of salvation we are moved and enabled to repent. In a sense we are forgiven before we repent, by God's grace, on God's initiative—not our own. Salvation is not a matter of bringing external influences to bear in order to change God's mind about us. Faith is a firm and certain knowledge of God's benevolence toward us (*Inst.* 3.2.7) This knowledge provides a confidence and security that frees us from ourselves—from being *incurvatus in se*. We no longer live in unbelief, having continually to secure ourselves. We have faith in God and know ourselves to be ultimately secured.

Not only are we justified, we are also sanctified. We experience a "double grace" of reconciliation and *regeneration*. In true repentance, what happens is a "mortification" of the flesh (dying to the old self-preoccupied way of being) and a "vivification" by the Spirit. The regeneration the Spirit works in us restores the image of God that has been disfigured and all but obliterated. Calvin assumes that our justification will have real effects in our lives, that faith will issue in good works. Yet all good works are, like faith, not our own—a cause for boasting—but are a gift of God.

Calvin did not see this *sanctification* as a state of sinless perfection but as a process in which our hearts, minds, and wills come ever more into agreement with God's purposes for us. We become children of God, receiving the spirit of *adoption*. "Christ is not outside us but dwells within us. . . . With a wonderful communion, day by day, he grows more and more into one body with us, until he becomes completely one with us" (*Inst.* 3.2.24). In this way of putting the matter, Calvin took a more modest line than Andreas Osiander, who claimed that Christ's righteousness is "infused" into us by our unity with God in Christ so we actually "are righteous." This essential righteousness enables God to justify us. Calvin countered that Christ's righteousness is "imputed" to us. One is justified when, excluded from the righteousness of works, one grasps the righteousness of Christ through faith and, clothed in it, appears to God not as a sinner but as righteous. There is both acquittal from guilt and imputation of righteousness (*Inst.* 3.3.10), but there is no hint of sinless perfection.

Calvin's third use of the *law is* as a guide for life under the Spirit's ongoing work of sanctification. The main stress is on the positive nature of the "saved" life. As mentioned above, the term carries the sense of health and wholeness of the human being. It is not only "safety" but essential soundness or completeness— the fullest realization of human powers and values. The saved life is the fully human life—not lifted out of its finitude and creatureliness but spacious and unhindered, authentic and spontaneous, no longer *incurvatus in se* but now set free for God and others.

ANNA CASE-WINTERS

Sanctification   The *doctrine* of sanctification has been a bone of contention in the *church* through the ages. Among areas of controversy are the interdependence of sanctification and *justification*; the relation of *faith* and love; the interplay of *grace* and works; the role of the

Christian life in our *salvation*; the tension between personal holiness and the righteousness of Christ; and the question of rewards.

Different understandings. The Roman Catholic view, developed by the mystics and the scholastic theologians, and formally articulated by the Council of Trent, tends to subordinate justification to sanctification. We are justified to the degree that we are sanctified. Justifying grace enables us to cooperate with the Spirit in living a sanctified life—a process often called deification or divinization. Faith by itself is deemed insufficient to justify us: Faith must be formed or fulfilled by love. In Catholic mysticism, metaphors of the ladder and mountain were often used to illustrate the ascent of the believer to divinity, an ascent involving purgation and illumination and finally culminating in mystical *union* and ecstasy.

Luther's emphasis was on the justification of the ungodly. *God* comes to us while we are yet in our sins and pronounces us just on the basis of the perfect righteousness of Jesus Christ. The mystical union with Christ, already realized in faith, enables us to do works that glorify God. Faith in itself is passive, but it becomes active in obedience as the Spirit works within us. We are justified by grace alone through faith, and good works flow spontaneously and inevitably out of the commitment of faith.

Luther was emphatic that our justification and sanctification are based on the alien righteousness of Christ, which covers our sinfulness and makes us acceptable before God. He made a firm distinction between the righteousness of faith, which justifies us, and the righteousness of life, which attests our sanctification. The latter is a consequence and fruit of the former, but it is always incomplete, for the old nature is never entirely extirpated. Christians are righteous and sinners at the same time—righteous because our *sin* is covered by the perfect righteousness of Christ and sinful because in and of ourselves we are still prone to follow the cravings of the flesh.

Whenever Luther employed the ladder imagery of Christian mysticism, it expressed the descent of Christ to sinful *humanity,* not the ascent of the Christian to divinity. Instead of the Augustinian synthesis of *caritas* (Lat.) in which grace makes possible the human ascent, Luther revived the NT motif of *agapē* (Gr.) in which God's love descends to the world of sin in order to serve and heal. Christians become instruments of divine love sent into the world to be servants of all. On the basis of faith we become sons and daughters of God, but through the power of love we become virtual gods, since we are now the hands by which God shapes a new world.

Luther also made use of the metaphor of the ship, representing *baptism.* If we but stay aboard, we will finally arrive at our destination—glorification with Christ in *heaven.* If we fall away from faith, we need simply to return to our baptism rather than seek a new means of grace such as penance or *confirmation.*

Calvin, like Luther, regarded justification as primarily a forensic act by which the holy and merciful God cancels our debts on the basis of the merits of Christ. He too viewed justification as the ground of our salvation, but Calvin tried to hold justification and sanctification in balance. Whereas justification is an event, sanctification is a gradual process. Justification is a change of status, sanctification a change in being. In justification we are covered by the righteousness of Christ; in sanctification (or *regeneration*) we are engrafted into this righteousness. The basis of sanctification is justification; the goal of justification is our sanctification and glorification.

Whereas Luther portrayed the life of the Christian as moving forward but often slipping backward, Calvin's emphasis was on moving upward to Christian perfection through divine grace. Yet this is a broken ascent, because the old nature, though dying, continues to reassert itself. Paradoxically, it is also an ascent that is realized through a descent to the needs of an ailing and lost humanity.

For Calvin, justification and sanctification are complementary, not parallel, terms. This is why he spoke of a twofold blessing. We are never justified apart from the blessing of regeneration. We are never recipients of faith without being motivated to practice love.

Yet even the works of the regenerate, Calvin insisted, are nondeserving of God's grace, accompanied as they always are by motives less than pure; at the same time, these works are not valueless. God crowns our works with God's grace and even rewards them. They are good because they are used by God to advance God's kingdom and give glory to Christ.

The message of the Protestant Reformation was revived by Karl Barth in the twentieth century but given a new thrust. For Barth, justification and sanctification are not successive acts of God but two moments in the one act of reconciliation in Christ. Our salvation was fully realized in its totality once and for all times, and for all humanity, in the sacrificial life and atoning *death* of Jesus Christ. In him we are justified, sanctified, and redeemed. Barth can even say that our *conversion* takes place in Christ, since through Christ's death and *resurrection* the whole world was converted to him. Yet Barth also acknowledges the need for the subjective response to God's act of mercy and redemption; otherwise God's redeeming work would have no practical efficacy in our lives. Barth affirms that we are justified by faith and sanctified by love.

Barth accepts Luther's understanding that the Christian is both righteous and a sinner but insists that sin is now behind us whereas righteousness is before us. In Christ we cannot sin, for we are now rooted in perfect holiness. But the ontological impossibility of falling away from Christ happens again and again, and this is why the life of the Christian is a continuous returning to the fount and anchor of our faith—the cross of Calvary.

As Christians, Barth insists, we can do works that are pleasing to God—not meritorious, since they are performed by sinners, yet nevertheless pleasing to God because they are made possible by God's grace and declare God's righteousness and mercy. Good works are works in which our sin is recognized and confessed. Human righteousness is not divine righteousness but will in some way correspond to it.

The paradox of sanctification. **Reformed theology** holds that our sanctification is a secret work of the Spirit within us, yet it never occurs apart from human effort. The paradox of human striving and *irresistible grace* is certainly evident in Paul (cf. 1 Cor. 15:10; Phil. 2:12–13). The Christian life is both a crown to be won and a gift to be received. We are summoned to run the race and attain the prize but give all the glory to God, since it is God who makes us run and ensures that the prize will be ours.

The role of the Christian is not to procure or earn salvation but to witness to a salvation already accomplished and enacted in Jesus Christ. We are called to work out the implications of our salvation through a life of loving service. The Christian life is a consequence of salvation (Luther), a sign and witness of our salvation (Barth), and also the arena in which the work of salvation is carried forward (Calvin). We are not coredeemers but coworkers in making God's salvation known. We contribute not to the achievement of salvation but to its manifestation and demonstration. We also contribute to its extension (Calvin), since our works may well be used by the Spirit of God to bring outsiders into the kingdom. We do not build the kingdom, but we can be instrumental in its advance.

Errors to be avoided. Among the errors that Reformed theologians have warned against are the following: confounding justification with sanctification, for then *forgiveness* is not entirely gratuitous; viewing justification as wholly extrinsic, thereby denying or underplaying its mystical dimension; equating sanctification with works of purification, and so opening the door to legalism and moralism; reducing sanctification to special experiences, such as the second bless-

ing—the error of experientialism and subjectivism; exaggerating the benefits of sanctification, which leads to perfectionism; minimizing the reality of sanctification, which fosters defeatism; and separating *law* and gospel, which denies the law as a guide for the Christian life.

Reformed theology, as set forth by Calvin and Barth, contends for the unity of the law and gospel, seeing one *covenant* in the Bible—a covenant of grace with two dimensions. The so-called covenant of works represents a misunderstanding, especially prominent in rabbinic Judaism. We are freed by grace for obedience to the law. But this is now the law seen in the light of grace—no longer a burden but a privilege, for, paradoxically, in our obedience we realize true *freedom.* In Reformed theology, the second face of the gospel is the law and the second face of the law is the gospel. The law leads us to the gospel, and the gospel directs us back to the law—yet no longer as a legalistic code but now as the law of spirit and life, the law that equips us for service to God's glory.

D. G. Bloesch, *Essentials of Evangelical Theology,* 2 vols. (1978).

DONALD G. BLOESCH

Savoy Declaration of Faith and Order

Some two hundred representatives of 120 Independent churches met at the Savoy Palace (September 29–October 12, 1658) to write this document. Participants included John Owen, Philip Nye, Thomas Goodwin, and William Bridge (the last three had been members of the Westminster Assembly [1643–48]). They prepared a Preface, a Declaration of Faith, and the "Savoy Declaration of the Institution of Churches and the Order Appointed in Them by Jesus Christ."

The Preface affirms the freedom of the Spirit, who does not "whip men into belief . . . but gently leads them into all truth." The Declaration answers the need for a clear articulation of gospel truth; demonstrate agreement with all who "hold fast the necessary foundations of faith and holiness"; and testify to "a great and special work of the holy Ghost," in that a large group of people completed in only eleven days. Finally, it will prove that the ascended Christ "will . . . be with his own Institutions to the end of the world." The objective is humbly to give an account of their *faith*, "and not so much to instruct others, or convince gainsayers." (However, in presenting it to Richard Cromwell on October 14, 1658, Goodwin said the authors wished to contradict the "scandal . . . affixed upon us, viz., That Independentism [as they call it] is the sink of all Heresies and Schisms.")

Doctrinally and verbally the Declaration largely follows the *Westminster Confession.* However, it strengthens Westminster's Trinitarianism, introduces the language of *federal theology,* and speaks of Christ's active and passive obedience. It revises the Westminster's "Of Repentance unto Life," adding "and Salvation" to the title. "Of the Gospel, and of the Extent of the Grace Thereof" (ch. 20) is entirely new. The power of the civil magistrate is curtailed compared with Westminster, and whereas the latter includes, Savoy omits the children of believers from the catholic church. Savoy adds a paragraph on the tranquillity the churches of Christ will enjoy in the latter days.

The concept of *covenant* is present throughout the Declaration's thirty paragraphs on church *polity,* but the term is not used. Particular churches are appointed by Christ's *authority,* and "Besides these particular Churches, there is not instituted by Christ any church more extensive or Catholique. . . ." Such churches comprise pastors, teachers, *elders,* and members, the officers being chosen by the members. The latter are "Saints by Calling," who "do willingly consent to walk together according to the appointment of Christ, giving up themselves to the Lord, and to one another by the will of God in professed subjection to the Ordinances of the Gospel." *Church discipline* is required, and "all Believers are bound to join themselves to particular Churches, when and where they have opportunity so to do." Provision is made for advisory synods comprising messengers sent by the churches (not comprising whole churches as advocated by Robert Browne) and for the reception of members of other true churches as occasional communicants.

A. G. Matthew, ed., *The Savoy Declaration of Faith and Order* (1959); Schaff, *Creeds* 3:829–33; A. P. F. Sell, "Confessing the Faith in English Congregationalism," in *Dissenting Thought and the Life of the Churches* (1990).

ALAN P. F. SELL

Scholasticism A term first used in a derogatory sense by humanists in the sixteenth century. It is now applied to any theology in which concerns with logic and method are prominent, where theology is conceived as a type of science.

A scholastic movement flourished during the Middle Ages (1050–1500). Anselm, Abelard, Bonaventure, Thomas Aquinas, Duns Scotus, and William of Ockham were prominent figures. They also influenced later scholasticism. Reformed scholasticism of the last half of the sixteenth century and the seventeenth century had contemporary parallels in a Lutheran and a Catholic scholasticism. Reformed scholasticism has had a major influence on the development of the Reformed/Calvinist tradition.

Erasmus popularized the negative image of the schoolmen as boring, tradition-bound professors who focused on useless subtleties. Calvin also refers to the schoolmen in derogatory terms, though on occasion concedes the value of their careful analysis. Erasmus and Calvin were reacting to late-medieval scholasticism in which debates had often grown sterile. Both wished to return to a study of the Bible itself, a study directed by the liberal arts.

After Calvin, a new scholasticism was inevitable, for every great thinker has followers who teach and interpret his thought. The seeds of Reformed scholasticism were sown with the founding of the Geneva Academy. Theodore Beza, called by Calvin to teach there, is an early Reformed scholastic. In many ways, Beza's thought is simply a clear, consistent exposition of Calvin's position, but the systematizing and ordering, the further elaboration of difficult points regarding the inspiration of *scripture*, *predestination*, and limited *atonement*, modified Calvin's position in significant ways.

Reformed scholasticism is, however, more than just a simplifying and systematizing of Calvin's thought. Calvin was only one of a number of significant Reformed leaders. Huldrych Zwingli, Martin Bucer, and John Oecolampadius preceded Calvin, and Peter Martyr Vermigli, Girolamo Zanchi, and Zacharias Ursinus, as well as Beza, were contemporaries. Their contributions, along with Calvin's, became known as *Reformed theology.*

While Calvin was most influenced by humanist attitudes and techniques, Vermigli and Zanchi, both Italians, were educated at Padua, the center of a great Aristotelian revival. In both, but especially in Zanchi, the influence of Aquinas is also evident. Like Beza, Vermigli and Zanchi order the *doctrine* of *God* in terms of divine decrees, resulting in predestination becoming a major point of contention. These three, more than Calvin, are responsible for the prominent place that predestination assumed in Reformed theology.

A notable example of Reformed scholasticism is the *Synod of Dort.* Its formulation of *Calvinism* was under five "heads of doctrine": *total depravity,* unconditional *election,* limited atonement, *irresistible grace,* and *perseverance of the saints.* The most prominent Reformed scholastics in the seventeenth century were Benedict Turretin and his son Francis. Benedict supported the views of the orthodox party at the Synod of Dort and promoted them in Switzerland. His son Francis also defended the

decrees of Dort and argued for the complete inerrancy of scripture. His view is found in the *Helvetic Consensus Formula* (1675) and is still influential today.

ARVIN VOS

Science (Physical)   Physical science includes physics, chemistry, and the earth sciences (astronomy is treated separately under "cosmology"). In the European West, physical science has progressed through four major phases: Aristotelian, post-Aristotelian (Paracelsus, Bacon, Descartes), Newtonian, and post-Newtonian (thermodynamics, field theory, and quantum mechanics).

Aristotelian *philosophy* dominated Western science from the thirteenth to the seventeenth century. It provided a comprehensive picture of the world as known without the aid of instruments that enhance human sense perception. John Calvin's interest in Aristotelian physics is reflected in his sermons and commentaries. Like Martin Luther and Huldrych Zwingli, Calvin accepted the basic Aristotelian picture as a description of universal *providence* but also appealed to phenomena such as the elevation of mountains and the confinement of the seas as indications of particular providence. These "gaps" in Aristotelian science evidenced the continuous activity of *God* in all of nature.

Calvin allowed a limited role for astrology in medical science but criticized what he saw as confusion of the natural and supernatural in Neoplatonism, Hermeticism, and alchemy. He wanted to affirm legitimate science as a *vocation* but was sensitive to any indication of vainglory in eccentrics such as Agrippa and Paracelsus. English reformers such as John Hooper and William Perkins held similar views. However, Reformed physicians of the sixteenth century such as William Turner and Oswald Croll revised the ideas of Paracelsus and helped pave the way for post-Aristotelian chemistry. Seventeenth-century chemists such as Samuel Hartlib and Robert Boyle successfully combined alchemical skills with ideas of the newer mechanical philosophy.

In Elizabethan times, the strategy of finding gaps in physical science was shunned by churchmen such as Thomas Cooper and Richard Hooker and by natural philosophers such as Francis Bacon. God's activity in the present was limited to universal providence. Bacon also stressed the social utility of legitimate science and provided it with a Reformed ideology that was instrumental in the success of the Royal Society of London in the late seventeenth century. Christianity was to be seen in such deeds as the healing of disease and the subduing of the forces of nature as much as in words of *faith* and *forgiveness.*

Much of the seventeenth century was dominated by the philosophy of Descartes, which required a strict separation of physical science and theology. This tactic was stoutly resisted by Gisbert Voetius at Utrecht but was defended by Johannes Cocceius at Leiden and later accepted by Francis Turretin of Geneva.

In the late seventeenth century, Isaac Newton revised the mechanical philosophy and combined the notion of inert matter with faith in a God who acts directly through space and force. In the eighteenth century, the son of a Swiss Reformed minister, Leonhard Euler, contributed to the foundations of mathematics and mechanics along more Cartesian lines. English Independent ministers who accepted the new science include Isaac Watts and Joseph Priestley, the latter being partly responsible for the discovery of oxygen. The American Congregationalist minister Cotton Mather and the son of a Dutch Reformed minister, Hermann Boerhaave, were able to combine the new physics with older ideas concerning the direct involvement of spirits in matter without any apparent sense of inconsistency. At a philosophical level, Jonathan Edwards tried to bring out a more direct dependence of all matter on God.

In the nineteenth century, science became increasingly technical and professional, while *Reformed theology* was influenced by romanticism and revivalism.

Some twentieth-century Reformed theologians who have treated scientific ideas seriously are Emil Brunner, John Baillie, T. F. Torrance, and Harold Nebelsick.

J. Dillenberger, *Protestant Thought and Natural Science* (1960); C. B. Kaiser, *Creation and the History of Science* (1990); E. Klaaren, *Religious Origins of Modern Science* (1977); D. C. Lindberg and R. L. Numbers, *God and Nature* (1986); R. Westfall, *Science and Religion in Seventeenth-Century England* (1958).
CHRISTOPHER B. KAISER

Scots Confession The proclamation and testimony of faith of the Scottish reformers, accepted by Parliament and the Reformed Church of Scotland (1560), accorded civil legal status in 1567. The confession belongs to the Reformed family of *confessions* and reflects the Geneva-Zurich doctrinal consensus. Militant, cordial, and evangelical in style, it became the chief subordinate doctrinal standard of the Scottish church, presbyterian or episcopalian, until superseded by the *Westminster Confession* (1647).

Decisive in the confession's composition and adoption was the intervention of Protestant England to help liberate Scotland from Catholic French interests. A companion text to the Book of Discipline, the confession was drawn up by the "six Johns"—Knox, Willock, Winram, Spottiswoode, Row, and Douglas.

The first ten of the confession's twenty-five articles embody the Catholic doctrinal traditions of the early *church.* The remainder reflect the characteristic controversial theology of the age, treating *faith, justification, sanctification, scripture,* the offices of Christ, the civil power, the church, and *sacraments.* Distinctive is the combination of systematic and biblical *heilsgeschichtliche* ("salvation history") theology. Notable also is the stress on ecclesiology, the sacramental eating of Christ's flesh and blood, and Christian ethics, the right to rebel against tyranny. *Predestination* is not highlighted.

The voice of John Calvin in the confession is clearly identifiable but less exclusive and authentic than usually assumed. A Latin translation was published (1572). Alongside the confession, the Scottish church also sanctioned the Genevan English Confession, the *Second Helvetic Confession* (1566), and the acrimonious Negative Confession or *King's Confession* (1581).

K. Barth, *The Knowledge of God and the Service of God according to the Teaching of the Reformation* (1938); A. C. Cochrane, ed., *Reformed Confessions of the 16th Century* (1966); W. I. A. Hazlett, "The Scots Confession: Context, Complexion, and Critique," *ARH* 78 (1987): 287–320; G. D. Henderson, ed., *The Scots Confession, 1560* (1960); P. Jacobs, *Theologie reformierter Bekentnisschriften in Grundzügen* (1959); J. Knox, *History of the Reformation*, ed. W. C. Dickinson (1949); W. Niesel, ed., *Bekenntnisschriften und Kirchenordnungen* (1938); E. Routley, *Creeds and Confessions* (1962).

W. IAN A. HAZLETT

Scripture   The *doctrine* of scripture has been prominent in the Reformed faith. Scripture is one aspect of the *Word of God* and the medium through which God's self-revelation in Jesus Christ is made present by the witness of the *Holy Spirit.*

Reformed confessions. Over against sixteenth-century Roman Catholicism, the *Scots Confession* maintained scripture's *authority* "to be from God," not from the *church* which established the canon (*BC* 3.19). *God* communicates through scripture, which presents "the holy gospel" of Jesus Christ (HC, q. 19) received by *faith,* whereby one accepts "as true all that God has revealed" in God's Word (HC, q. 21). "Scripture is the Word of God" (*BC* 5.003) where the church has "the most complete exposition of all that pertains to a saving

faith, and also to the framing of a life acceptable to God" (Second Helvetic Confession; *BC* 5.002). The scriptures are the basis for the church's *preaching*: "The preaching of the Word of God is the Word of God" (*BC* 5.004). Preaching is made effective by "the inward illumination of the Spirit" (*BC* 5.005); yet this "inward illumination does not eliminate external preaching" (*BC* 5.006).

The relationship of scripture and the Holy Spirit (Word and Spirit) is developed more fully in the *WCF* (*BC* 6.001–.005). There the canon of scripture is identified as "the Word of God written" and all canonical books said to have been "given by inspiration of God, to be the rule of faith and life" (*BC* 6.002). This formulation focuses attention on scripture's *scopus,* or purpose. God is said to be "the author" of scripture, a way of stressing that scripture "is to be received, because it is the Word of God" (*BC* 6.004). While many external considerations might move and induce people to esteem scripture, "yet, notwithstanding, our full persuasion and assurance of the infallible truth and divine authority" of scripture come from "the inward work of the Holy Spirit, bearing witness by and with the Word in our hearts" (*BC* 6.005). Scripture is to be interpreted in reliance on the Spirit, and while "all things in Scripture are not alike plain in themselves, . . . yet those things which are necessary to be known, believed, and observed, for salvation, are so clearly propounded and opened in some place of Scripture or other, that not only the learned, but the unlearned, in a due use of the ordinary means, may attain unto a sufficient understanding of them" (*BC* 6.007).

The *Theological Declaration of Barmen* emphasizes that the church is built on "the gospel of Jesus Christ as it is attested for us in Holy Scripture" (*BC* 8.05). It is "Jesus Christ, as he is attested for us in Holy Scripture," who is "the one Word of God which we have to hear and which we have to trust and obey in life and in death" (*BC* 8.11). The *Confession of 1967* indicates that Jesus Christ is known as the Holy

Spirit "bears unique and authoritative witness through the Holy Scriptures, which are received and obeyed as the Word of God written" (*BC* 9.27). While the scriptures are given under the "guidance of the Holy Spirit," they are nevertheless human words "conditioned by the language, thought forms, and literary fashions of the places and times at which they were written" (*BC,* 9.29).

Theological formulations. Three emphases on scripture have characterized various Reformed theologians. The **Princeton Theology** of Charles Hodge, B. B. Warfield, and A. A. Hodge saw scripture as a book of inerrant facts. Scripture's inerrancy—its complete accuracy on all matters of science, history, or geography on which it teaches—was considered a crucial part of scripture's authority, since scripture as "God's Word" shares in God's perfection of truth. This meant that scripture was "verbally inspired" and was the source for all doctrinal belief. Thus, "the Scriptures are the word of God in such a sense that their words deliver the truth of God without error" (Warfield).

Karl Barth stressed scripture as the "witness to Jesus Christ" that "becomes" authoritative as a form of the Word of God as through it one encounters the living Christ by the work of the Holy Spirit. Because scripture is written by humans who "witnessed" to God's *revelation* in Jesus Christ, the biblical texts are not to be perceived as inerrant in the sense of presenting unerring accounts, since they were written by fallible writers. Scripture was "inspired," for Barth, insofar as it witnesses to scripture's special content: the Word of God, Jesus Christ.

Calvin, Reformed *confessions,* and theologians such as Abraham Kuyper, Herman Bavinck, and Gerrit C. Berkouwer have emphasized scripture as presenting a divine message in human thought forms. The purpose of scripture is not to present inerrant facts; yet it is "infallible" in that it will not lie or deceive about what it is intended to focus upon: God's salvation in Jesus Christ. In this view, scripture is seen in relation to its central purpose, the proclamation of the gospel (John 20:31). The Spirit witnesses to scripture's content. Scripture is infallible in accomplishing its purpose.

Barth, *CD* I/1; I/2; G. C. Berkouwer, *Holy Scripture* (1975); D. G. Bloesch, *Holy Scripture* (1994); D. K. McKim, *The Bible in Theology and Preaching* (1994); Rogers and McKim, *AIB*; B. B. Warfield, *Inspiration and Authority of the Bible,* 2nd ed. (1948).

DONALD K. MCKIM

Sense of Divinity

Part of the theological attempt to understand the origin, condition, and value of the human aspiration toward *God* is the sense of divinity (*sensus divinitatis* or *deitatis*). In Western intellectual history, this powerful yearning toward the Eternal is classically described with the concept of *erōs* by Plato in his dialogue *Symposium.*

For Christians, the **doctrine** of **creation** includes the conviction that human beings are made in God's image (Gen. 1:26) and that evidences of deity are manifest and can be known in the external world and within the created self. This **natural theology** can be developed by the unaided human **reason** and differs from revealed theology based on God's **revelation** in **scripture** and made effectual by the inner testimony of the **Holy Spirit.** The **sin** of humankind against God, as it affects this original and natural condition, is variously evaluated. Roman Catholic theology, with its higher view of the capacities of human reason and will surviving the fall, distinguishes between natural and supernatural virtues. Likewise, the ability of natural reason to demonstrate the existence of God is generally more esteemed in Catholicism than in Protestantism. In Reformed thought, the category of natural theology is smaller than in Roman Catholicism because the effect of sin is considered greater. Concerning the fall, **Reformed theology** teaches "total depravity." This does not mean that every human being is entirely evil but insists that reason and will cannot be even relatively and successfully followed apart from God's guiding *providence* and the necessity of the *forgiveness* revealed in Jesus Christ. While vestiges of the original creation remain, sin results in complete, rather than partial, estrangement from God.

According to John Calvin, in our estranged condition God is known in a twofold way as both creator and redeemer. The *knowledge of God* the creator can be seen in creation and the knowledge of God the redeemer is seen in the face of Jesus Christ. The sense of divinity, referring to the knowledge of God the creator, is universally and indelibly imprinted within created nature. Thus, Paul (Rom. 1:19–24) is interpreted to teach that genuine knowledge of God the creator is objectively possible and valid but cannot produce *salvation* because human iniquity renders such natural knowledge inadequate and ineffective.

The Christian doctrine of God the creator as it has issued in a modest, but real, natural theology has led some Reformed thinkers to emphasize the doctrine of universal providence as a way of constructing a Calvinistic worldview (or philosophy) relatively independent of *faith* on the basis of "sanctified reason." In recent times, Karl Barth leveled a severe criticism of all "natural theology."

E. A. Dowey, Jr., *The Knowledge of God in Calvin's Theology* (1952; repr. 1964); B. B. Warfield, *Calvin and Calvinism* (1931).

CHARLES PARTEE

Shorter Catechism　*see* Westminster Confession of Faith

Sin The Reformed tradition has always contained a virulent idea of sin. Having entered the human condition by *original sin*, sin renders human existence both tragic and miserable and takes on a life of its own.

Most often the tradition regards sin as the human transgression of God's *covenant*, which represents God's active will for every human society and individual. Having sinned once, a person compounds the simple sin by rationalizing the behavior, typically: "I didn't do anything so bad; I'll do better next time." The first part fails to take God's will seriously. The second part fixes attention on doing more exactly what the covenant requires. Both parts gloss over the sin and its effects, justify the action, and set up a trap from which there is no human way out. Henceforth the sinner either sinks into gross and overt sins by ignoring the covenant altogether or becomes more sinful by trying to attain a self-sufficient goodness that comes from merely doing the works of the covenant. Attention to the covenant (and to the *sinner's* accomplishments) replaces attention to the covenant-maker, *God*, and the harder a sinner tries to be good according to the covenant, the more sinful the person becomes.

A person's first sin makes the person a sinner. But the trap puts the sinner into a condition of sin that leads to constant sinning with every thought, word, and deed. The sinner is not all bad, just never all good; and sinners alone or in society cannot discern clearly which part is which, since the good and the bad are intermingled. Every action of the sinner is at least partially skewed, no matter how well intentioned—the *doctrine* of total depravity.

Such sin perverts the good things God provides, none of which are intrinsically evil. The most notable items perverted are the God-given covenant, the sinner's own thinking-willing-acting capacities, and the larger world of nature. As a perversion of the good, sin lodges in certain focal points of human outlook, behavior, and relationship. Most often mentioned are pride (self-worth turned to ambition, power, fame), desire (become self-serving in sex, money, self-indulgence), truth (turned to ideology or unreality), *freedom* (independence without relationship or responsibility), obedience (as blind loyalty, disobedience), and *faith* (as an end in itself, unbelief). The list could be lengthened indefinitely.

Surrounded by sin and sin's effects, the sinner takes sin to be normal and natural for human life. The awareness of sin comes to sinners when God's *grace* breaks in, particular grace to particular people. Grace gives people the heart to see their lives as God sees them, loved and upheld by God but at the same time deformed and unworthy of love. Reformed *piety* builds on this dynamic of grace and sin, sin and grace *beginning with* the move from grace to sin.

Different views of sin correspond with views of the *atonement*. For the substitutionary atonement, wherein Jesus Christ on the cross takes upon himself the *punishment* due humans for their sins (forgives the debt, suffers the loss, pays the price), sin is disobedience, a moral misdeed, a violation of the covenant or some relational code. For the classical theory of atonement, wherein Jesus Christ *defeats death* by dying on the cross, occupying the space of *death* and transforming death into the gateway to life, sin in its extreme form is death ("the last enemy to be defeated"; 1 Cor. 15:26; cf. 15:56; Heb. 2:14–15), both physical and spiritual. For the moral influence theory of atonement, wherein Jesus Christ taught *how to live a transformed life before God* and exemplified that life in his own full *humanity,* sin is an insufficient consciousness of God reflected in imperfect understanding, ignorance, bad attitudes, psychological maladjustments, and/or the breakdown of basic relationships.

The three views of sin suggest different levels of scope and concern. As imperfect God-consciousness, sin pertains to the inner, relational life of the human both individually and collectively. As moral misdeed, sin entails the behavior of the whole person outwardly and socially as well as inwardly and individually. As victory over death, sin involves the continuing problem and impact of evil, rooted in nature as well as in human life.

Calvin and Barth successfully blended all three views of sin and atonement. Other Reformed Christians, however, have compartmentalized sin in one view held singly, each one competing with the other two. In the late twentieth century, sin was regarded variously as individuals' private moral misdeeds (emphasis on substitutionary atonement; seventeenth to twentieth century), the realm of the inner person and one's damaged relationships (emphasis on moral influence atonement, nineteenth to twentieth centuries), and the sins of particular social contexts (the social dimension of the two previous items, notably in the twentieth century: the poor in relation to the rich, mixed races, women and men, the use and abuse of personal, corporate, and military power).

Additional questions deserve to be raised. In an era of advanced technology, can any human technological accomplishment be morally neutral without restructuring further the cycles of natural and human life? Have the structures and inequities of human society become so large and self-serving that they invariably oppress people and particular groups of people? Has the scale of evil in the twentieth century—world wars, the Holocaust, genocide, the threat of nuclear annihilation, apartheid, unrelieved famines, the disruption of the environment, epidemics of substance abuse and AIDS—outstripped views of sin currently held singly? How have the varieties of people, ideologies, and ways of living complicated present attempts to identify and address what is sinful in particular situations and contexts?

Barth, *CD* III/3, 50; IV/1, 60; IV/2, 65; IV/3, 70; G. C. Berkouwer, *Sin* (1971); Calvin, *Inst.* 1.1–2 and bk. 2; Heppe, *RD*, 301–70; Schleiermacher, *CF*.
MERWYN S. JOHNSON

Social Gospel

Though Presbyterians in Scotland, Canada, and the United States had interest in "the social gospel," the Social Gospel movement was primarily an American phenomenon (1870–1913). The term was coined during the 1870s as a few clergy began to respond to social ills related to industrialization, urbanization, and immigration. Social Gospel leaders expressed concerns for labor problems, "workers," and the cities through sermons, lectures, books, and articles. Along with "progressives" and "muckrakers," they alerted the public to the excesses of laissez-faire capitalism.

Social Gospel leaders were also concerned about political unrest and the possibility of class warfare. Theirs was a world where church members were unsettled by social and intellectual change, especially by talk of Darwinism and higher biblical criticism.

Strictly speaking, there was no Social Gospel among Presbyterians in America. Social Gospel leaders included two Baptists, Walter Rauschenbusch and William Newton Clarke, and two Congregationalists, Washington Gladden and Josiah Strong. Though Baptists and Congregationalists can claim to belong to the Reformed family, it was differences in theology and *polity* between Presbyterians, and Baptists and Congregationalists, that explain why there was no Presbyterian Social Gospel movement.

The Reformed is a tradition "especially of the word, elevating preaching, teaching (doctrine), and ethical practice to the forefront of its concerns. Thus confessional documents have always had a prominent place in its history, especially in the education and ordination of ministers" (Purdy, 13). Social Gospel leaders considered confessional statements and Calvinist theology a hindrance to social and moral progress. They were caught up in a "new" theology, one that adjusted the scorned "old" Calvinist theology to "present-day living." They preached a gospel calculated to inspire believers to emulate the life and character of Jesus so "the church" would lend moral force to the social progress they expected to usher in the *kingdom of God* in America.

At a time when Social Gospel leaders were revising theology and their use of the Bible, Presbyterians reacted to the threat of higher biblical criticism with the heresy trial of David Swing, a Chicago pastor who was both a "modernist" and an "evangelical" (1874). Though Swing won the case, the point was clear: Presbyterians would continue to subscribe to the Westminster Standards. This was the same decade in which the Baptist Clarke would decide that the ethical propositions of the NT "sweep away" the "ancient truth" of the OT.

Church historians usually relate Presbyterian failure to participate in the Social Gospel movement to class commitments. "The reasons for the relative conservatism of this denomination are obvious. Its members, especially the influential city elements, were traditionally of the upper social and economic groups. Through the important part played by elders in Presbyterian church government, wealthy laymen had an especially influential role" (May, 193). Reformed polity's capacity to enforce doctrinal conformity also helps account for the extent to which the *Princeton Theology*—which served the interests of the status quo—was dominant.

Presbyterians were not unaware of the plight of the lower class and labor problems. But the denomination took no formal action until the 1910 *General Assembly* approved Thirteen Social Principles. Till then, most references to social problems were appeals to evangelism to overcome threats of "Socialist anarchy." The Social Principles called for an end to child labor, a minimum wage, better working conditions, shorter working day, and the right to organize unions. This agenda was the work of Social Gospel leaders from other denominations.

Presbyterians established a Department of Church and Labor in the Board of Home Missions (1903). Approval of the Social Principles and the Labor Department were primarily the work of one man, Charles Stelzle. An ordained clergyman, Stelzle was the son of working class immigrants. When the controversial Labor

Department he headed was discontinued (1913), he went into social work.

Stelzle belonged to a small minority of Presbyterians who wanted to "socialize" church teachings. Though Reformed *piety* includes a sense of responsibility for the public good, Presbyterians in the United States have rarely expressed concern about economic issues. Members are encouraged to be informed citizens who vote. Education is the usual response to social and moral issues. The Presbyterian confessional stance did protect *Reformed theology* from a naive social idealism that led to the demise of the Social Gospel (1913). But it also led to callous indifference to social injustice.

C. Evans, ed., *The Social Gospel Today* (2001); H. F. May, *Protestant Churches and Industrial America* (1949); J. C. Purdy, ed., *Always Being Reformed* (1985).

JANET F. FISHBURN

Socinianism   The religious movement named for Faustus Socinus (1539–1604). Socinus attempted to unify the various factions of Unitarianism. The chief symbol of the Socinians, the Racovian Catechism, was composed immediately after his death. The movement proceeded through Poland, Germany, the Netherlands, and Transylvania. It was frequently confronted with persecution.

Socinianism's unique teachings include the view that the *doctrine* of the *Trinity* was neither presented in nor deducible from *scripture*. Socinians said the *Holy Spirit* is nowhere called *God* in scripture. The preexistence of Christ was denied, and the view that while Christ was on earth the divine and human natures could not be fully united was affirmed (for certainly Christ could not have then died on the cross). Socinians generally held that a plurality of persons in one divine essence was not possible. Despite the ambiguity in Socinus's own teaching, Socinianism held to the total immersion of the adult believer and that Christians were not to use the sword.

J. H. S. Kent, "The Socinian Tradition," *Theology* (1975): 131–41; G. H. Williams, *The Radical Reformation* (1962).

RICHARD C. GAMBLE

Soteriology   *see* **Salvation**

Spirituality   *see* **Piety**

Stewardship   The biblical term "steward" (Gr. *oikonomos*) describes the office of one who is entrusted with the properties of another. While there are twenty-six direct references to stewards and stewardship in *scripture*, the concept was insufficiently developed in historical theology. In North America and other settings where the church could no longer count on public (state) support, stewardship practice as tithing or the donation of "time, talents, and treasures" to the church became an important aspect of ecclesiastical life. The deeper application of the biblical term as a symbolic expression for the whole Christian (and human) life has, however, only begun to inform theological discourse profoundly in our own time.

Biblical background. The OT usage confines itself to the technical meaning of the term but in doing so establishes the two dialectically related ideas that inform the more symbolic use of stewardship—accountability and responsibility. On the one hand, the steward is a servant (often a slave!) and strictly accountable to his master; on the other, he is given an exceptional range of freedom as one bearing high responsibility. Being accountable, he may be judged severely for the misuse of the trust placed in him (Isa. 22:15–16); yet this presupposes the honor of the office (e.g., Gen. 43; 44).

Some NT references are simple allusions to the office (Matt. 20:8; Luke 8:3; John 2:8); in others, a more explicitly theological connotation is present. Luke 12:42 links stewardship with "watchfulness" as a characteristic mark of Christ's true disciples. In 1 Cor. 4:1–2, Paul applies the concept of the steward explicitly to himself and implicitly to the *church* at large: "Think of us in this way, as servants of Christ and stewards of God's mysteries."

History. Despite its relative biblical prominence, stewardship did not achieve its potential for theological and anthropological significance in historical *doctrine.* Two factors contributed to its underdevelopment: (1) the spiritualization of Christian doctrine under the impact of Hellenistic thought and (2) the political establishment of the Christian religion from the fourth century onward. While there are of course exegetical references to the term in all periods, its capacity to transmit something of the worldly significance of Christian discipleship and function critically with respect to other "images of the human" was not explored. Though the Reformers advanced cognate ideas, only John Wycliffe made fairly extensive use of the steward metaphor as such.

With the loss of legal "establishment" in New World and other situations, Protestant churches found in stewardship a significant biblical basis for responsible financial and other support of the church's life and mission. This has kept the term alive, particularly in the North American context. At the same time, it has reduced its biblical profundity by applying it too exclusively to church giving.

Present status. Stimulated in part by secular appropriation of the metaphor, contemporary theology has begun to explore the potentiality of stewardship as a symbol of human *vocation* and meaning. The three "great instabilities" of the age (injustice, *war,* and environmental deterioration) have inspired many to see in the ancient biblical concept an alternative on the one hand to human *mastery* (we are *accountable*) and on the other to human *passivity* (we are *responsible*). The symbol is used extensively in the Confession of Faith of the Reformed Church of Cuba and in numerous recent documents of Presbyterian and other Protestant denominations in the United States,

Canada, and Europe. It was an integral component of the many documents that emerged from the WCC's "Justice, Peace, and the Integrity of Creation" process.

D. J. Hall, *The Steward: A Biblical Symbol Come of Age* (1990) and *Imagining God: Dominion as Stewardship* (1986); T. S. Horvath, *Focus on Our Identity as Stewards* (1987); T. A. Kantonen, *A Theology for Christian Stewardship* (1956); J. van Klinken, *Diakonia: Mutual Helping with Justice and Compassion* (1989).

DOUGLAS JOHN HALL

Supralapsarianism   One of the two main positions on *election* after the death of John Calvin. In dispute was the place of the fall in God's electing purposes. As the term implies (*supra,* "above" or "before," and *lapsus,* "fall"), supralapsarianism affirmed that *God* decreed both election and *reprobation* from all eternity without respect to the merits or demerits of persons. It differed from *infralapsarianism* (*infra,* "below" or "after," and *lapsus,* "fall"), which held that in *predestination* God had in view sinful *humanity,* of whom God elected some and passed by others. Expressed differently, the object of predestination in supralapsarianism was the human race as not yet created and not yet fallen (*homo creabilis et labilis*) and in infralapsarianism, the human race as already created and fallen (*creatus et lapsus*). For infralapsarianism, the temporal sequence of *creation,* fall, and *salvation* was also the logical order, while for supralapsarianism, the logical and temporal orders of God's purpose were reversed.

The controversy was subtle yet theologically significant, fiercely debated but not fundamentally divisive. While infralapsarianism became the dominant confessional position of Reformed churches, theologians such as Theodore Beza, Franciscus Gomarus, Franz Burmann, and William Twisse subscribed to supralapsarianism. At the *Synod of Dort,* infralapsarians were in the majority, and while the Canons do not exclude supralapsarianism, the bias is in favor of infralapsarianism. The same is true of the *WCF.*

Though both positions were ultimately unsatisfactory—because the connection between election and the fall is inscrutable—supralapsarianism was more consistent, coherent, and comprehensive in scope. It viewed salvation as God's primary purpose, while infralapsarianism was inclined to see salvation as God's reaction to *sin,* that is, as a kind of emergency measure or redemptive repair work—"Plan B" after "Plan A" had failed. On the other hand, supralapsarianism tended to rationalize sin and evil by viewing them as necessary elements in God's plan, and it was accordingly accused of making God the author of sin. In the eyes of Roman Catholics, Lutherans, and even some Reformed theologians, the God of supralapsarianism took on the appearance of a demon who arbitrarily saved some and damned others, a God who created in order to condemn. By making both election and reprobation unconditional, it was less ethically satisfactory than infralapsarianism, which represented election as unconditional but regarded reprobation as conditional upon human sinfulness.

Attempts to reconcile supralapsarianism and infralapsarianism have not been successful. Karl Barth sought to overcome their respective difficulties by arguing that supralapsarianism is relatively more nearly correct. If supralapsarianism is liberated from the dangerous presuppositions of an absolute decree and the symmetry of election and reprobation, and the doctrine of election is interpreted christologically, with Jesus Christ as the true object of predestination, then, according to Barth, supralapsarianism is preferable. So understood, election is solely and totally grace, "the sum of the gospel." Yet Barth's resolution of the problem is not without its own difficulties, especially with respect to reprobation and the ultimate force of the human creature's "no" to God. It appears that on

the question of the place of the fall in the electing purposes of God, a reverent agnosticism is advisable.

Barth, *CD* II/2, 127ff.; G. C. Berkouwer, *Divine Election* (1960); P. K. Jewett, *Election and Predestination* (1986).
WILLIAM KLEMPA

Synod   *see* **Polity**

Tetrapolitan Confession   The oldest *confession of faith* by the Reformed church in Germany was written (1530), chiefly by Martin Bucer, as a theological exposition of the views of four imperial cities: Strassburg, Constance, Memmingen, and Lindau.

The nascent Reformed church had hoped to effect a union with Lutherans and make common cause in opposition to Roman Catholicism. To this end, Bucer and Zwingli met with Luther and Melanchthon at the *Marburg Colloquy* (1529). Since the attempt to form a single Protestant front failed, Reformed Christians were thereby excluded from the discussions between Lutherans and Catholics at the pivotal Diet of Augsburg (1530).

Nevertheless, Zwingli wrote a confession of faith for the Diet, and the Tetrapolitan Confession was hastily prepared for presentation to the Holy Roman Emperor, Charles V. Later these four cities affirmed the Lutheran Confession and joined the Lutheran Smalcald League.

The irenic Tetrapolitan Confession contains twenty-three chapters. The first deals with the centrality of Holy Scripture in the life of the *church,* and chapters 3 and 4 set forth the *doctrine* of *salvation* by God's *grace* through *faith* and not by works of our own. Since it was on the doctrine of the *Lord's Supper* that Luther most sharply disagreed with Zwingli, Bucer attempted in the Tetrapolitan Confession, and throughout his life, to find a compromise formula that would satisfy both Protestant sides—but without success.

CHARLES PARTEE

Theocracy Apparently coined by Josephus (d. c. A.D. 100) to describe the government of Israel under Moses (Ex. 19:4–9; Deut. 17:14–20), the word "theocracy" literally means "the rule of God" (Gr. *theos*, "God"; *kratein*, "to rule"). Historically, the term has been used mainly to describe a form of government or state in which *God* (or a deity) is regarded as the immediate and supreme ruler, while temporal power is in the hands of an individual or priestly order that claims divine sanction. Some have wrongly regarded Calvin's Geneva, Cromwell's England, and Puritan New England as "theocratic." Calvin shared with theocrats the belief that in the ideal political system the secular authority should be responsible to God and that its goal should be the effectual operation of God's will. However, in Calvin's Geneva the clergy did not govern the state, church and state were separate though interlocking, and prerogatives of the church were jealously guarded. Further, Calvin taught that the ideal form of government was a republic in which the rulers were chosen by the citizens from among "the best people," who were then responsible to both God and their subjects in the execution of God's will. Calvinists since Calvin, with few exceptions, have favored representative government and opposed various forms of absolutism.

R. Hancock, *Calvin and the Foundations of Modern Politics* (1989); H. Höpfl, *The Christian Polity of John Calvin* (1982); J. T. McNeill, *The History and Character of Calvinism* (1954); W. A. Mueller, *Church and State in Luther and Calvin* (1954).

ROBERT D. LINDER

Theological Education Theological education refers to the education received by a minister or other professional church worker. Traditionally, this has included instruction in the scriptures, systematic theology, and pastoral practice.

The intellectual history of the Reformed churches began in the Renaissance of the fifteenth and sixteenth centuries. Advocates of a European intellectual rebirth demanded that scholars set aside their compendia of familiar quotations and standard authorities. In place of these handbooks, Renaissance leaders suggested that scholars return to the original sources. Inspired by this ideal, intellectuals began systematic study of the Latin classics and initiated the study of Greek and Hebrew literature. Part of this rediscovery of ancient literature was the availability of the Bible and the church fathers to educated Europeans.

Huldrych Zwingli, pastor of Zurich, was trained in the new methods of studying ancient texts at the Universities of Bern, Vienna, and Basel. Zwingli launched his reformation with a series of biblical studies and disputations that included an exposition of the complete book of Matthew. Once Zurich legally established the Reformation, Zwingli used small groups to retrain the existing ministry in correct exegesis. In his essay *The Pastor*, Zwingli argued that the best ministry was one attentive to study. The faithful shepherd first learned and then taught.

In Geneva, John Calvin conducted a similar Reformation. Before his *conversion,* Calvin was a young humanist, author of a commentary on Seneca's essay *On Clemency.* After Calvin became a Protestant, he applied his hermeneutical skills to the interpretation of the Bible.

Exegesis was the nucleus of Reformed church life. The first Reformed ministers believed *preaching* should be expository. A liturgical change further encouraged this style of preaching. Unlike Catholic and Lutheran churches, Reformed judicatories encouraged their *elders* to select their own texts. While some texts could be expounded in a single sermon, many required several Sundays before the pastor finished the biblical passage. Many Reformed preachers followed Zwingli's and Calvin's example by preaching through different books of the Bible on successive Sundays.

The need for correct exegesis determined much of the early history of Reformed theological education. Under Calvin's leadership, Geneva required all children to attend school. The more able were to advance to Latin or grammar schools. In 1559, the City Council of Geneva completed the educational system. In that year, the town fathers invited instructors of the University of Lausanne to move to their city and reorganize as the Geneva Academy. The new school required a heavy program of classical studies.

Few continental churches, however, had opportunity to begin new educational institutions. In most areas, Reformed churches inherited medieval universities. Though Reformed leaders modified these schools, they retained the basic outline of medieval theological studies, including dependence on Aristotle's logic.

By the seventeenth century, dogmatic theology had replaced biblical studies as the most important subject in many continental Reformed universities. Two motives underlay this change in educational focus. First, Reformed theologians needed to compete with the Catholic Counter-Reformation. Rejuvenated Catholicism presented its teachings in clear, concise, scholastic form. The Reformed had to answer in kind or risk losing the debate. Second, Reformed thinkers needed to answer such critiques of orthodoxy as that offered by the Dutch Arminians. Despite this shift in focus, continental Reformed churches continued to require the classical languages and Hebrew before the study of theology proper.

England had a different educational pattern than the Continent. The Reformation marked the triumph of humanism in the English universities. Though the scholastic programs—including theology—continued, instruction moved to the colleges. In the medieval period, the colleges were dining and residence halls. After the Reformation, college fellows and tutors assumed most of the teaching responsibilities. The tutors and fellows, often young men awaiting ecclesiastical preferment, drilled their charges in the classical languages. Strangely, the colleges neglected Hebrew, an important subject on the Continent.

In the American colonies, Reformed churches adopted various expedients. American Congregationalists and Presbyterians followed the English model. Harvard, Yale, and, later, the College of Rhode Island were modeled on English schools and followed established English patterns. Little theology was taught in the classrooms, even after the establishment of professorships in divinity.

The Great Awakening apparently created a new demand for more formal theological study. Many candidates studied for a period of time (three months to three years) with an established pastor. In turn, those who completed this training, called "reading divinity," taught others. Unfortunately, many who participated in "reading" programs scrutinized the very convoluted speculative theology of the New Divinity or neo-Edwardseans.

The Dutch Reformed maintained the same standard for their colonial ministers as for continental pastors. Initially, Dutch Reformed churches used a two-leveled approach. Candidates for the *ministry* received their classical education in America, often attending Harvard or Yale, and then went to Holland, where they were trained in Reformed dogmatics. As ethnic distinctions became less important, the denomination created its own liberal arts school, Queens College, and appointed a professor to prepare young men for the preaching office. John Livingston (1746–1825) served as both theological instructor and college president.

In the early nineteenth century, the various American Reformed churches moved toward a different institution for the training of ministers: the seminary. The first seminary in the United States, Andover, opened in 1808. Other Reformed denominations quickly established similar institutions. The new seminaries had many similarities to the European faculties of theology, including a multiple faculty, a specialized library, and a confessional basis. But, unlike European theological schools, the new schools were private institutions organizationally separate from other institutions of higher learning.

Scottish theological arguments also contributed to the development of another type of theological institution. After the enactment of the Patronage Act (1712), the *General Assembly* continually debated the role of presbytery in the appointment of ministers. Though a small group seceded from the Kirk in the eighteenth century, the most significant breach occurred in 1843. In this Great Disruption, approximately one-third of the ministers in the church withdrew. The new Free Church was numerous enough to establish its own educational foundations. New schools were founded at Aberdeen, Edinburgh, and Glasgow. These colleges combined the best features of Scotland's traditional university program with components borrowed from American seminary experience, such as boards of trustees.

By the beginning of the nineteenth century, more advanced scholars used the historical-critical method of biblical interpretation. The first notable Reformed thinker to struggle with the new approach was Friedrich Schleiermacher, professor of theology at the University of Berlin. Schleiermacher argued that scholars had to interpret the Bible historically, and his own discussions of the pastoral epistles and the life of Jesus influenced later research. Yet Schleiermacher also believed that theology could not be chained to the results of any historical investigation. Hence, he suggested that dogmatic theology needed to be grounded in the faith of the contemporary church.

For most contemporary Reformed churches, Schleiermacher's suggestions were too radical. In general, early nineteenth-century Reformed educators ignored the newer biblical studies. This policy of benign neglect, however, did

not last long. Throughout the first half of the nineteenth century, scientific studies indicated that the earth was far older than Genesis indicated. Charles Darwin capped these arguments with his brilliant *On the Origin of Species* (1859). While scientists' findings did not directly concern biblical scholarship, they strongly suggested the Bible was not, as the Reformed tradition affirmed, an inerrant and infallible guide to all knowledge. If so, then the theological schools needed a new method of biblical study.

While the leaders of Reformed theological schools were reevaluating their programs, historical-critical study matured. In the hands of such scholars as Julius Wellhausen (1844–1918) and Wilhelm Wrede (1859–1906), the new method seemed to offer reasonable solutions to difficulties in the biblical text.

The new biblical study also contributed to several Reformed *heresy* trials. In Scotland, William Robertson Smith was tried for his articles on the Pentateuch in the *Encyclopaedia Britannica*. In 1881, the General Assembly of the Free Church convicted Smith and deprived him of his living. In the United States, Charles Briggs of New York City's Union Theological Seminary was likewise tried and convicted for his understanding of the OT. However, Briggs's colleagues supported him. At the urging of the faculty, Union's trustees removed the school from the jurisdiction of the Presbyterian Church. Union became an ecumenical seminary. At Princeton Seminary, the leading conservative school, a 1929 decision to reorganize the school led J. Gresham Machen and other fundamentalist faculty members to establish Westminster Seminary in Philadelphia.

In Switzerland, the universities gradually removed the requirement that members of university theological faculties pledge themselves to teach according to a set theological tradition. Though conservatives established separate theological schools in many cantons, few of the schools survive today. In Holland, the debate became so heated that the conservatives established the Free University of Amsterdam (1880) to teach their point of view.

Though biblical conservatism continued to influence Reformed theological education throughout the twentieth century, the neo-orthodox theology of Karl Barth and Emil Brunner permitted many Reformed institutions to adjust to the new biblical studies. Both Barth and Brunner cut through the hermeneutical problem by separating the words of *scripture* from the *revelation* that supported the text. Thus, theologians could explore the historical world of the Bible as thoroughly as they wished without any substantial loss of theological substance. The American theologians H. Richard Niebuhr and Reinhold Niebuhr presented a similar solution to the biblical problem, and their *neo-orthodoxy* was more in line with the activism of the American Reformed tradition.

The most dramatic changes in Reformed theological education from 1965 to 1990 were in the composition of the institutions that trained pastors. In 1965, the schools were primarily male and most often white. Since then, significant numbers of women have completed their theological studies, and almost all Reformed schools have some female faculty members. Schools in Europe and North America have also enrolled students from third-world countries. This new openness to the world has led to an increasing interest in Reformed schools on such issues as the influence of race, *economics,* and gender on theology.

G. T. Miller, *Piety and Intellect* (1990) and "Christian Theological Education," in *Encyclopedia of the American Religious Experience,* vol. 3, ed. C. H. Lippy and P. W. Williams (1988), 1627–52.

GLENN T. MILLER

Theology, Reformed All Protestant theology may be called "Reformed," but the name is appropriately applied to the theology originating from Huldrych Zwingli, Heinrich Bullinger, John Calvin, Martin Bucer, and others, to distinguish their thought from that of other Protestants. The Swiss reformers were more radical in emphasizing biblical authority than were the Lutherans, and sought to eliminate from the life of the *church* not only what the Bible condemned but also all that did not receive confirmation in *scripture.* The background of the leading Swiss reformers, especially Zwingli and Calvin, was Christian humanism. Erasmus died a cardinal but spent his last years in Protestant Basel and exercised considerable influence over the Swiss theologians. Zwingli's and Calvin's intention, however, was not to create a unique theology but to proclaim the Christian (catholic) faith in the language and idiom of their time.

The seminal works of Reformed theology were all completed before Calvin's death (1564). The authors were preachers who directed their theological work to the edification of the church. The most important classical theologies include those of Zwingli, *On True and False Religion* (1525); Bullinger, *Fifty Godly and Learned Sermons, Divided Into Five Decades Containing the Chief and Principal Points of Christian Religion* (1549); Calvin, **Institutes of the Christian Religion** (editions 1536–59); Wolfgang Musculus, *Commonplaces of Sacred Theology* (1560); and Peter Martyr Vermigli, *Commonplaces* (posth. 1576).

The classic works of Reformed theology were followed by Reformed *scholasticism.* School theologians, unlike the preacher theologians of the first generation, were concerned with precision and clarity of definition, coherence, and comprehensiveness. They sought to relate the Protestant theology to the old theology, as it had developed in the ancient church and medieval scholastic theology.

This development was as necessary as it was useful. In the generation after Calvin's death, Reformed theology had to be defined in the light of conflicts with Lutherans over the person of Christ and the *Lord's Supper* as well as the carefully defined Catholic theology of the Council of Trent (1545–63). Within the Reformed community, disputes quickly arose over theological issues the Reformers had ignored or at least left open-ended. Jacobus Arminius (1560–1609) raised questions about human responsibility over against the very vigorous *doctrine* of *predestination* enunciated by Theodore Beza and Franciscus Gomarus (1563–1641). His theology also intensified the conflict over *supralapsarianism* versus *infralapsarianism*—a question Calvin did not really face—as to whether *God* in *election* viewed people as creatable or fallen. Among the Saumur theologians, Moïse Amyraut sought also to modify predestination. Joshua de la Place (Placaeus; 1606–65) opposed the doctrine of the imputation of Adam's *sin,* and Louis Cappel the younger (1585–1658) denied the Mosaic authorship of the Hebrew vowel points. *Covenant* theologians, especially Johannes Cocceius and Hermann Witsius (1636–1708) sought to organize theology around the various covenants, shifting the attention from the decrees of God to the working out of the decrees in *history,* modifying the arbitrariness of the divine activity and emphasizing human responsibility.

Covenant theology was the only modification of Reformed theology that became part of the official creedal life of the churches. The *Synod of Dort* (1618–19) adopted a moderate Reformed position on predestination, insisting on unconditional election but denying that the decree to elect and the decree to reprobate were equal and parallel decrees. Furthermore, it was infralapsarian in its theological perspective. The *WCF* included the doctrine of the covenants as one of the major organizing factors of its theology, but only alongside other theological rubrics.

Scholastic theology provided the Reformed community with a universal vocabulary that was carefully worked out and defined. It incorporated the accumulated wisdom of the church's theological *tradition* so that all theological questions were faced. Contemporary theologians may not agree with the answers the scholastics gave to theological questions, but they have to praise the theological acumen that lays out the issues so clearly and that, if used today, saves theologians much unnecessary work. Theologians as different as Karl Barth and Paul Tillich have both paid tribute to the high theological competence of the Protestant scholastics.

Among the most important scholastic theologies were those of Beza, *Confession of the Christian Faith* (1558); Girolamo Zanchi, *Commonplaces* (1617); Zacharias Ursinus, *Commentary on the Heidelberg Catechism* (1584); William Perkins, *A Golden Chaine* (1591); William Ames, *A Marrow of Sacred Theology* (1623); Johannes Wollebius, *Compendium of Christian Theology* (1626); James Ussher, *A Body of Divinitie* (1645); and Francis Turretin, *Institutio theologiae elencticae* (1679–85).

The works of Jonathan Edwards were the most influential Reformed contribution to eighteenth-century theology. Edwards wrote his theology in the light of the emphasis of Isaac Newton (1642–1727) on an orderly world that left little place for God; of the insistence of John Locke (1632–1704) on the empirical basis of all knowledge and the reasonableness of Christian faith; and of the revivals that raised anew the problems of *free will* and divine sovereignty. Edwards, who was unwilling to be called a Calvinist for the sake of distinction, wrote *A Treatise Concerning Religious Affections* (1746); *Freedom of the Will* (1754); *The End for Which God Created the World* (posth. 1765); and *A History of the Work of Redemption* (1739 sermons; pub. posth. 1774).

The Enlightenment and nineteenth-century intellectual and cultural events constitute one of the great divides—if not the greatest divide—in the history of Western culture. The churches' response generally was threefold: liberalism, which sought to incorporate the new wisdom into Christian faith sometimes at the expense of the faith; a conservative fundamentalism, which in protecting the faith sometimes destroyed its intellectual vitality; and the *Social Gospel,* to indicate how Christians should live in the new industrial society.

Some theologians in the Reformed tradition, such as Friedrich Schleiermacher, sought to relate Christian faith to the new intellectual and cultural situation. In doing so, they raised the question of whether their theology should be distinguished as Reformed or characterized primarily as nineteenth-century liberalism. On the other extreme, theologians defied the nineteenth century and lost intellectual credibility. Reformed theologians generally found it easier to relate the Christian faith to the new social situation than to reach unanimity about theological concerns. This was the basis of the ecumenical slogan that doctrine divides but work unites. In recent years, however, work more radically divides the Christian community than doctrine, in part because work is based upon doctrine.

The most influential nineteenth-century Reformed theologians, however, cannot be classified as either liberal or fundamentalist. Heinrich Heppe's *Reformed Dogmatics* (1861; ET 1950; repr. 1978) combined in one compendium much of the Reformed theological wisdom of various European traditions, and proved to be an influential textbook, even receiving Barth's commendation. In the United States, Charles Hodge's *Systematic Theology* (3 vols.; 1871–73) was the most influential theological text of any school of thought. Hodge's theology built on the Reformed tradition and particularly on the seventeenth-century formulation of Francis Turretin but united these traditions with the warmth of American revivalism.

Reformed theologies after World War II moved beyond the peculiar problems of the Enlightenment and the nineteenth century. On the one hand, they sought to take the Enlightenment seriously; on the other, they intended to reaffirm in the idiom of a new day the classical Christian theology of the ancient catholic *creeds* and the classic Protestant Reformation. The most influential twentieth-century Reformed theological works include: Barth, *Church Dogmatics* (1936–69); Emil Brunner, *Dogmatics* (3 vols.; 1946–60; ET 1950–62); and Otto Weber, *The Foundations of Dogmatics* (2 vols.; 1955; ET 1982–83).

What are the distinguishing marks of Reformed theology? Reformed theology intended to be catholic but was formulated in such a way that it can be recognized even though its uniqueness cannot be defined with precision. In the nineteenth century, in discussions between Reformed and Lutheran communities in Germany, some insisted that Lutheranism was directed against Judaism or works-righteousness, while Reformed theology was directed against paganism or *idolatry.* Others pointed to Luther's emphasis on the Christian's experience of *grace* and Reformed emphasis on the activity of God. Still others sought to define the uniqueness of Calvin in terms of some central dogma from which his theology was deduced.

Emile Doumergue, the great Calvin biographer of an earlier century, emphasized the theocentric character of Calvin's theology, a quality shared with Zwingli. The Swiss reformers all thought of God as energy, activity, and moral purpose. God is the Lord of nature and of history. They understood human history as the working out of God's purposes and the essence of human life as embodiment of the purposes of God. Calvin himself would insist, perhaps with a glance toward Luther, that *salvation* of a human soul was subordinate to the glory of God.

The theocentrism of Calvin's theology, however, is strictly qualified. It is the theocentrism of the triune God who is made known to us in Jesus Christ. The theocentric character of Reformed theology involves a radical rejection of any form of unitarianism as well as the exaltation of human concerns.

Reformed theology is distinguished by certain ways of doing theology:

1. It is always subordinate to the *authority* of the Bible as the *Word of God* written. Theology is a coherent explication of scripture in the language of ordinary discourse. The authority of scripture is the norm of all theological thinking and speaking.

2. Reformed theology has always sought to illuminate *experience* and the concreteness of the situation. Calvin subjected what he wrote theologically to the common sense wisdom of Christian experience. *Revelation* may go beyond human experience, but it cannot and does not contradict the clear facts of human experience or common sense. Reformed theology is not an explication of Christian experience, but it never takes place apart from it and the demands of the concrete situation. It is not speculative.

3. Theology is a practical, not a theoretical, science. The purpose of theology is to glorify God, to save human souls, to transform human life and society. Calvin's "rhetorical theology," as William Bouwsma has indicated, is directed to practical results rather than a systematic theology intended for the ages.

4. Reformed theology is characterized by simplicity. At its best it is written without ostentation, with transparent clarity, and in the language of ordinary discourse. It rejects the pompous, the artificial, and the contrived.

Reformed theology is also distinguished by certain theological perspectives or decisions. It has always made a sharp distinction between creator and creature. It is Antiochene rather than Alexandrian. This emphasis on the distinction between creator and creature and the peculiar way of relating transcendence and immanence characterizes all of Calvin's doctrine, from the person of Christ, to the presence of Christ in the *sacraments*, to the nature of the church.

Reformed theology is also distinguished by an emphasis on the activity of God and particularly the prevenience of God's grace. Predestination may not be the unifying principle of Calvin's theology, but this emphasis upon the priority of the activity of God pervades every doctrine.

A third theological perspective is the way God the creator and God the redeemer are related to each other. *Creation* and redemption cannot be opposed. Yet they cannot be identified, for redemption is more than creation—not simply as its completion but, in the light of sin, as its transformer. The practical priority in Reformed theology is always on redemption. Calvin, for example, refused to discuss the possibility of whether the Word would have become flesh if human beings had not sinned.

The fourth characteristic perspective is the refusal to confuse or separate gospel and *law, justification* and *sanctification.* Neither gospel and law nor justification and sanctification can be separated; for the gospel is in the law and the law is in the gospel. Salvation as God's mercy—justification by grace through faith—and salvation as God's power—sanctification—must never be separated or confused.

Reformed theology is also unified by a vision of the human community under the authority of God. Calvin, unlike Zwingli, wished to maintain the independence and distinction of church and state. Zwingli and Calvin were united, at least intentionally, in the sense that all society is under God's authority and should reflect God's glory. They sought to create the Christian community on earth. Hence, Reformed theology has never been satisfied with a pietistic definition of Christian faith.

No one distinguishing mark identifies any theology as Reformed. It is catholic in that it builds on the ancient creeds and protestant in its affirmation of Luther's writings (1520), as well as the early Swiss theses such as Bern (1528). However, any Reformed theology is distinguished by its emphasis upon God as energy, activity, and moral purpose, upon the Lordship of God over nature and history, upon the distinction between creator and creature, upon the refusal to separate, oppose, or confuse creation and redemption, law and gospel, justification and sanctification together with an emphasis on the life of the church in the world. Further, the style of Reformed theology is simple, and always in opposition to the pompous, the pretentious, and the ostentatious.

J. H. Leith, *An Introduction to the Reformed Tradition* (rev. ed. 1981); J. T. McNeill, *The History and Character of Calvinism* (1954).

JOHN H. LEITH

Thirty-nine Articles

The Thirty-nine Articles of Religion of the Church of England, which are substantially the same as Archbishop Cranmer's Forty-two Articles (1553), received their final form and authorization in 1571. Their purpose was "for the avoiding of diversities of opinions and for the establishing of consent touching true religion." They affirmed particularly the Reformed *doctrine* of *scripture, salvation,* and *sacraments* as a corrective to sixteenth-century Roman Catholic positions.

But not all the articles are polemical in this sense. The first five state briefly the historic faith regarding the *Trinity* and *Christology,* and the last three relate to certain civil and social matters, while the eighth declares acceptance of the classical *creeds.*

Articles 9–14 deal with *original sin, free will,* and *justification,* proclaiming that "we are accounted righteous before God, only for the merit of our Lord and Saviour Jesus Christ by Faith, and not for our own works or deservings" and that "Good Works, which are the fruits of Faith, and follow after Justification, . . . do spring out necessarily of a true and lively Faith." Article 17 states, "The godly consideration of Predestination, and our Election in Christ, is full of sweet, pleasant, and unspeakable comfort to godly persons." Other articles condemn the doctrine of purgatory, issuing pardons or indulgences, adoration of images and relics, invocation of saints, and conduct of public *worship* "in a tongue not under-standed of the people" as "repugnant to the Word of God" (arts. 22; 24). Transubstantiation "cannot be proved by Holy Writ; but is repugnant to the plain words of Scripture, overthroweth the nature of a Sacrament, and hath given occasion to many superstitions" (art. 28).

The insistence on the sufficiency of Holy Scripture for salvation reflected adversely on the papal attribution to *tradition* an *authority* equal with scripture's (art. 6). It was not denied that there is a place for various traditions and ceremonies in the church, but only subject to the condition "that nothing be ordained against God's Word" (art. 34). Likewise, "the Church hath power to decree Rites or Ceremonies, and authority in Controversies of Faith," but "it is not lawful for the Church to ordain any thing that is contrary to God's Word written" (art. 20). Again, in article 21 on the authority of general councils, it is stated: "Things ordained by them as necessary to salvation have neither strength nor authority, unless it may be declared that they be taken out of holy Scripture." The hallmark of the articles is the insistence on the supreme authority of Holy Scripture over the church and its affairs.

In recent times, the Thirty-nine Articles have suffered neglect and met with contemptuous comment. Current signs of a renewal of interest and willingness to pay attention to the message they convey are welcome insofar as they carry hope of a recovery of strength for a weakened and confused church.

Schaff, *Creeds,* vol. 3.

PHILIP E. HUGHES

Toleration, Religious

Religious toleration took on a new dimension with the onset of the Reformation. The *church* had always been concerned about *heresy,* but this became much more complex with the variety of Protestant dissent. Initially, toleration within the Reformed tradition was impeded by the corporate view of society where church and state were but different aspects of the Christian community. Thus, opinions other than the doctrines of the established church could not be tolerated. Toleration was realized within the Reformed tradition only in the eighteenth century.

Toleration was an issue from the very beginning of the Swiss Reformation. In early Reformed communities, dissenters were forced to conform, sometimes on pain of death, as with Felix Manz in Zurich and Michael Servetus in Geneva. Basel, the one exception, became the most tolerant of Reformed cities by the mid-sixteenth century, allowing a group of refugee scholars, several of questionable orthodoxy, to gather at the university. The most prominent was Sebastian Castellio, whom Calvin had forced out of Geneva.

Castellio began the open debate over toleration among the Reformed churches with *Whether Heretics Ought to Be Persecuted* (1554). Like Erasmus and Sebastian Franck, who influenced him, Castellio argued that the civil magistrate had no authority over souls. Castellio responded to Calvin's *Defense of the Orthodox Faith*, in which Calvin argued that it was the magistrate's God-given duty to put heretics to death. Theodore Beza, agreeing, wrote *Whether the Civil Magistrate Ought to Punish Heretics* (1554). For the next century, Castellio's descendants remained a small minority in the Reformed communities.

In the United Provinces, the toleration issue lay just below the surface of the Arminian/orthodox Calvinist debates. The major *Arminian* spokesman for toleration was Simon Episcopius. While the established Reformed church produced no one who advocated complete toleration, Johannes Althusius, chief magistrate of Emden, did argue for and practice a limited toleration of Christian dissenters and Jews. Many other Reformed magistrates followed his lead, so the United Provinces were the most tolerant of all European states in the seventeenth century.

In Poland, Reformed, Lutherans, and Bohemian Brethren joined with the Catholics in signing the Confederation at Warsaw (1573) to establish toleration in Poland for nearly a century. A practical toleration existed in Poland since the mid-sixteenth century, when the anti-Trinitarians broke with the Reformed Church. Faustus Socinus was the greatest toleration spokesman in eastern Europe.

In England, both Presbyterian Puritans and Separatists opposed the established Anglican Church, but neither advocated religious toleration. No Reformed advocated toleration until the Congregationalist John Owen, who argued for toleration of all dissenters (1649). Owen advocated toleration until his death (1683) and influenced John Locke in his *Essay on Toleration* (1689).

Among the American colonies, the basis for future U.S. *religious liberty* was set in Virginia. The toleration struggle that had begun in the mid-seventeenth century was carried on by the Presbyterians, among others. The resultant Act for the Establishment of Religious Freedom (1786) was the basis for the clause on religion in the First Amendment to the Constitution (1791).

S. H. Cobb, *The Rise of Religious Liberty in America* (1902; repr. 1978); H. R. Guggisberg, *Basel in the Sixteenth Century* (1982); W. K. Jordan, *The Development of Religious Toleration in England*, 4 vols. (1932–40); J. Lecler, *Toleration and the Reformation* (1960).

J. WAYNE BAKER

Total Depravity   *see* **Sin**

Tradition   From the Latin word *tradere* ("to hand over"). It primarily refers to an action or a process of transmission and reception. Most broadly, tradition is whatever the past gives to the present and the present receives from the past. Tradition includes, among other things, beliefs, documents, institutions, and rituals as well as ways of seeing, hearing, believing, doing, reading, writing, speaking, thinking, and acting. The word itself is neutral. It does not suggest anything normative about the past or about what we have received from it. In the NT, adhering to "tradition" (*paradosis*) is sometimes criticized:"Thus making void the word of God through your tradition that you have handed on" (Mark 7:13); or affirmed, as when Paul commends the Corinthians because they "maintain the traditions just as I handed them on to you" (1 Cor. 11:2). The verb "to hand over," in English, Greek, or Latin, means both to deliver and to betray. *Scripture* is ambivalent about tradition.

In Christianity's early centuries, tradition came to be considered "the deposit of faith." It became normative in the degree to which it was understood as coming from the apostles. Hence, the NT *canon* was received as consisting of authentic apostolic writings and teachings. In the fifth century, Vincent of Lérins argued that the "true faith" is to be determined from the authority of the biblical canon and from tradition of the *church.* In terms of contents, the biblical canon was sufficient, but its proper interpretation required the guidance of tradition. Therefore, he proposed that "we hold to that which has been believed everywhere, always, and by all." His norms—which themselves became traditional—were universality, antiquity, and consensus. In principle, with the emphasis on antiquity, the norms were conservative. In practice, however, the norms were used ever more frequently to legitimate the recent and novel. The criterion was no longer antiquity of source but became universality of acceptance. Some began to claim that, under the Spirit's impulse, through the church's teachings, the apostolic tradition may continue to unfold, even to grow and enlarge.

Increasingly in the Middle Ages, attention shifted from the distinction between text and interpretation, between source and unfolding, to that between the *written* traditions (in scripture and the *creeds*) and the *unwritten* traditions, supposedly transmitted, from apostolic times, orally and secretly. Thus, many

came to believe that divine *revelation* flowed through two streams: scripture and tradition. This notion was reinforced by the Council of Trent (1546), which "receives and venerates with the same piety and reverence all the books of both Old and New Testaments—for God is the author of both—together with all traditions concerning faith and morals."

Among the Reformers, Calvin was critical of Trent, arguing that it compromised the normative character of scripture not only by mixing it with tradition but also by deciding that in the use of scripture the traditional (but unreliable!) Vulgate version was to be the standard. Thus, while Calvin was quite open to using nonbiblical language in theology and suggested that Christianity was truer in the early centuries, centuries that were a "purer" time, a sort of "golden" age, for him, only scripture contains the authentic, reliable, and normative tradition in the truest sense (cf. *Inst.*, "Prefatory Address"). At the same time, within the Reformed tradition, there has been a willingness to use traditional theological language of the *Trinity* and Chalcedonian *Christology* as well as traditional documents such as the Nicene Creed. Further, the Reformers themselves clearly did not always recognize the measure to which they were the unwitting inheritors and practitioners of many quite recent traditions.

A significant statement of Reformed understanding appears in the *Second Helvetic Confession* (1566), "Of Interpreting the Holy Scriptures; and of Fathers, Councils, and Traditions" (ch. 2). Here, while the Fathers and the councils may be instructive in scripture's interpretation, scripture remains the norm; and "we reject human traditions, even if they be adorned with high-sounding titles, as though they were divine and apostolical . . . which, when compared with the Scriptures, disagree with them." The *WCF* affirmed that the *conscience* is "free from the doctrines and commandments of men which are in anything contrary to his Word, or beside it in matters of faith or worship" (20.2).

Y. M.-J. Congar, *Tradition and Traditions* (1966); E. Shils, *Tradition* (1981).

JOHN E. BURKHART

Trinity   The *doctrine* of the Trinity affirms that the one and only **God** is the threefold reality of Father, Son, and **Holy Spirit.** While classical Reformed theologians made no substantive contributions to traditional doctrinal formulae of the patristic era, contemporary Reformed theologians have contributed significantly to understanding the triunity of God as a "community" of divine being.

The principal elements of the doctrine of the Trinity were settled during fourth- and fifth-century Trinitarian controversies under the leadership of the Cappadocian Fathers and **Augustine.** Then the "grammar" of the doctrine was fixed, though the terminology took different forms in the Greek East and the Latin West. Eastern theologians referred to God as one essence in three hypostases, while Western writers said that God is one substance in three Persons. For some time this terminology caused considerable confusion because the Greek *hypostasis* was often translated by the Latin *substantia.*

As time went on, East and West divided over the way the relations among the Persons was described. The East preferred to speak of the Trinity as having one Source (or Font) and two issues: that is, the Father is the One who begets the Son and from whom the Spirit proceeds. The West attempted to reinforce its reading of the biblical references to the Spirit as the Spirit *of Christ.* Thus, the custom developed in the Latin-speaking church of adding the word *filioque* to the Niceno-Constantinopolitan Creed, or Nicene Creed, (the Spirit proceeds from the Father *and the Son*). This problem (and the authority by which the addition was made) led to the 1054 schism and has been a principal cause of East-West division ever since.

Among the most significant contributions to Trinitarian doctrine was Augus-

tine's *On the Trinity* (c. 425). He intended to explain and defend Nicene orthodoxy while also expounding the view of the relations among the Persons that led to the inclusion of the *filioque.* Augustine considered numerous analogies. Some are taken from nature (fire, heat, and light); some are social (parents and child). One extensively discussed is the psychological analogy to the operation of the human mind: God's triunity is compared to the relations between memory, understanding, and will. In the end, Augustine expounded the analogy of Lover, the Beloved, and Love, which binds them together, as the best description of the internal life of God.

Augustine's work and the defenders of Nicene orthodoxy laid the foundation for Reformation consideration of the Trinity. Few reformers questioned the Trinity's centrality, and its outlines were restated by the *confessions* and *catechisms.* Calvin defended Trinitarian orthodoxy primarily by emphasizing the divinity of Christ and Christ's centrality for the work of *salvation.*

Within the Reformed family, very little substantive discussion of the Trinity occurred until Karl Barth made this doctrine the theme both of his consideration of *revelation* and of his theological anthropology. He opened his *Church Dogmatics* by contending that the fact of God's self-disclosure makes clear that God *is* ("in unimpaired unity yet also in unimpaired distinction") Revealer, Revelation, and Revealedness. The revelation that stands behind *scripture* is the God who is at the same time: *who* is revealed, *what* is revealed, and *how* revelation is effected. The doctrine of the Trinity is thus not an exercise in abstract theological speculation. It is the church's reflection on its *experience* of God, who makes God's self known in the revelation that both *is* and is contained *in* the Bible (*CD* I/1, pt. 1).

In interpreting the event of revelation, the *church* discerns that God is an "indissoluble subject" who reveals God's self in three distinctive "modes of being" (Ger.

Seinsweisen). These ways of God being God subsist in their mutual relations as Father, Son, and Holy Spirit. Though it is from the one essence of God that the threeness of God occurs, yet the unity of God "is not to be confused with singularity or isolation" (*CD* I/1, 354). God's way of being one Subject is to be in real, internal relationship within God's self. It is in part to preserve this dynamic quality that Barth prefers the term "triunity" (*Dreieinigkeit*) in describing divine relatedness.

Because the triunity of God is reflection on God's self-disclosure that is the history of revelation as recorded in scripture, we discover that at the heart of God is the event of *election.* God's free choice to love and redeem *humanity* is far more than an act of God directed outward; election is not simply an act of God taken in response to humanity's fall into sin. Election is an act of God's eternal self-determination, for it entails a decision as to how God intends to be related to God's self, and, through that decision, how God intends to relate to all humanity. In the classical language, election is not one of the *opera ad extra*; election takes place first of all within the divine being. In election, God decides to be both the Elector and the Elected One. Thus, choosing and being chosen, redeeming and being redeemed, are ways in which the divine subject is self-related and has been from all eternity.

What Barth hopes to accomplish with this unusual description of God's triunity is to explain how the radically transcendent God can be really related to *creation* and to humanity. His solution to this dilemma is that creation is the external form of the covenant relationship that inheres in the being of God. The redemption of humanity is the repetition *ad extra* of the electing love with which the Father loves the Son and with which the Son responds in obedience to the Father.

A most interesting sidelight to Barth's consideration of the Trinity is how it functions in his anthropology. He begins from the premise that God is a subject distinguished by real relationships. The history of revelation shows that God is a being in correspondence or confrontation with itself. Using Martin Buber's language, there is within God "I and Thou." This means that "God Himself is not solitary, that although He is one in essence He is not alone, but that primarily and properly He is in connexion and fellowship" (*CD* III/2, 324).

The move from Trinitarian doctrine to anthropology centers on the exegesis of Gen. 1:26–27: humanity as created in the "image and likeness" of God. Barth argues that the point of correspondence between God and humanity is in the fact and form of human relatedness. As the human being is created to be God's partner, so the essence of humanity is found in partnership (or the relationship of I and Thou) among humans. The essential form this partnership takes is the relation of man to woman. In their relationship (in general and not simply in the covenant of *marriage*), male and female correspond to the relatedness that is at the heart of God. A curious implication of this is that their relationship thus takes the form of that between the Elector and the Elected One. Thus, Barth concludes that there is always between male and female a structure in which male precedes and female follows, in which male initiates and female responds. Barth admits that this is a structure of superordination and subordination but denies that this infringes on the equality of the male and the female any more than a similar structure of superordination and subordination threatens the unity and equality of the Persons of the Godhead.

While Barth has clearly made a significant contribution to the discussion by linking the structure of the divine being both to God's self-disclosure and to the human created in God's image, many have questioned the way the analogy is made to work. Feminist theologians argue that subordination, no matter how carefully defined, cannot be separated from the notion of inherent inequality between any superordinate and subordinate. They resist the idea that male and female are anything but created equally in God's image. It is also fair to suggest that Barth has, by defining God's primary internal relation as that of election, introduced a structure of superordination and subordination into the Godhead that stands at odds with the entire orthodox tradition. The difficulty with Barth's proposal is not that humanity reflects the divine relatedness (several modern Reformed authors have found this useful). The difficulty is in the way in which the divine relatedness is defined, for example, as command and obedience.

Several contemporary Reformed theologians have proceeded from Barth's foundation and continued the discussion of the triunity of God as a community of real relatedness in the one Godhead. Eberhard Jüngel has confronted various philosophical arguments about the impossibility of speaking about God in the modern world by a further exposition of Barth's thought. The doctrine of the Trinity leads us to see that God is "a being structured as a relationship" (Jüngel, 25).

Jürgen Moltmann's work is more extensive as he takes over Barth's notion that the work of redemption occurs first of all within God's own being. Moltmann makes a significant alteration, however, suggesting that what takes place with the Godhead is not election but crucifixion. To describe how God can be really related to human suffering, he concludes that the suffering of Christ is not an event that takes place in the life of the human Jesus and "outside" the Godhead. The love of God (which is compassionate and suffering love) can be understood only if the cross and suffering of Christ are at the heart of God's own experience and existence. Moltmann is so convinced of the need to affirm God's active sympathy with human suffering that he is willing to claim that God suffers not only through the human nature of the Son but in the Godhead itself. Thus, he claims that patripassianism (that the Father suffers along with the Son) should never have been declared heretical.

Two things are striking here: first, the way in which Moltmann follows Barth's suggestion that real relatedness is what characterizes the being of God; second, the distinctive way in which Moltmann defines the nature of that relationship. No longer are Father and Son related as Elector and Elected One (the One who commands and the One who is obedient). Now they are the One who hears the cry of abandonment and the One who is abandoned.

Moltmann moves on from this discussion of suffering love at the heart of God to discuss ways in which the divine community can serve as a model for human community. Here again, Moltmann follows Barth's form but with distinctive content. Rather than focus on the relationship of male and female as the primary form of human relatedness, Moltmann's concern is for humans in broader community. He suggests that the free self-giving and compassionate love manifested in triune relatedness can serve as a model for human life in community (both political and ecclesiastical). God's self-revelation of love is the history of *freedom*. The **kingdom of God** is the condition where humans share with one another in the community of God's free love for all creation.

Another Reformed theologian who reflects on the significance of triune relatedness for human relationship is Letty Russell. She suggests that the doctrine of the Trinity contributes to our understanding of partnership. The Christian message is that we are set free to live as partners not only with one another but with God in the ongoing work of creation. Thus, "the partnership of God in the persons of the Trinity also provides an image of mutuality, reciprocity, and a totally shared life. The characteristics of partnership, or *koinōnia*, may be discovered in their perfection in the Trinity, where there is a focus of relationship in mutual love between the persons and toward creation" (Russell, 35).

Among feminist theologians, both within and outside the Reformed tradition, considerable discussion has been given to the status of the triune formula. Many argue that naming the triune God "Father, Son, and Holy Spirit" (and using masculine pronouns for all three) reinforces the incorrect notion that God is male and that only masculine language is strictly appropriate when speaking about God. Various proposals for alternative formulae have been made, the most common being the identification of the Persons by their function: for example, Creator, Redeemer, and Sustainer; or Creator, Christ, and Spirit.

While having the advantage of removing exclusively masculine terms, these alternatives raise another difficulty. Early theologians argued that the Persons should not be distinguished by specific acts or functions, because this leads inevitably to a modalism (the threefold nature of God is found in the *roles* God plays toward us). In fact, they argued, the act of one is the act of all. Thus, the Creed says that God the Father is "Maker of heaven and earth," God the Son is the One "by whom all things were made," and God the Spirit is "the Lord and Giver of Life."

Others object to renaming the Persons of the Godhead because they hold that the triune formula "Father, Son, and Spirit" is in fact God's self-disclosed, *proper* name (cf. Bloesch). This view, however, seems contrary to the ancient notion that the triune names signified the relations between the Persons rather than the essences of the Persons themselves.

This discussion of how the triune Persons are to be named is likely to continue with significant contributions from those who wish to eliminate any confusion that God is male as well as from those who are concerned about the vast ecumenical significance of the triune formula, especially as Christians from East and West find themselves in closer theological as well as ecclesial relations.

D. G. Bloesch, *The Battle for the Trinity* (1985); C. M. Campbell, " 'Imago Trinitatis': An Appraisal of Karl Barth's Doctrine of the 'Imago Dei' in Light of His Doctrine of the Trinity" (diss., Southern Methodist University, 1981); E. Jüngel, *The Doctrine of the Trinity* (1976); J. Moltmann, *The Crucified God* (1974); and *The Trinity and the Kingdom* (1982); L. M. Russell, *The Future of Partnership* (1979).

CYNTHIA M. CAMPBELL

Ubiquity Reformed and Lutheran theologians agreed that Christ is everywhere according to his divine nature. The main controversy rose over whether Christ's presence in the **Lord's Supper** necessarily implies, as some Lutherans insisted, that Christ is everywhere bodily.

Calvin insisted that Christ be confessed to be "really," not just "sacramentally," present in the Lord's Supper. Calvin (e.g., 1563 Dedicatory Letter to Frederick, *CO* 20, col. 75) was content to rely on Peter Lombard's distinction (*Sentences* III, d. 22, 3) to hold that the whole Christ, but not everything that belonged to Christ (*totus Christus sed non totum*), is really present by the power of the **Holy Spirit.** To go further and argue that Christ's body had communicated to it the divine property of ubiquity was, according to Calvin, to threaten Christ's true humanity on which, no less than on his true divinity, our **salvation** depends.

Subsequent **Reformed orthodoxy** distinguished among several senses in which the communication of the divine and human properties in the **incarnation** can be understood. Heppe (*RD* 432–47) identifies three main senses considered by representatives of Reformed orthodoxy. In the first (*genus idiomaticum*), the attributes of each nature are ascribed to the entire Person; according to the second (*genus apotelesmaticum*), the redemptive acts proper to the whole Person are ascribed to one of the natures; and according to the third (*genus majestaticum*), the human nature is magnified by the properties of the divine nature. Reformed theologians affirmed the first and second senses but insisted that holding to the third sense, as many of their Lutheran opponents did, argued for

Christ's bodily ubiquity at the expense of the true humanity of the one Person.

Barth, *CD* II/1, 484–90, 515–45; E. Bizer, "Ubiquität," *Evangelisches Kirchenlexikon: Kirchlich-theologisches Handwörterbuch* 3 (1959): 1530–31; H. Chavannes, "La présence réelle chez St. Thomas et chez Calvin," *Verbum Caro* 13 (1959): 149–70; P. Jacobs, "Pneumatische Realpräsenz bei Calvin," *Revue d'histoire et de philosophie religieuse* 44 (1964): 389–401; K.-H. zur Mühlen, "Jesus Christus, IV: Reformationszeit," *TRE* 14:759–72; J. Städke, "Abendmahl, III, 3: Reformationszeit," *TRE* 1:106–22; D. Willis, "Calvin's Use of Substantia," in *Calvinus Ecclesiae Genevensis Custos*, ed. W. H. Neuser (1984), 289–301.

E. DAVID WILLIS

Union with Christ (Mystical Union)

Mystical union in Reformed understanding is that personal engrafting of believers into Christ which constitutes the foundation of the Christian life. As branches are joined with the vine (John 15), or members of a body with their head (Eph. 4), so the elect are united with Christ. This ingrafting does not entail dissolution of the believer's individuality in the divine, nor does it stand as the goal of a process of spiritual development. It is, rather, that work of the *Holy Spirit* which engenders *faith* and enables individuals to share in the fruits of Christ's saving work. *Baptism* is the sign and seal of this union; the *Lord's Supper* nourishes and sustains it.

Calvin sees personal union with Christ as the means by which we appropriate Christ's benefits; in this union Christ takes our *sin* as his own and we take his obedience as our own. Some Reformed theologians speak of a federal or judicial union in which *God* declares believers joined to Christ, the Second Adam, as their representative head. Karl Barth has emphasized union with Christ as the goal of Christian *vocation*.

Barth, *CD* IV/3, pt. 2, 520–54; L. Berkhof, *Systematic Theology*, (4th rev. and enl. ed. 1949); A. A. Hodge, *Outlines of Theology* (1878); L. Smedes, *Union with Christ* (1983); R. S. Wallace, *Calvin's Doctrine of the Christian Life* (1959).

P. MARK ACHTEMEIER

Universalism

Universalism affirms the *salvation* of all *humanity* and rejects the Christian *doctrine* of *eternal punishment.* Hints of it are found in Gnostic writings. The Greek theologians Clement of Alexandria, Origen, and Gregory of Nyssa taught it, while *Augustine* and the medieval tradition strongly opposed it. Sixteenth-century Anabaptist writers Hans Denck and Hans Hut promoted it, though their tradition has largely distanced itself from universal salvation. Martin Luther and John Calvin opposed it.

During the European Enlightenment, the view found new favor in a variety of theological streams. The pietist mystic Jakob Boehme, the Puritan Philadelphians, the Wesleyans James Relly and his disciple John Murray, liberal Congregationalists Jonathan Mayhew and Charles Chauncy, and ex-Baptist Elhanan Winchester all promoted universalism during the seventeenth or eighteenth century.

Attempts to unite universalists through common publications and doctrinal statements have occurred in the United States. Doctrinal compatibility with Unitarianism yielded formation of the Unitarian Universalist Association (1961). However, many with universalist inclinations remained outside this movement.

Karl Barth represents a latent or implied universalism through his emphasis on Christ as simultaneously elected and rejected by the Father. Since Christ is the *covenant* head of all humanity, like him all are simultaneously elect and reprobate. Barth refrains, however, from speculating on the eternal consequences of this position.

Some Roman Catholic emphases on Christ's hidden presence in non-Christian religions and Protestant ecumenism's theory of dialogue with other faiths suggest a universalism incompatible with historic Reformed teaching.

S. Mark Heim, *Salvations* (1995).

JAMES A. DE JONG

Vocation The affirmation that each person in society is called by *God* to a specific vocation or function is a hallmark of the Reformed tradition. This conviction undergirds and strengthens those who perform even the lowliest daily tasks. Both Martin Luther and John Calvin developed a *doctrine* of vocation.

Calvin uses "calling" (Lat. *vocatio* "vocation") for the choosing of the elect but specifically in relation to God's appointing human beings to certain occupational or family positions. He writes: "The Lord bids each one of us in all life's actions to look to his calling. For he knows with what great restlessness human nature flames, with what fickleness it is borne hither and thither, how its ambition longs to embrace various things at once. Therefore, lest through our stupidity and rashness everything be turned topsy-turvy, he has appointed duties for every man in his particular way of life. And that no one may thoughtlessly transgress his limits, he has named these various kinds of living 'callings' " (*Inst.* 3.10.6).

That each person receives a calling from God was not the pre-Reformation understanding of "vocation." Calvin stood in direct opposition to those who withdrew from business and entered the contemplative life on the ground that they alone received a call. "On the contrary," he observes, "we know that men were created for the express purpose of being employed in labor of various kinds, and that no sacrifice is more pleasing to God than when every man applies diligently to his own calling, and endeavors to live in such a manner as to contribute to the general advantage" (*Commentary on a Harmony of the Evangelists* 2:143).

The conviction that one is called gave courage to people in a society in dramatic flux. In sixteenth-century Geneva, structures from medieval society had broken down, peasants were given new powers, refugees streamed into the city fleeing persecution, and a feeling of uncertainty pervaded the changing order. In such rootlessness, the knowledge that God calls people provides the ingredient necessary for a fulfilled life, namely, courage: "Nothing can fill us with courage more than the knowledge that we have been called by God. For from that we may infer that our labor, which is under God's direction, and in which He stretches out His hand to us, will not be in vain. Thus, it would be a very serious accusation against us to have rejected God's call. It should, however, be the strongest encouragement to us to be told, `God hath called thee to eternal life. Beware of being distracted by anything else or of falling short in any way, before thou hast obtained it' " (*Commentary* on 1 Tim. 6:12).

Moreover, whether a person is president or slave, no labor is too high or low that it is not blessed by God. "From this will arise also a singular consolation: that no task will be so sordid and base, provided you obey your calling in it, that it will not shine and be reckoned very precious in God's sight" (*Inst.* 3.10.6).

When each person fulfills the function or occupation to which he or she has been called, a certain orderliness in society results. It is incumbent upon each person who has received a calling to "keep within the limits" of that calling, thus preventing confusion and disorder. Peace is the result: "The best way, therefore, to maintain a peaceful life is when each one is intent upon the duties of his own calling, carries out the commands which the Lord has given, and devotes himself to these tasks; when the farmer is busy with the work of cultivation, the workman carries on his trade, and in this way each keeps within his proper limits. As soon as men turn aside from this, everything is thrown into confusion and disorder" (*Commentary* on 1 Thess. 4:11). Such an injunction, however, was not offered as a means of control but so that society as well as the inner self might be at peace. If we "claim more for ourselves than we ought," care and worry are the result. Work, therefore, should not be carried to excess but be kept under control. A sense of calling counters our restlessness and anxiety. "Immoderate care is condemned for two reasons: either because in so doing men tease and vex themselves to no purpose, by carrying their anxiety farther than is proper or than their calling demands; or because they claim more for themselves than they have a right to do, and place such a reliance on their own industry, that they neglect to call upon God" (*Commentary* on Matt. 6:25).

But Calvin does not insist that a person born in one station or calling in life must never seek to change it. Commenting on Paul's advice, "Let each one abide in that calling," Calvin says: "But at this point someone is asking if Paul wishes to impose something binding on people, for what he says may seem to suggest that each one is tied to his calling, and must not give it up. But it would be asking far too much if a tailor were not permitted to learn another trade, or a merchant to change to farming." The doctrine of vocation attacks the "restlessness which prevents individuals from remaining contentedly as they are" (*Commentary* on 1 Cor. 7:20).

The doctrine of vocation, God's calling, affirms all work, for it is the work of God. Our work has meaning because, seen as God's calling, it is the very work of God in human society.

A. Biéler, *The Social Humanism of Calvin* (1964); W. J. Bouwsma, *John Calvin: A Six-teenth-Century Portrait* (1988); R. S. Wallace, *Calvin's Doctrine of the Christian Life* (1959).
                    JOHN R. WALCHENBACH

War   Few issues have divided Christians more than the question of war. Three major historical positions have emerged.

1. *Pacifism.* The unwillingness of its members to participate in war character-ized the early church and created some of the earliest "church-state" conflicts.

2. *The just war theory* provided criteria for determining whether or not a war was just, for example, declared by a legitimate authority, fought with a right intention, undertaken only as a last resort, waged with respect for the principle of propor-tionality (the end to be gained must out-weigh the evil means employed), offering a reasonable chance of success, and waged with the greatest possible moder-ation. If all the criteria could be met, Christians could participate.

3. *The holy war or crusade,* in which the moral stakes were considered so high that any action necessary to bring victory was legitimate, particularly if the war was between God's partisans and the "infidels."

The Protestant Reformers had little use for pacifism, but its tradition was kept alive by many "left-wing sectarians" (Quakers, Anabaptists, etc.). De facto, the major Reformation groups implicitly affirmed the just war theory, convinced that wars often had to be fought to sup-port the right and oppose the wrong. But the line between a just war and a crusade was often blurred, and excesses of vio-lence marked the "wars of religion" that raged in the wake of a divided church.

The duty to obey the state is fre-quently invoked as a reason for Chris-tians to bear arms, though Calvin provided a tiny loophole at the end of the *Institutes* (4.20.32) in which "lesser mag-istrates" were encouraged to rebel if the cause of the king was clearly against God's will. Today most churches support the right of "conscientious objectors" to war to be excused from military service.

In the nuclear era, terms of the discus-sion have shifted, for wars can no longer be limited in scope or so waged that only professional soldiers are killed. Everyone is now a target. Entire cities can be exter-minated with a single bomb, and the pos-sibility of a chain reaction that would destroy the planet is real. As a result, a new position, "nuclear pacifism," has emerged, claiming that no "good" coming out of a nuclear war could justify the destruction involved.

War is now interrelated to all other issues; the ruinous cost of arms means lack of revenue for social services; the possession of nuclear weapons as "deterrents" threatens to escalate into use; large nations not wanting to risk global war turn to "low-intensity conflict" as a way of controlling the destinies of small nations at an "acceptable" cost.

As the social and human costs of modern war become less and less acceptable, the ancient biblical vision assumes new relevance: "Nation shall not lift up sword against nation, neither shall they learn war any more" (Isa. 2:4).

R. H. Bainton, *Christian Attitudes toward War and Peace* (1960); A. Marrin, ed., *War and the Christian Conscience* (1971); J. Nelson-Pallmeyer, *War against the Poor* (1989).
ROBERT MCAFEE BROWN

Westminster Confession of Faith

The work of an English assembly and Scottish commissioners (1647), the WCF was a fair summary of the theological consensus among British Protestants. But it never played a significant role in the future of Protestantism in England.

Yet the confession did become the most influential and, for centuries, the sole confessional authority among most English-speaking Presbyterians. This remarkable influence of a confession written under the authority of an assembly called by an English Parliament is due to the high technical competence of the confession itself and its success in embodying a consensus of *Reformed theology* as modified by English Puritanism. It unites the work of the classical Reformed theologians such as Zwingli, Bullinger, and Calvin with the ancient *Augustinian* tradition in England as well as the prolific theological work of the Puritans.

The confession embodies the theological achievements of Protestant *scholasticism* that produced in the seventeenth century a universal Reformed vocabulary along with clearly defined theological terms and carefully analyzed theological issues. The scholastics, in seeking clarity and precision, became increasingly abstract, and the WCF lacks the historical qualities of the *Scots Confession* (1560) or the experiential emphasis of the *Heidelberg Catechism* or even the *Second Helvetic Confession.*

The opening chapter, "Of the Holy Scripture," is an introduction to the confession's theology, laying out the sources of theology and directing how the theologian moves from sources to theological confession, that is, to what must be said in a particular time on the basis of what is said in the Bible. The confession's authors were sure *God* was revealed through "the light of nature," a *revelation* of God implanted in the human heart as well as in the created order. The confession did not denigrate this revelation, but insisted it was not sufficient for human *salvation.* The scriptures are indispensable, and they are the norm of all theological work. The chapter predates historical criticism but is so carefully done that it does not require revision in the light of what is known as the critical study of the scriptures today.

A second characteristic of the confession is the emphasis upon the Lordship and sovereignty of God. When the writers attempted to say who God is, they declared their belief in the "one only living and true God . . . working all things according to the counsel of his own immutable and most righteous will." When they spoke of God's eternal decree, that is, God's eternal purpose, they declared that "God from all eternity did by the most wise and holy counsel of his own will, freely and unchangeably ordain whatsoever comes to pass." The ease with which the confession speaks of the decree of God creates a difficulty for contemporary Christians. But when "purpose" is substituted for decree, the writers' intention becomes clear. The confession emphasizes throughout the personal activity of God in the created order.

The most striking innovation in seventeenth-century Reformed theology was the development of *covenant* theology. Along with *election*, covenant is a preeminent expression of God's saving activity among human beings. Biblical faith can be reduced to neither election nor covenant. The WCF remarkably unites election and covenant without making either one the single dominating, unifying principle of the theology. Covenant theologians focused attention away from the decrees of God abstractly considered to the working out of those decrees in human history, and they related the decree of God to the responsible action of human beings.

A fourth characteristic of the confession is an emphasis on the Christian life. The writers knew that the end of Christian faith is not *forgiveness* but the *sanctification* of the forgiven person, the transformation of the sinner into the image of Christ. The confession's emphasis on sanctification, *adoption,* and finally glorification—the completion of the transformation of human life in the *kingdom of God*—is supplemented by the extensive treatment of the commandments in the Westminster Larger Catechism and Shorter Catechism. Two-thirds of the confession is devoted to an analytical description of the Christian life and its practices and responsibilities in the world. The primary purpose of the Christian life is the glory of God, not the realization of human identity or potential or even the service of human beings.

The confession fully reflects its origin in the struggles of English society (1643–47). Its statements about church and state are very dated. But even in the midst of these most dated sections, there are remarkable affirmations: "God alone is Lord of the conscience, and hath left it free from the doctrines and commandments of men which are in anything contrary to his Word, or beside it in matters of faith or worship. So that to believe such doctrines, or to obey such commandments out of conscience, is to betray true liberty of conscience; and the requiring an implicit faith, and an absolute and blind obedience, is to destroy liberty of conscience, and reason also" (*BC*, 6.109).

A. I. C. Heron, ed., *The Westminster Confession in the Church Today* (1982); J. H. Leith, *Assembly at Westminster* (1973); A. F. Mitchell, *The Westminster Assembly: Its History and Standards* (1883); A. F. Mitchell and J. B. Struthers, eds., *Minutes of the Sessions of the Westminster Divines* (1984); R. S. Paul, *The Assembly of the Lord* (1985).

JOHN H. LEITH

Witness of the Holy Spirit

The witness of the *Holy Spirit* (*testimonium Spiritus Sancti*) enables Christians to know the truth of reality and the reality of truth. In opposition to the Roman Catholic Church, John Calvin stressed the importance of this teaching. Scripture's believability is based not on the (authority of the) *church* but on the Spirit's external witness in *scripture* and internal witness in Christians. Although scripture is *autopistic,* that is, carries its own credibility and evokes respect for its inherent majesty, it does not seriously affect believers until the testimony of the Spirit seals it upon their hearts (*Inst.* 1.7.5). Through this internal witness, Christian believers obtain the *faith* necessary to acknowledge, with indubitable certainty, the *theopneustic* (inspired) character of scripture (2 Tim. 3:16; 1 Peter 1:21) and its divine *authority.*

Through this witness, Christians not only accept scripture as God's Word but also acknowledge (John 15:26; 16:13; Rom. 8:16) the entire *revelation* of *salvation,* that is, the promises of the gospel, the *grace* of God, their *election* in Christ, and their acceptance as God's children.

The inner testimony of the Holy Spirit is not a separate, isolated, or additional revelation, nor is it a proof based on psychic experience or rational proof. According to the *WCF,* it is a power that convicts and assures Christians of the infallible truth and divine authority of scripture. This witness of the Spirit is important not only for personal faith but also for ecclesiastical acceptance of scripture as canon. Believers accept "without a doubt all things contained in Scripture—not so much because the church receives or approves them as such but because the Holy Spirit testifies in our hearts that they are from God" (*Belgic Confession,* art. 5).

Herman Bavinck stated that the basis for acknowledging the *canon of Scripture* lies in scripture itself as the Spirit's *external* witness and that Christians actually recognize this canon of the written Word through the Spirit's *internal* witness in their hearts. Although not the basis, this inner testimony (*testimonium internum*) of the Spirit is the deepest reason for the *faith* of Christians (Acts 16:14; 1 Cor. 2:14).

Calvin rejected the intellectualism inherent in medieval *scholasticism.* Knowing does not precede the witness of the Spirit, nor does it merely confirm in the heart what is already known in the head. Revelation is not rational, nor is faith intellectual. Believers are not first rationally convinced by the formal credibility of scripture and only afterward convicted in their hearts by the internal witness of the Spirit concerning the message of the written Word.

The *autopistic* character of scripture is not isolated from and preparatory to the Spirit's witness. Unlike the theologians of Protestant scholasticism, Calvin did not think of *reason* and Spirit's witness as constituting two forms of faith, scripture and Spirit as providing two sources of knowledge, or scripture (as external object) and witness of the Spirit (as internal subject) producing two kinds of witness.

Scripture is not prior to and complemented by the internal witness of the Spirit. The Spirit's witness continues and completes the witness of scripture. Though not identical, these two forms of witness are intimately related to each other. Believing scripture is impossible without believing in Jesus Christ, and believing in Jesus Christ is impossible without believing scripture (Luke 24:27). Believing scripture presupposes and expresses itself in believing in Christ.

Scripture is not something rational apart from the Spirit, nor is the Spirit something mystical apart from scripture. The inner testimony of the Holy Spirit is the basic reason for and essence of scripture's pointing to Christ.

By being grounded in Christ through the Spirit's witness, Christians appropriate the truth of scripture. It prevents them from separating scripture and Christ and from succumbing to three dangers—namely, *spiritualism,* which separates Jesus and Spirit from scripture and *creation*; *secularism,* which ignores the Spirit's witness and scripture; and *biblicism,* which relativizes general revelation and the witness of the Spirit and places ultimate certainty in a set of rationally accessible teachings. The Spirit that causes scripture to be inspired by its authors also causes it to be accepted by its readers. Not of themselves, but through this testimony of the Holy Spirit, Christians are immediately convinced of scripture's divine authority (1 Cor. 2:14).

H. Bavinck, *Gereformeerde Dogmatiek* (1928), 1:552ff.; H. Berkhof, *The Doctrine of the Holy Spirit* (1967); E. Doumergue, *Jean Calvin,* vol. 4 (1910); S. Greijdanus, "Karakter van het Testimonium Spiritus Sancti volgens Calvijn," *Gereformeerd Theologische Tijdschrift* 14 (1914): 519–43; A. Kuyper, *The Work of the Holy Spirit* (1900); T. Preiss, *Das innere Zeugnis des Heiligen Geistes* (1947); G. Vandervelde, ed., *The Holy Spirit: Renewing and Empowering Presence* (1989).

JOHN C. VANDER STELT

Word of God   The Word of God is God's eternal Wisdom, itself fully divine, which subsists eternally as the Second Person of the triune being of the Godhead. Directed outward toward the world, this Word becomes the active instrument of God's creative and redemptive power: The Word is the active agent in *creation* (Gen. 1) and the embodiment of God's redeeming power in *history* (Isa. 55:10–11).

The Word of God revealed. The Word

functions as the vehicle of God's self-disclosure. It came in "many and various ways" to the patriarchs and prophets of old and appears finally incarnate in human flesh in the person of Jesus (John 1:1–14; Heb. 1:1–2). The distinctiveness of the Reformed *doctrine* of the Word lies less in any novel conception and more in the doctrine's centrality both in theology and in the life of the *church.* Though Reformed theologians differ over the extent to which a natural *knowledge of God* is theoretically attainable within the created order, most agree that the only effective means for sinners to attain a saving knowledge is through God's self-disclosure in the Word. The attempts of fallen human beings to reach upward to *God* are ultimately futile, whether the point of contact with the divine is conceived as nature, history, *reason, tradition, experience,* or even religion itself. Access to the one true God is given in the form of a divine initiative, a sovereign Word that comes to us from One who is other than ourselves. As such, it is a gift of divine *grace,* utterly beyond the reach of human striving and wholly beyond human control.

Attentiveness to this revealed Word thus becomes the central focus of life and *worship* among the Reformed: Their churches are reformed "according to the Word of God" and sustained by it; their worship centers around the proclamation of the Word; their *sacraments* are understood as inseparable in principle from the Word.

The Word of God written. Reformed theologians affirm that the Word of God is contained in the scriptures of the OT and NT, though the sense in which this is the case is subject to varying interpretations. Barth speaks for much of the recent tradition in describing scripture as authoritative testimony to the Word of God that was given directly only to the prophets and apostles. Another strand of the tradition, typified by the so-called high orthodoxy of the late seventeenth century, posits a more mechanical theory of inspiration in which the text of *scrip-ture* is dictated word for word by the *Holy Spirit,* with the biblical writers acting as little more than recording secretaries. Both strands claim Calvin as a forebear, and one can indeed find isolated passages in the *Institutes* that appear to support either view (see McNeill).

Reformed understandings of scripture are characterized by an emphasis on the essential unity of OT and NT. Christ, the incarnate Word, is the unifying content of both, though the manner of his presentation differs from one to the other: The OT foreshadows Christ under signs and types; the NT presents him directly.

The Word of God proclaimed. The Word of God manifests itself in the church's proclamation. The *Second Helvetic Confession* states: "The preaching of the Word of God is the Word of God" (ch. 1). Human language, however, whether the biblical text or the church's proclamation, becomes the bearer of God's Word only by the active power of the Holy Spirit. Calvin insists (*Inst.* 1.9.3) that the Word of God in scripture and proclamation is joined inseparably with the work of the Holy Spirit: God's Word comes to us effectively through these human media only as the dead letter of the text is vivified by the life-giving Spirit. Thus, the Spirit causes believers to hear and respond to God's authoritative address in the human words of scripture and *preaching,* and these words in turn give positive content to the inward testimony of the Spirit.

Barth, *CD* I/1–2; J. T. McNeill, "The Significance of the Word of God for Calvin," *CH* 28 (June 1959): 131–46; R. S. Wallace, *Calvin's Doctrine of the Word and Sacrament* (1953); U. Zwingli, "Of the Clarity and Certainty of the Word of God," in *Zwingli and Bullinger,* ed. G. W. Bromiley, LCC, vol. 21 (1953).

P. MARK ACHTEMEIER

Work   In the Reformed tradition, work is viewed positively as part of everyone's call to serve and glorify God. Worshiping

God, however, rather than work is our ultimate purpose in life. The creation of the Sabbath as the day of rest was intended to put the meaning of work in perspective. Work is an expression of our *stewardship*; *worship* is the culmination of our *vocation*. Whenever work is separated from worship, the former loses its purpose and becomes the curse that alienates and dehumanizes us (Eccl. 2:4–11, 20–22; Luke 12:16–21). Work that becomes an end in itself is a form of *idolatry.*

This why Calvin insisted that a person's work be seen as one's calling. We were created and called to be stewards of God's *creation*; we live by *grace* and our response daily ought to be one of thanksgiving and gratitude. To those who do not work, the biblical charge is clear: "Anyone unwilling to work should not eat" (2 Thess. 3:10). Such a biblical admonition was taken seriously by the Reformers, for they saw work as both a duty and a discipline under God.

However, in contrast to an earlier agrarian society, the realities in our technologically oriented world may make this admonition to work more difficult to fulfill. Is there sufficient and meaningful work today for everyone? Should work be understood as a basic human right? These are some of the perplexing theological and ethical questions confronting us as we seek to understand the future meaning of work while remaining faithful to our biblical heritage.

All work, to be meaningful, must not only fulfill the human search to be needed but also contribute an added value to society. Work must reflect and uphold the intrinsic worth of persons, lest individuals become treated as commodities. Also, the worker must realize that work is created to meet the real need of society and not simply work for the sake of work.

All work should come with some sense of "calling." This understanding of Christian vocation has always been a significant theme in Reformed thought. Along with the sense of calling for whatever work one does, the worker also brings a dimension of creativity to the situation. Creativity with a sense of calling is what makes work meaningful. We were created to create, and there can be no creation without a God-given sense of calling, no matter how modest that contribution may be. In short, the Reformed understanding of work celebrates every worker who labors to God's glory.

G. Baum, "Toward a Theology of Work," *The Ecumenist*, Sept.–Oct. 1989; R. A. Calhoun, *God and the Day's Work* (1943); J. Moltmann, *Creating a Just Future* (1989); J. C. Raines and D. Day-Lower, *Modern Work and Human Meaning* (1986); A. Richardson, *The Biblical Doctrine of Work* (1952).

CARNEGIE SAMUEL CALIAN

World Religions

World Religions It is difficult to discuss views of other religions within the context of the Reformed faith and its history. This is because both circumstances and perspectives in the early years of that history were so different from those more recent, as well as different from those of the early *church.*

Differently from the Mediterranean orientation and increasing access to the wider world of Roman Catholic lands after the Reformation, central European Protestants had little or no existential knowledge of the great non-Christian world of their time. Luther had evidently read Theodor Bibliander's Latin translation of the Qur'an, at least in part, and deemed it an "accursed, shameful and desperate book." Calvin, on the basis that the name of the one *God* was everywhere known, concluded that "the heathen, to a man, by their own vanity either were dragged or slipped back into false inventions" and were therefore without excuse (*Inst.* 1.10.3).

Neither Calvin nor Luther, however, in the widely eclectic scholarly as well as religious world of the sixteenth century was fully consistent in his perceptions or views. This was also the time of "spiritual" writers such as Sebastian Franck, who wrote, "God is no respecter of persons but instead is to the Greeks as to the barbarian and the Turk, to the lord as to the servant, as long as they retain the light which has shined upon them and gives their heart an eternal glow" (G. H. Williams, *Spiritual and Anabaptist Writers* [1957], 150). Above all, the whole range of Protestant Reformers drank deeply from and contributed to the cultural humanism of their day. Thus, Calvin saw the liberal arts, the contents of whose studies were very largely of non-Christian origin, as gifts of God and felt free to borrow from any source he could regard as having come from God. He believed that philosophers in all times and places had been stimulated by God, "that they might enlighten the world in knowledge of the truth" (*Inst.* 1.3.1). Calvin had some genuine respect for the religious insights of persons everywhere, of "even the most remote peoples." At the same time, he was careful to discriminate, regarding the religion of the Greeks as qualitatively superior to that of the Egyptians or the Romans.

The way out and up from the limitations of common Reformation thinking has been long and even tortuous. Within the specifically Reformed tradition we may note the Dutch Arminian Remonstrants of the second half of the seventeenth century. Like the Cambridge Platonists in England with their emphasis on "inner illumination," the Dutch Remonstrants, who had long and close associations with the English Platonists, showed a "general courtesy and politeness, . . . reasonableness and breadth of view" in their personal and theological posture. This tradition of profound *spirituality*, relatively conservative biblical scholarship, and religious understanding open to the data of natural science, minority a view as it was in its time, came to be the attitudinal foundation for broader understanding in the following centuries. Protestant foreign mission activity, in which Reformed churches played an increasingly important role, contributed greatly to larger perspectives. Often missionaries who left their homelands believing that non-Christian

religions were simply the work of Satan were forced by their field experiences to modify these views. As early as 1710, the German pietist missionary in India, Bartholomäus Ziegenbalg, wrote that he did not reject everything taught by the Hindus but, rather, rejoiced that for them "long ago a small light of the Gospel began to shine" and that "one will find here and there such teachings and passages in their writings which are not only according to human reason but also according to God's Word" (W. R. Hogg, "Edinburgh 1910—Perspective 1980," *Occasional Bulletin of Missionary Research* 4, no. 4 [Oct. 1980]: 149).

At the present time, a rather weighty consensus among Reformed theologians regarding world religions is emerging from renewed studies of the early church and recent biblical studies. The biblical *covenants* that played a central role in the faith life of both Israel and the Christian church are seen to begin with universal covenants. Some scholars hold that the divinely initiated covenants begin with *creation* itself. Others prefer to see the first biblical covenant in the promise of God to Eve (Gen. 3:15–16). All agree that the divine covenant with Noah and his family includes not only all *humanity* but also "every living creature of all flesh" (Gen. 9:8–17). These covenants are now seen as both revelatory and salvific in meaning and as constituting the framework of the entire biblical story.

We now see that the mainstream of theologians in the early church shared in this perception of the "wider work of God in the world." The Logos theology of Justin Martyr (100–165) with its view of a "seed" (Gr. *sperma*) of the Logos given to every human being long before the manifestation in Jesus of Nazareth made it possible for Justin and other early Christians to recognize some qualities of the Logos—seen perfectly in Jesus—in noble pagans. Justin dared identify as worthy of the name Christian pre-Christian philosophers of Greece such as Socrates or Heraclitus. Irenaeus (fl. 185) taught that God is one and the same to all humans and has aided the human race from its beginning by various economies or arrangements (Lat. *variis disposition-ibus*). Clement of Alexandria (150–215) wrote that "all authentic understanding or wisdom is sent by God and that the true teacher of the Egyptians, the Indians, the Babylonians and the Persians, indeed of all created beings, is the first-begotten Son, the Fellow-counselor of God. . . . Many are the different covenants of God with men" (*Stromateis* 6.7).

A major contemporary responsibility of Reformed churches is to combine these wider perceptions of the presence and work of the triune God throughout human *history* with a renewed and Reformed commitment to the Christian world mission. To realize that no human being is a blank sheet of paper before our Maker and that a wise missionary is prepared to learn from as well as to teach persons of other backgrounds does not call for the abolition of that mission but for its purification in both motive and practice.

RICHARD H. DRUMMOND

Worship   In Reformed churches, worship is the service of God's glory. This service is in Jesus Christ, continuing his *preaching* of the gospel, his acts of mercy, his *ministry* of *prayer,* and celebration of the *sacraments* he instituted. It is both in Christ's name and in the fellowship of his body. Finally, worship is a divine work initiated, inspired, and constantly supported by the *Holy Spirit* at work in the individual human heart and the assembled congregation.

The Reformed approach to worship is most easily understood from certain key scripture passages. A fundamental principle of *Reformed theology* is that worship must be formed and constantly reformed according to *scripture.* That worship be according to God's Word follows from the perception that it is God's work. Our worship is at Christ's bidding and therefore bears the promise of his presence (Matt. 28:20). In working this out, the Reform-

ers—notably John Oecolampadius—intended to steer a middle course between the strict principle that what is not commanded by scripture is forbidden and the lax principle that what is not forbidden is permitted. By the end of the sixteenth century, this had become a major plank in the Puritan program for liturgical reform as in the Admonition to Parliament (1572). William Ames affirmed the principle of *Augustine* and Calvin that nothing glorifies *God* quite so much as that which comes from God—that is, our worship should reflect God's glory. A most balanced statement of this principle is in the *Westminster Confession* (1.6).

Already in the first tablet of the law of Moses, Israel is called to serve God's glory. This service is to be to the one true God and no other. Neither idols, which could confuse God's nature, nor magical formulas, which would profane God's name, are to be used. Rather, God's people are to gather each Sabbath in remembrance of God's mighty acts of creation and redemption. For a Reformed theology of worship, a Christian understanding of the first four commandments has always been fundamental (cf. Zacharias Ursinus on the *Heidelberg Catechism* [qq. 93–103]). As Calvin said, the first tablet of the *law* was summed up by Jesus as the first and greatest commandment, the commandment to love God. Worship is, therefore, in terms of the love relationship between God and the people of God (*Inst.* 2.8.11–34). Paul treats several liturgical questions in 1 Corinthians 10—14 in terms of this covenant love. For this reason, many Reformed preachers, such as New England's Thomas Shepard, Scotland's John Willison, and New Jersey's Gilbert Tennent, often preached on the wedding feast of the Lamb at Communion. They understood worship in terms of covenant love.

When Martin Bucer set down the program of liturgical reform of the Church of Strassburg in his *Grund und Ursach* (1524), he drew from Acts 2:42 that worship should consist of (1) reading and teaching the scriptures; (2) fellowship, expressed especially in giving alms; (3) celebration of the sacraments of *Baptism* and the *Lord's Supper*; and (4) the service of daily prayer. Strassburg developed a very full diet of prayer, including the singing of psalms and hymns, prayers of confession and supplication, prayers of intercession, thanksgivings, and benedictions. Place was given both to set forms of prayer and to extempore prayer. Bucer, as the Reformed tradition generally, was not so concerned for the sequence of these elements as that they all be included.

The Reformed approach to worship can be explained in terms of several dimensions of worship. First, there is the kerygmatic dimension. Jesus came preaching the gospel of the kingdom. The preaching of the gospel is worship because it proclaims God's rule and witnesses to God's sovereignty. In the worship of the Temple, many of the psalms were acclamations of God's sovereign presence (e.g., Ps. 93; 96–99), not only in regard to Israel but all nations. In the same way, evangelism glorifies God by proclaiming the Lordship of Christ over all nations and cultures. The missionary and evangelistic preaching of the nineteenth and twentieth centuries understood well the kerygmatic dimension of worship. Just as many of the ancient psalms were kerygmatic, so many Christian hymns are kerygmatic. One thinks of Isaac Watts's paraphrase of Psalm 72: "Jesus Shall Reign Where'er the Sun," or of Joachim Neander's "Praise to the Lord, the Almighty, the King of Creation." Much church music is kerygmatic. Organ preludes and postludes emphasize the kerygmatic dimension of Christian worship just as the sounding of the shofar and the blowing of trumpets announced the Sabbaths of ancient Israel.

Worship has an epicletic dimension: It calls on God's name for our help and *salvation.* (An epiclesis is a prayer calling upon or invoking God.) Just as it was important for OT worship not to use God's name in vain, so it was important for NT worship to hallow God's name. God is worshiped when the faithful call

upon God in time of need. Many psalms are lamentations, supplications, and *confessions* of *sin* (e.g., Ps. 22; 42; 51; 102; 130). Jesus prayed them in his own worship, and in the Lord's Prayer he taught his disciples to pray for the *forgiveness* of their sins, for the supplying of their daily bread, for deliverance from evil, and for the coming of the kingdom. Reformed worship gives great attention to the invocation of God's name at the beginning of worship and the invocation of the Holy Spirit before the reading and preaching of the scriptures. In the celebration of both Baptism and Communion, God the Father is called upon to send the Holy Spirit so that what is signified in the sacramental action becomes a reality in the lives of those who receive it.

Worship has a prophetic dimension. Jesus and the apostles no less than the prophets insisted that while God's glory is obscured by injustice and immorality, it is magnified when the worshiping community reflects God's holiness (Micah 6:6–8; Amos 5:21–24; Isa. 6:3–8). The service of God's glory entails the service of mercy toward the neighbor (Matt. 22:36–39; Rom. 12). The collection of tithes and alms, therefore, has a place in worship. It is in the diaconal ministry that the service of mercy and the service of worship are tied together. Theodor Fliedner and the German Reformed deaconesses developed this in a notable way. From this prophetic dimension of worship, Reformed churches have developed a simple, orderly worship and have avoided sumptuous liturgical forms. As Calvin put it, "Humility is the beginning of worship" (*Commentary* on Micah 6:8).

The wisdom tradition of the Old and New Testaments shows us yet another dimension of worship. The wisdom tradition delighted in the *Word of God* (Ps. 1:2–3). In studying the Word, memorizing it, teaching it, preaching it, and living it, God was glorified. As in Psalm 19, the law, God's Word, glorifies God in the same way as the order of *creation.* In fact, God delights in wisdom (Prov. 8:30). In Johannine Logos *Christology,* we find how the wisdom tradition approached worship (John 1:14–18; 2:1–11; 6:25–69; 20:29–31). The wisdom dimension helps us understand the importance of preaching in Reformed worship. Sermons of Huldrych Zwingli, Thomas Goodwin, or Charles H. Spurgeon delight in scripture. Thomas Manton's 190 sermons on Psalm 119 can best be appreciated in terms of this delight.

Finally, there is a covenantal dimension. This is found in the worship described in Exodus 24. The Book of the Covenant is read, and with the making of vows of faith, the covenant is sealed both by the sprinkling of the blood of the covenant and by the sharing of a meal. Early in the Reformation, Heinrich Bullinger developed a covenantal understanding of the sacraments. Ever since, Reformed theologians encouraged by 1 Cor. 11:25 have seen these covenantal assemblies of the OT as types of Christian worship where the breaking of bread and the sharing of the cup unite Christians in the new and eternal covenant. So also with baptism, which, because it was a sign of the covenant as was circumcision, was appropriately given to the children of the covenant community. From this baptismal understanding, Horace Bushnell derived his ideas on Christian nurture. One place where this covenantal dimension is seen most clearly is in the Scottish Communion season. There the vows of faith were made and renewed. From New England's Jonathan Edwards and Virginia's Samuel Davies, it was clear that those who came to faith during the Great Awakening formally professed that faith at the **Lord's Supper.**

E. B. Holifield, *The Covenant Sealed* (1974); J. H. Nichols, *Corporate Worship in the Reformed Tradition* (1968); H. O. Old, *Worship That Is Reformed according to Scripture* (1984). H. Rice, *Reformed Worship* (2001).

HUGHES OLIPHANT OLD

Selected Resources

Benedetto, Robert, Darrell L. Guder, and Donald K. McKim. *Historical Dictionary of Reformed Churches.* 1999.

Cochrane, Arthur C., ed. *Reformed Confessions of the 16th Century.* 1966.

Gerrish, B. A. *Tradition and the Modern World: Reformed Theology in the Nineteenth Century.* 1978.

Heppe, Heinrich, ed. *Reformed Dogmatics Set Out and Illustrated from the Sources.* Repr. 1978.

Hesselink, I. John. *On Being Reformed: Distinctive Characteristics and Common Misunderstandings.* 1988.

Johnson, William Stacy and John H. Leith, eds. *The Reformed Reader: A Sourcebook in Christian Theology.* Vol. 1. 1993.

Leith, John H. *An Introduction to the Reformed Tradition.* Rev. ed. 1981.

McKim, Donald K., ed. *Encyclopedia of the Reformed Faith.* 1992.

———. *Introducing the Reformed Faith.* 2001.

———, ed. *Major Themes in the Reformed Tradition.* Repr. 1998.

———, ed. *Readings in Calvin's Theology.* Repr. 1998.

Muller, Richard A. *Post-Reformation Reformed Dogmatics.* 2 vols. 1987 and 1993.

Osterhaven, M. Eugene. *The Spirit of the Reformed Tradition.* 1971.

Presbyterian Church (U.S.A.). *The Book of Confessions.* 2000.

Rohls, Jan. *Reformed Confessions: Theology from Zurich to Barmen.* 1998.

Sell, Alan P. F. *A Reformed, Evangelical, Catholic Theology: The Contribution of the World Alliance of Reformed Churches, 1875–1982.* 1991.

Stroup, George W., ed. *The Reformed Reader: A Sourcebook in Christian Theology.* Vol. 2. 1994.

Torrance, Thomas F., ed. and trans. *The School of Faith: The Catechisms of the Reformed Church.* 1959.

Vischer, Lukas, ed. *Reformed Witness Today: A Collection of Confessions and Statements of Faith Issued by Reformed Churches.* 1982.

Walker, Williston. *Creeds and Platforms of Congregationalism.* Repr. 1960.

Willis, David and Michael Welker. *Toward the Future of Reformed Theology: Tasks, Topics, Traditions.* 1999.